PATERNOSTER BIBLICAL MONOGRAPHS

God, Order and Chaos

René Girard and the Apocalypse

PATERNOSTER BIBLICAL MONOGRAPHS

A full listing of titles in this series and Paternoster Theological Monographs appears at the end of this book

PATERNOSTER BIBLICAL MONOGRAPHS

God, Order and Chaos

René Girard and the Apocalypse

Stephen Finamore

Foreword by Christopher Rowland

WIPF & STOCK · Eugene, Oregon

Wipf and Stock Publishers
199 W 8th Ave, Suite 3
Eugene, OR 97401

God, Order, and Chaos
Rene Girard and the Apocalypse
By Finamore, Stephen
Copyright©2009 Paternoster
ISBN 13: 978-1-60608-604-9
Publication date 4/20/2009
Previously published by Paternoster, 2009

This Edition published by Wipf and Stock Publishers
by arrangement with Paternoster

PATERNOSTER BIBLICAL MONOGRAPHS

Series Preface

One of the major objectives of Paternoster is to serve biblical scholarship by providing a channel for the publication of theses and other monographs of high quality at affordable prices. Paternoster stands within the broad evangelical tradition of Christianity. Our authors would describe themselves as Christians who recognise the authority of the Bible, maintain the centrality of the gospel message and assent to the classical credal statements of Christian belief. There is diversity within this constituency; advances in scholarship are possible only if there is freedom for frank debate on controversial issues and for the publication of new and sometimes provocative proposals. What is offered in this series is the best of writing by committed Christians who are concerned to develop well-founded biblical scholarship in a spirit of loyalty to the historic faith.

Series Editors

I. Howard Marshall, Honorary Research Professor of New Testament, University of Aberdeen, Scotland, UK

Richard J. Bauckham, Professor of New Testament Studies and Bishop Wardlaw Professor, University of St Andrews, Scotland, UK

Craig Blomberg, Distinguished Professor of New Testament, Denver Seminary, Colorado, USA

Robert P. Gordon, Regius Professor of Hebrew, University of Cambridge, UK

Tremper Longman III, Robert H. Gundry Professor and Chair of the Department of Biblical Studies, Westmont College, Santa Barbara, California, USA

Stanley E. Porter, President and Professor of New Testament, McMaster Divinity College, Hamilton, Ontario, Canada

For Rebecca

Contents

Foreword	xiii
Preface	xvii
Acknowledgements	xix
Abbreviations	xxi
Introduction	xxv

Chapter 1 History, Theology and Visions of Chaos:
A Review of the Literature on Revelation's Plague Sequences   1
A. Introduction   1
B. The Interpretation of Revelation until 1850   4
   1. *The Early Church*   4
   2. *Joachim of Fiore and His Followers*   15
   3. *The Reformation Period*   17
   4. *The Early English Protestants*   21
   5. *The Sixteenth and Seventeenth Century Jesuits*
     and their Successors   24
C. Critical Readings of Revelation since 1850   26
   1. *Church and World Historical Methods*   27
   2. *Spiritual Methods*   29
   3. *Futurist and Eschatological Methods*   32
   4. *Preterist and Contemporary Historical Methods*   35
   Excursus: Recapitulation or Progression?   38
   5. *Historical Critical Investigations*   41
   6. *New Critical Approaches*   49
   7. *The Theology of Revelation*   51
D. Conclusions   54

Chapter 2 Mimesis, Culture and Apocalypse:
The Thought of René Girard   59
A. Introduction   59
B. Imitation and Representation: Mimesis   61
C. Text and Reality: Reading Strategy   63

D. Mimesis and Scapegoating: Anthropology	69
1. *Prohibition*	75
2. *Ritual*	76
3. *Myth*	79
E. Violence and Truth: Teleology	83
F. Revelation and Renunciation: The Gospel	85
G. Conclusions	93

Chapter 3 Praise, Criticism and Interpretation:
The Reception of Girard's Theory in Contemporary Thought   95

A. Introduction	95
B. Social and Cultural Anthropology	98
C. Literary Criticism and the Philosophy of Language	105
D. Feminism	107
E. Theology	109
F. Biblical Studies	120
G. Conclusions	127

Chapter 4 Revelation, Illumination and Liberation:
The Results of Jesus's Ministry According to
the Book of Revelation   131

A. Introduction	131
B. Μάρτυς (Witness) and Νικάω (Conquer) and Cognates	135
1. *Μάρτυς (Witness) and Cognates*	135
2. *The Verb Νικάω (Conquer)*	141
a. Νικάω in Revelation 4-22	141
b. Νικάω in the Rest of the New Testament	143
c. Νικάω in the Old Testament and Other Jewish Writings	143
d. Νικάω in Revelation 2-3	145
3. *Conclusions*	146
C. The Book of Revelation and *Christus Victor*	151
Excursus: Images of Atonement in the New Testament	153
The Synoptic Gospels	153
The Fourth Gospel and the Johannine Letters	155
The Pauline Corpus	156
Other New Testament Writings	158
Concluding Remarks	159

Contents

Chapter 5 Outline, Interpretation and Exegesis:
Reading Revelation in the Light of Girard's Thought   161
A. Introduction   161
  1. *Language*   161
  2. *Genre*   163
  3. *Literary Structure*   165
B. Outline   166
  Excursus on the Date of Revelation   168
C. Interpretation   169
  1. *Transfer of Sovereignty*   171
  2. *The Unique Quality of the Renewed Creation*   174
  3. *Conclusions*   177
D. Exegesis: Revelation 4:1-6:17   178
  1. *Introduction*   178
  2. *Chapter 4:1-11*   179
  3. *Chapter 5:1-14*   186
  4. *Chapter 6:1-17*   196
  Excursus: Romans 1:16-32   205
    Romans 1:17-31   206
    The Views of Some Exegetes   207
    Girard's Ideas as an Interpretative Grid
    for Romans 1:18-32   212
E. *Conclusions*   221

Chapter 6 Conclusions   223

Bibliography   227

Scripture Index and Index to Other Ancient Texts   271

Author Index (prior to AD 1850)   279

Author Index (since AD 1850)   281

Subject Index   289

Foreword

An influential approach to the interpretation of the Bible, which has appealed to those who espouse non-violence, has been in the work of René Girard. I have Steve Finamore to thank for introducing me to it.

At the risk of oversimplification, according to Girard human cultures have their origin in that basic human tendency to imitate (mimesis) which provokes conflicts of desire which are resolved by the murder or scapegoating of an arbitrary victim, whether or nor the victim is guilty of any offence. Events like this are remembered and retold by societies. Myths grow up which narrate the murder from the perspective of the killers, and, along with such myths, sacrificial rites provide a means of dealing with the violence generated by mimetic desire.

In the gospels, however, we have a story of a victim and a killing, when society deems that it is expedient for 'one man to die for the people'. In the gospels the story is told from the perspective of the scapegoated person, asserting his innocence. This, according to Girard, has the effect of unmasking cultures based on violence. Humanity is thereby challenged to initiate a way of renunciation of violence advocated and practised by Jesus, lest they destroy themselves. In contrast with human society's version of the story of the fate of the victims who are regarded as troublemakers and subversives. The words of Caiaphas (to which I have already alluded) 'it is fitting for one man to die for the people' (John 11:50) represents the sentiments of the leaders of state security forces down the centuries. Jesus identifies with the victims in his society and as a result sets in train a process of victimization of him, which leads to a violent reaction as the political elite, plots to rid himself or herself of a troublemaker.

The gospel gives the perspective of the victim, the Abel's of this world who otherwise remain silent, as it tells the story from the perspective of a victim. In these texts we have a situation which challenges the old African proverb, 'Until lions have their historians, tales of hunting will always glorify the hunter.' The story of the life and death of the lion of the tribe of Judah who is a Lamb who is slain (Rev 5:5-6) exemplifies a different kind of story. The story of Jesus, therefore, becomes fundamental for interpreting all human history and the distortions and delusions we tell about ourselves, the violence we use to maintain the status quo, and our ways of disguising from ourselves the oppression of the victim and the way we maintain a lie in order to keep things as they are.

The story of Jesus' death, therefore, is not about a sacrifice for sin but of a revelation of the false consciousness of the efficacy of the scapegoat mechanism, which is endemic in society and the violence, which it institutionalizes. The gospel unmasks the fact that violence lies at the base of all human culture and does so by proclaiming the innocence of the victim. It offers an alternative pattern for humanity. To bear witness to this alternative way is to risk the violence of the old system. The story of Christ's life and death subverts the 'lie' of culture based on violence as do the lives of those lived according to this pattern. That provokes a violent crisis as the lie is revealed accelerating the process of cultural disintegration. With the gospel there can be no resolution other than acceptance of its alternative way. Culture based on violence is inherently unstable. Religion, myth and ritual can only paper over the cracks of society. The revelation of the gospel reveals the extent to which human culture based on violence:

> We can see why the Passion is found between the preaching of the Kingdom and the Apocalypse.... It is a phenomenon that has no importance in the eyes of the world - incapable, at least in principle, of setting up or reinstating a cultural order, but very effective, in spite of those who know better, in carrying out subversion. In the long run, it is quite capable of undermining and overturning the whole cultural history and supplying the secret motive force of all subsequent history.[1]

The relevance of this for the interpretation of the Apocalypse has been strangely neglected. Indeed, Girard and his followers explicitly exclude the Apocalypse from their canon of texts, which subvert the culture of violence. Steve Finamore introduced me to the work of René Girard ten years ago when he was doing a doctoral thesis on the Apocalypse. One way of reading the New Testament's primary apocalyptic text is to regard it as the unmasking of the violence of human culture by the gospel of the slain Lamb. The lamb's death and exaltation unmask the violence of the world, which in Rev 6 and following is described in all its horror as the vindication of the lamb provokes a violent reaction in an unjust world. Such an interpretation has its roots in the history of interpretation, as the earliest commentator on the Apocalypse, Victorinus of Pettau, came close to seeing the gospel as a challenge and to the violence and injustice of the world in the way in which the rider on the white horse is seen as the effect of the gospel on a violent world.

Whatever value we attach to this way of approaching the Apocalypse it represents the way in which modern attachment to non-violence reads even this most violent book as (to use Girard's own words) is 'very effective, in spite of those who know better, in carrying out subversion [and] capable of undermining and overturning the whole cultural history and supplying the secret motive force of all subsequent history'. As I read chapter after chapter of Steve's dissertation I realized that not only did Steve have something very

---

[1] Girard 1987.209

Foreword

important to say but also in his usual understated way a voice had emerged in biblical studies, which needed to be heard. My only regret as I write this enthusiastic endorsement of Steve's wonderful book is that it has taken so long for the book and the author to be more widely known. Steve's self-effacing character will make him cringe to read this, but if the Apocalypse was a book for its times to enable what the Spirit was saying to late first century people, Steve's reading of the Apocalypse, through the lens of Girard's theory, is an equivalent wake up call for a world addicted to violence and coercion in the pursuit of human flourishing and a plea to consider the 'better way' of the victim, the story of whose death, supposedly expedient for the wellbeing of the people is recorded in the New Testament gospels.

Christopher C. Rowland
Oxford, 2007

Preface

On a Sunday afternoon in August 1989 I sat on the lawn in the courtyard of a restaurant in Cajamarca in the Peruvian Andes talking to two young historians from Lima. Their research had brought them to the city where agents of the Christian Spanish Empire deceived and betrayed Atahualpa, the last Inca. We discussed the latest crisis facing their homeland and they, like most of the Peruvians to whom I had spoken, believed that a large scale civil war was almost inevitable. I asked if nothing could be done to avert such a catastrophe. Their reply was that war was not only inevitable, it was also necessary; it would be for the best. There was so much tension, so much injustice and so much anger in the experience of the Peruvian people; they possessed so many emotions which needed to be purged; only widespread violence could conceivably resolve the situation. A war would act as what they called *una catarsis*; it would enable Peruvians to expunge their negative collective attitudes, and provide the new beginning necessary if the just, peaceful Peru which every Peruvian desired was to come into being.[1]

At the time I was a little shocked by an attitude which seemed a counsel of despair. However, I was also conscious that I had for some months been living with a deep sense of fear and foreboding. I was aware that the guerrilla insurgency of Sendero Luminoso was moving progressively closer to the area in which I lived and worked. My concern went beyond the thought of the physical harm to which I, my friends, colleagues and family might come. I experienced the fear that all order would be lost and that we would find ourselves caught up in the impending anarchy. I was afraid of disorientation, of the loss of the markers by which we live. My sense of foreboding was all the greater because I was unable to name the thing of which I was afraid. It occurred to me that this thing which I most feared was the very thing which the young historians believed must come if Peru's many tensions were to know any resolution.

When I returned from South America in order to read theology, I was encouraged to think again about the Old Testament stories in which God is said to act, in creation and in redemption, so as to confront chaos and to bring forth order. I learned to name the thing of which I had been afraid: chaos. It seemed to me that, because of the circumstances in which they lived, some of the people of Peru stood looking into the abyss, at once repelled by and fascinated by the chaos which might emerge. It also occurred to me that, in a rather different way, our own culture might be facing its own confrontation with such forces.

---

[1] They may have been influenced by the anti-colonialist analyses of Fanon 1967.

I was aware of the apostolic assertion that "God is a God not of disorder but of peace",[2] but as I pondered these issues I found myself wondering if it was possible that violence, chaos, even death could ever have a therapeutic effect and if so, whether this might be relevant in any way to Christian ideas about atonement or to older Jewish ideas about the sufferings which were expected to be the herald of the dawn of the messianic age. I also wanted to know if the New Testament's chaos imagery, for example the plagues described in the Book of Revelation, bore any relation to such issues. I was fortunate enough to have the opportunity to undertake doctoral research which began as an attempt to address such questions. This book is a revised version of that thesis. I have attempted to supplement it with references to works by Girard and major works on Revelation which have been published since the thesis was submitted. However, the material and the argument are the same and the intervening years of reading and of the observation of world events have only made the work seem more relevant.

---

[2] 1 Corinthians 14.33. *NRSV*.

Acknowledgements

There are many people whom I must thank for their help in enabling me to write this thesis. Many friends and colleagues have helped me to find publications, engaged helpfully with ideas or simply listened patiently when I needed to try to put a thought into words. Dr Paula Gooder, who read and commented on an earlier draft of this thesis, Professor Paul Brickell and the Revd Dr Sean Winter were all particularly supportive. I am pleased to have this opportunity to express my gratitude to all of them.

I owe a huge debt of thanks to the two bodies which have provided me with the grants which made it possible for me to study for the last few years. The Scholarship and Ministerial Training Bursary Committee of the Baptist Union of Great Britain and the Dr Williams's Trust have both been generous in their support.

There are many people associated with the study of theology at Oxford whom I would like to thank. My first teachers were the staff of Regent's Park College and I am grateful for all I have learned from them and for their continuing support. In addition, I would like to thank those who taught me as a postgraduate, especially Mr Robert Morgan and Dr John Ashton. I am also grateful to my friends, colleagues and teachers in the New Testament graduate seminar for the stimulating papers and discussions, the patience with which they listened to early versions of some of the sections of the thesis of which this book is a slightly revised version, and the suggestions which they made as a result. I have a particular debt to Dr Graham Ward who helped me to understand the thought of Girard and to appreciate the background to his ideas. My debt to my teacher and supervisor Professor Christopher Rowland is incalculable. He has been a constant source of help, encouragement, support, advice, suggestions and wisdom. Such good ideas as there may be in this thesis almost certainly originate with either Chris or Graham. However, the flaws in the use to which I have put those ideas are, like the other deficiencies in this work, fully my own responsibility.

There are also many people outside of the University whom I would like to thank. In particular I am grateful to friends and colleagues at the Baptist Union of Great Britain and at Tearfund, to the members of Baptist churches in South Battersea, Abingdon, Bayworth and Westbury-on-Trym, and to my colleagues and students at the Bristol Baptist College. In addition, the staff at Paternoster Press have been both patient and understanding and I am particularly grateful to the Revd Dr Anthony R. Cross for his help and encouragement as I prepared the book for publication.

Finally, I would like to thank all the members of my family. In particular, my parents have continued to be a wonderful source of support. My daughters,

Deborah and Jennifer, are a great delight to me and have been remarkably patient with my need to spend time reading and writing. And my appreciation of my wife Rebecca goes beyond words. Without her I could not even have contemplated this project. This book is therefore for her.

Stephen Finamore
Bristol Baptist College, 2008

Abbreviations

AARSSR	American Academy of Religious Studies Studies in Religion
AB	Anchor Bible
ACW	Ancient Christian Writers; the Works of the Fathers in Translation, Newman Press, London 1956
A.H.	*Against Heresies*
ANL	The Ante-Nicene Library, T & T Clark, Edinburgh 1869
ANRW	*Aufstieg und Niedergang der Römischen Welt*
ATANT	Abhandlungen zur Theologie des Alten und Neuen Testaments
AUSS	*Andrews University Seminary Studies*
AV	Authorized Version
BA	*Biblical Archaeologist*
BETL	Bibliotheca ephemeridum theologicarum Lovaniensium
BGBE	Beiträge zur Geschichte der Biblischen Exegese
Bib	*Biblica*
BNTC	Black's New Testament Commentaries
BR	*Biblical Review*
BS	Bollingen Series
BTB	*Biblical Theology Bulletin*
BZNW	Beihefte zur *Zeitschrift für die neutestamentliche Wissenschaft*
CBC	Cambridge Bible Commentary
CBQ	*Catholic Biblical Quarterly*
ConB	Coniectanea Biblica
CSEL	Corpus Scriptorum Ecclesiasticarum Latinorum
CSIR	Cambridge Studies in Ideology and Religion
Douai	Douai-Rheims Bible
EQ	*Evangelical Quarterly*
ET	English Translation
ETL	*Ephemerides theologicae lovanienses*
EstBib	*Estudios bíblicos*
Exhort	*An Exhortation to Martyrdom*
ExpT	*Expository Times*
FC	The Fathers of the Church, Catholic University Press of America, Washington 1959
GNS	Good News Studies
H.E.	*Church History*
HTR	*Harvard Theological Review*
IBS	*Irish Biblical Studies*

IC	Interpretation Commentary
ICC	International Critical Commentary
IDB	*Interpreter's Dictionary of the Bible,* Abingdon, Nashville, 1962
Int	*Interpretation*
JB	Jerusalem Bible
JBL	*Journal of Biblical Literature*
JNES	*Journal of Near Eastern Studies*
JSJ	*Journal for the Study of Judaism*
JSNT	*Journal for the Study of the New Testament*
JSNTSS	*Journal for the Study of the New Testament* Supplement Series
JSPSS	*Journal for the Study of the Pseudepigrapha* Supplement Series
JSS	*Journal of Semitic Studies*
JTC	*Journal of Theology and Church*
JTS	*Journal of Theological Studies*
KTR	*King's Theological Review*
LF	A Library of Fathers of the Holy Catholic Church, Parker, Oxford 1861
LXX	The Septuagint
MLN	*Modern Language Notes*
MNTC	Moffatt New Testament Commentary
MT	The Masoretic Text
NASB	New American Standard Bible
NCB	New Century Bible
NCBC	New Cambridge Bible Commentary
NEB	New English Bible
NICNT	New International Commentary on the New Testament
NIGNT	New International Greek Testament Commentary
NIV	New International Version
NovT	*Novum Testamentum*
NovTSup	Supplements to *Novum Testamentum*
NRSV	New Revised Standard Version
NRT	*Nouvelle revue theologique*
NTA	*New Testament Abstracts*
NTS	*New Testament Studies*
OHM	Oxford Historical Monographs
RB	*Revue Biblique*
RevExp	*Review and Expositor*
RHPR	*Revue d'histoire et de philosophie religieuse*
RSV	Revised Standard Version
SBL	Society of Biblical Literature
SBT	Studies in Biblical Theology

SJT	*Scottish Journal of Theology*
SL	A Select Library of Nicene and Post-Nicene Fathers of the Christian Church, Parker, Oxford 1905
SNTSMS	Society for New Testament Studies Monograph Series
SP	Sacra Pagina
SUNT	Studien zur Umwelt des Neuen Testament
T.Ab.	*Testament of Abraham*
TAPSNS	Transactions of the American Philosophical Society New Series
TDNT	*Theological Dictionary of the New Testament*, edited by Gerhard Kittel and G. Friedrich, Eerdmans, Grand Rapids, 10 volumes, 1964-19761967, ET of *TWNT*
TEV	Today's English Version (Good News Bible)
TWNT	*Theologische Wörterbuch zum Neuen Testament*
TynB	*Tyndale Bulletin*
UCOP	University of Cambridge Oriental Papers
UPPMAS	University of Pennsylvania Press Middle Ages Series
VT	*Vetus Testamentum*
WBC	Word Biblical Commentary
WCC	World Council of Churches
ZKTh	*Zeitschrift für katholische Theologie*
ZNW	Zeitschrift für die neutestamentliche Wissenschaft

Introduction

The Book of Revelation lies on the margins of the church's life. It is the last book of the Christian Bible and thus on the fringes of the canon. It has only a limited place in the lectionaries of the church,[1] and is therefore rarely expounded within the mainstream denominations. The theologians of the church in every age have distrusted and criticized this text.[2] Revelation, with its unusual symbols and its violent images, seems to have little relevance to the Christian message. Centuries of effort have produced many interpretations but have failed to deliver a hermeneutic which will guarantee a reading compatible with orthodox theology or ethics. The text's language adapts too readily to sectarian interpretations. The sectarian hermeneutics are rarely self-evidently inferior to those of the orthodox. It is for reasons of this kind that Hadorn acknowledges that for many, "The Apocalypse remains a book locked with seven seals".[3] O'Donovan is right to say of Revelation that, "the universal prejudice of church and scholarship is against it."[4] Instead, the book has appealed to those concerned that church and state should be renewed or even overthrown. Those excluded by the establishments of both these institutions have often turned to Revelation in order to find resources for their struggle.[5] It has provided them with ways to interpret their own history and encouraged them to persist in their hopes for a better world.[6] Revelation is a marginal text fully embraced only by the marginalized and their sympathizers.

Yet in other ways Revelation has a central role in the life of the church. It is difficult to think of any other book of the Bible, with the exception of Psalms, which has had such an influence on the church's hymnody. The Christophanies of 1:12-18 and 19:11-16, the throne vision of 4:1-11, the praise of God and the Lamb at 5:6-14 and 7:9-17, the declarations of 11:15-18, 15:3-4 and 19:1-8, and the visions of the new Jerusalem at 21:1-22:5 have inspired hymn writers and poets throughout the Christian era. Revelation fires the creative imagination and as a result its symbols lie at the heart of the church's experience of the God it encounters in worship. Equally significantly perhaps,

---

[1] Rowland points out that Revelation is rarely found in the lectionary for the Sunday Eucharist of the Church of England. 1988a.66, 1993.2. Cranmer required the rest of the New Testament to be read three times a year while Revelation, like the Old Testament (except the Psalms), was to be read once a year. The book is classified with the prophets. Brightman 1915.lxxvii.
[2] See Ch1 on, e.g., Eusebius, the Reformers, Bultmann and Dodd.
[3] "blieb die Ofbg ein mit 7 Siegeln verschlossenes Buch" 1928.1.
[4] 1986a.61.
[5] See Rowland 1988.66-88.
[6] Cohn 1993a. On millenarian movements generally see B.R. Wilson 1973.

Augustine's understanding of the book provided him with the framework, especially the teleology and epistemology, for his *The City of God*, a work whose influence on Christian theology is incalculable. Revelation is thus in some senses marginal and in others central to the life of the church. It seems that it is experienced as 'two-edged' and this raises the question of whether a fully coherent reading is possible.

In some books of the Bible, the authors express God's action in creation and redemption in terms of a confrontation with the hostile forces of chaos, an overcoming of those forces and the establishment of order in their place. Revelation draws on traditions and uses images which include or involve such ideas. However, it does not regard God and God's agents as sources of order alone; in certain passages they also appear to be responsible for at least some of the chaos which is experienced by the earth and its inhabitants. This is true of the plague sequences which are the subject of this thesis. These passages are integral to the structure of the book and so cause difficulties to sympathetic reviewers and generate hostility in others.

One purpose of this thesis is to investigate the relationship between God, God's agents, order and chaos as they are expressed in Revelation's plague sequences, in particular the sequence of seal openings. Exegesis inevitably relies on patterns derived from outside of the text itself and most readings use an understanding of history or theology as a framework and interpret the details of the text in accordance with it. The first chapter of this thesis reviews the history of the interpretation of the plague sequences from the early church to the present day. It pays particular attention to the early church, Joachim of Fiore, the reformers and critical readings of the last 150 years. The conclusions suggest that another perspective may help contemporary readers to find meaning and value in the book. A new critical tool is needed as the basis for such an approach and it is proposed that the textual and cultural theories of René Girard may be appropriate for the task.

Girard has presented his ideas in a number of different publications and within a number of different disciplines. His work has attracted a considerable response and scholars from a variety of fields have engaged with it. An important part of this thesis is the attempt to present Girard's theories, and the criticisms and uses made of it, as a coherent whole. Particular attention is paid to Girard's views that *mimesis* is a fundamental human drive; that mimesis induces the scapegoating phenomena to which human cultures owe their origin and maintenance; that myths and rituals all have their provenance in such phenomena and therefore share a common structure; that the Gospels expose the truth about human culture; and that this revelation has necessary consequences for human history. This presentation allows the key ideas which can be used in reading biblical texts to be identified and two hermeneutical methods to be defined as means of aiding the exegesis of Revelation.

From the perspective of biblical studies, one of the key features of Girard's system is his insistence, at least in his major works, that the Gospels do not portray the death of Jesus as a sacrifice. This raises a number of questions about theological understandings of the work of Jesus and the ways his death is treated in the New Testament. A study of Revelation's presentation of the work of Jesus is necessary in order to determine whether or not Girard's ideas can help improve our understanding of the text.

The final chapter attempts to apply the hermeneutical methods derived from Girard to some key texts from Revelation. It shows that Jesus is portrayed as the martyr whose vindication exposes culture to the truth and so initiates a crisis which is experienced as chaos and articulated as such. The new reading of Revelation's first plague sequence, based on the work of Girard, is an exercise in theological exegesis. It seeks to allow it to speak in a way which, it is hoped, is both consistent with the book as a whole and meaningful to readers in the first decade of the twenty-first century. It is not an attempt to impose yet another rigid structure upon the book and to interpret every detail accordingly. Nor does it rule out other readings and the conclusions which they reach. Instead it seeks to understand the structure of the text and the story it tells. It offers a flexible framework which may allow readers to enter imaginatively into the world generated by the text and engage with it in such a way that they are confronted by the word of God in their own particular contexts. This word of God may prove to be two-edged, to be something which brings both judgement and salvation. If so, it may help to account for some of the ambivalence associated with the reception of the book. The word may also turn out to be spoken through a victim driven to, indeed beyond, the margins of human social life. Should this be the case, there may be some reason this text is rejected by those at the heart of collective human relations and embraced by those who feel themselves to be at the edges.

Chapter 1

History, Theology and Visions of Chaos: A Review of the Literature on Revelation's Plague Sequences

A. Introduction

In 1963, when Feuillet reviewed the scholarly literature on the Book of Revelation, one of his conclusions was that "Saint John's Apocalypse today exercises less attraction than at other times to professional exegetes. This disfavour, albeit relative, is regrettable." He expressed the wish that "scientific research should increase".[1] By 1980, when Vanni reviewed the scholarship since Feuillet wrote, the prayer appeared to have been answered.[2] Vanni himself later acknowledged this saying, "Fortunately, the lack of interest from scientific research that Feuillet had lamented in 1963 appeared by 1979 to have been overcome".[3] Since then there has been no reduction in the flow of books and articles published on Revelation and there is every reason to suppose that attention, both scholarly and otherwise, will increasingly be paid to the book as the third millennium continues.

The principal argument of this chapter is that despite their continuing interest in Revelation, and in apocalypses and apocalyptic thought generally, scholars have so far failed to offer an adequate account of the chaos imagery found in the book. In particular, the interpretations offered of the series of plagues loosed at the breaking of the seven seals (6:1-17, 8:5), at the sounding of the seven trumpets (8:2-9:21, 11:15-19) and at the pouring out of the seven bowls (15:1, 15:7-16:21) have proved unsatisfactory.[4]

Commentators often use the term *chaos* with respect to the imagery found in Revelation but its meaning and helpfulness are rarely discussed. Issues of order

---

[1] "L'Apocalypse de saint Jean exerce aujourd'hui moins d'attrait qu'autrefois sur les exégètes de profession. Cette défaveur, d'ailleurs toute relative, est regrettable", "les recherches scientifiques se multiplient." Feuillet 1963.109.

[2] 1980b.

[3] "Lo scarso interesse della ricerca scientifica che A. Feuillet aveva lamentato nel 1963, appariva, nel 1979, felicemente superato." 1988.7. As late as 1986 Georgi wrote of Revelation, "The work of John has gained the attention of critical exegetes only recently". 1986.121.

[4] There is no consensus about the points in the text where the series begin and end.

and disorder play a significant part in the argument of this thesis and it is therefore important that the use made of the term be explained. Chaos, involving as it does the abolition of differences and distinctions, is inevitably difficult to define acceptably; in a sense it may be taken to refer to that which cannot be defined.

In the discussion of ancient myths, chaos is often used for the state of the universe prior to the act of creation. Gunkel, in seeking to demonstrate its debt to an ancient Babylonian creation myth, applied the German word *Chaos* to the imagery of Revelation 12.[5] He identified the dragon with the monster whose defeat in battle preceded the act of creation. Yarbro Collins[6] and Day[7] have questioned the Babylonian provenance of the version of the myth adapted in Revelation. However, both agree that an ancient myth about a chaos monster lies behind some of the images in 12:1-17.[8] Thus, the term chaos is sometimes used for the condition of the universe as it was before creation, the agents which maintained it in that state and, by extension, any forces or events which tend to return the world to its primeval condition. Similar understandings of creation are found throughout the ancient Near East.[9]

Traditional Christian theology interprets the Bible so that it is understood to teach *creatio ex nihilo*, but most contemporary scholars agree that traces of a version of the chaos myth may be found in its pages.[10] Some share Gunkel's view that the creation story of Genesis 1 is a demythologized version of such an account.[11] It seems probable that a belief in a chaotic stage in the process of creation, before God imposed difference and order upon the material which made up the universe, was held by the writers of the Old Testament and perhaps by some of the authors of the New Testament. The position of Genesis 1 on the nature of creation is disputed,[12] but the words תהו ובהו[13] at 1:2 suggest that at one stage in the creation process, the earth, if not the heavens, was characterized by undifferentiation. The Greek word χάος and the Egyptian word transliterated *isfet* express similar ideas.[14] Thus, chaos is a term used to describe the undifferentiated state of the universe prior to creation and for anything which tends to move the universe back towards such a condition.

---

[5] 1921.
[6] 1976.
[7] 1985.
[8] The material is also discussed by Abir 1995; Delcor 1977b; Wakeman 1973; H. Wallace 1948.
[9] See N. Cohn 1993c.
[10] The relevant material is discussed by Day 1985, Wakeman 1973.
[11] 1921.
[12] See bibliographies and discussion in G. Wenham 1991.1-17.
[13] The usual translation is 'formless and void'.
[14] These ideas are discussed by N. Cohn 1993c. The themes as they relate to biblical ideas of creation are discussed by B.W. Anderson 1987; Gunkel 1921; R. Murray 1992; Niditch 1985; Oden 1992.

When aspects of the created order lose their distinctive characteristics, the things which allow them to be distinguished, the effect is one of chaos.

There are, of course, differences between Hebrew thought and that of neighbouring peoples, but the work of Hengel[15] and Glasson[16] suggests that mutual influence between Jewish and Hellenistic thought should not be ignored. Furthermore, J. Barr has offered a helpful criticism of the idea that languages possess an implied metaphysic which prevents the accurate translation and interchange of religious ideas.[17] There is thus no reason why the word *chaos*, though derived from Greek, when defined in this way, should not be used as a tool for the investigation of images in a text which, though written in Greek, betrays evidence of having been influenced by Semitic patterns of thought and grammar.[18] In Chapter 5 an attempt is made to demonstrate that the process described in Revelation, drawing as it does on the language and imagery of Old Testament ideas about the Day of the Lord, is one of 'uncreation', that is, of the breakdown of the order which sustains creation and its reversion, partial at least, to chaos. The distinguishing and naming which took place at creation is undermined.

The three series of plagues of Revelation are full of images of chaos. Court has described these sections as "often neglected".[19] This is less the case for the first series than the others which are sometimes passed over as though they merely repeated the content of the first. The series are used by commentators for a wide range of purposes, many of which are discussed in this chapter, but few attempts have been made to understand what these parts of the text convey to the reader nor to understand the relationship of the imagery they contain to the development of the narrative of which they are a part. For example, while it is occasionally acknowledged that the three series all flow from the vision of the heavenly throne and the exalted Lamb at 4:1-5:14,[20] little attempt is made, other than through assertions about early Christian beliefs, to understand why the text understands these things to be related to one another.

This chapter offers a review of opinion, from the early church to the present day, about the chaos imagery found in the relevant sections of Revelation. It covers the principal methods of interpretation and the views of influential commentators. It does not pretend to be exhaustive. Even Allo, whose commentary includes an extensive history of interpretation, in justifying his decision to discuss only some of the Protestant commentators, and referring the reader to Bousset for details of the rest, observes that "A person's life does not

---

[15] 1974.
[16] 1961.
[17] 1961.
[18] See Ch5.A.
[19] 1979. vii.
[20] See Ch5.D.

allow them to read all the commentaries on the Apocalypse".[21]

For ease of presentation, the material is presented in a roughly chronological order, beginning with the earliest commentators and making use of the generally accepted, but admittedly somewhat arbitrary, division of church history into periods. In the same way, while no two commentaries are exactly alike, it is necessary to discuss them in terms of the generally accepted categories of interpretation. However, even though such methods are adopted, the flow of this chapter cannot be straightforward. The history of the interpretation of Revelation is not a seamless robe flowing from the millennialism of Justin Martyr, through the spiritualizing interpretations of the later church Fathers to the church historical views of the Protestants, and on to the historical and literary-critical views of our own day. Any such presentation would be unacceptably schematized and fail to do justice to the many and varied interpretations of Revelation which have been made and which continue to be made. Furthermore, in many instances it was the overall interpretation of Revelation that was the matter debated. The view taken of the plagues was dependent on exegetical decisions taken on other grounds. This means that overall approaches and interpretative methods, in addition to comments on the chaos imagery itself, must sometimes be discussed.[22]

B. The Interpretation of Revelation until 1850

1. The Early Church

Most scholarly work on the interpretation of Revelation in the Patristic period emphasizes the different attitudes of the Fathers to chiliasm.[23] Chiliasm, or millenarianism, refers to the belief in a concrete, historical and temporary

---

[21] "Une vie d'homme ne suffirait pas à lire tous les commentaires de l'Apocalypse." 1921. ccxxxi.

[22] Fuller histories of interpretation are in the introductions to the major commentaries. Allo 1921.s14, Bousset 1896a.51-141 are particularly helpful. E.B. Elliott 1862 includes an extensive history of interpretation at 4.275-563 and devotes considerable space to a refutation (4.564-700) of interpretative approaches other than his own church and world historical view. Beckwith 1919; Böcher 1988; Charles 1913.1-78, 1922; Court 1979.Ch1; Feuillet 1964a; Schüssler Fiorenza 1968, 1977b, 1985.12-26,160-164; Vanni 1980b have also written helpfully on the subject. Prigent 1959, on Revelation 12, inevitably includes helpful comments on the development of different readings of Revelation as a whole. Wainwright 1993 is an excellent review of the literature but focuses on the issue of the millennium and scarcely mentions the interpretation of the plagues. See Koester 2001. Kovacs and Rowland 2004 is especially interesting.

[23] General discussions of Patristic interpretations of Revelation and of eschatological expectation in the early church include Bietenhard 1953; Daley 1991; Helms 1991; Kelly 1977.459-489; Mackay 1978; McGinn 1984, 1995; Simonetti 1994.

future reign of Christ upon earth. The advocates of this doctrine claim that it is taught by Revelation 20:1-7 where the phrase χίλια ἔτη (a thousand years) is used six times. As a consequence, scholarly attention tends to focus on the interpretation of Chapters 20-22 and relatively little attention is paid to the rest of the book.[24]

It is usually argued that that the earliest interpretations, such as those of Justin Martyr (died c.165) and Irenaeus (c.130-200), were millenarian.[25] It is claimed that they found such an approach necessary to counter the spiritualizing tendencies of the Gnostics which they wished to oppose.[26] However, when the Gnostic threat declined, such an interpretation became less necessary. In fact, after the conversion of Constantine and the establishment of Christianity as the official religion of the Roman Empire, its anti-imperial implications made it an embarrassment, especially to those seeking a rapprochement with the authorities. The distaste for millennial ideas, which came to be regarded as carnal and Jewish,[27] led some to reject Revelation altogether, while others developed the spiritualizing methods that, following the work of Tyconius (c.380), who influenced the views of Augustine (354-430), eventually came to dominate the exegesis of Revelation. These methods were not seriously challenged until the Medieval period brought the development of the church and world historical methods of interpretation under the impetus of the exegetical ideas of Joachim of Fiore (c.1135-1202).

Eusebius (c.260-340) appears to have been somewhat ambivalent about Revelation. Sometimes he appears to be positive about the book.[28] However, his relationship with the Emperor would not allow him wholeheartedly to endorse a text which could be understood to relativize the imperial claims to earthly sovereignty.[29] Eusebius questions the apostolic authorship of

---

[24] Allusions to other parts of Revelation exist in early apocryphal works: e.g. *Epistle of the Apostles* 34 refers to a trumpet in heaven and stars that fall to earth (8:2, 8:6, 8:10, 9:1); the Gnostic *Gospel of Truth* 3 refers to Jesus taking up a book that nobody else could open and may reflect 5:1-7. Parts of *Sibylline Oracles* may reflect Revelation e.g. 8:190-200 and 8.341, 353. There is an interesting parallel between Revelation 6:14 and the *Gospel of Thomas* 111 which states, "Jesus said, 'The heavens and the earth will be rolled up in your presence.'" It is possible that these texts draw on the same or similar traditions to those which influenced Revelation.

[25] *Dialogue with Trypho* 81. *A.H.* 5.

[26] Newman 1963-1964 suggests that Revelation itself has anti-Gnostic purposes. Simonetti 1994 argues that Irenaeus had at least one other motive; his literalistic understanding of the millennium is connected with his concern to relate protology and eschatology.

[27] The idea of a temporary messianic reign in the Jewish literature is discussed by Bailey 1934 and Kreitzer 1987.29-91.

[28] E.g. *H.E.* 3.18.

[29] His view of Constantine is stated in the oration he gave on the thirtieth anniversary of his reign. Eusebius claims imperial rule is ordained by God and that the emperor's

Revelation, suggesting it is the work of a different John.[30] Elsewhere he cites the work of Dionysius of Alexandria who contested the apostolic authorship of the book on literary grounds.[31] He does not reject the text outright, although others did so because of the use allegedly made of Revelation by the Montanists. Eusebius's views proved influential and caused the authority of the work to be doubted by many, especially in the East. Helms claims that Eusebius was motivated by the fact that he "cannot abide the millennium."[32]

The view that the prevailing early church interpretation of Revelation was determined by doctrinal and political considerations has been challenged, in part at least, by the thesis of Helms. He believes that a different, Christological, interpretation of Revelation existed alongside the one which stressed chiliasm, and that this reading may be traced in the writings of Justin, Irenaeus, Origen (c.185-255) and Eusebius. Helms asserts that this was the original and generally accepted interpretation and that the chiliastic interpretation was adopted only because of its usefulness in providing polemical material for use against the Gnostics. Literalistic approaches to the millennium were little more than a temporary aberration. Those who adopted them were well aware that orthodoxy had previously interpreted the millennium in terms of the past or had understood it spiritually.

Helms argues that Irenaeus used two different and largely unreconciled ways of reading Revelation. The better known is literal and chiliastic and may be found in *A.H.* at 2.31.3 and from 4.20.11 through to the end of Book 5. However, in the rest of the work Irenaeus understands Revelation to refer to the first coming of Christ and to his dispensation for the saints; the interpretation is rarely oriented towards the future. The reading remains eschatological, but in the sense that the church is understood to be living in the last days, a period inaugurated by Christ. This was, according to Helms, the better established interpretation. Irenaeus uses it and offers no defence of it for none is needed. However, it allows a spiritual understanding of the eschaton and could therefore be used to support some of the positions associated with Gnosticism.

---

earthly rule reflects heavenly reality. Eusebius says of the emperor "The kingdom with which he is invested is an image of the heavenly one. He looks up to see the archetypal pattern and guides those whom he rules below in accordance with that pattern...The basic principle of kingly authority is the establishment of a single source of authority to which everything is subject. Monarchy is superior to every other constitution and form of government. For polyarchy, where everyone competes on equal terms, is really anarchy and discord. This is why there is one God, and not two, three or even more." Wiles 1975.230-234. Kee discusses the function of religion and the church in Constantine's imperial ideology and strategy and claims the emperor accomplished "the replacement of the norms of Christ and the early church by the norms of imperial ideology." 1982.4.

[30] *H.E.* 3.39.
[31] *H.E.* 7.25.
[32] 1991.29.

Since it does not serve his anti-Gnostic purposes, it is occasionally abandoned in favour of the more literal interpretation.[33]

In his conclusions Helms attempts to reconstruct what he regards as the established non-eschatological reading of Revelation in the early church, a reading he regards as being obscured in the texts because it served no polemical use in the arguments with the Gnostics. He acknowledges that this interpretation is nowhere extant but argues that it can be reconstructed. In it the millennium is understood to refer to the old economy; Satan was bound and was freed for the time of Christ's ministry. Thus Satan was able to crucify Jesus, an event which had results Satan had not anticipated; it was the cause of his crushing defeat. The remainder of the book refers largely to the experience of the church in the present; a time of persecution and the threat of persecution. Helms regards this reading as more established than the eschatological reading because the authors who refer to it feel no need to defend their interpretation. This is not the case with those who adopt the eschatological readings. Thus, the latter are innovative, being motivated by the struggle against Gnosticism, while the spiritual readings are traditional.

Although Helms makes his case effectively, he depends on an argument from silence with respect to the failure of the Fathers to defend the alleged non-eschatological reading. The citations below will show that Tertullian at least was unembarrassed by the literal understandings of Revelation which he frequently adopted. It is certainly the case that Irenaeus, despite his chiliasm, which might imply a literalistic approach to the text, and his own warnings at, *A.H.* 5.35, against allegorical interpretations, allegorizes certain sections of Revelation.[34] At the very least this suggests that no established reading of Revelation existed at this stage. Perhaps Helms stretches the evidence when he speaks of two irreconcilable readings. The view depends on a subsequent classification of approaches to the book; such constructs should not necessarily be read back into the writings of the early church. The views of Eusebius do not necessarily help Helms's case for he must have believed that the chiliastic view was the dominant one, or was likely to become so, or he would not have felt moved, as Helms claims he did, to challenge the authority of the book on such grounds.

There were no fixed rules for the interpretation of Scripture in the early church and many Fathers were content to use a text to prove their case without necessarily considering whether such a use fitted with their understanding of the book as a whole. The Bible had been given for teaching the church. Revelation, like any other book, could be mined for useful texts. So, while it is possible that two alternative approaches to the text existed side by side, it is not necessarily the case that the early Fathers found the two views to be in tension. It may be the modern tendency to classify and a corresponding desire for

---

[33] 1991.Ch4.
[34] E.g. *A.H.* 2.31.3 allegorizes the action of the dragon's tail.

consistency, which produces the apparent problem in the first place.

Irenaeus certainly uses texts from Revelation as proof texts for the unique status of Jesus. Some of these come from the sections which include chaos imagery. For example, he uses texts from Revelation, including 5-8, in this way.[35] However, he makes little reference to the context and it is difficult to demonstrate that there is any consistent reading behind the texts. Helms argues that the reading is Christological but there is no reason why a person holding the view that 19:11-16 and the subsequent visions lie in the future should not use these texts in such a manner.

Tertullian (c.155-235) was undoubtedly largely literal in his approach to Revelation. Like Justin and Irenaeus, he was a chiliast.[36] His literalism is perhaps most apparent in his attack on the spiritualizing tendencies of Hermogenes. For instance, he insists that the events described at the opening of the sixth seal at Revelation 6:12-17 are to be taken literally.[37] In *Treatise on the Resurrection* 25 he discusses Revelation 6:9-11 and argues that the souls of the martyrs must await their vengeance because the world must first experience the plagues which remain; the events which have been prophesied must take place. Elsewhere, he returns to this text to urge his readers not to fear martyrdom but rather to fear the consequences of fearing it.[38] He refers to the same text to prove his contention that the human soul is visible and therefore that it must have a corporeal nature.[39] The text was certainly a favourite.

So, Tertullian's approach to Revelation appears to have been fairly literal and this probably reflects his concern to defend orthodox eschatology. Certainly, his use of passages from the plague sections is mainly to give scriptural support to positions arrived at on other grounds. Sometimes these are orthodox positions, at other times, as is the case in the last text cited, he uses Scripture to defend Montanist prophecy. There are only limited indications of an overall reading.[40]

The views of Hippolytus of Rome (c.160-235) have been reconstructed from fragments and are discussed by Helms and Prigent.[41] The plagues are not to be understood literally but they will have a concrete fulfilment in the future. They will complete the process begun when God sent the plagues of the Exodus against Egypt. The Exodus is understood as a type of the experience of Christians described in Revelation. In both cases God acts decisively to rescue God's people from danger and lead them to safety. The use of Exodus as a key

---

[35] E.g. *A.H.* 4.20.2, 11; 4.21.3.
[36] See e.g. *Treatise against Marcion* 3.24.
[37] *Treatise against Hermogenes* 34.1-3.
[38] *Antidote to the Scorpion's Bite* 12.
[39] *On the Soul.* 8.5.
[40] Helms cites *Treatise on the Resurrection.* 26.11 and 27.1 as evidence that Tertullian knew and used a spiritual and allegorical interpretation of Revelation.
[41] 1991, 1959.

to the reading of Revelation enables Hippolytus, if the reconstructions are accurate, to offer a coherent reading of the text. The plagues released at the sounding of the fifth and sixth trumpets[42] refer to the kingdoms which were the ancient enemies of Israel and which rise again. Rome is regarded as an enemy of God's people so that Hippolytus's exegesis is anti-imperial. He regards 6:9-11 as offering some rationale for the delay of the Parousia. Hippolytus rejects the idea of a literal millennium while preserving an eschatological understanding of the text.

Cyprian (c.205-258) on the other hand, according to Prigent, avoids an eschatological approach, preferring to understand Revelation in terms of the present and the past. Cyprian refers a number of times to 6:9-11; to calm those eager for vengeance,[43] to demonstrate the benefits of martyrdom,[44] and to discourage over-reliance on the merits of the martyrs who may not command God.[45] He generally offers Christocentric interpretations which offer ethical and theological guidance. Thus 19:11-16, for example, does not refer to a future event but to the initial coming of Jesus.

Such a spiritualizing approach seems to have been present in the comments of Clement of Alexandria (c200) and is most certainly found in Origen. Clement cites Revelation 6:9-11 to demonstrate that Christians should reject dyed clothes for these are made to be looked at. They should wear only simple, white garments.[46] His concern is not really to spiritualize the text so much as to draw ethical teaching from it.

Origen (c.185-253) provides the first clear-cut evidence of a non-eschatological approach to the text and a rejection of chiliasm through the offering of an exegetical alternative for understanding Revelation 20:1-7. As Simonetti points out, Origen's reading deprived the millennialists of the scriptural basis of their teaching.[47] The thousand years are not a future prospect nor even a present reality. They refer to the previous economy which ended with the crucifixion of Jesus and the subsequent fall of Jerusalem, events which Origen regards as related. The new Jerusalem of chapters 21-22 is not a future hope but a present spiritual reality, the school of the saints becoming perfect.[48] The rest of the book is interpreted accordingly. It is about the coming of Christ and the spiritual consequences of his coming. It is not concerned with the future. The plagues are to be understood accordingly.[49] Origen's interest is in

---

[42] 9:1-21. Biblical references are to Revelation unless otherwise specified.
[43] *The Good of Patience* 21.
[44] *Testimonies* 3.16
[45] *The Lapsed* 18.
[46] *The Instructor* 2.11.
[47] 1994.45.
[48] *On First Principles* 2.11.2, 3.
[49] Corsini 1983 revives an interpretation of this type. Its guiding idea is that Revelation is about the first coming of Jesus Christ, not about his coming at the end of time.

Christology rather than in predictions of things to come. He understands the images to speak symbolically of the growth of Christians into salvation in a step by step process.[50] In fact Origen deals little with the plagues because he prefers to pass over texts which deal with destruction and damnation. For him, the time of the apocalyptic catastrophe was the time of the crucifixion and the destruction of the Temple. This option may reflect his opinion about the ascription of wrath to God.[51]

According to Helms,[52] Origen's views are criticized by the moderate chiliasm of Methodius (c.270-315). However his interpretation remains an essentially spiritualized one. He uses an Origenistic method to interpret Revelation 20:1-7 in a way which allows a defence of orthodox eschatology.

Although commentaries were apparently written by Melito of Sardis (c.175) and by Hippolytus, the earliest extant commentary is that of the martyr Victorinus of Pettau (died c.303). His work was adapted by Jerome (c.345-420) who removed its millenarian sections. The work had considerable influence in its revised form. A critical edition of Victorinus's text was not published until early in this century.[53] The interpretation mixes methods without necessarily reconciling them. Bruce describes the interpretation as contemporary-historical and allegorical, while Helms calls it spiritual and eschatological.[54]

As far as the plagues are concerned, Victorinus regards those associated with the seven seals as being things which must happen in order to fulfil the prophecy of Jesus recorded in Mark 13 and parallels. The scroll of 5:1 is the Old Testament, the true contents of which are hidden until Christ breaks open its seals to reveal the true meaning which includes a description of the events of the end times. The plagues are a part of God's end time judgement on the world. Victorinus discusses the first five seals. The rider on the white horse, regarded by Irenaeus as Christ[55] and by Tertullian as an angel crowned by God,[56] is interpreted by Victorinus as referring to the Holy Spirit and to the proclamation of the Gospel. These things are associated with the ascension of Jesus into heaven. The next three riders are said to refer to events which must take place before the eschaton but after the Gospel has been preached to the whole world. These riders represent war, famine and death and so the four riders together represent the Christian era from the coming of the Spirit to the return of Christ. In contrast to Victorinus's understanding of the texts about the millennium, these interpretations are clearly not literal. The fifth seal reveals

---

[50] *On First Principles* 3.6.6-9.
[51] Origen discusses the ascription of anger to God and understands it as an accommodation to humanity in *Homilies on Jeremiah* 18.6. Wiles 1975.7-10.
[52] 1991.Ch9.
[53] Haussleiter 1916.
[54] 1938, 1991.Ch10.
[55] *A.H.* 4.21.3.
[56] *On the Soldier's Chaplet.* 15.

the fate of the saints who have died during this time.[57]

As far as the other plagues are concerned, Victorinus offers no explanation as such. Both series lead up to and depict the eschaton and therefore Victorinus is credited with making a major contribution to the interpretation of Revelation; recapitulation. This is the idea that successive sections of the book describe the same events from different perspectives. Some subsequent exegetes have applied this idea to all three series of plagues, arguing that the seals, trumpets and bowls tell the story of the same events.[58] However, Victorinus himself limits recapitulation to the trumpets and the bowls, with the prophecies of the former being made less opaque in the latter. Helms argues that in Victorinus, "Through recapitulation, the dominant, figurative interpretation accommodates a literal, chiliastic eschatology."[59]

Whatever may have been the most common interpretation of Revelation during the first three or four centuries of the Christian era, it is without doubt the case that the spiritual reading dominated until the ideas of Joachim of Fiore became influential. The success of this reading is usually attributed to its adoption by Augustine. It is generally accepted that Augustine's position was highly influenced by the work of the lay African Donatist Tyconius,[60] whose commentary is lost. However, so many subsequent interpreters refer to it, depend upon it and repeat its arguments that some scholars have attempted to reconstruct its text. Steinhauser, for example, discusses the influence of the commentary and its subsequent use by other commentators. He concludes that Tyconius wrote a coherent verse by verse commentary. While it is impossible to reconstruct a critical text, a synopsis of the commentary can be produced, albeit with some missing sections.[61] His own synopsis takes the form of references to texts in the work of later commentators from Jerome's revision of Victorinus to the work of Beatus, whose commentary contains the greatest amount of raw material drawn from Tyconius.[62]

Tyconius reinterpreted the millenarian tradition and offered a spiritualized understanding of the text in which the eschaton need not be understood as being

---

[57] Jerome's revision includes an allegorical interpretation of the sixth seal in which, e.g., the earthquake represents persecution and the figs falling from the trees refer to people being separated from the church as a consequence. This interpretation is probably derived from Tyconius.

[58] Bruce 1938, e.g., thinks that the extension of recapitulation to include all three series of plagues is justified. Hendriksen 1939.28 regards the book as having seven parallel sections, including each of the three series of plagues, every one of which describes history from the first to the second comings of Christ.

[59] 1991.251.

[60] See Mackay 1978; Fredriksen, 1991, 1992; the opening sections of Matter 1992. Reflections on Augustine's eschatology can be found in Bonner 1993. Tyconius is also the author of the earliest extant Western treatise on biblical hermeneutics.

[61] 1987.265-266.

[62] 1987.267-316. Fragments of Tyconius have been published by Lo Bue 1963.

particularly close at hand. Thus Babylon is taken to refer not to Rome but the world in its hostility to the Christian church. The millennium is not a future, temporary, earthly reign of Christ but a description of the present age, that of the church. The majority of the plagues are not regarded as prophecies of future eschatological events but as representations of the church's and humanity's present experience. For example, the first trumpet (8:7) refers to the consequences of human concupiscence and luxurious living. The series of plagues recapitulate one another and the things which they describe have already begun and apply not to some future judgement but to the present sufferings of God's people. Nevertheless, Tyconius's thought does have an eschatological dimension for he believed himself to be a contemporary of the last persecution.

As a Donatist, Tyconius believed that the Catholic Church was the ally of the beast and that his was the true church whose experience Revelation describes. Despite this Augustine adopted the basic idea of his interpretation and gave it a degree of influence which belies its sectarian origins. Thus Simonetti remarks that Tyconius's commentary "marked a turning point in Western interpretation of this difficult text."[63] Augustine's principal reason for adopting this method seems to have been related to his concern about unduly literal, even carnal, understandings of the nature of the future millennium. The explicit discussion of Revelation in *The City of God* is almost wholly concerned with its closing chapters.[64] Corsini argues in his introduction that the concentration of attention on the millennium encouraged the erroneous view that the book as a whole is full of eschatological messages and that this caused the author's profound observations on God, Christology and the church to fade in importance.[65] In the course of his discussion Augustine lists the eschatological events but refuses to be drawn on how, when or in what order they will happen. He does not discuss the plagues of Revelation specifically. However, since he follows Tyconius in understanding the events described in Revelation, he probably understood the plagues to refer to present experience rather than to any future eschatological happenings. His view is that Revelation deals with the time which separates the first and second comings of Christ. This period is described in different ways and from different points of view. Augustine's writings occasionally show evidence of the influence of Revelation.[66]

Augustine had once held millenarian views[67] and he retains the idea of the cosmic week and understands himself to be living in the sixth day, the one prior to the seventh day of rest which will in its turn lead to the eighth and eternal

---

[63] 1994.96.
[64] 20:7-17.
[65] 1983.
[66] E.g. his view of the martyrs, *City of God* 22.9.
[67] E.g. *Sermon* 259.2.

day.[68] The present sixth day cannot, unlike the preceding ones, be measured in numbers of generations.[69] It may be that in Augustine's understanding the seventh day is not temporal but consists in the saints themselves and is thus in some sense contemporaneous with the sixth day.[70]

As Fredriksen has pointed out,[71] many contemporaries of Tyconius and Augustine were unconvinced by their interpretative strategy, yet such was the latter's influence that their tradition knew eight centuries of almost uncontested success and remains influential today. This situation has not been universally welcomed. E.B. Elliott, for example, speaks with lament of "With what misleading effect it (Augustine's reading) past downward into the middle age, as the received system of interpretation".[72]

In the East the suspicion of Revelation derived from Eusebius seems to have endured. The oldest extant Greek commentary on Revelation is that of the military official, Oecumenius (c.500-600), a Monophysite.[73] The interpretation appears to be largely independent in its thought but has been influenced to some extent by the work of Origen (although not by either Tyconius or Augustine) and it is clear that those for whom Oecumenius writes need to be persuaded of the canonicity of Revelation. The commentary is notable as the first to offer a Marian interpretation of the woman of Revelation 12, a view that subsequently became influential and remains so in certain Roman Catholic circles.[74] Unlike Origen, Oecumenius understands the thousand years of Revelation 20:1-7 to refer to the time of Christ's incarnation; the devil was bound for this period and was released at the ascension. As far as the plagues are concerned, Oecumenius regards the first six seals as references to the events of Christ's earthly life, while the seventh refers to his Parousia. Nevertheless, the other series of plagues are to be understood eschatologically, if not literally, for they refer to events which will take place either just before of just after the second coming. Thus the commentary understands Revelation to work on two levels, one which is concerned with the first coming of Christ and one which refers to the end of the world.

Another Greek commentary from the same period is that of Andrew of Caesarea (c.563-613).[75] It became the standard commentary of the later Byzantine church. This commentary takes Augustine's position on the millennium seeing it as a reference to the length of time, known to God but

---

[68] The idea of an eschatological Sabbath in Revelation is discussed by Johnston 1987.
[69] *City of God* 22.30.
[70] See Fredriksen 1991.
[71] 1991.
[72] 1862.4.336.
[73] See the discussion in DuRoussea 1984 and the comments in Daley 1991; Prigent 1959; Simonetti 1994. The commentary was discovered early last century.
[74] See McHugh 1975.404-408.
[75] Also discussed by DuRoussea 1984; Prigent 1959; Simonetti 1994.

undefined so far as humans are concerned, which lasts from Christ's incarnation until the end of the world. Revelation as a whole refers to this period, a time characterized by the existence of the church. Andrew's interpretation is not original and cites its predecessors. It understands Revelation to refer to events which are to occur in the last days. Andrew finds reference to seven great empires and believes that the last two are those of Rome and Constantinople and therefore thinks that the last times are approaching.

Thus Tyconius's view of the millennium, through the mediation of Augustine and Andrew, succeeded in rehabilitating Revelation in the East and his views dominated subsequent exegesis there as they did in the West. In spite of its renewed acceptance, Revelation received relatively little attention from the Greek church, in terms of commentaries at least, until the fall of Byzantium in 1453. This event was, given the prestige of Andrew's commentary and his views about the Roman and Byzantine Empires, regarded as an eschatological and apocalyptic event of cosmic significance and led to a renewed interest in Revelation.[76]

In the West, interest in Revelation continued unabated. The Augustinian advocacy of the views of Tyconius meant that spiritualizing and allegorical interpretations, with little stress on imminent eschatological events, dominated the reading of Revelation until the Medieval period. Perhaps no other interpretation was conceivable at a time when church and government were so closely associated with one another.[77] In any event, the spiritual reading is reflected in Jerome's revision of Victorinus and the commentaries of Apringus (wrote c. 531-548), Primasius (died c.540-550), Caesarius (c.540), Cassiodore (died c.583), Bede (672-735), Ambrose (wrote c.758-767), Beatus (wrote 776-786)[78] and Bruno (1049-1123). There is a certain irony in the last of these which uses the text to attack heretics including Tyconius on whose work the method of interpretation is based.

Prigent hints that the spiritualizing interpretation derived from Tyconius contained the seeds which eventually led to its dominance being challenged.[79] Its tolerance of allegory permitted the Marian reading of Revelation 12. This meant that historic events rather than atemporal spiritual truths could enter the system. Once past events were accepted, there seemed no reason why a work which describes itself as a prophecy[80] could not contain references to future history. So it is that many of these commentaries contain a spiritualized

---

[76] Eastern exegesis of Revelation after the fall of Byzantium is described by Argyriou 1982.
[77] For the relationship between church and society during this period, see Southern 1970.15-23.
[78] Discussed by Reeves 1984; J. Williams 1992.
[79] 1959.
[80] E.g. 1:3; 22:7; 10, 18, 19.

understanding of Revelation in which the series of plagues associated with the seals, trumpets and bowls recapitulate one another and in which each is understood to lead up to the end of the world. So, historical understandings of aspects of Revelation were never entirely lost. However, they came to the fore in the West through the method of interpretation initiated by Joachim of Fiore.[81]

2. *Joachim of Fiore and His Followers*

Towards the end of the twelfth century a wholly new method for the interpretation of Revelation was proposed by the Calabrian abbot, Joachim of Fiore. It challenged the established reading derived from Tyconius and Augustine, generated an extensive following and fed, or was fed by, a significant popular interest in prophecy.[82] Lerner calls his work "an extraordinary assertion of doctrinal independence."[83] For Joachim's interpretation made history and eschatology central to the understanding of Revelation.

Joachim developed a view of history based on alternative, though mystically connected, patterns of twos and threes. The former finds its type in the two testaments of the Bible while the latter has its basis in Joachim's Trinitarian ideas. In the latter system the first status or age, pertaining to God the Father, lasted from Adam until Christ. The world of his own day is in the second status, the age of God the Son, but will soon make way for the coming third age, the status of God the Holy Spirit. This is to be a Sabbath age and will precede the

---

[81] McGinn 1995 suggests that non-Augustinian understandings of the last things persisted and were influential in the period AD 400-1,000, but as he himself says elsewhere, "It is not totally unfair to dismiss the next seven centuries as a series of footnotes to Augustine...from the viewpoint of the theory of history, it was not until the twelfth century, and really not until Joachim of Fiore, that a total re-thinking of the different ways that the Christian tradition had structured history allowed for movement beyond the Augustinian paradigm." 1994.24.
This study concentrates on European interpretations of Revelation, at least insofar as periods prior to this century are concerned. However, other schools and traditions of interpretation exist, one of which pertains to the Ethiopian Orthodox Church. See Cowley 1983.

[82] See the extensive literature on Joachim, his followers and influence. In addition to the histories of interpretation mentioned above, there are the works of Daniel 1992; Lee 1989; McGinn 1979.126-285, 1985, 1994; and Reeves 1954, 1969, 1972, 1976, 1995. 1954 is a helpful introduction to Joachim's main ideas. D. Burr 1992 considers the work of his followers, Rowland 1988a.83-88 discusses his influence. More general articles about the importance of Revelation in medieval culture and church life include Reeves 1984; Camille, Christe, Emmerson 1992b, Flanigan, Klein, Lerner, Lewis, Matter, Morrison, Szittya all 1992. Some of these, and others on related issues, are collected in Emmerson 1992a. Discussions of millennial movements may be found in Cohn 1993a.

[83] 1992.58.

final tribulation which itself heralds the end of history. In the former system, the two ages, conforming to the old and new covenants, are regarded as exhibiting a series of parallels with each era culminating in a final tribulation.

At Revelation 5:1, the scroll in the hand of God is said to have writing on both sides and Joachim understands this to refer to the events of the two ages. He interprets the seven seals of Revelation so that they correspond to the seven divisions which he discerns in the history of each age. The seals themselves, in their unbroken state, refer to events of the old dispensation, the opened seals relate to the corresponding parallel events in the age initiated by the birth of Christ. Each is characterized by a conflict with a different foe, the sixth and seventh being a double conflict which lead to a Sabbath period itself brought to an end by a great tribulation. In the case of the old covenant, Joachim identifies the final tribulation with the persecution of the Jews by Antiochus Epiphanes, the event which he regards as bringing the Old Testament period to a close. Each of the events of the old dispensation has its parallel in the new. This two-age system is dovetailed into the three-age, trinitarian system by identifying the future third age or status of the Spirit with the coming Sabbath period.

This system varies a little between Joachim's principal publications and in those of his followers.[84] Sometimes the twofold structure of history is stressed and sometimes the threefold. However, the basic pattern remains. The seven seals are understood to refer to different periods of biblical and church history, and history itself is moving towards a goal ordained by God. The double pattern of seven, derived from Revelation, is one of the basic concepts of Joachim's thought. Revelation, on this view, is a description of history. The idea that Revelation presents a periodization of history in a series of parallels has proved hugely influential. The church and world historical interpretations which are derived from it were the principal Protestant readings of the book from the sixteenth to the nineteenth centuries. While most twentieth century interpreters have rejected this approach, it must be acknowledged that the periodization of history is a feature of apocalyptic literature and so such an interpretation of Revelation is at least conceivable.

One feature of this approach was that it encouraged the reader of Revelation to look to the events and to the major figures of his or her own day and to find references to them in the text.[85] This enables the radical and the discontented to identify their oppressors with the opponents of God in Revelation. Most famously, some of Joachim's followers came to believe that the papacy was the beast of Revelation 13. The Franciscan Spiritual Olivi (c.1247-1298) wrote a

---

[84] The significant works are *Liber Figurarum*, *Liber Concordie* and *Expositio in Apocalypsim*. The tract *De Septem Sigillis* is an introductory work and is regarded by Reeves 1954, 1976.27 as authentic. A select bibliography of Joachim's work is at Reeves 1976.198-199.

[85] Joachim's understanding of Revelation 7:2 was read by Bonaventure as a prediction of the coming of Francis of Assisi. D. Burr 1993.28.

commentary which implies this and which was subsequently condemned by Pope John XXII.[86] This understanding subsequently became extremely important in Protestant exegesis.[87]

3. The Reformation Period

The magisterial reformers are known for a suspicious attitude towards the Book of Revelation.[88] The statement of Luther (1483-1546), that his spirit could not abide the book, is widely cited in the literature.[89] In the preface to Revelation written in 1522 Luther states,

> I...consider it to be neither apostolic nor prophetic...it befits the apostolic office to speak clearly of Christ and his deeds, without images and visions...I can in no way detect that the Holy Spirit produced it...let everyone think of it as his own spirit leads him. My spirit cannot accommodate itself to this book. For me this is reason enough not to think highly of it: Christ is neither taught nor known in it. But to teach Christ, this is the thing which an apostle is bound above all else to do.[90]

It is less commonly noted that Luther subsequently came to see the value of the book although he continued to doubt that it was written by an apostle. His editions of the New Testament from 1530 onwards contain a wholly new preface which offers a view on the correct interpretation of Revelation. Luther argues that given that the book is,

> a revelation of things that are to happen in the future, and especially of tribulations and disasters that were to come upon Christendom, we consider that the first and surest step toward finding its interpretation is to take from history the events and disasters that have come upon Christendom till now, and hold them up alongside these images, and so compare them very carefully. If, then, the two perfectly coincided and squared with one another, we could build on that as a sure, or at least an unobjectionable, interpretation.[91]

Luther's partial change of heart may have come about, in part at least,

---

[86] See D. Burr 1976, 1989, 1993.

[87] Chapter 25.6 of The Westminster *Confession of Faith* of 1647, for example, holds it as an article of faith that "the Pope of Rome...is that Antichrist, that man of sin and son of perdition, that exalteth himself in the church against Christ and all that is called God." The notes refer the reader to Matthew 23:8-10, 2 Thessalonians 2:3-9 and Revelation 13:6. The relationship between Joachim and Protestantism is discussed in Reeves 1976.136-165.

[88] See Pelikan 1984.

[89] E.g. Kümmel 1975.473; Megivern 1978; Firth, who cites the original, "mein geist kan sich inn das buch nich schicken". 1979.7.

[90] Bachmann 1960.398-399.

[91] Bachmann 1960.401.

because when interpreted in the church historical method derived from Joachim of Fiore, which Luther outlines, Revelation could readily be used in polemic against the Roman Catholic Church in general and the papacy in particular. As Bainton notes, Revelation in Luther's editions of the Bible was copiously illustrated, as though a picture might do what words could not.[92] In the 1522 edition the great whore of Revelation 17 is depicted wearing the papal tiara demonstrating that even at that stage Luther was aware of the book's polemical potential.[93]

With respect to the series of plagues, Luther believes that the seals and trumpets refer to events in church history from the beginning until the time of Mohammed. The seals refer to bodily tribulations faced by the church. The rider on the white horse (6:2) refers to persecution of believers by the temporal government. The other riders (6:3-8) are war, famine and plague. The martyrs described at the fifth seal (6:9-11) cry out for the last day which is depicted on the opening of the sixth seal (6:12-17). Each of the first five seal openings depicts events which continue until the sixth. The seven trumpets, on the other hand, announce spiritual tribulations, the heresies which afflicted the church and which run parallel to the bodily tribulations described in the seals. The church, having been sealed by the good angels, that is by the orthodox fathers like Athanasius, Hilary and the bishops gathered for the Council of Nicea, is confronted by a series of heretics such as Tatian, Marcion, Origen, "who embittered and corrupted the Scriptures with philosophy and reason",[94] and Novatus.

Luther hints that contemporary clergy may be all the first four trumpets at once. The last three trumpets are the three great woes. The first Arius, the second Mohammed, and the third the Papal Empire or Imperial Papacy; the bowls are a part of a prophecy of the rise and eventual fall of the papal empire. Luther was not above finding references to his opponents in these sections of the text of Revelation. He identifies the frogs coming from the mouth of the dragon, beast and false prophet on the pouring out of the sixth bowl at 16:12-14 with his opponents, Faber, Eck and Emser.

Luther concludes that "With this kind of interpretation we can profit by this book and make good use of it",[95] and that "As we see here in this book, that through and beyond all plagues, beasts, and evil angels Christ is nonetheless with his saints, and wins the final victory."[96] At points, especially in his understanding of Revelation 11-12, Luther shows an awareness of another way of interpreting the text. He understands these passages as offering general and timeless promises of divine protection and provision of pious teachers to the

---

[92] 1978.329.
[93] Bainton 1978.332-333.
[94] Bachmann 1960.403.
[95] Bachmann 1960.409.
[96] Bachmann 1960.411.

church during periods of suffering.

Luther's church historical method of interpretation, if not the details of his decoding, became normative for Protestantism until the nineteenth century. Although Luther was never completely at ease with Revelation, he was quite prepared to exploit it where it served his purposes. He certainly believed that he was living through some of the events described in the book. It is far from inappropriate then that in the course of the message preached at Luther's funeral, Johann Bugenhagen identified the reformer with one of the angels mentioned in Revelation.[97]

One aspect of Luther's wariness of the book, and his unwillingness to endorse it unless it was tied to a particular method of interpretation, may have been due to the use made of the text by some of his more radical contemporaries. Thomas Müntzer, for example, believed that he was living in the times prophesied in Revelation, that its text was being fulfilled in and around him, and that the peasants of Germany would be the human agents of divine wrath.[98] In 1522 he wrote to Melanchthon arguing that "The phial of the third angel has already been sprinkled on the fountains of the waters".[99] In 1524, in encouraging the people of Allstedt to revolt, he argued "Go to it, go to it, while it is day! God goes before you; follow, follow! The whole business can be read up in Matthew 24, Ezekiel 34, Daniel 7, Ezra 16[100], Revelation 6..."[101] In a similar way, the following year he addresses the people of Eisenach, Mühlhausen, "Now that God has moved the whole world in a miraculous way towards a recognition of the divine wrath, and...is proving this by great and earnest zeal against the tyrants, as Daniel 7 says clearly: that power should be given to the common folk; Revelation 11 also points out that the kingdom of this world is to belong to Christ."[102] Luther wished to dissociate his own movement from what he regarded as the excesses of Müntzer who relied heavily on apocalyptic expectation and symbolism and this may have affected his view of Revelation.[103]

Zwingli's attitude to Revelation is not dissimilar to Luther's. He too is reluctant to grant it apostolic authority but is prepared to allow that it has some value. He offers no system for interpreting the book. In opposing the view that the saints in heaven mediate the prayers of Christians to God, Zwingli notes that "the Apocalypse was not reckoned by the early church to be among the sacred books...Secondly it is ascribed to John who was the Bishop of Ephesus,

---

[97] See Pelikan 1984.
[98] See Goertz 1993 and Rowland 1988a.89-102.
[99] Matheson 1988.45.
[100] Presumably a reference to the deuterocanonical 4 Ezra.
[101] Matheson 1988.142.
[102] Matheson 1988.150.
[103] For one of his public reactions to the Peasant's War see, *Against the Murdering Thieving Hordes of Peasants*, 1525.

for it does not have the manner, heart and spirit of the evangelist." Nevertheless, he argues that the author "sought to paint the salvation of Christ, his teaching which God opened for us through him, the calling of all Jews and heathen, the glory and honour of Christ, the joy of the saints, several punishments and signs which God is about to send over us, in obscure words."[104] At certain other points Zwingli refers to Revelation as an authority but it is unclear if this is because he himself regards it as such or because he knows that it is accepted by those whose views he is opposing.[105]

Calvin's approach was rather different. Where Luther demoted the book, yet offered an interpretation, Calvin acknowledged its position within the New Testament but rendered it noteworthy by allowing it to become (with the exceptions of 2 and 3 John) the only book of the Bible on which he failed to publish a commentary.[106] Nevertheless, there are some forty references to Revelation in Calvin's writings, the majority of which are in either his *Institutes* or in *Psychopannychia*. Most of these use the text for paraenetic purposes or to attack the papacy. Calvin undertook no systematic exegesis of the book. While this may have been because he could write nothing that would conform to the prevailing Protestant interpretation, it may also reflect his own distaste for Revelation.

The views of radical reformers other than Müntzer are less straightforward and too varied to be readily systematized. The Anabaptists certainly made use of symbols and images drawn from the Book of Revelation. The many who rejected Müntzer orientated life in the light of the coming end through a theology of mission and martyrdom.[107] Menno Simons, for example, writes a good deal about life in the new Jerusalem.[108] He also exhibits the tendency found in Luther and Müntzer to interpret the text of Revelation as though it was in the process of being fulfilled in his own time. The plagues are doctrinal errors and their advocates. Simons sees himself living among the locusts of the fifth trumpet. In the preface to his reply to Martin Micron he writes,

> Apollyon of the Apocalypse has so corrupted things by the locusts of the bottomless pit that but little truth remains with man. It is manifest that not only the Turks and the papists, but also those of whom one might expect better things, are those who hate the brightness of the most holy birth of Jesus Christ on which true faith depends.[109]

In Chapter 5 of the same work Simons identifies his opponents with the

---

[104] Furcha 1984. 166-168.
[105] E.g. Furcha 1984.44, 356.
[106] There is some evidence that Calvin did write a commentary on Revelation. It is discussed by Parker 1971.75-76, who finds it unpersuasive.
[107] See Bauckham 1978.Ch2.
[108] See Isaak 1992.
[109] Wenger 1956.839.

locusts of the text, arguing that "Justly has the Holy Spirit likened this generation to the fearful locust of the Apocalypse...with crowns on their heads...of which Micron and Hermes have each placed one on their heads by their writings."[110]

The successors of the reformers were not nearly so restrained in their approaches to Revelation as those they claimed to follow. Most Lutherans adopted and embellished the method of Luther or, as Allo puts it, they "Repeat the same mistakes."[111] The standard Protestant position remained the historical one which Luther had exploited and which permitted the identification of Pope and Antichrist. That position tended to be the fixed point of each interpretation. The remaining details were worked out differently by each writer as each generation found that more and more church history needed to be, and indeed could be, fitted into the text; and nearly every one finding that his or her own was the last before the ending of the world.

4. The Early English Protestants

The early English Protestants adopted similar methods.[112] An example is offered in Tyndale's annotations to his translation of the New Testament. He believes that Revelation tells the history of doctrine. The note to Chapter 7, which is his only extended comment on Revelation, states

> Angell is a greke worde and signifieth a messenger. And all the angelles are called messengers, because they are sent so ofte from god to man on message: euen so prophetes, preachers and the prelates of the churche are called angelles: that is to saye messengers, be cause their offyce is to bringe themessage of god vnto the people. The good angelles here in this booke are the true bysshopes and preachers, and the euell angelles are theheretyckes and false preachers which euer falsify gods worde, with which the church of Christ shalbe thus miserablye plaged vnto the ende of the worlde as is paynted in these fygures.[113]

Most Protestants believed that their own generation was living in the last days before the return of Christ and that few of the prophecies of Revelation

---

[110] Wenger 1956.864.

[111] "suivirent les mêmes errements", 1921.ccxxxiii.

[112] Discussions of English Protestant interpretations of Revelation in the sixteenth and seventeenth centuries include Bauckham 1978; Brady 1979, 1983; Firth 1979; Murrin 1984; Popkin 1995; Patrides 1984a, including Capp's discussion of the political dimension of apocalyptic thought. Burdon discusses the period 1700-1839. The relationship between Revelation and literature in this period and in the following century is discussed by Abrams 1984 (Blake, Milton, Western culture generally); Korshin 1984 (Bunyan, Swift and Pope); Patrides 1984b (Milton); Sandler 1984 (Spenser); Shaffer 1995 (Wordsworth); Tannenbaum 1982 (Blake); Wittreich 1984a (Shakespeare). Herzman 1992 discusses the influence of Revelation on Dante.

[113] Wallis 1938.539-540.

remained unfulfilled. It was common ground that the various plagues of Revelation referred to particular events or periods in the history of the church or the world but there was rather less agreement about the particular things described by each plague. Nevertheless, despite the somewhat arbitrary means by which the system allocated references, it endured until the nineteenth century and is not without its advocates today.[114]

The system was frequently used to justify already existing beliefs that the end of the world was at hand. Expectations of this kind played a part in promoting the social and political disorder which characterized much of seventeenth century England, especially the period of the commonwealth.[115] Knappen, while not devoting a great deal of space to the issue, speaks of, "the great importance of eschatology in the history of the seventeenth-century Puritan movement".[116] Firth claims that

> The intellectual atmosphere of the 1640s was charged with a belief that a great change was imminent. The crisis of the Reformation demanded the allegiance and single-minded efforts of all good men to fulfil the promises of prophecy. The trumpet had sounded.[117]

Writing in 1548, John Bale argues that the seven seals are seven periods of church history and are recapitulated in the seven trumpets which refer to specific preachers.[118] The sixth of each series concerns the Reformation. The Antichrist is to be recognized in the form of papal aggrandizement, and has, with the overthrow of the papacy in England, now fallen. Bale understands history in dualistic terms through the doctrine of the two churches derived from Augustine's doctrine of the two cities. The Roman Catholic Church is accused of having taken the side of the devil in history. By these means the Protestants developed a theology of history which enabled them to see their own battles in the last times as an embodiment of the fundamental conflict between good and evil which was on the verge of its final resolution. The Protestants would triumph for they would be vindicated even though they had been killed. These ideas were expressed in ideas drawn from Revelation. Bauckham cites Bale,

> the godly number (reigneth) most of all, when they seme to the wicked least of all to reigne, as whan they suffre persecucion and death for Christ. For after none

---

[114] Brogan 1990; French 1968; Tout 1992; have attempted to revive the method.
[115] See, e.g. C. Hill 1975, a discussion of the radical ideas of the English revolution. Ch6.87-106, is entitled, "A Nation of Prophets".
[116] 1939.376.
[117] 1979.241.
[118] *The Image of Bothe Churches.*

other sorte reigneth his churche here, than he reigned afore them, whose tryumphe was greatest upon the crosse[119]

and Marlorat, "The sainctes overcome by beeing overcome."[120]

The approach Foxe takes finds references to the Old Testament period and to world history as well as church history.[121] Thus the first four seals are equated with the four empires mentioned in Daniel, Christ is born at the time of the fifth seal and the sixth seal refers to the corruption of the church. The seven trumpets are God's judgements upon the enemies of the church. Firth argues that "Foxe was the first British author to write a Protestant apocalyptic history that attempted to explain changes in time in terms of an unfolding pattern of events."[122]

The influence of this method of interpretation was enhanced by its use in the notes to the Geneva Bible published in 1560. These hold, for example, that the great earthquake of the sixth seal "signifieth the chãge of the true doctrine, w' is the greatest cause of motions and troubles that come to the worlde", and that the star of the fifth trumpet represents "the Bishopes and ministers, w' forsake ye worde of God, & fall out of heaven, & become Angels of darkenes."

In 1593 John Napier wrote that Revelation was a prophecy of the matters that would concern the church from its beginnings until the return of Christ. He worked out the three series of plagues run in parallel and therefore that one of the trumpets sounds about every two hundred and forty-five years. The seventh has already been blown. He tries to show that prophecy has a regular and observable pattern and therefore that future events may, within limits, be predicted. Similar methods were adopted by subsequent exegetes who included Joseph Mede the second edition of whose *The Key of the Revelation* was published in 1650.[123] He attempted to systematize the method and his approach proved tremendously influential. His famous followers include William Whiston (1706) and Isaac Newton (1733).[124]

Perhaps the most impressive exposition of the system is the four volume work of E.B. Elliott which ran to five editions between 1851 and 1862. He writes to defend the traditional Protestant interpretation from the increasing number of futurist interpretations being published. He believes that 6:1 onwards

---

[119] 1978.117.

[120] 1978.117.

[121] 1563.

[122] 1979.110.

[123] Discussed by Murrin 1984 and Firth 1979.203-241.

[124] Subsequent exegesis found references to the French Revolution in Revelation. See Nelson 1981. Stein 1984 discusses Revelation's influence among New England colonists in the seventeenth and eighteenth centuries. Secular millennialism in the nineteenth century, including the thought of Owen and Marx, is discussed by Tuveson 1984.

offers a treatment of the continuous fortunes of the church and the world.[125] The three series of plagues are connected; the events of the seventh seal unfold in the descriptions of the seven trumpets and the events of the seventh trumpet in those of the seven bowls. The first six seals cover the years up to the fall of Rome. The first six trumpets describe the destruction of Christian Rome and its subsequent apostasy and division. The Reformation occurs in the course of the sixth trumpet. The bowls are concerned with judgement upon, and the overthrow of, the papacy and of the Mohammedan Turks. Elliott suggests that the seventh bowl refers to events of his own lifetime, in particular the revolutions of 1848 and their consequences. He therefore concludes that the world is but a short time from the end of the present dispensation.

While it may have been the finest hour of the church historical interpretation, Elliott's work also turned out to be in some sense its last.[126] Scholarly work came to be dominated by source critical methods and preterist interpretations while conservative Protestants increasingly adopted futurist methods. There is some irony in the fact that both the preterist and the futurist readings, ultimately adopted by different wings of Protestantism, may be traced to sixteenth century Catholic attempts to discredit the church and world historical method which provided such a powerful anti-Papal polemic to the reformers and their successors.[127]

5. The Sixteenth and Seventeenth Century Jesuits and their Successors

The futurist method of interpreting Revelation is often traced to the work of Ribeira (1591). According to this school of thought, the plagues are references to future events associated with the end of the world. In fact Ribeira is not wholly futurist. The first five seals describe historical events from the time of the author. The sixth seal and all the subsequent material are about future eschatological events. The first seal's rider on a white horse is a reference to the preaching of Christ by the apostles while the fifth is about the persecution of the church at the time of the emperor Trajan. Thus, according to Ribeira, there is a gap between the early Roman persecutions and the events of the end when the secular government in Rome would break with the Roman see and would thus face judgement. Ribeira finds a break between Chapters 11 and 12. The

---

[125] 1862.1.111.

[126] Of course, church historical interpretations continued, e.g. Forster 1853. New variations were occasionally offered. E.g. Gascoyne 1875 suggests 4-11 should be interpreted in an anti-papal sense. The scroll of 5:1 is the pretence of the church to offer extra-biblical doctrine and the Lamb of 5:6 is not Christ but power; a principle worshipped by the papal church. The whole is apparently to be read as an unexaggerated description of the corrupt doctrines and practices which obtained in the Church before and during the fourth century.

[127] This concern is reflected in the attempts, published 1581-1593, of the English Jesuit, Cardinal Bellarmine, to refute the charge that the Pope is the Antichrist.

first eleven chapters tell the story of the church until the coming of the Antichrist while the following chapters are about Antichrist's reign and the last trials. While Ribeira notes the significance of the spiritualizing exegetes, his reading acknowledges that Revelation is about history. His achievement is to have found an historical method that can be used to counter the Protestant church and world historical methods.

Alcazar (1614 and 1619), drawing on the work of Hentenius (1547), is credited, despite the amount of moral allegorizing in which he engages, with establishing the preterist method of interpretation; the view that all, or at least the great majority, of the events described in Revelation happened before, or soon after, it was written. Like Ribeira he makes a division between Chapters 11 and 12, but argues that 6-11 deal with the conflict between the church and the synagogue while 12-19 are a prophecy, fulfilled by the time he wrote, of the church's ultimately successful conflict with paganism. The closing chapters are a description of the present experience of the triumphant Roman Catholic Church. This position has been extremely influential and the idea of Revelation as a description of a conflict first with Judaism and then with heathenism has been advocated more than once during the course of this century.[128] According to Alcazar, each of the first four seals reveal the victories of the gospel in the early church, the fifth depicts the experience of the martyrs while the sixth represents the siege of Jerusalem. 8:1-9:21 describes the evil behaviour of the Jews during the course of the war against the Romans, culminating in the fall of Jerusalem in 11.[129] Once the church had established itself in relation to Judaism, the story of its battle with the beast, that is the pre-Constantinian Roman Empire, may be told. In fact, since the author is thought to have described the conflict with Judaism but prophesied the one with heathenism, it is fair to say that only the first is strictly speaking a preterist reading while the second is better described as church historical. The preterist/church historical approach held an appeal to some Protestant interpreters and was adopted by Grotius (1644), the first to break with the established anti-papal reading. The interpretation was introduced to Britain by Hammond (1653).

Naturally, commentaries were written which concentrated on the philological and grammatical questions and made little attempt to interpret the book. However, the main lines of interpretation were established and endured until and beyond the rise of the historical-critical method. The difficulty with all the readings is essentially the same. They all attempt to decode the text but all the codes are derived from outside the text and the details are forced to fit. Even Mede's attempt to systematize the church historical reading must categorize whole centuries of Christian experience in terms of one image. The difficulty applies to historical and spiritualizing readings alike. The only ones which do not appear arbitrary are those which are wholly futurist, but these

---

[128] E.g. Hopkins 1965.
[129] A view revived by Giet 1957.

imply that a book which the reader is told has not been sealed is,[130] in its detail if not in its overall purpose, meaningless to every previous generation which ever lived. Furthermore, every futurist interpreter seems to have regarded his or her own generation as the one upon which the end would come and thus the one to which the meaning of Revelation would be revealed.

C. Critical Readings of Revelation since 1850[131]

In many respects the traditional divisions of approaches to Revelation, as they are discussed by most commentators, while broadly acceptable and helpful in terms of bringing some sense of order to the apparent chaos which is the interpretation of the Apocalypse,[132] are becoming less and less helpful. Few are now followed in their pure form.[133] They are retained for the purposes of this discussion on pragmatic grounds. They divide, broadly speaking, into historical and non-historical interpretations. The historical approach sub-divides into the church and/or world, the contemporary, and the future historical approaches. The non-historical include spiritual interpretations of different kinds. The distinctions derive from the pre-critical period and while some critical readings broadly fit one of the categories, others do not. Some of the latter are therefore discussed within a section on historical critical research. An excursus covers different understandings of the way the sequences of plagues relate to one another. The plague sequences are the root cause of many criticisms of Revelation's theology and these are discussed in their own section. Recent years have seen the development of new interpretative models and these are referred to in a separate section and in the course of the conclusions. Some system of classification is necessary but it is acknowledged that many of the readings find their place in the discussion because of their relationship to one another and could readily have been categorized differently.

It is worth noting that the issue of the millennium still dominates exegesis in conservative protestant circles where interpreters are often categorized as premillennialist, amillennialist or postmillennialist depending on where their scheme places the parousia in relation to the millennium.[134] The premillennialist

---

[130] 22:10.

[131] In addition to the histories of interpretation already mentioned, brief discussions of some recent work on Revelation include Beasley-Murray 1963; Paulien 1988.

[132] Beckwith claims "It is doubtless true that no other book, whether in sacred or profane literature, has received in whole or in part so many different interpretations." 1919:1.

[133] This is illustrated by Blevins 1980, 1984 who believes the structure of Revelation is essentially that of Greek drama. In his commentary he argues that it combines a Greek cyclical view of history with the Hebrew idea of history as something which moves towards a goal. The interpretation should be aware of the work's true genre and be both timeless and conscious that it has its goal at the end.

[134] Two such views are reflected in Beasley-Murray 1977. See also Clouse 1977. Amillennialist positions are presented in Grier 1970 and Hendriksen 1971. I.H. Murray

camp then subdivides according to the point during the great tribulation that the rapture of the true church into heaven will occur. One is thus pre-tribulationist, mid-tribulationist or post-tribulationist while remaining in the premillennialist camp.[135] And this is before the various forms of dispensationalism have been considered. However, these views tend to be reserved for popular rather than scholarly presentation.

1. Church and World Historical Methods

The traditional methods of the interpretation of Revelation have all survived into the exegesis of the last one hundred and fifty years, although scholarly use of the church and world historical methods has died out.[136] The method retains some advocates. Warner, for example, while his approach is basically premillennial and futurist, believes that "A general elementary knowledge of world history" is one of the things needed in order to understand Revelation.[137] Whitwell attempts to combine a church historical approach with a spiritual reading.[138] Tatford allows that the historical view may be true insofar as Revelation's prophecies may have known partial and preliminary fulfilment in past history even though their complete fulfilment remains future.[139] Brogan, who regards the futurist interpretations found in popular, conservative Protestantism as papist, has recently attempted to revive what he calls the Protestant continuing historicist interpretation of the Apocalypse.[140]

The church and world historical interpretations have fallen out of favour for two main reasons. Firstly, if such readings were correct, Revelation would have

---

1971 discusses the amillennialist and postmillennialist views of the British Calvinists. The conservative Protestant positions are discussed by Milne 1979.78-96, Ross 1977. An example of the lengths to which millennialists will go in predicting life in the millennium is Wood 1954.76-80, who speculates about the movement of cats and the intelligence of animals in the millennium. Caines 1960 uses the numerology of Revelation to prove that the world is 5,764,801,000 years old. More restrained discussions of Revelation's number symbolism include Bauckham 1993a.Ch1; Yarbro Collins 1988b. A. Johnson 1981 classifies the main commentators.

[135] See Ross 1977.122.

[136] Vestiges of the church historical view remain in futurist readings such as those of *The New Schofield Reference Bible*, 1352-1353.n4 and Lindsey 1974.31-70. These understand the events from 4:1 onwards to be in the future; the church age is described in the letters to the seven churches of 2-3. Each letter is believed to reflect the general spiritual state of the church in a particular period. Warner, on the other hand, holds that the four riders released on the opening of the first four seals (6:1-8) form a description of world history from the ascension of Christ until his second advent. 1944.

[137] 1944.9.

[138] 1942.

[139] 1947.18.

[140] 1990. See n.112.

had little relevance to its original audience and secondly, commentators who used this method were unable to agree which events, individuals or historical movements were represented by the different plagues. After all, each generation of such interpreters believed that they were living in an epoch proximate to the last days and so tended to identify their own times with the pouring out of the bowls of Chapter 16 and of course each had more and more history to include within their frameworks. A further difficulty is that the prophecies are normally thought to begin at the time the book was written, sometimes c.AD 68 but more usually c.AD 96. No explanation is given as to why Christ might have waited some sixty years after his ascension before receiving the sealed scroll from the hand of God (5:1-7).

Benson and others have attempted to evade some of these difficulties by arguing that Revelation does not prophesy particular events, but presents key points in the development of the church in terms of a cosmic struggle between truth and the enemies of truth.[141] This is a spiritualizing version of the church historical approach. Féret, for example, argues that the events of 6:1-17 are at work in all of history and culminate in the other plagues which are a history of the end times. The prophet is not interested in "phenomenal events in history"[142] but gives an account of "The progress of truth's victories in history",[143] his purpose being to "enable the Christian to follow and apply the essential affirmations of faith".[144]

In a similar way, J. McKay believes 6:1-8 does not reflect a chronological progression but offer illustrations of things which regularly happen on earth, while 6:12-17 describes God, responding to the pleas of the martyrs, expressing his wrath in history.[145] Harrington is concerned that the images of Revelation should be allowed to stand as symbols and not be pressed too far; the temptation to interpret the details in terms of historical events or concrete reality should be resisted. Unfortunately he is unable to resist linking 6:1-2 with the Parthians.[146]

A variation on this view found in the work of Torrance. In discussing 6:9-11 he reflects on the human tendency to find others to blame for their own deficiencies and argues that the powers of the world therefore persecute the vulnerable.[147] He goes on to argue that the subsequent series of plagues illustrate the effects of the prayers of the saints and the way in which the

---

[141] 1900. See also Bonsirven 1951 who sees Revelation as a manifestation of the invisible history of a war between spiritual powers; Scullion 1969 who believes that in Revelation the apostolic kerygma is transferred into an apocalyptic key in order to provide the church with a theology of history.
[142] 1958.173.
[143] 1958.221.
[144] 1958.172.
[145] 1994.
[146] 1969.
[147] 1960.

message of the cross of Jesus disturbs the world, for the gospel discovers the secrets of the human heart and pushes all latent human evil to the surface; Jesus reveals "the bottomless pit of evil in the human heart".[148]

A.T. Hanson,[149] deriving his main idea from the work of Dodd on Paul,[150] understands the plagues in terms of the outworking within history of the consequences of human sin. Similar themes are found in the commentary of which Hanson is a co-author.[151] According to Hanson, the events of 6:1-17 are precipitated by the cross and martyrdoms. He writes that

> the power and judgement of Christ are manifested in the disastrous consequences working out in history of his rejection by the Jews and the persecution of his followers by the authorities of the Roman Empire. The wrath here is not purely eschatological; it is a process stretching from the Cross to the Parousia.[152]

Despite Dodd's own views on Revelation,[153] he has also, through his views on realized eschatology,[154] affected the influential work of G.B. Caird.[155] Caird believes that in Revelation, as elsewhere in the Bible, eschatological language is used to describe historical events. This is because some events, such as the coming of Jesus, "can be adequately viewed only through the lenses of myth and eschatology."[156] Thus, Revelation is not about the end of the world but, as the text expressly says, ἃ δεῖ γενέσθαι ἐν τάχει (Those things which must soon take place 1:1). According to Caird, the author uses eschatological language to express his conviction that, by attacking the church, Rome was bringing about its own downfall. The use of such language gave theological depth and urgency to the present crisis.[157]

Such theological-historical readings of Revelation have some features in common with the spiritual and sometimes associated ahistorical approach to the text which is derived from one stream of patristic exegesis.

2. Spiritual Methods

The use of contemporary history as the key field of discourse through which the

---

[148] 1960.77.
[149] 1957.
[150] 1978.66-70, 1932.20-24.
[151] Preston and Hanson 1949.
[152] 1957.172. similar ideas are briefly explored by Brooks 1988.
[153] See below.
[154] 1961.29-61, 1963.95-117.
[155] 1984. For the influence of Dodd on Caird see 1980.201-271.
[156] 1980.271.
[157] Caird is mentioned here because of his link to other theological-historical interpretations. He could have been included in the section on preterist or contemporary-historical readings.

New Testament is to be interpreted has also meant that the decline of the ahistorical, spiritual approach to Revelation has continued in the period since 1850. Nevertheless, a number of spiritual readings have been published and these include the work of Whitwell, Carrington and Corsini. Whitwell has historical and spiritual understandings operating in parallel. The series of plagues record both the experience of the human soul and the history of human life on earth from Adam, who rides the horse of 6:2, until the end. Thus, the seven trumpets refer to the kingdom of God coming into a person's life. At the same time the first three trumpets refer to events in the course of the fall of Rome, the fourth to the church's subsequent loss of spirituality and the fifth to the Renaissance.[158]

Carrington, on the other hand, combines spiritual and contemporary-historical readings.[159] He wishes to avoid being forced to understand Revelation's symbols as either eschatological future facts or as myths. He believes the book has the form of an apocalypse but that it does not convey an apocalyptic message. The author wrote around AD 95 but did so as though he were writing in AD 69 with Jerusalem on the verge of destruction and a new world on the brink of emerging. Thus, any future events which are described in the text have already begun to happen at the time the book was written. The opening of the seven seals shows what truly dominates the world. It reveals the process behind history in which the lawless spirit of humanity is ruining creation. The seals offer a kind of outline of history while the events which accompany the first four trumpets demonstrate that evil is something which was originally something good and noble, but which has now fallen.

An example of a purely ahistorical, spiritual approach is offered by Corsini who advocates understanding Revelation through symbolism, allegory and typology; the book describes the move from the old economy to the new one.[160] He believes that his interpretation revives the dominant patristic understanding of Revelation. Contrary to the majority of post-Reformation exegetes, he believes that Revelation is not about the end of the world or the coming of Jesus to the world at the end of time, but about the first coming of Jesus into the world. The concern of the author is to promote loyalty to the covenant now. Revelation is about Christology not eschatology. It is concerned with the death and resurrection of Jesus and the end of the earthly Temple; it is about the end of the cult not the end of the world. 4:1-11 is an allegory of creation while 5:1-14 is an allegory of redemption. The events which occur at the opening of the seven seals flow from this vision; the first four seals being "an allegory of the spiritual history of man before the coming of Christ".[161] They represent the creation and fall of humanity. The souls seen and heard at

---

[158] 1942.
[159] 1931.
[160] 1983.
[161] 1983.140.

the opening of the fifth seal are the martyrs of the old economy while the events of the sixth seal refer to the death of Christ. Silence comes with the seventh seal because "The ancient cult administered by the angels has come to an end; all creation waits for the new cult that will begin with the resurrection of Christ, the new Passover."[162]

In the light of this, the seven trumpets are not to be regarded as an eschatological signal but a prehistorical judgement. The first four trumpets refer to the corruption of creation by fallen angels while the next two tell how the corruption spreads. The seventh trumpet is a further reference to God's salvific intervention; the death and resurrection of Christ and the effects of those events. The seven bowls receive a similar interpretation; the first four are an allegory of the effects of original sin while the next two describe its condemnation and its spiritual consequences. The last bowl is once again a reference to the death of Christ and to the judgement of God upon the effects of the fall of Satan. Thus, Corsini regards Revelation as a reading of the Old Testament in the light of the coming of Christ.

Another determinedly non-historical approach is the one produced by Ellul which attempts to bring modern society under the word of God.[163] He argues that the text must be read as a whole and not divided up for the purpose of examining each part separately. To divide it is to miss the way the meaning is driven by the structure of the work. The subtitle of the French original is "Architecture in Movement". Revelation is not about judgement and calamities but is an allegory of the manifestation of all that has been successively revealed about God in the Old and New Testaments.[164]

One of the principal difficulties with allegorical and other ahistorical approaches is that there is no control over the range of interpretations which can be offered for the different images. This may be illustrated through the commentary of Bock which is influenced by the thought of Rudolph Steiner.[165] The three series of plagues are related to pictures, speech and reality, Steiner's three phases of supersensible suggestion. The seven churches in Chapters 2 and 3 are "stages in the evolution of mankind",[166] while the seven related messages are "a catechism of exercises for the soul".[167] The overall purpose of Revelation being "to show men the way to the true fulfilment of their being."[168] Further examples are provided by P.W. Wilson, who argues that the scroll of 5:1 is sealed with the seven deadly sins,[169] and by Barnwell who regards

---

[162] 1983.163.
[163] 1977.
[164] Ellul is discussed by Megivern, 1978, 1981.
[165] 1957. See also Capel 1989.
[166] 1957.25.
[167] 1957.39.
[168] 1957.14.
[169] 1921.

Revelation as "a window on the soul",[170] and "a record of spiritual initiation of a Christian genre. An initiation is a direct experience of what life is about behind the surface level of consciousness",[171] with the overall purpose of allowing us to progress from our lower to our higher selves. A similar approach is taken in the work by Lorie who writes of the rider of 6:2 that "Metaphorically, the power of the white horseman who carried a bow and a crown could indicate the transformation of consciousness, giving free access to higher levels of conscious freedom."[172] In addition, Firebrace has interpreted Revelation in terms of the teachings of Christian Science,[173] while Vollmann thinks that the book was received by John the Baptist after his death on the Isle of Patmos that lies in the spiritual realm, and that it is concerned with the holy grail which is currently located at the boundary of the divine realm and is to be identified with the fountain of 21:6.[174]

As with the historical methods, the spiritual method is over-dependent on a framework of ideas derived from a source external to the text and through which the text can be read. This might be the history of salvation, and so one would find references to Adam, his fall, the fall of the angels, the ministry of Christ and so on. On the other hand, it might be ideas about the evolution of human enlightenment, in which case the text will be allegorized in another way. The text tends to be subjected to forced interpretations so that it can be made to fit the commentators' framework; some framework is necessary but not one so rigid that forced interpretations of some of the texts details become inevitable.

3. Futurist and Eschatological Methods

Another effect of the dominance of the historical-critical method in academic circles has been to restrict futurist interpretations to conservative writers. Generally speaking, futurists are less concerned that the text should have been meaningful to its first hearers and more concerned that it should have some relevance to their own audience. So Cho thinks that the events described at the sounding of the first trumpet represent the effects of a hydrogen bomb being exploded and that much of the remainder of this series is about the technological destruction of the planet.[175] Lindsey offers a similar approach.[176] He tends to follow the lead given by the Schofield Reference Bible. One of the most thorough presentations of the futurist method may be found in Walvoord's

---

[170] 1992.7.
[171] 1992.6.
[172] 1995.118.
[173] 1963.
[174] 1987.6-14.
[175] 1992.
[176] 1973, 1974. See also Bancroft 1994.

commentary.¹⁷⁷ The three series of plagues describe events which will take place in the future. The descriptions are as literal as possible for a person from the first century attempting to convey unique future happenings some of which are the effects of a then unknown and scarcely imaginable technology.

One of the principal criticisms levelled at the futurist interpretation is that the text could have meant little either to its author or to the Christian communities to whom it was originally addressed. The force of this argument within scholarly circles is such that thoroughgoing futurist interpretations are rarely found. However, the interpretation is sometimes combined with preterist or contemporary historical readings. This is particularly common among conservative scholars who believe that Revelation is authentic prophecy which must be fulfilled. Since they do not believe that it has yet been fulfilled, they hold that the fulfilment of some at least of its prophecies must lie in the future.¹⁷⁸

In some respects, it is difficult to distinguish the work of futurists from those who claim to interpret Revelation eschatologically. Both hold that the majority of the events in Revelation have yet to occur. The difference may lie in the perspective of the commentators themselves. The futurist believes that the text consists of genuine prophecies which must be fulfilled and tends to assume that the long delay between the prophecy and its fulfilment was anticipated by the author or, at the very least, is allowed for by the text. Those who read Revelation eschatologically believe that the text anticipates the imminent arrival of the events it prophesies but may accept that these arrivals failed to materialize. Thus, Schüssler Fiorenza, who rejects history altogether as a medium for interpreting Revelation,¹⁷⁹ criticizes the futurist reading (and by implication some eschatological readings) for seeing in Revelation "a description of the sequence of real events which will occur at the end of the world."¹⁸⁰

Strongly eschatological readings may be found, for example, in the work of Zahn,¹⁸¹ Giblin, Lohse and Lilje. For Giblin, the trumpets mark the stages in God's war against evil. Giblin's interpretation relies on the idea that Revelation is concerned with three moments; that which is (the present state of the churches), that which was (the death and resurrection of Christ), and that which will be (the rest of the book). This last includes both proximate future and the end results.¹⁸² Lohse has a similar approach, arguing that that which is to come is revealed in 4:1 onwards. The seven seals are an overture of themes and the cosmic events of the sixth seal opening are merely the introduction to

---

[177] 1966.
[178] E.g. Beasley-Murray 1974a; Bruce 1979; Ladd 1972; Morris 1969; Mounce 1977.
[179] 1968, 1985.35-67.
[180] 1985.37.
[181] 1924-1926.
[182] 1991.

the apocalyptic dramas still to come. The seven trumpets bring an intensified and more awful catastrophe.[183] Lilje regards Revelation as testimony to the end of the world.[184] It presents the death and resurrection of Jesus as the turning point of history. Lilje offers a theological interpretation of the book which insists that it is about the end and should not be read in any other way. He concludes that "The world cannot remain the same as it is because Christ did not remain in the grave."[185] Revelation is to be understood as a testimony to this fact. Lilje regards the opening of the first four seals as presenting the prelude to the end of the world, the acts of judgement which are the prelude to the end of history. He compares them to the games with which the official reign of a new emperor was inaugurated.

The majority of the exegetes who take an eschatological approach attempt to find ways to read the text in terms of its historical context. They try to find referents for the images used in the experience of the author and the original audience who are understood to have regarded their own time as the eschatological time, the last days or at least as the time immediately before the last days. Thus, historical events of their own day might be understood to have a cosmic and eschatological meaning or dimension. Some exegetes think the author believed that these events were themselves a part of the end while others hold that he used them as symbols or types of events which would occur in future. Even Schüssler Fiorenza, who wants to understand the book without reference to past or future history, but to something beyond history, "the eschatological reality of God's Kingdom",[186] finds that parts of the text allude to imperial enthronement,[187] and cannot escape identifying Babylon (17-18), to some degree, with Rome.

As with futurist readings, therefore, eschatological approaches tend to be combined, to a greater or lesser extent, with contemporary-historical understandings. The futurist readings have the greater difficulty with this. They have to deal with the issue of the great length of time which has elapsed between the prophecy and its fulfilment and the consequent lack of relevance of the text for its initial hearers. The eschatological interpreter, on the other hand, usually believes that the world of the text is a world in which the events of the last days have already begun; the events of eschatological promise are already a part of historical experience. The futurist view imposes an external factor - the historical fact of the delayed eschaton - onto the text and interprets it accordingly. The eschatological approach allows the text more integrity but still must wrestle with the question of how any contemporary community could

---

[183] 1960.

[184] Lilje says of Revelation, "its essential content, the matter which is its heart, is the testimony to the 'End'." 1957.8.

[185] 1957.286.

[186] 1985.56.

[187] 1991.57-58.

regard as true such a text understood in this way.

4. Preterist and Contemporary Historical Methods

The terms preterist and contemporary-historical are both used to describe approaches to Revelation which understand it in terms of the history of the time it was first composed. The terms are sometimes used interchangeably, but it is probably better to reserve the designation *preterist* for those readings which regard Revelation as largely a prophecy of events which had taken place at the time the text was written or were to do so shortly. These tend to be linked to the view that some chapters are prophecies of events which came to pass in the succeeding centuries. Contemporary-historical readings, on the other hand, are those which interpret the text in terms of the historical background but which do not necessarily regard the prophecies as having been fulfilled or having some future fulfilment. The two approaches are related but are clearly not the same.

The traditional preterist position asserts that the great majority of the prophecies of Revelation refer to events of the author's own time and to the period immediately following, with the claim that the prophecies have, by the time of the commentator, been fulfilled. This position retains some adherents. The view of Alcazar that Revelation Chapters 4-11 recalls the victory of Christianity over Judaism, has been supported, in whole or in part, by Giet, Feuillet, Siegman and Hopkins. Giet finds parallels between Josephus's account of the Jewish War and the three woes of Revelation 8:13-11:15.[188] Feuillet remarks that Giet's view is that "so many historical allusions could hardly be pure accident."[189] Hopkins argues that one characteristic feature of the apocalyptic genre, of which he assumes Revelation to be an example, is the description of past history under the guise of a prophecy. The story of Christianity's triumph in a past battle provides the author with the basis for arguing that the current struggle with heathen Rome will also be successful. In his view, the seven seals reflect the same traditions as those found in the synoptic apocalypse (Mark 13 and parallels) while the seven trumpets show how the Exodus plagues are to be turned on the Jews. On this view, the truly prophetic section begins at 12:1 and refers to Christianity's subsequent defeat of paganism and its acquisition of the power of Rome; the majority of the prophecies of the second half of the book have been fulfilled.[190] A similar view is taken by Siegman[191] and by Newbolt.[192]

While a case can be made for dividing the book into two sections with the

---

[188] 1957.
[189] 1964a.46 see also 1964b.183-256.
[190] 1965.
[191] 1967.
[192] 1952.

second beginning at 12:1,[193] and while Jerusalem is indicated at 11:8 and Rome appears to be behind the image of Babylon in 17:1-18:24, the preterist understanding is not without its difficulties. Even if one were to accept that Giet has found allusions to the Jewish War in 9:1-21, one is still left with the need to find contemporary referents for the other plagues. In fact, the allusions are too vague and not all the data can be made to fit. There are two further difficulties with the view that Revelation begins with prophecy against Judaism and then goes on to prophecy against the nations. The first is that it makes a distinction between Judaism and Christianity which the text does not necessarily share.[194] There is some evidence that Christians are clearly distinguished from the Jews (2:9, 3:9) but other sections suggest a continuity between the Christians and Jewish identity (7:1-8). The second is that it must ignore 2:1-3:22 in which there are prophetic oracles directed against the church and which come before any, if any there be, directed against the Jews.

Contemporary-historical approaches of different kinds have, until recently, been the leading academic readings of Revelation, fitting as they do into the dominant historical-critical paradigm. Authors have, without necessarily engaging with the issue of whether the prophecies have been or will be fulfilled, attempted to understand the book as they believe its author and/or its original audience, would have understood it. Some writers who take this approach explicitly state that they believe the author's expectations were not fulfilled. Quispel, for example, understands the author to have believed that the east would, through the Parthians, bring down Rome and dominate the world again. The seven trumpets are a prophetic account of this anticipated campaign by an eastern power which culminates in the final and decisive victory of Israel. These events would occur in human history and should be understood as divine judgement.[195]

Where this method of interpretation is used, decisions must be taken about authorship, genre, date, context, audience and so on. The historical background can then be investigated thoroughly, including an examination of the archaeological and literary sources, and the text read with such a background in mind. Specific images of Revelation are understood as allusions to things within the historical background which appear likely to have been known to and to have been mentioned by the author. These may be natural phenomena like the eruption of Vesuvius in AD 79, referred to by Swete as an event which might have suggested the image found at 8:8:[196] or human actions such as the edict of Domitian which decreed that half the vineyards of the imperial provinces should be destroyed, which Charles and others suspect may have

---

[193] This is the view, e.g., of Swete 1907.
[194] Beagley 1987 believes Revelation's polemic is directed against non-Christian Jewish opponents.
[195] 1979.
[196] 1907.

prompted the thought expressed in 6:6:[197] or fear of foreign invasion; it is often suggested that an invasion of the Parthians from east of the Euphrates was anticipated and that this lies behind the images at 6:2, 9:14 and 16:12.

Beckwith is a major commentator who seeks to relate the content of Revelation to the historical events of the author's own day.[198] He argues in his preface that to know the meaning of Revelation one must put oneself into the world of its author and those to whom it is addressed. Glasson also finds the meaning of Revelation is linked to the circumstances of the first century. The book is about the struggles of the church and the judgement of God on the enemies of the church and it is set in the time of the author.[199] Barclay's approach is similar.[200] There is a sense in which such interpretations are allegorical. Our knowledge of the historical background offers some control over the range of possible allegorizing but the text is nevertheless treated as a form of allegory in which each symbol stands for a specific historical referent. Furthermore, the series of plagues of Revelation have a function within the book as a whole, yet some contemporary historical exegesis appears to believe that to have determined the nature of each image's historical referent is to have explained its meaning. The best exegetes tend to combine this method with others.

Charles, for example, in a major commentary noted for its exploration of the Jewish literature comparable with Revelation, argues for a combination of contemporary historical, eschatological and other methods.[201] He understands the seal-openings of 6:1-17 as preliminary signs of the end, the messianic woes which precede the destruction of the present world. The first four seals (6:1-8) show the breaking up of the existing political and social order and the sixth (6:12-17) describes the partial destruction of the present cosmic order but should not be understood in a literal way. Charles rejects a straightforward contemporary-historical reading because he does not believe that these verses are a free composition by the author. Rather, the text follows a pre-existing tradition, a version of the synoptic apocalypse (Mark 13 and parallels) which the author has adapted and into which he has inserted a number of allusions to contemporary events. Charles sees the three series of plagues as chronological with each referring to a different period. The plagues associated with the trumpets and the bowls are regarded as future and eschatological and are treated as literal.

Allo also regards Revelation as essentially eschatological.[202] The author

---

[197] 1920.
[198] 1919. An earlier example is Maurice 1861.
[199] 1965.
[200] 1976. Hemer 1986; Ramsay 1904; Scobie 1993; discuss 2-3 from this perspective. Their method is critiqued by Friesen 1995.
[201] 1920.
[202] 1921.

regarded his own time as the period leading up to the last times about which he prophesied. From the perspective of the twentieth century therefore, the whole of church history is included in these last days. Allo finds some evidence for recapitulation suggesting that 12:1 onwards reviews, from a new perspective, things already described; the second section describes "the events already prophesied in a more general and schematic way in the first."[203] The seven seals are parallel to the seven trumpets, the former being preparatory and anticipatory of the latter. Apart from the first seal which shows the word of God being loosed, nothing actually happens on earth as a result of the opening of the seals; they represent judgements prepared in heaven and only realized on earth at the sounding of the seven trumpets. Allo is followed by Giblin on this point; the seals offer previews but nothing can be executed until the scroll is open.[204] According to Allo, the seven trumpets blow when the scroll of 5:1 is unsealed (during the silence of the seventh seal) and judgement commences. They are neither literal nor successive but each embraces the whole age of redemption. The eschatological trumpets are recapitulated in a more severe manner by the bowl pourings of 16:1-21. The symbols have no particular historical referents and refer to general and universal events of the church age.

Excursus: Recapitulation or Progression?

In addition to discussing the interpretation of the plague sequences, scholars have also asked about their relationship to one another.[205] The debate has focussed on the issue of recapitulation; the idea that the three series of plagues recapitulate one another, a position which is often contrasted with the view that the author expected them to follow one another in chronological order. The idea of recapitulation can be traced back (at least so far as the bowls and the trumpets are concerned) to Victorinus. The idea has been revived in the twentieth century in the light of the parallels which exist between the different series. Allo used a form of the idea. The revival is often attributed to Bornkamm who argued that the scroll could not be read until all the seals had been opened and that its content is therefore to be found at 8:2-22:6 and proceeds in parallels with the plagues of 16:1-21 recapitulating those of 8:6-9:21, 11:15-19, with the latter being provisional and the former intensified.[206]

Yarbro Collins adopts a similar approach to the plagues. She follows Allo and Bornkamm in the idea that what is presented in a more obscure way in the first half of the book is presented in clearer and more final terms from 12:1. All three series of plagues tell the whole of the story of the end of the world,

---

[203] "les événements déjà prophétisés d'une manière plus générale et plus schématique dans la première". 1921.ccxlix.
[204] 1991.
[205] E.g. W.S. Taylor 1930.
[206] 1937.

although there is some escalation as the end draws closer.²⁰⁷ Yarbro Collins argues that, from the author's perspective, the future starts at 6:1. 6:1-17 tells the whole story of the end and the story is told again by the second series of plagues. She acknowledges the difficulty of restricting the interpretation of the individual plagues to particular events but nevertheless believes that their primary referents should be sought in the historical context. Thus 6:2 refers to the Parthians whom the author believed would destroy Rome.

Other writers who believe that the series of plagues recapitulate one another include Bonsirven who writes that "The three groups of seven must symbolize three series that are simultaneous rather than successive";²⁰⁸ Bruce;²⁰⁹ Torrance, who believes that the second series is a repetition of the first from a new angle;²¹⁰ Beasley-Murray, who argues that the three are series of judgements portraying different aspects of a single short period of judgement in history;²¹¹ G.B. Wilson, who argues that since both 6:12-17 and the seven trumpets describe the end of the world, they must be synchronous;²¹² Krodel, who claims that 6:1 onwards sees the Lamb enact the events of the end time by putting the content of the scroll into effect in three parallel cycles of different intensities and perspectives;²¹³ and Schüssler Fiorenza who argues that the second and third series are parallel and refer to the writings on the two different sides of the scroll (5:1) and that both "symbolically illuminate different dimensions of the 'Great Day of the Lord'".²¹⁴ Some of these authors acknowledge some intensification and development between the series. The argument in favour of recapitulation depends largely on the many parallels which exist between the series in terms of both content and structure.

Other scholars maintain a contrasting view. Without denying the parallels between the series, they stress the differences between them, the intensification in the effects of the plagues (for example the increase in the amount of the world which is affected from τὸ τέταρτον τῆς γῆς [a fourth of the earth] at 6:8 to τὸ τρίτον [a third] at 8:7 to the apparently universal effects of 16:1-21), and the progress which these things imply. This group includes Charles, who regards the apparent arrival of the end of the world at 6:12-17 as non-literal and the proclamation of the transfer of sovereignty at 11:15-19 as proleptic;²¹⁵ Court, who points to the different purposes behind the three series in order to argue that they are a consecutive account of the history of salvation and

---

²⁰⁷ 1976, 1979, 1989b, 1992.
²⁰⁸ "Les trois septénaires...doivent symboliser trois séries, non pas successives, mais simultanées" 1951.44-45.
²⁰⁹ 1938, 1979.
²¹⁰ 1960.
²¹¹ 1948, 1974.
²¹² 1985.
²¹³ 1989.
²¹⁴ 1991.93.
²¹⁵ 1920.

judgement;[216] Farrer, who points to the progressive destructiveness of the plagues;[217] and Rowland, who uses the absence of precise parallels and the explicit statement at 15:1 that the third series is the last of the wrath of God, to argue that there is a definite progression within the book.[218]

Some authors have attempted to resolve the issue by arguing that Revelation should be understood as a spiral. C.A. Scott, for example, argues that since the author expected the end to come in his own time, we should not look for a straightforward chronology. Instead, reading the book may be compared to "upward progress around a circular mountain";[219] after each circuit you are back where you started and at a point where the peak can be seen. Each circuit takes you higher up the mountain. A similar position with respect to the book's structure is taken by Schüssler Fiorenza, who writes that

> By integrating the plague septets into the narrative structure, the author combines a cyclic form of repetition with the end-oriented movement of the whole book...The narrative movement of the seven-sealed scroll is therefore best diagrammed as a conical spiral moving from the vision of the Lamb's enthronement as the eschatological ruler to that of the Parousia, Christ's coming.[220]

Others have taken a different approach and have argued that the earlier sequences of plagues contain within them the later ones.[221] Ladd, for example, suggests that the second series of plagues give the content of the seventh seal-opening while the third series is the content of the blowing of the seventh trumpet (11:15-19).[222]

There is much to be said for all these points of view. There are parallels and there is intensification and if a satisfactory solution exists it must take both these things seriously. It is also important to ask how the plagues series should be understood to relate to the remainder of the book and why sequences which include chaos would be appropriate to such a context. These issues are less commonly addressed.

With all these systems of interpretation, these different attempts to understand the series of plagues, an assumption is made about the external network of ideas which can be referred to in order to interpret the text. However, none of them has offered a wholly successful decoding and it is therefore legitimate to ask whether the symbols truly have referents outside of the text and, if they do, which realm of discourse they might be found in.

---

[216] 1979.Ch3.
[217] 1964.19-23.
[218] 1982.
[219] Undated 69.
[220] 1985.171.
[221] This view can be traced to Mede.
[222] 1972.122.

Attempts have been made to define such a realm through the investigation of the origins of the types of literature and the symbols found in the text of Revelation.

5. Historical Critical Investigations

In the case of the plague sequences, the most significant work on their literary form is Müller's form-critical analysis of the accounts given of the individual plagues.[223] He concentrates on the pouring out of the seven bowls (Revelation 16:1-19) and identifies five motifs within each vision, although he acknowledges that not every element is wholly apparent in each item of the series. His purpose is to establish the literary form of the plagues.[224] One conclusion is that like the plagues of Exodus, they follow an ancient pattern of magical action.

Another means of pursuing the source of Revelation's symbols and language has been through the history of religions. Researchers have found the range of imagery in Revelation provided many opportunities for investigation. Bousset's commentary is written from this perspective[225] as is his work on the antichrist legend.[226] The work of Gunkel is also very significant.[227] Boll has attempted to trace much of the imagery found in Revelation to its origins in the synoptic gospels, the Old Testament, apocalyptic literature and Hellenistic astrology.[228] The riders of 6:1-8 are traced to pagan astral symbols and are related to signs of the zodiac and to ideas about the four winds. He sets out the sequences of trumpets and bowls in parallel and treats them as examples of a *Grundschema*. Of course this approach, while fascinating, does not necessarily aid the interpretation of the images as they are used in the text of Revelation. Aune shows its relevance when he argues that Revelation conducts a polemic against pagan revelatory magic by depicting Jesus as the usurper of the claims of pagan figures. The pagan images are appropriated and invocations parodied in order to make claims about the authority of Jesus.[229]

Hooke, of the myth and ritual school, tries to demonstrate that the different elements of Revelation can be traced to the rituals of kingship found throughout

---

[223] 1960.
[224] See also Staples 1972. Form-critical studies of other parts of Revelation include, Aune 1990; Enroth 1990; O'Rourke 1968; van Unnik 1962-1963, Vanni 1976, 1991. See also the rhetorical-critical discussion in Kirby 1988.
[225] 1896a.
[226] 1896b.
[227] 1921, 1930.
[228] 1914.130-135.
[229] 1987.

the ancient Near East.²³⁰ Members of the school had sought to demonstrate that the pre-exilic temple in Jerusalem was the site of a cult similar to that found in other temples of the region.²³¹ Hooke identifies the common elements in the known rituals and seeks to demonstrate that most, if not all, can be found within Revelation. He argues that

> The general plan to which apocalyptic visions conform is based on the early myth and ritual pattern...and is evidence for its persistence long after the social structure and outlook of the civilizations which had given birth to it had decayed and passed away.²³²

Unfortunately, Hooke devoted only a couple of pages to his demonstration and the case remained to be proven. However, Yarbro Collins was influenced by his basic contention and devoted her doctoral research to establishing that the combat myth, of which elements may be found in many myths and rituals throughout the ancient Near East, lies behind the images and pattern of thought of Revelation. She argues that the myth is most apparent in 12:1-18, the structural midpoint of the book, and that it is used to interpret the religious-political conflict between the church and the empire. Yarbro Collins claims that the persecution facing the church is seen as a part of the universal and systematic rebellion of chaos against order, a rebellion which began in primordial time. The myth structures the rest of the book as well.²³³ Her case is certainly well made with respect to Chapter 12 and reinforces the work of Gunkel on this point. However, there must be some doubt as to whether the combat myth as such lies behind all of Revelation. Certainly, from her perspective, it is hard to see why God, the source of order, should be responsible for loosing so much chaos upon the earth.

History of religions research has also been done by Betz.²³⁴ He uses a plague vision to demonstrate the influence of Hellenistic thought on Revelation and argue that apocalypticism is not a purely Jewish phenomenon but a part of Hellenistic-Oriental syncretism. He seeks to show this from a study of the words of the angel of the waters at 16:4. He compares this with a text in the *Corpus Hermeticum* in which the spirit of the water is depicted as pleading with the high god to intervene because human violence is having a polluting effect. After discussing similar Jewish texts Betz concludes that Revelation's angel derives from a tradition related to the liturgy of the mystery cults. On these grounds he claims that Revelation cannot be understood on the basis of the

---

²³⁰ 1935b. P.D. Hanson 1973 claims archaic forms from ancient Near Eastern ritual were mediated to the apocalyptic tradition through the Jerusalem cult. See also Barker 1987, Paulien 1995.
²³¹ A.R. Johnson 1967. See also Mowinckel 1956, Day 1990.67-87, 101-106.
²³² 1935b.213.
²³³ 1976.
²³⁴ 1969.

Hebrew Bible alone but that Hellenistic influences must also be taken into account. Staples has criticized Betz's argument on form-critical grounds.[235] He points out that Revelation 16:4-6 has the form of a judgement doxology, a form not normally found in apocalyptic texts. It therefore cannot serve as a helpful example for Betz. The vindication formula which it contains is derived from the Hebrew Bible and is common in martyrological texts. Staples suggests that the angel of the waters may ultimately be derived from Ezekiel 1:24 and 43:2. He concludes that, while not wishing to deny that later apocalypticism has been influenced by Hellenism, this text cannot be used to support the idea that apocalypticism had its origins in Hellenistic-Oriental syncretism. Yarbro Collins argues that there are no literary forms peculiar to apocalyptic and tries to find a mediating position between Betz and Staples by showing that the interpretation of apocalyptic texts should not be limited by using resources from either Jewish or Hellenistic forms and categories.[236] Nevertheless, she does acknowledge that the ideas found in this particular text and which Betz traces to Hellenistic thought, can readily be traced to the Old Testament, although one motif within it may have been borrowed from Hellenism. The debate is an interesting one but it is doubtful whether it helps us to interpret the text.

While the history of religions school acknowledges the influence of the Hebrew Bible on Revelation, its members tend to concentrate on the influence of non-Jewish religions in their analyses. However, the majority of commentators on Revelation discuss the use of the Old Testament in Revelation[237] and most attempt to identify the Old Testament origins of the different images found in its series of plagues. Sweet, for example, lists numerous suggestions of texts which may lie behind the images used in Revelation.[238] These and others are discussed by Beagley[239] and by Mazzaferri who seeks to demonstrate that the Hebrew Bible is Revelation's primary source and that it derives its genre from the Old Testament prophetic tradition.[240] Buchanan regards Revelation as a collection of midrashim on various parts of the Hebrew scriptures.[241] Most writers agree that the plagues of Revelation

---

[235] 1972.
[236] 1977a.
[237] Other discussions of the influence of the Old Testament on Revelation generally or on specific texts include Beale 1980, 1984, 1985, 1988, 1992, 1996; Casey 1987; Craddock 1986; Draper 1983; Farrer 1949; Fekkes 1994; Fitzmyer 1960-1961; Hre Kio 1989; Lust 1980; Mowinckel 1956; Moyise 1992-1993 and 1995; Strand 1984a; Trudinger 1966; Ulfgard 1989; Vanhoye 1962.
[238] 1979.
[239] 1987.27-112.
[240] 1989.
[241] 1978, 1993.

draw on the plagues of Exodus 7-11 for much of their content.[242] There is no rigid following but parallel ideas occur. The existence of allusions to Exodus elsewhere in Revelation suggest that the influence of Exodus on the plague sequences is likely and that the Exodus is to be understood as a type of the process being described in Revelation.[243] However, it is also clear that other texts have influenced the details of the plagues and that the overall structure of the book owes a great deal to the classical prophets, especially Ezekiel.[244] The origin of the name Ἁρμαγεδών (Armagedon) at 16:16 is often traced to the Old Testament. The options are discussed by Day 1994 who traces it to Zechariah 12:11. One study suggests that the term is a word puzzle made up of Nod and Gomorrah spelt backwards.[245]

Given that the consensus of scholarship is that Revelation is a Jewish-Christian apocalypse, it is inevitable that the sources of its imagery have been sought in the pseudepigraphal texts of second temple Judaism and in some subsequent works. Charles's commentary explores these sources in some depth.[246] Among other things, he suggests that the plagues of Revelation should be understood in terms of the messianic woes, the birth pangs which precede the destruction of the present world and which have to be endured if the new age is to come into being. Bauckham's study suggests that Revelation manifests no literary dependence on any extant apocalypse but that it makes free use of images from the apocalyptic tradition.[247] In addition, there is some evidence that Revelation draws on material found in the Targums.[248]

It is frequently argued that Revelation has been influenced by other parts of the New Testament or by traditions which have found their way into other parts of that collection. The synoptic gospels are the most frequently mentioned in this respect. Bauckham, for example, traces references to parousia parables.[249] Charles and others discuss the relationship between Revelation 6 and Mark 13 and parallels.[250] Charles thinks that both derive from the same origin while Harrington holds that the whole of Revelation 4-11 "is a commentary on the synoptic apocalypse".[251] The issue is discussed by D. Wenham who argues that Revelation 6 and 13 refer to the same period and that it is plausible that the author of Revelation knew a version of the eschatological discourse that

---

[242] Ford 1986-1987 claims the third plague sequence is based on the whole Exodus event.
[243] Clear allusions to Exodus occur e.g. at 1:6 and 15:3. The Exodus pattern is discussed by Casey 1987, Hre Kio 1989, Ulfgard 1989.35-41.
[244] See Lust 1980, Mazzaferri 1989.85-156, Vanhoye 1962.
[245] Oberweis 1995.
[246] 1920.
[247] 1993a.Ch2.
[248] R.P. Gordon 1983.
[249] 1977b, 1983, 1993.92-117.
[250] 1920.
[251] 1969.55. Feuillet 1964b.233-256 expresses a similar view.

included elements attested separately by the three synoptic evangelists.²⁵² The work of Vos suggests that the author of Revelation knew some of the traditions about Jesus which lie behind the synoptic gospels.²⁵³

Traditionally, Revelation has been ascribed to the Apostle John who is also regarded as the author of the Fourth Gospel and of the Johannine Epistles. It was therefore natural, despite the obvious differences between these works, to look for connections between them. The links most commonly cited are the Christological titles Lamb and Word. One form or another of the word ἀρνίον (lamb) occurs 29 times in Revelation and 28 of these refer to Christ, the exception being 13:11 where the second beast appears having two horns ὅμοια ἀρνιῳ (like a lamb). Naturally, the link is made to John 1:29 but there the word used is a different one, ἀμνός (lamb). As Whale points out, the word ἀρνίον does occur in the Gospel but is used there (21:15) to describe Jesus's followers rather than Jesus himself.²⁵⁴ At 19:13 Christ is named as ὁ λόγος τοῦ θεοῦ (the word of God). While the parallels with the prologue at John 1:1-18 are obvious, the phrase as such is never used. The links between the three sets of texts have been sufficient for some scholars to propose the existence of a Johannine school. This issue is discussed in some depth by Schüssler Fiorenza who concludes that it is unlikely that Revelation can have originated in such a context.²⁵⁵

Occasionally, comparisons are made between Revelation and Paul, particularly the sections of his letters regarded as apocalyptic such as parts of the letters to the Thessalonians. Schüssler Fiorenza compares aspects of the theology of Paul with that of Revelation.²⁵⁶ Remarkably few attempts have been made to compare Revelation with the thought of Hebrews although Hurst compares it to that of Jewish apocalyptic,²⁵⁷ and the eschatology of the letter is discussed by Barrett.²⁵⁸

Where Hooke tried to trace the elements of Revelation to the rituals of the temples of the ancient Near East, other scholars have attempted to understand the structure and contents of Revelation on the basis of the liturgy of the primitive church, sometimes thought to be derived in whole or in part from the liturgical and ritual practices of the Jerusalem temple and of the synagogue. Shepherd for example, proposes that the text is structured according to a paschal rite. The plagues are all a part of the vigil with the first six seals corresponding to the lessons, the first six trumpets to the reading of the Law

---

²⁵² 1984.205-210.
²⁵³ 1965.
²⁵⁴ 1987.
²⁵⁵ 1977a, 1985.85-113.
²⁵⁶ 1973, 1985.114-132.
²⁵⁷ 1990.21-42.
²⁵⁸ 1956.

and all seven vials to the reading of the gospel.²⁵⁹ Farrer understands Revelation to be structured in accordance with the Jewish ritual year;²⁶⁰ Niles takes a similar approach,²⁶¹ while Goulder, arguing that "we need an explanation of the symbolism of the seals, trumpets and bowls, which is in no obvious sense given",²⁶² believes that Revelation is an annual cycle of prophecies aligned to the Jewish calendar. A number of other scholars discuss liturgical elements within Revelation or the text's liturgical function.²⁶³ Some are within the plague sequences, particularly 11:15-18 and 15:3-5 where the third sequence is thought to have begun by this point. Certainly, it is difficult to escape the idea that the text of Revelation describes a heavenly performance of some kind and that a liturgy or ritual is being carried out.

Other writers have argued that the performance described in Revelation has the structure of Greek drama. Bowman claims that it is a drama in seven acts each made up of seven scenes, with the whole being a chiasm.²⁶⁴ Blevins agrees that Revelation is a prophetic message in dramatic form and relates the structure of the book to the seven-windowed stage of the theatre known to have existed in Ephesus.²⁶⁵ While the issue of Revelation's structure is not so readily resolved,²⁶⁶ it is true that Revelation has links with Greek drama. In particular the heavenly songs interpret the action telling the hearers what has happened and what is going to happen; Schüssler Fiorenza points out that this is the function of the words of the chorus in Greek tragedy.²⁶⁷

In addition, a number of scholars have examined the relationship between Revelation and the ceremonies associated with the Roman imperial court and cult.²⁶⁸ This idea has been taken up by Moore who uses it to critique the theology of Revelation and to suggest that it presents a hypermasculine God who must compete with the emperor like a contestant in a body building

---

[259] 1960.
[260] 1949.
[261] 1962.101-115.
[262] 1980-1981.342.
[263] D.L. Barr 1986a; Cabaniss 1953; Carnegie 1982; Comblin 1953; Deichgräber 1967.44-59; Delling 1959; Mowry 1952; O'Rourke 1968; Paulien 1995; Piper 1951; Prigent 1964; Ruiz 1994, Thompson 1969, 1990.53-73; Vanni 1976, 1991; Waddy 1935. Carrington thinks the trumpets and bowls are modelled on the temple liturgy. Seel 1995 is a theology of music for worship derived from Revelation.
[264] 1955, 1962. Kepler 1957 suggests seven acts with ten scenes plus prologue and epilogue.
[265] 1980. Brewer 1952 also argues for the influence of Greek theatre on Revelation.
[266] Theories of Revelation's literary structure are discussed in Ch5A. The three plague sequences are key components in most of them.
[267] 1985.172. Later she notes the affinity of Revelation's structure with that of Greek drama and also with both Roman and Israelite literature. 1985.176.
[268] Aune 1983b; Janzen 1994; Scherrer 1984; see Kreitzer 1988; Wilkinson 1988. Lilje claims the symbolism of 6:1-8 is derived from the imperial games.

competition. He argues that "in and through Revelation, the emperor ascends into heaven and becomes a god, and the god he becomes is none other than Yahweh." [269] Moore entertains but fails to observe that the imperial cult is just one source among many from which Revelation draws for its structure and content, and he fails to discuss the way the symbol of the Lamb might affect the way the imagery should be understood.

While recent scholarship has explored the Jewish, early Christian and Graeco-Roman background for things which might have influenced the text of Revelation, the sources of its structure, its images and so on, earlier scholars were confident that they could identify literary sources which had been redacted to produce the canonical text. The series of plagues were particularly important for this field of research. Scholars noticed that each series includes a moment, the sixth seal opening (6:12-17), the sounding of the seventh trumpet (11:15-19) and the pouring out of the seventh bowl (16:17-21), which leads the reader to anticipate that proceedings are about to be brought to a close. It seems that the end has already come and the reader is surprised to find that the ending is deferred. Some consequently assumed that these series were once part of independent apocalypses which were used as sources by the author of Revelation. Source-critical theories of this kind were very common in the closing decades of the nineteenth century. These hypotheses present a variety of viewpoints. Many suggest that Revelation as we have it is a redaction of one or more earlier apocalypses. Some writers believe that these earlier works were Christian while others suggest that they were probably Jewish and that the explicitly Christian sections such as the letters to the seven churches were added by a Christian redactor.[270]

Weizsäcker, for example, regards Revelation as a composite document which includes elements of an earlier Jewish Christian prophecy and other materials. He says that the author, "took up visions of varied origin, and intended to bring them into some kind of connection".[271] In other words, the text as we have it includes a collection of recognizable, existing first century material, some dating from before AD 70 and some from after. Others took a different approach. Völter and Erbes find evidence of two Christian sources which have been redacted together. The former believes there was also a later revision. Vischer, on the other hand, believes that the core of Revelation was originally a non-Christian Jewish document written in Hebrew or Aramaic and which was translated and edited by a Christian. He defines the Christian additions, including the letters to the seven churches, and claims that their removal will demonstrate the Jewish nature of the work. Von Soden takes a similar line but believes the first plague sequence was also the work of the

---

[269] 1995.49.
[270] See the histories of interpretation; Charles 1913.59-75; Schüssler Fiorenza 1977b, 1985.160-164.
[271] 1895.173-180.

Christian redactor and that the whole was subsequently revised. Weyland's view is also similar to Vischer's but he suggests that there were two Jewish sources which were subjected to Christian redaction. Then again, J. Weiss claims that Revelation is a Christian redaction of two sources, one Jewish and one Christian, while Spitta finds a Christian redaction of a Christian source and two Jewish sources. Briggs believes that he has found evidence of four different redactions of six originally independent apocalypses. These theories have proved influential. Even an author such as Charles, who is generally credited with having demonstrated the essential unity of Revelation, believes he has found evidence of a redaction, somewhat unsuccessful, by a later editor. Thus, he believes, as did Weiss,[272] that the original text excluded the first four trumpets. He also believes that the seven seals, while not a written source as such, are not a free composition, but rather "the subject matter of the seals, which is derived from a pre-existing eschatological scheme, is recast under new forms."[273] Other scholars, who regard Revelation as a unitary composition, follow Weizsäcker in believing that existing sources have been incorporated by the author within his own literary structure although they do not necessarily agree about the extent to which the author has adapted the sources so that they fit within the overall form of the work.[274]

While it is no longer as common as it was, advocacy of multiple source theories has continued this century. Boismard has been particularly influential. He argues that the parallels and repetitions that exist between Chapters 4-9 and 12-16 may be explained by assuming that Revelation is a redaction of two apocalypses written by the same author at different times, one from the reign of Nero and the other from the reign of Domitian.[275] He writes that Revelation is the result of "the fusion of two parallel series of prophetic visions."[276] Boismard has been followed by Harrington[277] and Scullion.[278] More recently, source theories have been revived by Ford and Buchanan both of whom regard the sources used as Jewish. Ford believes 4-11 can be traced to a tradition originating with John the Baptist while 12-22 are an interpretation by one of his disciples written in the mid-60s. 1-3 are, of course, a Christian addition.[279] She denies that there is any link to Mark 13 in 6:1-17 which she believes marks the beginning of the Holy War. Giblin also thinks background to the thought of

---

[272] Charles 1913.65-66, 1920.
[273] 1920.160.
[274] E.g. Yarbro Collins 1976.Ch3, 1979; Beckwith 1919; Kraft 1974.17; Schüssler Fiorenza 1985.162-164.
[275] 1949, 1959.719-726, 1966.
[276] "la fusion de deux séries parallèles de visions prophétiques." 1949.509.
[277] 1969.
[278] 1969.
[279] 1975. Similar views are held by Whealon 1981 who lists the supposed Christian interpolations.

Revelation is to be found in the idea of Holy War.²⁸⁰ Buchanan, in a major commentary, argues for a reappraisal of the meaning of eschatological language in general and of the Book of Revelation in particular.²⁸¹ He identifies the bulk of Revelation as a nationalistic Jewish text concerned with events in Palestine. ἡ γῆ should be understood as referring to the land rather than the usual translation, the earth. This means that 5:13, where the traditional translation is clearly correct, must be treated as an interpolation. The text as a whole is an anthology and only the first three chapters, the epilogue and some of the interpolations were written by a Christian.

Other recent commentaries have regarded Revelation as a compilation. Barker compares it to the Book of Enoch and regards it an 'anthology of high priestly material describing mystical experience in the holy of holies.'²⁸² Aune's major commentary states that

> Revelation was not written over a period of a few days, weeks, or even months, but rather was the product of years of apocalyptic-prophetic proclamation, writing, and reflection, including the appropriation and adaptation of a variety of types and forms of earlier traditional material, both written and oral.²⁸³

Aune offers a *diachronic composition criticism*²⁸⁴ which understands the composition of Revelation as the result of an extended literary process. He identifies textural units which appear unrelated to their immediate context and posits three major stages of composition.

The views of Ford, Buchanan, Barker and Aune which revive, in different ways, the source-critical ideas of the last century, fail to deal adequately with the unity of Revelation's language and its consistent treatment of the Old Testament through allusion rather than direct citation. Furthermore, most of the theories must rely, nearly always without manuscript evidence of any kind, on the idea that numerous interpolations were made by a Christian redactor. Few source and redaction hypotheses, or attempts, such as that of Oman,²⁸⁵ to rearrange the existing text, have found support from other scholars.

6. New Critical Approaches

In opposition to readings which stress the Jewishness of Revelation are the canon-critical approaches which consciously decide to interpret it as a Christian book because of its status as a part of the New Testament. Childs notes the shortcomings of historical-critical methods and speaks of a growing

---

[280] 1991.
[281] 1993.
[282] 2000.
[283] Aune 1997.xci.
[284] Aune 1997.cxviii.
[285] 1923, 1928.

dissatisfaction with the easy way in which biblical imagery and historical figures are correlated. The issues of symbolism, literary genre, and fluctuating tradition pose a complexity which does not allow for a simple method of 'decoding the text.'[286] He calls for an approach which sees Revelation as a part of the New Testament's Johannine corpus and which offers canonical control over the theology of the text. A canon-critical reading has been attempted by Wall who sees his approach as an example of a post-critical hermeneutic.[287] He acknowledges that canonical intent differs from authorial intent. Clearly such an approach, while it may be interested in sources that may be discerned within Revelation, will be concerned with the final form of the text and with its meaning as a part of the Scriptures of the church.

A number of scholars have argued that its apocalyptic genre is the key to the interpretation of Revelation. Robbins,[288] Efird,[289] and Metzger[290] offer examples. Such approaches tend to treat the text as symbolic and then to seek to explain the symbols. Metzger's title, *Breaking the Code* is symptomatic of this approach. In a sense it treats the text as an allegory of past, present and anticipated historical events. Thus Efird identifies the rider of 6:1-2 with Domitian, while Metzger writes that "What is suggested here is a Parthian invasion that meets with success."[291] In fact a decision about genre need not necessarily determine interpretation. In any case, the category or type of literature that Revelation belongs to is by no means as clear and straightforward as the so-called apocalyptic readings usually imply.[292]

Beale, while taking the historical context of Revelation seriously, calls his approach 'eclecticism'. However, but his general understanding is that, the Apocalypse symbolically portrays events throughout history. With one or two minor exceptions, the only specific historical event portrayed is the second coming of Christ.[293] Meanwhile Garrow, Resseguie and Barr[294] have attempted narrative readings of the text. Witherington's commentary claims to be socio-rhetorical but is firmly grounded in the historical context of the first century.[295]

There have been a number of attempts in the last few years to give political readings of Revelation.[296] These include some of the authors who have

---

[286] 1984.504.
[287] 1995.36-39.
[288] 1977.
[289] 1989.
[290] 1993.
[291] 1993.58.
[292] Revelation's genre is discussed in Ch5A.
[293] 1999.
[294] 1997, 1998, 2001.
[295] 2003.
[296] See, e.g., Boesak 1987, a reading in the context of apartheid; O'Donovan 1986a; Pippin's feminist readings 1992a,b,c.; Rowland 1988b; M. Williams 1989; Yarbro

preferred to understand some of the plagues, particularly those of the first series, as descriptions of the contemporary world rather than as prophecy of future events. The plagues describe the true state of the world as it may be seen in the light of the exaltation of Christ represented in 5:1-14. This was the view taken by Swete at the beginning of the century. He argues that 6:1-8 "describes the condition of the Empire as it revealed itself to the mind of the Seer."[297] Niles, Hanson and Caird see this passage as a description of the consequences of human sin seen from the perspective of heaven.[298] Sweet, who understands the work of the rider of 6:1-2 in part as the exposure of false consciousness,[299] believes that 6:1-8 evokes the true state of the world, "insecure beneath its affluence and power".[300] Elements of Caird's thought have a similar dimension. In the introduction to his commentary he writes that

> Any political or religious system which is not constantly subjected to a rigorous critique may seem nonsense to those who stand outside it, but to those who are locked within the system it operates with a logic so compelling that they cannot understand why others fail to be persuaded by it. John knows of only one way of avoiding being sucked into that vortex. Over against the realism of earth he sets the realism of heaven.[301]

Mealy thinks that these plagues are not divine chastisements but the bringing into the open of the true character and disposition of human beings.[302] Schüssler Fiorenza, whose commentary is "a critical feminist-political interpretation and theo-ethical assessment" of Revelation, argues that 6:1-17 describes the actual situation of the churches from the perspective of the risen Christ. 6:1-8 "reveal and highlight the true nature of Roman power and rule", and she states that "Revelation's visionary rhetoric reveals the true nature of the reality and power of Babylon/Rome in its inevitable collapse."[303] Rowland's view is broadly similar; he believes that the exaltation of the Lamb demonstrates the extent of the world's injustice and so reveals "the reality of the disorder of the world."[304]

7. The Theology of Revelation

Many Christians have expressed considerable disquiet about the views of God

---

Collins 1977b, 1993 (responding to Pippin). Richard 1994 interprets Revelation using a hermeneutic derived from liberation theology.

[297] 1907.89.
[298] 1962, 1957, 1984.
[299] 1979.138.
[300] 1979.136.
[301] 1984.xiv.
[302] 1992.67.
[303] 1991.63.
[304] 1993.80. Howard-Brook 2001 addresses imperialistic ideologies past and present.

and of ethics that are taught in Revelation. The discussion is often focussed on passages drawn from the series of plagues. For example, the prayer of the martyrs at the opening of the fifth seal (Revelation 6:9-11) is regarded as vindictive and indicative of a failure to understand the ethical imperative of forgiveness, while the wrath of the Lamb from which the people of earth flee during the sixth seal (6:12-17) is treated as an expression of a sub-Christian theology which has failed to grasp the nature of God's love.

Bultmann's view that the Christianity of Revelation is a "weakly Christianized Judaism" is widely cited in the literature.[305] His grounds for asserting this, that the book fails to grasp "the peculiar 'between-ness' of Christian existence",[306] are only rarely mentioned. In a similar way, Dodd regards Revelation as "a work deeply Jewish and only superficially Christian".[307] It is worth noting that the views of Ford, Buchanan, Whealon and other scholars who believe that Revelation consists mainly of one or more Jewish apocalypses which have been subjected to some minor redaction and then incorporated in a Christian epistolary structure, offer an exegetical defence for the position advocated by Bultmann and Dodd.[308]

D.H. Lawrence's criticism of Revelation is derived from his own experience of the use made of the text in English non-conformity. He believes that the text has a particular appeal for the working classes. He writes,

> Down among the uneducated people you will still find Revelation rampant. I think it has had, and perhaps still has, more influence, actually, than the Gospels or the great Epistles. The huge denunciation of Kings and Rulers, and of the whore that sitteth upon the waters, is entirely sympathetic to a Tuesday evening congregation of colliers and colliers' wives, on a black winter night, in the great barn-like Pentecost chapel.[309]

Revelation is "the work of a second-rate mind. It appeals intensely to second-rate minds in every country and every century."[310] The book represents a popular religion of the frustrated power-lust of the lower orders, directing hate, envy and resentment at the wealthy and the powerful, "the revelation of the undying will-to-power in man, its sanctification, its final triumph".[311]

---

[305] E.g. Laws 1988.80. See Bultmann 1955.175.
[306] 1955.175.
[307] 1960.180. It is interesting that these two adjectives should be regarded as mutually exclusive.
[308] The same might also be said of Couchard 1932. This states that Revelation was the first New Testament book to be written, that its Jesus is not and never was an earthly being, and that it has no link at all to the Gospels.
[309] 1932.9.
[310] 1932.22.
[311] 1932.23.

History, Theology and Visions of Chaos 53

Revelation knows nothing of the thoughtful, tender spirit of Jesus;[312] it is the Judas Iscariot of the New Testament[313] and gives "the death kiss to the Gospels."[314] It advocates Christianity founded on "Self-righteousness, self-conceit, self-importance and secret envy",[315] one which threatens the whole Christian project.[316] If a religion teaches self-realization to the masses they are made envious, grudging and spiteful. No doubt Lawrence reacted against the interpretation of Revelation offered in some Primitive Methodist circles while he was growing up. Nevertheless, it is hard to escape the view, acknowledged in a sympathetic introduction by Aldington,[317] that the work tells us more about the older Lawrence than it does about Revelation.[318]

Another especially fierce criticism of Revelation's theology is that made by Baker.[319] In particular, he regards Revelation 6-20 as an "obscene, sadistic fantasy"[320] in which God destroys evil by means that cannot be justified. He suspects that the writer was "not quite sane."[321] Ulrich has replied specifically to Baker's article.[322] Many others have defended the theology of Revelation.[323] Nevertheless, even staunch defenders of Revelation's theology and politics, such as Rowland,[324] confess to misgivings about the language of the wrath of God and acknowledge that this issue needs to be discussed.[325] He writes, "we are still faced with the issue of why it is that God countenances such aweful things to happen in the name of messianic salvation."[326] The three series of

---

[312] 1932.60.
[313] 1932.24.
[314] 1932.30.
[315] 1932.210.
[316] 1932.211.
[317] 1932.
[318] Other authors use the book in their own work. Victorian examples are discussed by Wilson Carpenter 1984. Contemporary novels influenced by Revelation include West 1982 and Eco 1984. Morrice 1985-1986 attempts a narrative exegesis of Revelation. Films like *The Omen* and its sequels draw on ideas from Revelation. The number 666 (13:18) has found its way into some popular songs.
[319] 1983.
[320] 1983.2.
[321] 1983.2.
[322] 1984.
[323] In addition to the major commentators, especially Caird 1984.284-301, the theology of Revelation has been described and defended by, among others, Bauckham 1993b; especially 22-53, Beasley-Murray 1974b; Boring 1986; Congar 1962.204-235; Court 1994.109-122; Laws 1988; Weber 1988. Carrington advises, "do not let us disgrace our birth and breeding by calling the Apocalypse crude or materialistic or vindictive." 1931.xvi. The issue of vengeance in Revelation is discussed by Klassen 1966, Le Grys 1992-1993 and Yarbro Collins 1988a, 1989a.
[324] E.g. 1988a.
[325] E.g. 1993.85-88.
[326] 1993.85.

plagues which see God and God's agents launch wave after wave of chaos upon the earth cause particular difficulty and trouble interpreters who wish to defend the status of Revelation as part of the canon of the Christian church.[327]

D. Conclusions

This range of differing interpretations of Revelation demonstrates the difficulty that exegetes have had in understanding the book. The shortcomings of pre-critical and critical methods have been indicated in the course of the discussion. There is scarcely a single issue on which scholars are agreed: authorship, date, genre, unity, literary structure, provenance, social context, theology and ethics remain disputed. The three sequences of plagues have proved particularly difficult to interpret and are the root cause of many of the disagreements. There are a number of reasons for this.

Firstly, while it is possible to point to Old Testament, pseudepigraphal and even New Testament texts from which ideas have been drawn, and while some case can be made for finding the meaning of the plagues in the historical events of the first century, and while one may demonstrate that a debt is owed by the text to both Semitic and Hellenistic traditions and myths, none of these things tell us what the text means. They may be aids to its interpretation, but they are too often treated as ends in themselves.

Secondly, scholars have often relied too heavily on an interpretative framework derived from outside the text. Some have used history for this purpose and have imported as a frame of reference the Jewish War; or the events of the first century in Palestine, Asia Minor or the Empire as a whole; or the history of the European and Near Eastern world and church to date; or a framework of salvation history derived from the rest of the Bible and systematic theology; or a framework of future events or of eschatological events divined from an understanding of prophecies from other parts of the Bible. All can be used to understand Revelation. Others have found the framework from elsewhere: the pattern of ancient myth or ritual; the structure of the liturgy of the early church; the shape of Greek tragedy; a pattern derived from Jewish apocalyptic texts; sometimes even a structure which purports to be internal to the text but into which the text must to some extent be forced: in every case the framework determines the subsequent meaning found in the text.

Of course, some form of framework is necessary if a text is to be interpreted at all. It provides a limit to the infinite range of possible referents that any given symbol might otherwise possess. However, most frameworks prove too

---

[327] Extensive bibliographies may be found in most of the major commentaries and monographs. An especially thorough one, which attempts to be exhaustive in dealing with Renaissance commentary and interpretation and is selective elsewhere is Wittreich 1984b. Böcher 1988 mentions many relevant publications since 1700. Brütsch 1966 lists many European works.

inflexible; they treat the text as though it were an elaborate code or allegory, the key to which has been lost. They attempt to impose a pattern on the text and then require that every image be interpreted in accordance with it. Many work adequately for some elements of the text but strain to provide adequate explanations of others so that the interpretations of some of the text's symbols can appear arbitrary. It is not possible to know that any given referent could have been in the mind of the author or the first readers. The results are therefore speculative. All exegesis will involve some form of decoding but the 'this is that' approach required by most readings may prevent the reader from engaging imaginatively with the text as a whole. The text as a whole may be treated as a metaphor without requiring that its every detail must have one specific, concrete referent.

Finally, and linked to all the preceding points, while scholars have made great efforts to understand how the plague sequences relate to one another, there has been relatively little work on how they relate to the rest of the book. In particular, it is clear that the first sequence at least flows out of the events described in 5:1-13. Yet few discussions of the text connect the interpretation of the seal openings to the nature of those events as they have been explicated. Sometimes it is claimed that the sealed scroll of 5:1 contains within it one or more of the plague sequences. However, few attempts are made to explain why the events of 5:1-13, for example the opening of a scroll or the worship of a lamb, should have such consequences. The exegesis of 5:1-13, and of 4:1-11 to which the vision is linked, is a vital first step towards an appropriate understanding of the subsequent plagues.

It is possible to argue that the sequences are judgements. This is the position taken by Yarbro Collins.[328] Others see them as warnings designed to promote change. Brütsch writes of the author's purpose with respect to the plagues of 16:1-21,

> He wishes to demonstrate that before the end God will warn humanity by every means and will make those who worship the beast understand the false path they have taken; at the same time he underlines the obstinacy of humans in their refusal to accept God and to recognize their sins.[329]

On the other hand, they can also be seen as the fulfilment of prophecy in the Old Testament and the teaching of Jesus. Beasley-Murray claims, "The conviction that judgements must fall prior to the coming of the kingdom of God is rooted in the teaching of the Old Testament prophets concerning the Day of

---

[328] 1989b.

[329] "il veut montrer qu'avant la fin Dieu avertira l'humanité par tous les moyens et fera comprendre aux adorateurs de la «bête» dans quelle fausse voie ils se sont engagés; en même temps, il souligne l'obstination des hommes dans leur refus d'accepter Dieu et de reconnaître leurs torts." 1966.263.

the Lord."³³⁰

However, while any or all of these things may be true, they do not necessarily help us to see why such things should have been expected to flow from the visions of 4-5. Something has happened which leads to chaos, but the nature of the event and the reason for its consequences remain unclear. Furthermore the explanations of the plagues so far encountered offer no explanation of why God, who elsewhere in the biblical tradition acts in the world to bring order out of chaos, should here be the source of disorder. God casts chaos upon the world and it is hardly surprising that some have found this difficult to reconcile with Christian theology.

In the last few years a number of scholars have concluded that the historical-critical method alone cannot provide an adequate interpretation of Revelation and have turned to literary criticism and the social sciences for new means of approaching the text. Burch attempted to apply the findings of social anthropology to Revelation.³³¹ More recently Gager has used sociological concepts and Lévi-Strauss's understanding of myth to interpret the text.³³² Thompson uses tools drawn from the social sciences to understand the context which gave rise to the text.³³³ Yarbro Collins investigates the psychological effect that the reading of the text would have on its hearers.³³⁴ Stanley makes use of the sociological understanding of sectarian groups to understand Revelation.³³⁵ Schüssler Fiorenza argues that

> All scholarly attempts to arrive at a definite one-to-one interpretation of certain passages or of the whole book seem to have failed. This failure suggests that the historical-critical paradigm of research has to be complemented by a different approach that can do justice to the multivalent character of the language and imagery in Rev.³³⁶

D. Barr makes a similar point when he advocates methodological pluralism, the integration of the perspectives of several disciplines, in the interpretation of Revelation.³³⁷ Of course, as Aune points out, such an approach represents a secondary application of the theories of social science and is "primarily of heuristic value in that it enables the scholar to see correlations, functions and explanations which would not otherwise be apparent."³³⁸

This book falls into this broad category of social scientific and literary

---

³³⁰ 1974.129.
³³¹ 1939.
³³² 1975. Critiqued by Thompson 1985.
³³³ 1990.
³³⁴ 1984.
³³⁵ 1986.
³³⁶ 1985.21.
³³⁷ 1986b.
³³⁸ 1981.16.

critical approaches. It will attempt to interpret Revelation through the use of the social, cultural and literary theories of René Girard. He is appropriate because he is one of a number of contemporary thinkers whose work possesses a teleological dimension,[339] because his work is concerned to restore the idea of transcendence to discourse about human culture and society,[340] and because his work privileges the Bible, especially the New Testament, as a revelatory text. His ideas have been used in the interpretation of a number of biblical texts,[341] but, surprisingly, only limited attempts have been made with respect to Revelation.[342]

What follows attempts to make as few presumptions as possible about the likely historical or social context of the text and therefore, without denying the possibility that sources played a part in the development of the text, interprets the canonical form of the text.[343] Before the interpretation can be offered, it will be necessary to describe Girard's approach to texts, his theory and its context in some detail, and to discuss his reception in scholarship generally and in theology and biblical studies in particular. These issues are addressed in the next two chapters.

---

[339] Others include Derrida who has written on Revelation and speaks of "an apocalyptic tone newly adopted in philosophy." 1992. See Andrews 1996.232-243. Sacks 1991 cites a number of thinkers who regard our own culture as standing on the brink of chaos.
[340] A number of such writers are discussed by Milbank 1990.
[341] See Ch3.
[342] E.g. Pippin 1992.a.
[343] Watson 1994 offers a theological and hermeneutical rationale for reading the final form of the text.

Chapter 2

Mimesis, Culture and Apocalypse: The Thought of René Girard

A. Introduction

In a series of books and articles,[1] René Girard[2] has promoted, expounded and defended a theory of the processes which determine human behaviour and which created and now sustain human societies and cultures. His analyses rely on readings of material from a number of disciplines including social and cultural anthropology, psychology and philosophy. However, his own primary field of discourse, the one in which he first outlined the key features of his thought, is that of literary criticism.

Girard believes that many texts, including those which are designated myths, are representations of historical events. While he does not regard the relationship between the text and the event as straightforward, Girard claims that his theory allows the text to function as a window onto elements of history; his theory makes it possible to read texts in such a way that certain significant aspects of the historical circumstances which gave rise to the text can be discerned.

Girard does much of his work through engagement with other texts. He reaches conclusions on the basis of, for example, literary critical methods or anthropological findings, and then defends them by reference to material drawn

---

[1] See bibliography. Bibliographies of Girard's work may be found in Deguy 1982.316-333; Juilland 1986a.iii-xxxii; Swartley 2000.321-322; Wallace, M. 1994a.ix-xiv: all volumes of articles which engage with Girard's work as are Dumouchel 1985, 1988a and *Semeia* 33. Helpful summaries of Girard's thought may be found in Dumouchel 1988b; McKenna 1985; J.G. Williams 1988. Frémont 1985, Orsini 1982 introduce his major works. Alison 1993 attempts to write Christian, essentially Roman Catholic, apologetics on the basis of Girard's theories. Kirwan 2005 attempts to introduce Girard's ideas to a popular audience.

[2] Girard is French and has lived and worked for many years in the United States of America. Some limited biographical information may be found in Deguy 1982.315; North 1985.

from other fields of discourse.³ This is a method associated with postmodernism,⁴ and which he has derived from his own engagement with structuralism.⁵ However, Girard uses the method to promote what amounts to a *metanarrative*: an overarching telling of the human story which includes and explains the whole of human experience; an interpretative grid capable of ascribing every human life to its place within a defined historical process. This is remarkable because the refusal of all metanarratives is often stated to be one of the defining characteristics of the postmodern condition.⁶ Furthermore, the

---

³ E.g., Girard acknowledges that his view of imitation "binds together literary and anthropological questions." 1988a.vii. Elsewhere, he speaks of using the Bible to reinforce the conclusions drawn from cultural anthropology. 1987a.176.

⁴ Wallace, M. 1989 discusses Girard's postmodernism.

⁵ Structuralism is the intellectual movement derived from the linguistic theories of Saussure who understands language as a system of signification made up of signs which consist of two elements, a signifier and the signified. The two are related only by convention, the relationship between them being, in reality, arbitrary. Signs possess meaning only because they are part of a system and by virtue of their difference from one another. The most straightforward differences are those which exist between binary oppositions and structuralists regard the construction of such oppositions as a fundamental operation of the human mind. It is by distinguishing things from one another that the human mind brings order out of the chaos of the vast number of impressions which are perceived through the senses, and so produces meaning. The structuralist project concerns the application of elements adopted from structural linguistics to cultural phenomena other than language, including texts, kinship systems, and mythology. It is concerned with the uncovering and systematization of the rules of the structures which underlie human cultural phenomena. When applied to texts, the purpose of structuralism is to identify their *poetics*, to make explicit the underlying system which makes their literary effects possible. In this sense it is a methodology. However, the term is sometimes used interchangeably with terms such as semiotics and semiology which refer to the study of signs. In addition, especially in France, structuralism has been the term used to describe a particular philosophical orientation, one which objects to the notions of Cartesian individualism and Hegelian dialectics. Structuralism examines systems which are shared by groups of humans and so provides a philosophical basis for rejecting understandings of humanity derived from the study of the experience of individuals. It is characterized by its use of synchronic perspectives.

Girard too is concerned to oppose understandings derived from Cartesian individualism and to expose the structures of texts and rituals. He also engages in the search for the *transcendental signifier*, the origin of systems of meaning. However, his break with structuralism may be seen in his adoption of diachronic perspectives in his understanding of culture. In the introduction to 1994a Hamerton-Kelly calls Girard's method "radical structuralism". Elsewhere, in 1994b, he calls the theory *poststructuralist* in the sense that it assumes the insights of structuralism. Girard's differences from the post-structuralist school are discussed below.

⁶ Lyotard, for example, writes "simplifying to the extreme, I define *postmodern* as incredulity towards metanarratives". *The Postmodern Condition*, xxiv, cited by Lyon 1994.12.

idea that texts can offer any access to reality runs counter to the key ideas of post-structuralism.[7]

B. Imitation and Representation: Mimesis

Since his theory is based on an understanding of the way in which texts represent reality, the process which literary critics call *mimesis* is crucial to Girard's case. Mimesis is widely acknowledged to be a slippery term. Graham Ward, for example, has described it as having "the body of an eel".[8] Girard himself says that it is "undecidable and worse than undecidable".[9] Within literary criticism, mimesis is usually understood to refer to the process by which a world, perceived or imagined, becomes presented in a text, and by which a world, as it is presented in a text, generates a representation of reality in the minds of those who read or hear the text. Mimesis, in this sense, is clearly crucial to Girard's position and, as one would expect, his work is full of references to mimesis and to the mimetic qualities of different phenomena. In fact, mimesis is the central and essential idea in Girard's theory. However, he uses the term in a rather different and much broader sense than most literary critics. He believes that his own usage is one which incorporates all other meanings but which is not restricted to them or by them. Girard writes of mimesis,

> Throughout its long history, the word has meant or appeared to mean many different things, and I would like to believe I mean it myself in a sense that is different and even unique and that can make sense out of all previous senses. This is the one problem of 'literary theory' that really interests me at this time. I would like to study all literary acceptations of the word from the standpoint of mimetic anthropology.[10]

Girard is clearly aware of the different ways in which the word mimesis has been used and knows its accepted meaning within literary criticism. Nevertheless, his interest in anthropology and his desire to use that field of discourse to defend his theory have motivated him to use the term in a new way which, he believes, incorporates all the existing meanings. As a result of his idiosyncratic use of a term which is central to his thought, Girard is prone to being misunderstood. It is important to clarify what Girard intends to convey by his use of the term mimesis and to discuss the role played by mimesis, both as he understands it and in its more restricted literary critical sense, in his theory.

---

[7] See, e.g., the discussion of Girard in Derrida 1989 and Lacoue-Labarthe 1978 and 1989.
[8] 1994a.3.
[9] 1988a.204. See also 1988a.105 where Girard agrees with Derrida 1981 that mimesis in Plato is undecidable.
[10] 1988a.225.

This will involve some comparison of Girard's views with other understandings of mimesis.

The Greek word μίμησις has the root meaning of imitation or emulation, just as its cognate μιμέομαι means imitate, emulate, follow or use as a model, and the noun μιμητής means an imitator.[11] The last term is also used of an artist, his or her work being seen as an imitation of reality. The cognates are used in corresponding ways.

In the scholarship of this century, the term mimesis has a range of meanings and these vary between disciplines. Zoologists, for example, have used the term *mimetic* in the past to describe the tendency of some animals to mimic other animals.[12] Thus, when a harmless insect evolves the colours of a stinging insect in order to discourage predators, using its new colouring to deceive them by representing itself as something else, the process involved is mimetic. The lie, the false representation, is responsible, to some extent at least, for the insect's improved prospects of survival and thus for its improved performance as a species.[13] The term might also be used in the behavioural sciences for the process by which animals learn to behave from models, usually one or both of their parents.[14] Ethologists[15] and neurologists are aware of the role played by such a phenomenon in the conduct of humans. Girard says that the latter regard the "human brain as an enormous imitating machine".[16] We have a fundamental drive which causes us to imitate one another; it enables us to learn to behave and to acquire language.

Used in these ways, mimesis refers to the tendency of animals, human and non-human, to imitate models, either in terms of appearance or of behaviour. In either case this may amount to a misrepresentation; the animal purports to be something which it is not. The animal may be unaware that it is misrepresenting itself. Thus, mimesis has the power to generate either true or false perceptions of reality whatever the intention of those involved.

Girard draws a distinction between imitation and mimesis in this ethological sense. He discusses this in the course of a dialogue in which he sets out his "fundamental anthropology".[17] At one point, one of his interlocutors says to Girard, "Your constant use of the term mimesis will perhaps create certain misunderstandings." Girard agrees, acknowledging that "It might be better to speak only of imitation".[18] His reason for not doing so is that modern theorists

---

[11] Bauer 1979.521-522.
[12] Poulton 1929.
[13] Girard believes something similar happens in human societies; we use mimetic phenomena to protect ourselves from our own proclivity to violence.
[14] Girard discusses mimesis among non-human animals in 1987a.85-98.
[15] Ethology is the study of behaviour.
[16] 1987a.7.
[17] 1987a.3-124.
[18] 1987a.16.

of imitation limit the scope of that term to certain kinds of activities; gestures, speech and behaviour that conform to socially-recognized models. According to Girard these activities contain no risk of generating conflict. Since his view is that the imitative drive does indeed generate conflict and that this is one of its most significant characteristics, he chooses another word for the phenomenon: *mimesis*. He says that "The only advantage of the Greek word is that it makes the conflictual aspect of mimesis conceivable."[19] So, Girard regards imitative behaviour as a category of mimetic behaviour generally; the term imitation is reserved for mimetic behaviour carried out consciously or deliberately as opposed to mimetic behaviour of which the perpetrators are unaware. Girard's main interest is in the latter forms of mimesis.[20]

Of course, in attempting to avoid misunderstanding with ethologists, Girard has courted it with literary critics, the more so since he is one himself and would be expected to use the term mimesis in the same way as his colleagues. However, he does not regard mimesis in his own sense as being at odds with the senses in which it is employed by other literary critics. Rather, he regards that sense as a category of his own; as a particular, specialized form of a wider phenomenon.

Mimesis, therefore, is the word which Girard uses for the animal drive to imitate and this would appear to be a legitimate use of the term. Nevertheless, it clearly does not exhaust the range of possible meanings which the word can convey. At first sight, it does not even cover all the meanings with which Girard invests the term, for, as a literary critic, he uses the word to refer to the function of representational media such as texts. Thus, the term is used to refer to the related phenomena of imitation and representation. Its effects can often be misleading or deceptive, indeed that is sometimes its very purpose, although it need not be intentionally so. However, where there is sufficient knowledge and understanding, the deceptive effects of mimesis can be exposed. These observations provide a key to understanding Girard's use of the term mimesis and to grasping the direction of his thought as a whole.

Mimesis, both in its restricted sense and in the wider sense understood by Girard, plays the crucial role in the functioning of human cultures as Girard understands them. The following account of Girard's theory attempts to avoid possible confusion by limiting the use of the term mimesis and, where it is necessary, categorizing its primary meaning as either imitative or representational, although of course it is recognized that, for Girard, these things are aspects of the same phenomenon.

C. Text and Reality: Reading Strategy

One aim of Girard's work is to give a coherent and consistent account of the

---

[19] 1987a.18.
[20] 1987a.16-17. Dumouchel speaks of it as "this disposition without intention". 1988.

origins and functioning of human cultures and of the ways in which individuals behave within those cultures. The theory which he develops draws on texts from the canon of Western literature including Plato, Sophocles, Dante, Shakespeare and Dostoievski, and on work in the social sciences, especially Durkheim, Freud and Lévi-Strauss. Girard also finds a special place for the Christian Bible, particularly the four Gospels, claiming that it reveals the same truths as those explicated in his own theory.

The origins of Girard's approach to texts can be traced to his first book which is a literary critical study of a number of European novels.[21] In it he develops the concept of *imitative desire*. In the French original he speaks of la *nature imitative du désir*[22] (the imitative nature of desire) and of the vaguely Hegelian-sounding *désir selon l'Autre* (desire according to the other).[23] The thesis is that the novels analysed share a common structure; a subject imitates a model and so desires what the model desires. Where the model, as in Cervantes's *Don Quixote*, inhabits a different world from the subject, the desire is said to be externally mediated and there is no prospect of conflict. Where this is not the case as, for example, in Stendhal's *The Red and the Black*, the desire is said to be internally mediated and conflict and violence are likely to result. The fact that both subject and model desire the same object renders them rivals and hence potential enemies. Therefore, desire has three elements: the subject, the desired object and the model who mediates desire for the object to the subject. Hence Girard's talk of the triangular structure of desire.[24]

An important consequence of this structure is that it leads to what Girard calls the *double-bind*. Subjects understand models to be saying, 'imitate me'; however, this leads subject and model into rivalry over the same object, in which case the model may be heard to say, 'don't imitate me', leaving the subject confused and disorientated.[25] This double-bind occurs in both texts and in reality; all young children are subjected to it by their parents and are permanently affected.[26] The idea is fundamental to Girard's understanding of human psychology.[27]

This triangular structure reflects the truth about human motivations and can be discerned in the work of the great novelists. Romantic individualism, on the other hand, promotes the false idea that desire for an object springs without mediation from within the subject and ignores the social dimension of human

---

[21] 1965.

[22] 1961.23.

[23] 1961.89. Butler 1987 offers a helpful discussion about the reception of Hegel's *Phenomenology of Spirit* among French intellectuals.

[24] 1965.1-52.

[25] 1979.147.

[26] 1979.175.

[27] 1987a.283-298. The importance of this concept to Girard is implied in the title of 1988a.

motivations. Hence the French title of the work, *Mensonge romantique et verité romanesque* (romantic lie and novelistic truth).[28] Girard also hints at the religious and revelatory dimension that was later to become more central in his thought.[29] Many of the protagonists of the novels discussed undergo a conversion experience towards the end of their adventures as a result of which they renounce their previous models.[30] The transcendent may thus have a role in revealing the triangular structure and imitative nature of desire and in offering some prospect of escape from the rivalry and conflict generated by the drive to imitate.

Certain features of Girard's subsequent approach to texts can be discerned in this first book. Firstly, there is the search for the underlying structures in texts. This is behind much of the discussion in *Violence and the Sacred* and is given some methodological basis, outlined below, in *The Scapegoat*.[31] Secondly, there is the idea that imitation (later called mimesis) is the key to understanding the behaviour of the characters whose actions are described in texts, an idea worked out in some detail in Girard's work on Shakespeare.[32] The conviction that this is true in reality as well as in texts is central to all Girard's subsequent work. Next is the idea that some texts, in this case novels, speak the truth about the human condition whereas others, in this case romances, obscure it. In subsequent work, Girard distinguishes between the Gospels, which, he claims, reveal the truth about the roles of imitative mimesis and violence in human culture and which declare the innocence of its victims, and myths which conceal or deny those things. The idea that some texts convey truths about historical reality is crucial to Girard's theory. He holds that the reading of a text can, in some circumstances, generate a perception of the world which is related to the historical reality from which the text arose.[33] Finally, Girard is aware that some means must be found to bridge the gap between the reality which generated a text and the representation of reality which is generated by reading the text, the more so since he believes that the authors of many of the texts he discusses were themselves mistaken about the nature of the reality that their texts represent. In other words, Girard must offer some account of the process of representational mimesis.

Accounts of mimesis which allow a connection between reality and representation certainly exist. They range from Aristotle's *Poetics*, through

---

[28] 1961.
[29] 1965.290-314.
[30] See the discussion of Proust. 1977b.11-12.
[31] Girard is anxious to go beyond approaches, which he regards as *Platonic*, that merely classify phenomena, and to arrive at an understanding of the "structuring force" (1979.88) which underlies them. 1979.90; 1986a.165; 1987b.Ch15.
[32] 1973b, 1987d, 1990, 1991. See also 1976a.41-135, 1976b on Dostoievski; 1976a.137-175 on Camus; 1976a.177-185 on Dante; 1976a.187-197 on Hugo; 1977b on Proust; and 1988a.Chs1-4.
[33] 1987a.105-124; 1988a.Ch9,

Auerbach's analysis of the representation of reality in Western Literature,[34] to the sophisticated threefold process of mimesis described by Paul Ricoeur.[35] Girard, however, appears at times to dismiss the question,[36] sometimes he takes refuge in pragmatism,[37] occasionally he resorts to the revelatory function of the transcendent. This last approach is implicit in his early work[38] and becomes explicit later on.[39] It is Girard's insistence that texts can offer access to reality that distinguishes him from those other former structuralists who make up the school known as post-structuralism.[40]

---

[34] 1968. Like Girard, Auerbach gives a central role to the Gospels. He claims that they break down the generic limitations on the ways in which reality could be represented in texts and make textual realism possible.

[35] 1984.52-94. Ricoeur discusses mimesis in the context of the relationship between time and narrative. He argues that the human experience of existing in time is connected to the representation of human experience in narrative form. Narrative has a mimetic function; by means of mimesis, narrative enables plots to re-configure our confused, unformed and mute temporal experience. Ricoeur describes three levels of mimesis. The first is figuration. Shared pre-understandings derived from social identity and fundamental anthropology allow the move from object to representation; an object or event is figured in representational form. The second level is refiguration which is accomplished by textuality. Words, style and rhetoric combine to re-present an object or an event to a reader. The plot mediates between individual events and the overall story thus giving a context and a meaning to each isolated event. This means that in the act of reading, the events and the objects represented can be refigured. The final level is configuration. The reader recreates the whole process and so is enabled, in some sense, through the medium of the text, to return to and to experience the events and objects which are represented in the text. Schweiker 1994 compares the theories of mimesis of Ricoeur and Girard.

[36] E.g., 1978a.18, where Girard claims he has better things to do than amuse himself with paradoxes. Elsewhere, Girard's interlocutor accuses him of dismissing too lightly the epistemological question and having no clear rationale for his truth claims. Girard's response is to "refute the frame of current theory", and claim to be using the "traditional framework of scientific research." He argues that if his epistemological assumptions can be challenged, so can the general consensus in favour of finding evidence of real persecution behind the texts of medieval anti-Semitism. 1988a.215-216. He makes the same argument, using much stronger rhetoric in 1986a.124

[37] E.g. 1979.316 and "From the technique of irrigation in ancient Egypt to the recipe for *boeuf bourguignon*, there is an immense linguistic domain whose practitioners never experience that titillating *glissement du signifié sous le signifiant* (sliding of the signified under the signifier) that is quite real, no doubt, in some domains, but that cannot be presented as characteristic of all language." 1988a.174.

[38] 1965.290-314.

[39] 1986a.100-212; 1987a.Bk2.

[40] Girard insists on the point in 1987a.105-124 and 1988a.Ch9. He is well aware that he is challenging the post-structuralist consensus that language can refer to nothing other than itself, 1988a.xi-xii, and that the concept "of a textuality entirely closed upon itself and for which no extra textual referent and origin can be reached has become an

Girard's most thorough defence of his own reading method is set out in the opening four chapters of *The Scapegoat*. He analyses a medieval poem in which the killing of Jews is mentioned. The Jews are blamed for the plague that threatens the author's community. Girard points out that the author believed the accusations brought against the Jews and that their murder was therefore justified. The modern reader sees clearly that the charges are false and that the Jews are the innocent victims of a persecution. Thus, an accurate representation of an historical reality can be gained from a text whose author unintentionally misrepresented that reality. The author's misconception generated a text which makes false assertions about the historical events in which it is grounded. A modern reader is able to make decisions about what really happened. Girard says that this approach is commonplace and that it would be disputed by few. He goes on to offer an account of how such a reading takes place.[41]

Girard argues that in times of crisis, all human societies experience a stereotypical instinctive reaction; they use violence against particular classes of victims and justify that violence by accusing them of certain categories of crimes. In other words, they persecute *scapegoats*.[42] Girard outlines four stereotypes of such persecution within the texts which it generates.[43] The first such stereotype is marked by reference to a crisis which threatens to undermine the society concerned. The responsibility for the crisis is either ascribed to the moral fault of the community as a whole or to the crimes of an identifiable group or individual. A second stereotype is found in accusations of certain categories of crimes. That the accusations are true goes unquestioned in the

---

unchallengeable absolute". 1988a.189. Girard has the post-structuralists in mind when he writes, "When we turn language into a prisonhouse...we ignore its true mystery just as much as when we take it for granted, when we assume it is always perfectly adequate to its task. The true mystery is that language is both the perfectly transparent milieu of empiricism and the prisonhouse of linguisticism. Sometimes it is the one, sometimes it is the other; often it is an inextricable mixture of both." 1988a.175. Of course, Girard is aware that his own theory demands that language is an inexact tool; "The hypothesis I propose makes these difficulties understandable." (1988a.175). E.g., he believes that our languages can play us false because they are constructed to contrast the mimetic and the spontaneous when in fact they are related. 1987b.Ch15. Useful introductions to post-structuralism may be found in Culler 1975.241-254; Eagleton 1983.127-150; B. Johnson 1981; Sarup 1993.

[41] Texts of persecution are also discussed in 1987a.126-138.

[42] Girard makes the same point elsewhere, e.g. 1987b.118-123. He sets out three possible meanings of the word *scapegoat*. 1987c.73-74. One of these is the victim of unjust violence or discrimination. Girard uses the term in this sense. The other possible meanings are related. The first refers to the ceremony described in Leviticus 16 and the second, a use now discredited in anthropology, to the large number of religious rites in which guilt or suffering is transferred to a ritual victim. Girard refers to Job as a scapegoat, "the innocent party who polarizes a universal hatred". 1987b.5. See also 1985. His view of Job is criticized by Levine 1985.

[43] A similar list is set out in 1987a.119.

text. They include: violence against those whom it is a most heinous crime to attack, such as kings, one's own father, young children; sexual offences such as rape, incest and bestiality; and religious offences, particularly the transgression of the strongest taboos. What these offences have in common is that each amounts to an attack upon the foundation of the social order. It is this that relates the second stereotype to the first. The third stereotype is found in the choice of victims. This is entirely arbitrary in the sense that the choice bears no relation to reality, but will usually be related to the vulnerability of a particular group to persecution; the disabled, the weak and those who, by virtue of their nationality, religion, age, marital status, wealth or some other factor, are only poorly integrated into the mainstream of the culture concerned.[44] Their lack of integration makes these people appear likely to commit offences against the social order; this stereotype is therefore linked to the first two. The final stereotype is found in references to violence itself. Girard next asserts that wherever two or more of these stereotypes are found in a text, it is arguable that the text represents an historical persecution.

Since many myths include these stereotypes, Girard is able to claim that they too are distorted representations or "retrospective transfigurations" of persecutions and murders.[45] Girard is aware that many myths deal with the issue of origins and that they understand this in terms of the emergence of order from chaos. He believes that the chaos images of the myths are a representation of the experience of social undifferentiation undergone in the course of violent primitive social crises.[46] Language, being a system of differences,[47] cannot directly express undifferentiation and so non-difference, which cannot be signified, is expressed in terms of the monstrous,[48] plagues,[49] floods,[50] and images of chaos. Thus, Girard claims, "The original chaos of the Greeks, the *tohu wa bohu* of Genesis, Noah's flood, the ten plagues of Egypt, and the companions of Ulysses turned into swine by Circe are all examples of mythical undifferentiation."[51]

The order which emerges from chaos in creation myths is a reflection of the

---

[44] A similar list of scapegoats and ritual victims is found at 1987a.122-123.

[45] 1979.64. Girard admits that this, "amounts to treating mythology as if it were a text of persecution." 1988a.211. A text of persecution which is seen to be such is thus, "a myth that failed". 1988a.212. A scapegoat who appears in a text as innocent is a failed scapegoat. 1987c.35.

[46] See D.

[47] This view, like Girard's understanding of culture, is derived from structuralism.

[48] 1979.64, 160-61; 1986a.33. Girard discusses hallucination and the experience of monsters and doubles in crises and in corresponding rituals in 1979.119-168.

[49] 1979.77, 1987a.12-13, 1988a.Ch8: "The plague is universally presented as a process of undifferentiation, a destruction of specificities." 1988a.136. "The distinctiveness of the plague is that it ultimately destroys all forms of distinctiveness." 1988a.137.

[50] 1987a.12-13.

[51] 1988a.156.

new or renewed structural, cultural differentiation which arises when the crisis is resolved. Girard believes that this resolution is achieved by violence, by the murder of one or more members of the community by the other members of the community; that is to say, the crisis is resolved by persecution. In mythology, order emerges from chaos through violence. Girard says,

> Everywhere, in 'primitive' texts, the collective murder is associated with the confusion of day and night, of the sky and the earth, of gods, men and animals. Monsters swarm. Everything begins with the abolition of differences...the mixing of what should be distinguished.[52]

This violent resolution of cultural crises is a key feature of Girard's anthropology. He accounts for the entire process in terms of mimesis.

D. Mimesis and Scapegoating: Anthropology

In the preface to *The Golden Bough*,[53] Frazer acknowledges that his anthropological research began with a desire to account for the role played by violence in a particular ritual. Subsequent social and cultural anthropologists have been reluctant to address this question. Girard's work is distinctive because it takes Frazer's original question as its starting point, although it is interested in the general phenomenon of ritual violence rather than the particular instance referred to by Frazer.[54]

Girard has been influenced by the structuralist view that both language and culture are symbolic systems built on the principle of differentiation.[55] In structuralist thought, it is this underlying system of distinctions and conventions that makes meaning possible.[56] For Girard, it is the possession of such systems which distinguishes humans from other animals.[57] Humans produce systems of signs and then confuse those signs with reality.[58] The pre-symbolic, pre-cultural state of 'pre-human' anthropoids was characterized not by a lack of differentiation but by a different, unsymbolized, form of differentiation.[59] Girard is interested in discovering what event, process or quality led to the

---

[52] 1988b.235-236.

[53] 1922.v.

[54] 1979.1-38.

[55] Girard writes, "cultural order is nothing more than a regulated system of distinctions in which the differences between individuals are used to establish their 'identity' and their mutual relationships". 1979.49. Discussions of structuralism and its influence can be found in Culler 1975, Descombes 1980, Eagleton 1983.91-126, Pavel 1989. Classic texts of structural anthropology include Lévi-Strauss 1963 and 1973.

[56] Culler 1975.4-8.

[57] 1987a.5-7.

[58] 1987a.6.

[59] 1987a.90-93.

creation of symbolic systems of differentiation, or "the origin and genesis of signifying systems".[60] He calls this the issue of *hominization*.[61]

Girard regards mimesis, the capacity and tendency, one might call it a drive or an instinct, to imitate, as fundamental to animal motivation. Animals learn to behave by copying others. This applies to the acquisition of objects and violent rivalries can develop where two or more subjects seek to acquire the same object.[62] Girard calls this *acquisitive mimesis*[63] or *mimesis of appropriation*. He writes of "The mimesis of appropriation, the main source of conflicts among humans as among the animals".[64] Non-human animals resolve these conflicts by means of dominance patterns; these patterns check dissension and prevent rivalries from being perpetuated. The pattern has no symbolic representation; the positions within it have no existence outside of the individuals who hold them.[65] Girard states that while humans and apes alike submit to the dominant animal within their group, it is only humans who also talk about 'monarchy'; human systems have representation as a characteristic. The system exists as a systematic whole beyond the individuals who have positions within it.[66]

Whereas structuralists usually argue that symbolic forms can be deciphered only from within their own system by means of a synchronic analysis, Girard demonstrates the freedom of his thinking from structuralist constraints by offering a generic and diachronic solution to the issue of the origin of symbolic systems and hence to the question of human origins. He believes that the structural differentiation which is the basis of all symbolic thought, and hence of all culture, is derived from acts of primal violence in which all the members of a social group join together in killing one of their own number.[67]

---

[60] 1987a.6-7.

[61] 1987a.7, 84-104.

[62] "When any gesture of appropriation is imitated, it simply means that two hands will reach for the same object simultaneously: conflict cannot fail to result." 1988a.201.

[63] 1987a.8-19.

[64] "le mimétisme d'appropriation, source principal des conflits chez les hommes comme chez les animaux." 1978b.37.

[65] 1987a.91.

[66] 1987a.91-92.

[67] 1987a.24-29, 84-124. This is one of many areas where Girard is indebted to Freud. Freud argues that the incest taboo is non-instinctive and that its origin marks the beginning of human culture. He traces it to the murder of their father by the younger adult males excluded from his primal horde and thus from access to women. The adoption of the incest taboo proved the only way to prevent hostility between fathers and their sons generated by their competition for sexual access to the most accessible females; their mother and sisters. Hence the need for exogamy. 1950.140-146. While Freud argues that this acquired taboo must have been inherited by subsequent generations, one of his last works suggests that the repetition of the original trauma might account for the continuation of culture. 1939. Girard develops this idea by suggesting that rites and myths represent the original murder to each generation.

Mimesis, Culture and Apocalypse

Girard argues that dominance patterns like those of other animals must have failed to contain rivalries and thus violence in communities of pre-human anthropoids. There were two reasons for this. Firstly, the mimetic drive in pre-humans was too strong.[68] While mimesis links humans to other animals, it also provides the means to distinguish them. Humans are "the hypermimetic primate".[69] Girard is seeking to demonstrate the dictum of Aristotle which he cites as a part of the heading to Book 1 of *Things Hidden since the Foundation of the World*; "Man differs from other animals in his greater aptitude for imitation."[70] He argues that one of the consequences of this intensification of imitative behaviour is increased rivalry, increased conflict and, in consequence, increased violence. Secondly, pre-humans used tools which could act as weapons and this ability adversely affected the instinctive brake on violence which prevents most animals from killing other adults of their own species.[71]

In these circumstances, mimetic violence escalated beyond the level found in animal social groups, "and must have caused, when it first appeared, the breakdown of societies based on dominance patterns."[72] So, once acquisitive mimesis had generated a violent conflict among pre-humans, there was nothing belonging to animal experience which could be used to prevent its uncontrolled reciprocal imitation throughout the social group.[73]

As with other higher primates, when acquisitive mimesis among pre-humans became acute the rivals were apt to forget the object which each had sought to acquire and instead to concentrate attention on one another. They were no longer driven by acquisitive mimesis but by what Girard calls *conflictual mimesis*[74] or *reciprocal violence*.[75] Whereas the former divided the group, the latter united it as all become imitators of one another's violent behaviour and a mimetic frenzy developed in which all differentiation was lost.[76] As Girard says, "the mimetic character of violence is so intense that once violence is installed in a community, it cannot burn itself out."[77] At this point

> Mimesis generates violence and violence accelerates mimesis. An offspring of mimesis, violence exerts a mimetic fascination without equal. All violence is modeled on earlier violence and in turn serves as a model. Between mimesis and

---

[68] 1987a.7. Girard speculates that the strength of the drive corresponds to the size of the human brain.1987a.84, 95; 1988a.201.
[69] 1988a.202.
[70] *Poetics* 4.
[71] 1979.221. 1987a.87. 1988a.200-202. Girard seems unaware of evidence suggesting that the great apes occasionally kill adults of their own species. Wrangham 1997.
[72] 1988a.201
[73] 1987a.84-98, 1988a.201-202.
[74] 1987a.26.
[75] 1988a.94.
[76] 1987a.26.
[77] 1979.81.

violence there exist relationships that still remain hidden. With reciprocal violence we enter a critical phase that opens upon delirium and madness, of course, but also upon destruction and death.[78]

The effacement of differences makes antagonisms readily interchangeable[79] and little is therefore needed to provoke violence or a change in the object of violence. The crisis is only resolved when two or more individuals converge on the same adversary and the effects of mimesis draw in everybody else so that all are united against one.[80] The undifferentiated and unified mob converges on one arbitrarily selected adversary. Thus,

> Once there is nothing left but doubles in confrontation, the slightest accident, the tiniest sign can cause all reciprocal hatred to be fixed on one of them. What mimesis has fragmented and infinitely divided can be in one motion unified again through a collective transference made possible by a general nondifferentiation.[81]

The murder acts as a catharsis, expelling hostile and violent emotions from the group and producing a sense of calm, harmony and peace.[82] Since the death of the victim has resolved the crisis, the group, being ignorant of the role played by imitative mimesis in the events which have taken place, regards him or her as having been responsible for it.[83] It feels that something supernatural has taken place.[84] Even though the scapegoat only affects human relations, he or she gives the impression of affecting external causes too, including plagues and droughts.[85] The victim is regarded as the source of the new order and the continuance of the order prompts the thought that he or she has survived or transcended death.[86]

The victim is therefore seen as being different from the rest of the group and is thus the source of the primary symbolic differentiation. He or she becomes the first signifier, representing both the chaos of the crisis and the order brought about by its resolution.[87] The passive victim becomes perceived as being the active founder of the human society concerned.[88] Humans instinctively give attention to food, sex and dominant group members; the victim is the recipient

---

[78] 1988a.93-94. Girard also discusses the relationship between mimesis and violence at 1987a.8-19.
[79] 1979.79.
[80] 1987a.26.
[81] 1988a.103-104.
[82] 1979.235, 1987a.26, 28, 1987c.91-92.
[83] 1987a.27, 100; 1987c.91-92.
[84] 1987c.92.
[85] 1986a.43.
[86] 1987a.108, 1987c.92.
[87] 1987a.100.
[88] 1987a.99-104.

of the first non-instinctual attention.[89]

Girard argues that a series of such murders taking place within a social group over a period of time changed human instinctive behaviour and produced symbolic differentiation and hence cultures. A spiral of these crises, each of which was resolved in the same way and which produced rudimentary signifying effects linked to prohibitions on excessive mimesis, eventually humanized the anthropoid.[90] Each of these crises activated the phenomenon which generated symbolic thought. Girard calls this phenomenon, which prevents humans from destroying themselves and through which disorder and undifferentiation is transformed into order and from which symbolic systems of differentiation and hence human culture develop, the *mechanism of the surrogate victim*,[91] *the generative mechanism*,[92] or *the scapegoat mechanism*.[93]

Of course, it is the imitative drive of the entire group which was really responsible for both the crisis and its resolution; the choice of victim is arbitrary and the victim has no more reason to be regarded as responsible for the crisis, or for signifying anything, than has any other member of the group. The effect is nevertheless real. Girard's claim is therefore that "we are indeed dealing, not simply with an illusion and a mystification, but with the most formidable and influential illusion and mystification in the whole range of human experience, one whose consequences are real and manifold."[94]

The mechanism itself is driven by mimesis and arises spontaneously in the course of a crisis. Such an important event is inevitably remembered and subsequently represented. However, if it is to be effective in structuring society, it must be misapprehended for true knowledge of it would contradict the system of meaning built upon it.[95]

Each separate group of humans went through such a process in different ways in different parts of the world.[96] There are no exceptions.[97] However, since each misunderstands the mechanism, as they must if it is to function, each interprets it in a different way. Religions are the different understandings of the mechanism found in different cultures,[98] "the deluded interpretation of most

---

[89] 1987a.99.
[90] 1987a.95-96, 100.
[91] 1979.235.
[92] 1979.311.
[93] 1986a.Ch9.
[94] 1979.82.
[95] 1979.310-311; 1986a.100; 1987a.28, 164; 1988a.169. Girard believes that a true apprehension of the mechanism will prove very dangerous. See 1988a.204.
[96] Girard speaks of "The Unity of All Rites".1979.274-308. See also 1979.92
[97] 1979.256, 280; 1987a.104, 164. "There is a unity that underlies not only all mythologies and rituals but the whole of human culture, and this unity of unities depends on a single mechanism". 1979.299.
[98] 1988a.209.

powerful scapegoat effects, by those who benefit from them."[99] So all human cultures have shared characteristics, but no two are ever exactly alike.[100]

Thus, all symbolic systems, all the characteristics which distinguish humans from other animals, have their origin in the scapegoat mechanism.[101] Girard claims,

> Mimeticism is the original source of all man's troubles, desires and rivalries, his tragic and grotesque misunderstandings, the source of all disorder and therefore equally of all order through the mediation of scapegoats. These victims are the spontaneous agents of reconciliation, since, in the final paroxysm of mimeticism, they unite in opposition to themselves those who are organized in opposition to each other by the effects of a previous weaker mimeticism...These are the underlying dynamics of all mythological and religious beginnings.[102]

Girard argues that humans possess points of continuity and discontinuity with other animals. They have mimesis in common but the strength of human mimesis drives them into the scapegoat mechanism and hence into symbolic thought. Girard thus claims his anthropology is

> the first to do away with the metaphysical postulate of absolute human specificity, still present in Marx and Freud, without espousing the simplistic assimilation of man and animal practiced by the ethologists. Mimetic phenomena provide the common ground between human and animal society as well as the first concrete means to differentiate the two, concrete in the sense that all observable analogies and differences between the two types of organization become intelligible.[103]

So, Girard argues that all symbolic thought is founded upon a primal misrepresentation of acts of unanimous arbitrary violence.[104] The unanimity is vital if the misrepresentation is to go unchallenged.[105] Human cultures are built on a misunderstanding. The scapegoat mechanism "is a fundamental instance of 'arbitration' that gives rise to the dual presence of the *arbitrary* and the *true* in all symbolic systems."[106] All cultural differentiation is derived from an arbitrary

---

[99] 1988a.xiii.

[100] Girard claims his theory, "accounts both for the variables of religious systems and for such constants as the universal existence of prohibitions, rituals, and the belief in something like the 'sacred'. The presence of such constants is incompatible with the now popular tendency to see each culture as an almost absolutely singular phenomenon." 1988a.209-210.

[101] "all the rules of culture stem from it".1987a.27. See also 1987a.103-104; 1988a.228; "Reason itself is a child of the founding murder". 1991.208.

[102] 1986.165. See 1979.307.

[103] 1988a.204.

[104] 1979.256, 1986.177.

[105] 1987b.111-117.

[106] 1979.235.

differentiation and is itself arbitrary. It is a necessary falsehood for it is all that protects humans from self-destruction.[107]

Imitative mimesis leads to representational mimesis, the defining characteristic of human culture.[108] The founding victim is thus the 'transcendent signifier', or acts as such,[109] which structuralists had sought in order to account for the origin of signifying systems of representation; the sign which anchors the system and gives meaning to all the other signs within it.[110] Yet this signifier which grounds everything else is far from secure. The original sign not only represents both order and disorder, but is also arbitrary. Human cultures, being founded on a misrepresentation, are inherently unstable. The differentiation generated by the founding murder is prone to being undermined by the drive to imitate which tends to abolish differences, provoke conflict and produce violence.

As a result, cultures develop means to limit imitative mimesis and to preserve differentiation. All these are derived from the scapegoat mechanism and relate to the realm of symbolic ideas called the *sacred*. Girard writes that "The sacred is the sum of human assumptions resulting from collective transferences focused on a reconciliatory victim at the conclusion of a mimetic crisis."[111] Humans succeed in positing their own violence as an independent and transcendent being: the sacred.[112] These means which cultures use to limit mimesis and preserve differentiation and which they regard as means of controlling or obeying the power of the sacred are the three pillars of primitive religion; prohibition, ritual and myth.[113] According to Girard, all three can be traced back to the founding murder:[114] these are the common possession of all cultures although their form and content varies.

1. Prohibition

A prohibition is a rule which proscribes behaviour that generated or is thought to have generated the crisis which ended with the operation of the scapegoat mechanism.[115] Taboos and purity rules all have the purpose of limiting mimesis, restricting opportunities for rivalries to develop and thus preventing

---

[107] 1979.236-237, 273.
[108] 1987a.6-7, 92.
[109] 1987a.103.
[110] Eagleton 1983.131.
[111] 1987a.42.
[112] 1979.31. Hence Girard's dicta, "Violence is the heart and secret soul of the sacred." 1979.31, and "Violence and the sacred are one and the same thing." 1979.262, an assertion for which Girard produces some lexicographical evidence. 1979.262-265.
[113] 1987c.
[114] 1987a.40.
[115] 1979.219; 1987a.10, 14, 19, 25; 1988a.105, 202.

violence. Girard speaks of "the antimimetic character of all prohibitions".[116]

Of the three things which characterize human cultures, prohibition is unique in not depending on representational mimesis to achieve its ends. Instead it preserves the differences between the members of the community, and so prevents rivalry and violence, by making certain aspects of mimesis, both imitative and representational, taboo. Cultures develop rules about the behaviour of men and women and of adults and children. They have regulations about access to members of the opposite sex and laws that govern all changes of status.

Girard regards Plato's notorious fear of artistic representation and his desire to exclude most forms of it from the ideal society discussed in *The Republic* as a reflection of his temporal proximity to cultures with active taboos against all forms of mimesis, even though Plato himself was unaware of the function of the taboos.[117] In fact, while he thinks "Plato is right to see it (mimesis) as both a force of cohesion and a force of dissolution",[118] Girard regards Plato's failure to understand the relationship between mimesis and violence, his failure to discuss, in the course of his writings on mimesis, the potential of imitative acquisition to generate rivalry, as having misled nearly all subsequent Western thought on the issue.[119]

2. Ritual

According to Girard, the function of rituals is to reinforce and renew cultural differentiation by group participation in a representation of the act on which the differentiation is founded.[120] The acting out of the founding murder (a ritual sacrifice) renews the symbol system which was generated by that murder. "*Rite* is the reenactment of mimetic crises in a spirit of voluntary religious and social collaboration, a reenactment in order to reactivate the scapegoat mechanism for the benefit of society".[121] It is a function of what Girard calls *imperative mimesis*.[122] The events of the original crisis and its resolution are reproduced in acts that breach normal taboos[123] and which culminate in a sacrifice, so that the original crisis and the benefits of the founding murder can be experienced in the present.[124] The community does not understand how its rituals produce their

---

[116] 1987a.19.
[117] 1987a.15.
[118] 1987a.17.
[119] 1987a.8, 15-16, 1988a.vii. Girard and Plato are discussed by Orsini 1985.
[120] 1979.92.
[121] 1986a.140
[122] 1987a.19-23.
[123] The breaking of taboos signifies the loss of differentiation. It survives in practices associated with carnivals and feasts, the exchanging of roles between masters and servants at Christmas, activities organized under the 'Lord of Misrule' etc.
[124] 1988a.105, 202. Girard cites numerous examples

effects and does not know which details are important. Therefore, the attempt is always made to follow the tradition as accurately as possible.[125] The tradition itself is derived from the founding murder. The murder was preceded by a cultural crisis and led to cultural differentiation. The pattern of ritual follows this. The first stage is that of normal social differentiation. Then, during the ritual, the prohibitions which sustain this condition are breached. This represents the state of undifferentiation experienced in the social crisis which led up to the founding murder. This period of the ritual is ended by a sacrifice which signifies the murder which resolved the original crisis. This sacrifice renews the differentiating effects of the original murder. The pattern of ritual is thus a move from social differentiation to renewed differentiation through a representation of undifferentiation resolved by the mechanism of collective violence.[126]

Since the imitative drive is constantly undermining differentiation and causing feelings of anger and frustration which need to be appeased, cultures need the outlet for internalized violence that ritual provides.[127] The violence of the group is deflected onto the sacrificial victim who represents the original founding victim. Girard writes that in the practice of ritual sacrifice, "society is seeking to deflect upon a relatively indifferent victim, a 'sacrificeable victim', the violence that would otherwise be vented on its own members, the people it most desires to protect."[128]

Thus, rituals are imitations of real events. However, for a number of reasons, the imitation is imperfect. Firstly, it is based not on the event itself but on a distorted interpretation of the event. The main distortion arises from the fact that the community is unaware that its original victim was arbitrarily chosen.[129] Secondly, a double transfer is in operation. The ritual victim is a substitute for the original victim. The ritual victim represents the original victim whose death

---

[125] 1987a.28. Girard has been influenced by the work of Eliade who argues that rituals (and myths) enable humans to participate in the origins of their world, the time and space of divine action. 1954, 1958, 1961, 1963. For Girard this is an effect of imperative mimesis, for Eliade it is the result of the existential need, an "unquenchable ontological thirst...for *being*." 1961.64. See Mason 1993, Olsen 1992. Douglas suggests that ritual is an attempt to create and maintain culture. 1966.128.

[126] Compare van Gennep's 1960 description of rites of passage as involving the stages of separation, liminality and incorporation. See Turner 1967.93-111. The first and last involve ordered society; the second is separate from the normal rules of society and involves the transitional phenomenon Turner calls *communitas*. This is the quality of life experienced by those who find themselves outside of existing social structures. 1969.Ch3-4. See also Douglas 1966.Ch10 who suggests that rituals harness destructive forces for good purposes, and the work of Stetkevych 1986a, 1986b who shows the way the stages of rites apply in sacrifice and in rituals of blood-vengeance.

[127] 1979.249.

[128] 1979.3.

[129] 1979.103.

provided a catharsis for the violence of the whole community.[130] Next, if internal reprisal is to be avoided, the sacrificial victim must be somebody not wholly integrated into the community. The victim must be a foreigner, a prisoner, a child, a disabled person or even a king.[131] Finally, all these factors cause rituals to evolve over time.[132] The imperfect representation becomes progressively poorer and less effective with each successive repetition. Eventually, since they are imperfect copies, rituals cease to be effective and become forgotten or degenerate. At this point a primitive society may have no means by which to restore the structural differentiation on which it is founded and so may face a new crisis which, in its turn, can only be resolved by a further act of all-against-one violence.[133] This may cause new myths and rituals to be generated or lead to variations of the old ones. Order relies on difference, even though the differences on which it relies are arbitrary.[134] The slow disintegration of a society's structure is experienced as a breakdown in the natural order too.[135] Furthermore, once the crisis becomes serious and reciprocal violence afflicts the community, the cosmic order itself may appear affected for human experience of the world is mediated through a system of differentiation that is socially determined.[136] In this sense at least, the cult really does keep the world in existence.

Representational mimesis is clearly at work in this theory. An historical event is (mis)represented in order to bring its effects to bear in the present. Yet the imitation, while effective, is never as effective as the original murder itself.[137] Cultural order is therefore inevitably subject to decay.

If Girard is right then there are a number of paradoxes at work in rituals. Firstly, one form of mimesis - representational - is being used to ameliorate the effects of another form of mimesis - imitative; representation is being used to

---

[130] 1979.269, where Girard also states that, "Ritual sacrifice is defined as an inexact imitation of the generative act."

[131] 1979.12.

[132] 1987a.48-82; 1987b.Ch15.

[133] 1979.39-67.

[134] 1979.51.

[135] 1979.94. People stop co-operating and so the hunt becomes less successful, less food is gathered. Though these things have social causes, they are perceived as being caused by a change in nature. When they are remedied by ritual or by all-against-one violence, a social event is perceived as having a positive effect on nature itself.

[136] See notes 48-51.

[137] Here it is possible to trace the influence of Plato's views on the imitative nature of art: art is the imitation of an imitation; it takes its hearer or viewer a step further away from the true world of forms; "the tragic poet is an imitator, and therefore, like all other imitators, he is thrice removed from the king and from the truth". *The Republic* Book 10.

prevent imitation.[138] Secondly, violence, that is sanctioned, ritual, sacrificial, unanimous violence, is being used to control violence, that is the unsanctioned violence generated by imitative mimesis.[139] Next, the abandonment of cultural differentiation and hence of social order, a part of rites the world over, is essential to the re-establishment or re-creation of the social order.[140] "Primitive societies abandon themselves, in their rituals, to what they fear most during normal periods: the dissolution of the community in the mimetic crisis."[141] For Girard it is a rule of culture that "For order to be reborn, disorder must first triumph."[142] This applies to myth and ritual and to all cultural forms derived from them. Finally, the system functions because nobody understands its true function; participants explain the effectiveness of their activities by reference to myths and in the metaphorical terms known as religion, in terms of the sacred. If the misrepresentation, the double transfer and the true arbitrary status of the victim at the heart of the mimetic act, is grasped, ritual becomes ineffective and the community loses an outlet for its violence.[143] Therefore, misrecognition is at the very heart of the way in which human cultures work and the truth, should it ever be revealed, would have the potential to undermine cultural differentiation and precipitate a crisis.

3. Myth

In addition to being acted out in rituals, founding events are also told as stories;[144] these are myths, the "retrospective transfiguration of social crises, the reinterpretation of these crises in the light of the cultural order that has arisen from them."[145] These recount the origins of a society and are used to account for the structural differentiation on which the society is based; they may be said to provide an ideology. The story of the original murder is told from the perspective of those who carried out the murder and who therefore regard the victim as having caused the original crisis.[146] In this way, the violence of the group is projected onto the victim and the violence is always justified;[147] the accusation against the victim is at the heart of the myth and is not open to

---

[138] Girard says "Rite, therefore, is itself mimesis" and "Unanimous, ritual mimesis...constitutes a real preventative of wandering and conflictual mimesis. Against bad mimesis, therefore, culture knows no other remedy but good mimesis." 1988a.105.
[139] 1979.23.
[140] See 1987a.29; 1988a.103.
[141] 1987a.22.
[142] 1979.79.
[143] 1979.5-7, 1988a.202-3.
[144] See 1986a.Ch3; 1987a.105-124.
[145] 1979.64.
[146] 1987a.38. In myths "the lynching is represented from the standpoint of the lynchers themselves". 1988a.188.
[147] 1987c; 1988a.188-189.

challenge.[148]

The murder took place at the climax to a crisis of differentiation and so, when the event is recalled, the victim may be regarded as lacking differentiation, as having a monstrous aspect. Furthermore, the victim cannot be seen as an ordinary member of the community (indeed it is possible that the primal victim may have been singled out because he or she was not an ordinary member) and is therefore often represented as having some mark which identifies him or her as a victim; royal blood, a limp, one eye, foreign birth etc. Since the lasting beneficial effects of the murder are also ascribed to the victim, he or she comes to be regarded as the founder of the community. Finally, since the community's order continues and this, it is assumed, must be due to the continuing work of the victim, the stories told often assert that the victim has survived death and remains responsible for the order of the society concerned.[149]

On this view, myths are "communal recollection",[150] highly distorted versions of unanimous founding murders. They give an account of events as they are perceived in retrospect by those who were actively involved. However, even though the events which generated the myth are historically real, the perception is largely false and therefore myths misrepresent reality; they enshrine in the stories which found human cultures the primal lie about the guilt of surrogate victims and thus fail to acknowledge the true roles of imitation and violence in human origins.

Thus, as Girard puts it,

> These episodes of victimage are not reproduced and remembered such as they really happened but such as they must be (mis)understood by the community they reunified. The victim must appear not as a random instrument of a mimetic shift in the collective mood from conflict to peace but as both a troublemaker and then a peacemaker, as an all-powerful manipulator of all human relations inside the community - in other words, a divinity.[151]

The structure of myths preserves the pattern of the emergence of differentiation from undifferentiation - of order from chaos. Language, since it is a system of differences, is not a tool which can express undifferentiation. It must resort to images of chaos, to the monstrous. Girard notes that myths begin with a lack of differentiation, in which, for example, day and night are confused. This represents a great crisis of social undifferentiation which engendered collective persecution.[152] Creation myths which begin in this way may purport to tell the story of the origin of the world but in fact tell the story

---

[148] 1979.78.
[149] 1986.Ch3.
[150] 1988a.xiii.
[151] 1988a.xiii-xiv.
[152] 1986.Ch3

of the origin of a human social world; the beginning of a culturally-mediated experience of the world. The same applies to images of chaos in myths which are not about the birth of the cosmos.[153]

As is the case with ritual, representational mimesis is at work. An historically real event is represented, this time in the form of a narrative, in order to reproduce the effects of the event itself. However, since the story is told from a false perspective, the relationship between myth and event is far from straightforward. It is a false perception of reality that is found in myths and it is this false reality which is mimetically represented to the minds of the hearers of myths. The lie which is at the heart of every human culture is, by means of mimesis, imparted to each successive generation. As in the case of ritual, the myth becomes less effective with each repetition until the point is reached where the myth fails to reinforce differentiation and imitative mimesis generates a fresh crisis.[154] Since the way in which myths function to distort reality is now known, it is possible to read myths in such a way as to discern some features of the historical events that generated them. By means of mimesis, the historical reality may be perceived in the present in spite of the misperceptions of those who composed the texts concerned.

A similar paradox to the one which operates in his view of ritual is at work in the functioning of myth as Girard understands it. Representational mimesis is used to counteract the effects of imitative mimesis. Girard regards both as different manifestations of the same phenomenon. 'Good' mimesis is used to counter 'bad'.

The drive to imitate exists in tension with order based on differentiation. Differentiation is defended by prohibition, myth and ritual but, as has been indicated, they are not completely effective and social differences are eventually overcome by the effects of imitative mimesis. When this occurs, the culture concerned experiences a crisis which Girard calls a sacrificial crisis, a crisis of differentiation, or a crisis of degree. The lack of differentiation and the consequent violence is experienced as chaos by those involved. However, the

---

[153] Girard is indebted to Lévi-Strauss's attempts to apply the insights of structuralism to cultural phenomena. Lévi-Strauss attempted to define the structures common to myths. He argues that the structure of myths reveals the attempt to reconcile fundamental oppositions. 1963, 1973. See Strenski 1987. Lévi-Strauss's refusal to take narrative into account is criticized by Douglas 1967. However, Lévi-Strauss recognized that the beginnings of many myths are characterized by lack of differentiation. He sees this as the necessary background for the display of the differences the myth seeks to reconcile. Girard sees it as a representation of a social crisis.

[154] Once again, certain parallels with the thought of Plato can be discerned, in particular the idea that literature, since it is an imitation, misrepresents reality. Both Girard and Plato argue that the mimetic process leads to a false rather than to a true perception of reality. They differ inasmuch as Girard believes that it is possible to overcome the distorting effects of mimesis and recover truths about the historical events represented in texts. See the discussion of literature and other art in *The Republic* Books 3, 10.

weakness of social differentiation at this stage means that the truth about society, that its order is arbitrary and based on a lie, is liable to be discerned. The crisis can only be resolved by unanimous collective violence which re-establishes differentiation and hence order.

Human society therefore has a cyclical character. Each culture is born in a crisis, characterized by undifferentiation, which is resolved through violence; it experiences a period of stability when the effects of its myths, rituals and prohibitions remain strong and reinforce the cultural order founded upon a misrepresentation of that violence; eventually the order-reinforcing effects of representational mimesis are undermined by imitative mimesis and another crisis arrives which, in its turn, can be resolved only by a further act of collective violence.

To sum up, Girard believes that human origins lie in crises resolved by the unanimous collective murders of arbitrary victims who are subsequently represented as sacred; the source of both chaos and order, evil and good, violence and peace and who are regarded as being both present in the community and absent from it. The crises, their resolution, the maintenance of cultural order and the slow undermining of that order, are all effected by the imitative drive that Girard calls mimesis. Girard thinks all cultures are founded this way and are based on a similar misrepresentation.[155] Therefore, they all tend to react in the same way when faced with a crisis; they look for scapegoats, accuse them of undermining society and kill or expel them.[156] Persecution is a cultural response to a cultural crisis. Thus, the reading strategy adopted by Girard purports to allow the reader to understand the ways in which certain texts distort the reality which generated them and so allow access, potentially at least, to an undistorted version of that reality.

Girard's argument, then, is that human systems of representation have their origins in acts of collective violence generated by imitative mimesis, and that representational mimesis, in the forms of myth and ritual, has an essential function in such systems. He tries to substantiate these ideas, derived from reading texts, by reference to another realm of discourse; social and cultural

---

[155] The idea that a culture's ideology may distort reality and generate false consciousness is found in Marx 1977. J.J. Collins 1977b, in discussing sacrifice, approves of Lévi-Strauss's comments on Sartre. Sartre knows that both Marx and Freud argue that humans have meaning only on the condition that they view themselves as meaningful. This is true but the meanings humans give themselves and their actions are never the right ones. Collins claims that 'superstructures' are faulty acts which have acquired social acceptance. Hence the social scientist goes in vain to historical consciousness when searching for the truest meaning. Girard too thinks that ideologies misrepresent reality. He has been influenced in this position by Dumézil's comparative studies of the myths of different Indo-European peoples. Dumézil argues that they all refer to a social structure which reflects a common underlying ideology. 1980, 1983. See Littleton 1982.

[156] 1987b.Ch17

anthropology. He reaches the same conclusions by means of the social sciences as he reached through literary criticism. The conclusions drawn from the two fields reinforce one another.

As seems to be the case in Ricoeur's first level of mimesis, Girard appears to be arguing that humans share a certain pre-understanding derived from our social identity prior to language and from fundamental anthropology. Mimesis, in Girard's sense, is a pre-cultural phenomenon which also has cultural manifestations; mimesis precedes representations and sign-systems.[157] It is this which permits access to the historical events on which our systems of representation are founded.

E. Violence and Truth: Teleology

Although Girard's thought seeks to demonstrate the cyclical nature of human cultures, it also sees human history moving towards an end - or towards one of a number of possible ends. Until now, all human cultures have been cyclical and humans had no resources with which to free themselves from the cultural process.[158] "The destruction of the old religion culminates in the collective murder and the collective murder, through the intermediary of rites, produces the new religion."[159] This is the eternal recurrence.[160]

It is interesting to note the relationship between order and truth in this understanding. At the beginning of the cycle, in the period when the effects of the founding murder are strongest, cultural differentiation is clearly pronounced and rituals are effective in strengthening it; as a result cultural order is stable. At this point in the cycle the founding lie is firmly believed. As the cycle progresses and imitative mimesis slowly undermines cultural differentiation, the cultural order becomes weaker and the founding myths start to appear less self-evidently true and the mythological and ritual victims less self-evidently guilty. These hints of the truth limit the effectiveness of myth and ritual and so serve to further undermine the cultural order.[161] Thus, in Girard's system, order and truth appear to be incompatible; to expose the truth about cultural order is to contribute to its collapse.

The world today, led by the dominant Western culture, is entering its own crisis of differentiation. There are no ritual or sacrificial resources available to

---

[157] 1987a.15-16; 1988a.203, where Girard speaks of "my real non-Platonic and non-Hegelian starting point, at the more primitive level of appropriation common to all primates."
[158] 1979.93; these issues are explored in dialogue with Nietzsche in 1988b. Girard also discusses Nietzsche in 1970, 1976b, 1984, 1986b.
[159] 1988b.236-237.
[160] 1987a.226; 1988b.242.
[161] "During periods of crisis and widespread violence there is always the threat of subversive knowledge spreading." 1986a.100.

help restore cultural difference. We are experiencing "a gradual loosening of legal constraints in proportion to the declining efficacy of ritual mechanisms".[162] The truth about cultural origins is gradually being exposed and the cultural order is threatened. So far most societies have escaped the worst consequences of violence's law of retribution "for reasons unknown".[163]

Nevertheless, the mimetically influenced escalation of human violence or potential for violence manifested in the destructive power of stockpiled modern weapons has reached the point where it must be doubted whether the crisis can be resolved by means of the scapegoat mechanism. If mimetic violence continues to develop we are likely to destroy ourselves before the mechanism can operate. The world today possesses what was once the prerogative of the gods; the power of absolute vengeance. Humanity therefore faces a "choice between total destruction and the total renunciation of violence."[164] Girard agrees with the suggestion that the scapegoat mechanism which has resolved previous crises has ceased to function.[165] Elsewhere he discusses the same issue and claims that in a situation such as our own, sacrificial resources, like fossil fuel, become a non-renewable commodity.[166] This is not a position faced by any previous culture.

> The genuinely new element is that violence can no longer be relied upon to resolve the crisis. Violence no longer guarantees a firm base. For violence to be capable of carrying out its cyclical development and bringing back peace, there must be an ecological field that can absorb the damage done in the process. Nowadays that field covers the entire planet, but even that has probably ceased to be enough. The environment can no longer absorb the violence humans can unleash.[167]

The contemporary world has many scapegoats and many victims, yet they have lost their power to reconcile; they are no longer effective.[168] Girard argues that "There must be several reasons for this, but they must all go back ultimately to the unforgettable knowledge we have acquired and are still acquiring of our violence and all its works, and of our propensity to victimize other human beings."[169] This suggests that truth, the truth about humanity, is the agent of teleology; truth is the engine of the eschatological process.

Clearly, Girard's hypothesis raises a number of questions for theology and for biblical studies. One might assume that if Girard has explained the origin of

---

[162] 1987a.253.
[163] 1979.260.
[164] 1979.240.
[165] 1987a.257.
[166] 1988a.226-227.
[167] 1987a.258.
[168] 1988a.219.
[169] 1988a.219.

all religion, then he has also accounted for Christianity. After all, the Christian story of a man who was violently killed at the instigation of the mob but who returned to life to bring peace and reconciliation, looks suspiciously like an historicized version of the story found in all mythology. As Girard says,

> In the second half of the nineteenth century ethnologists discovered the unity of the central drama at the heart of the world's religions, the extreme frequency with which violence appears, often in collective manifestations, in the myths and rites of the whole planet. They also perceived that the most violent rites, those which they judged to be the most primitive, were the ones which were structurally closest to Christ's Passion.[170]

At the end of *Violence and the Sacred* Girard states, "No attempt will be made here to consider the Judaeo-Christian texts in the light of this theory, or vice-versa; that must be left to a future study. However, I hope to have suggested here the course that such a project might take."[171]

The reader may well assume that the stories of the Bible will be read to reveal that they take their own origin from the same mechanism which, according to Girard, has produced all other myths.[172] However, such an assumption would be mistaken. With the benefit of hindsight, the words *vice-versa* quoted above suggest the direction Girard was to take. His readings of the Bible in general and of the Gospels in particular represent a remarkable apology for Christianity and a bold attempt to vindicate the status of the Christian Scriptures as revelatory texts.[173] The unforgettable knowledge of our own violence and of the innocence of our scapegoats has its source in the Bible.

F. Revelation and Renunciation: The Gospel

Girard is faced with a dilemma. If the scapegoat mechanism generates the lie essential to human culture and structures all human symbolic thought, how is it possible for the truth about the mechanism to be known and to be articulated? There is an apparent need for an agency outside of human culture to intervene so that the true nature of culture can become known. It is for this reason that Girard has recourse to the ideas of transcendence and revelation. These enable him to argue that it is conceivable for the truth to become known. Indeed the

---

[170] 1988b.241-242.

[171] 1979.309.

[172] On the other hand, if one knew of Girard's Christian commitment one might assume with White 1978 that Christianity will be defended on the grounds of its unique sublimation of the sacrificial system in the sacrament of the eucharist, something which White regards as a return to medievalism. In fact he has wrongly anticipated Girard's direction, even if some of his other criticisms are pertinent. However, White's criticism might apply to aspects of the interpretation of Girard in Alison 1993.

[173] 1987a.Bk2, 1986a.

argument is occasionally that since the truth has become known, it follows that an agency outside of human culture must have revealed it.[174]

Girard acknowledges that a number of similarities exist between myths and the stories found in the Bible, particularly the Passion.[175] However, he points to one vital distinction; while myths always obscure the innocence of the victim of collective violence, the Bible consistently, although not invariably, takes the side of the victim. The stories of Romulus and Remus and of Cain and Abel may be compared. In both one brother murders the other and founds a city. Both provide support for Girard's contention that societies are founded on acts of violence. However, while Remus is regarded as responsible for his own death because he breached the symbolic boundaries of the unbuilt city of Rome, the biblical text consistently asserts the innocence of Abel. Girard argues that myths justify the founding murder but the Bible exposes it and thus reveals the true origins and nature of human culture. [176]

In a similar way, Girard understands the prophets, especially Deutero-Isaiah, to take the side of the victims against those who use violence and rituals based on violence to maintain the social order. The prophets subvert the pillars of ancient religion; myth, sacrifice and prohibition. So Israel's calling, not necessarily fulfilled, was to protect those who might be treated as victims; the poor, the widow, the orphan, the foreigner.[177]

According to Girard, this biblical theme reaches its climax in the canonical Gospels which he regards as revelation *par excellence* for in them the scapegoat mechanism at the root of culture is revealed as a lie and the victim vindicated. His argument is that whereas, on the one hand, "Human culture is predisposed to the permanent concealment of its origins in collective violence",[178] on the other hand, "The Gospels constantly reveal what the texts of historical persecutors, and especially mythological persecutors, hide from us: the knowledge that their victim is a scapegoat."[179] Thus, mythology conceals but the Gospels reveal; religion lies but the Gospels expose the truth. Each tells the same story but while myth tells it from the perspective of the persecutors,[180]

---

[174] Girard speaks of the Bible as a counterforce in our culture, one which "tends towards the revelation of the immemorial lie." 1986a.100.

[175] 1986.101, 1993.340.

[176] 1987a.144-149. Augustine compares Cain and Romulus and states that the founder of the earthly city is a fratricide. *City of God* 15.5. Winstanley, for whom the first sin is the development of private property brought about by the covetousness which induces violence, uses the story of Cain and Abel as a typological example. He asks, "whether all wars, blood-shed, and misery came upon creation, when one man indeavoured to be a lord of another?" Hayes 1979.152. Contrary to Genesis 4:1, Josephus claims Cain's name means *possession*; he also calls him "covetous". *Antiquities of the Jews* 1.2.1.

[177] 1987a.154-158.

[178] 1986.100.

[179] 1986.119.

[180] 1988a.189-190.

the Gospels tells it from the point of view of the innocent victim.[181]

Girard develops his case on the basis of readings of a number of texts. One example is John 11:49-53 where the words of Caiaphas, speaking as high priest, expose the sacrificial nature of religious thinking which advocates violence against a scapegoat so that greater violence might be avoided. However, it is the Passion narratives which form the basis of Girard's case for there he finds Jesus presented as the archetypal victim. The Passion reproduces the founding event of all rituals and so is linked to every ritual and parallels between them may be traced.[182] The key difference is that in the texts which represent the Passion, the innocence of the victim is not hidden, rather it is asserted, indeed proclaimed, throughout.[183]

> The Gospels do indeed center around the Passion of Christ, the same drama that is found in all world mythologies...This drama is needed to give birth to new myths, to present the perspective of the persecutors. But the same drama is also needed to present the perspective of a victim dedicated to the rejection of the illusions of the persecutors. Thus the same drama is needed to give birth to the only text that can bring an end to all mythology.[184]

It is this reproduction of the founding murder in texts which show the one murdered to be innocent which exposes the lie in all the other texts which represent founding murders. It is this which signals the existence of a non-violent God who rejects human behaviour derived from sacrificial thinking and who is driven out by human violence.[185] This means that Girard rejects the traditional Christian understanding of the death of Jesus as a sacrifice.[186] He does not deny that Jesus's death is a sacrifice in the sense that it was a death

---

[181] 1987b.154-168; the God of the Gospels is the God of victims.

[182] This accounts for Girard's stress on the role of the crowd in the death of Jesus and his stress on the unanimity of the decision to have him killed. 1987c, 1986a.Ch9 and "What is astonishing about the Gospels is that the unanimity is not emphasized in order to bow before, or submit to, its verdict as in all mythological, political, and even philosophical texts, but to denounce its total mistake, its perfect example of nontruth...This is what constitutes the unparalleled radicalism of the revelation." 1986a.115.

[183] "The Gospels constantly reveal what the texts of historical persecution, and especially mythological persecutors, hide from us: the knowledge that their victim is a scapegoat". 1986.117. And see 1986.165-166; 1987a.194; 1993.346-348

[184] 1986.100. This is the "only textual mechanism that can put an end to humanity's imprisonment in the system of mythological representation based on the false transcendence of a victim who is made sacred because of the unanimous verdict of guilt." 1986.166.

[185] "A non-violent deity can only signal his existence to mankind by having himself driven out by violence - by demonstrating that he is not able to establish himself in the Kingdom of Violence." 1987a.219. "a God of victims cannot impose his will on men without ceasing to exist." 1987b.154. See 1987a.Bk2Ch4 and 1987b.154-168.

[186] 1987a.180-223.

which has the potential to have beneficent effects on others; he rejects it in the sense that it was required by God. Girard most especially rejects the idea that God, or God's anger, or God's tendency to respond to humans in a violent way, (a characteristic which Girard holds that God does not possess) was propitiated or appeased by the death of Jesus on the cross.[187]

Girard develops this idea in one of his more recent publications, one which is perhaps his most self-consciously theological book.[188] Rejecting what he calls Medieval and modern theories of redemption that look to God (the satisfaction of God's honour, justice or anger) for the causes of the crucifixion, he advocates a demythologised version of the theory of the duping of Satan found in Greek Patristic thought. Satan is identified with the mimetic contagion and its corresponding victim mechanism. In its operation on Jesus, this inadvertently reveals itself. Satan overturns "his own lie; he has rendered the truth of God universally understandable." He continues

> The trick that traps Satan does not include the least bit of either violence or dishonesty on God's part. It is not really a ruse or trick; it is rather the inability of the prince of this world to understand the divine love...Satan himself transforms his own mechanism into a trap.[189]

God's involvement is to have the wisdom and foresight to foresee this outcome and to allow "himself to be crucified for the salvation of humankind."

When Girard turns his attention to the present state of humanity, his analysis takes on dimensions which may be described as apocalyptic.[190] He believes that our own culture has entered into a crisis of differentiation in which the truth about cultural origins is gradually being exposed and, as a consequence, the cultural order threatened. One would expect, given Girard's cyclical view of human culture, that he might think that this crisis might be resolved in the usual way and culture reborn. Interestingly, Girard's analysis of Aphorism 125 from *The Gay Science* suggests that this was in fact Nietzsche's view. The Madman holding a lantern at midday in the market square accuses his hearers of the collective murder of God. Girard, following what he takes to be Nietzsche's line of thought, writes,

> If religion once again dies a violent death in our world it will certainly be reborn in another form, it matters little which. The crisis of the modern world is but an episode in the middle of an unending process. The prodigious importance which we attach to our history is due to the narrowness of our vision...The eternal recurrence crushes all claims to absolute singularity. It relativizes our world in the

---

[187] 1987a.180-185.
[188] 2001.
[189] 2001.152
[190] 1987a.185-190, 202-205, 253-262; 1988a.204,227; Wallace, M. 1994b; Green 1995 (a review of Bailie 1997).

midst of an infinity of worlds. It contradicts the Judaeo-Christian conception of a unique history dominated by the divine determination to ensure the salvation of humanity. There is no alpha and omega.[191]

Nevertheless, Nietzsche is, in Girard's view, less than sure of this position. He recognizes that Christianity has some potential to discredit the collective murder which generates the eternal recurrence. Girard continues, "Far from taking Christianity to be just another sacrificial religion, Nietzsche reiterates several times that its great fault is to 'prevent sacrifice', to render impossible the acts of violence necessary to the smooth functioning of society."[192]

So, Girard finds Nietzsche to be ambiguous on this point, sometimes implying that Christianity is simply another sacrificial religion but on others suggesting that it might have a disrupting effect on human culture. Girard continues,

> One finds the same ambiguity at the conclusion of the Twilight of the Idols. One does not know if the colossal finish marks the end of the cycle only, the promise of a thousand renewals, or if it is truly the end of the world, the Christian apocalypse, the bottomless abyss of the unforgettable victim.[193]

And these observations reflect Girard's own view. The Gospels account for the state of Western culture in our day. Girard suggests that it is the Gospels which have generated our awareness of the innocence of the scapegoats of others and even of our own victims. The Gospels have spread the subversive knowledge which is preventing the operation of the scapegoat mechanism. We have reached the point where our knowledge of the truth will prevent us from restoring a cultural order of the kind we have had in the past. Girard writes,

> mankind has become, for the first time, capable of destroying itself...The whole planet now finds itself, with regard to violence, in a situation comparable to that of the most primitive groups of human beings, except that this time we are fully aware of it. We can no longer count on sacrificial resources based on false religions to keep this violence at bay. We are reaching a degree of self-awareness and responsibility that was never attained by those who lived before us.[194]

So, human history has, until now, been cyclical. However, the effects of the Gospels have now given it a linear trajectory. Now humans must find a means to escape the influence of the way in which our cultures are founded and on which all our systems of representation are built, for these make us imitate acquisitive acts, react to crises by searching for scapegoats, and respond to violence with more violence. In other words, we must find the means to found a

---

[191] 1988b.243.
[192] 1988b.244.
[193] 1988b.246.
[194] 1987a.260-261.

non-violent cultural order. And, since mimesis is inescapable, we must find a new model to imitate; one based on truth rather than upon a lie so that it has the prospect of being stable.

Girard's suggestion is found in the Gospels; it is the kingdom of God as proclaimed and exemplified by Jesus. It involves the universal renunciation of violence, the elimination of every form of vengeance, retribution and reprisal from human relations.[195] To do this is to escape from the realm of violence, which involves enslavement to the pervasive lie, into the domain of God.[196] The Gospels tell us "all that people must do in order to break with the circularity of closed societies, whether they be tribal, national, philosophical or religious".[197] To escape from the realm of the lie to the kingdom of God is possible; "Mankind can cross this abyss, but to do so all men together should adopt the single rule of the Kingdom of God."[198] This is a call to conversion, to secede from the mimetic consensus.[199]

The Gospels begin with the announcement by John the Baptist that his own culture faces a crisis.[200] Then Jesus offers the kingdom of God, God's way in which the crisis can be escaped.[201] The message is announced with some urgency for at the time of the crisis, "when violence is at its peak, when the community is one (*sic*) the brink of dissolution, the chances of succeeding are at their greatest, as are the dangers".[202] The rejection of the offer results in the announcement of apocalypse and the crucifixion,[203] for an unprecedented cultural crisis will follow without any sacralized victim to prevent its worst consequences.[204] This crisis is announced in the Gospel apocalypse. To those who have refused the offer of the kingdom, Jesus appears as a destructive and subversive force which threatens the community, the corrupter of the cultural order they wish to maintain or restore.[205] Jesus becomes the ideal victim. There seems to be every reason to pick on him yet he is in fact wholly innocent.[206] People killed Jesus because they could not be reconciled without killing. However, his death does not have that effect and the community is exposed to its own unlimited violence.[207] This human violence is prophesied in the Gospel

---

[195] 1987a.197-198. Comparisons of love and violence in Girard's thought are found in Dumouchel 1982, D'Iribane 1985.
[196] 1987a.197.
[197] 1987a.198.
[198] 1987a.199.
[199] 1993.348-350.
[200] 1987a.199.
[201] 1987a.201.
[202] 1987a.202.
[203] 1987.202-203.
[204] 1987a.203.
[205] 1987a.206-208.
[206] 1987a.208-209.
[207] 1987a.213.

apocalypse.

Thus, for Girard, apocalyptic violence is not the violence of God but human violence.[208] Humans are responsible for their own history.[209] God is not uninvolved however, for God's intervention, the offer of the kingdom (once it is refused) and the exposure, through the death of Jesus, of the scapegoat mechanism, provoke the crisis and deny it any prospect of resolution.[210]

The crisis which confronted first century Israel, prepared as it was by the Old Testament,[211] did not immediately confront the rest of the world, although it threatened to do so. The reason it did not do so was because of the sacrificial interpretation of the New Testament which gave rise to historic Christianity. This reading provided enduring sacrificial resources which are only now becoming exhausted.[212] Now the whole world faces a crisis generated by the diffusion of the Gospel text and its slow penetration into human awareness.

> In our interpretation, divine intervention no longer violently changes the course of human history and suspends its ordinary laws of development. On the contrary, a text does disturb those laws, but only to the extent that it gradually reveals the state of sacrificial misapprehension protecting people from their own violence.[213]

This is the work of the Spirit in history.[214] The Spirit is at work in history through the Gospels, disintegrating the world and provoking the crisis which confronts humanity.[215] This is a function of the text which represents, from a new perspective, the story at the heart of human culture. Representational mimesis is therefore essential to its effectiveness. It is the means through which the Spirit works. Girard occasionally hints that the Gospel writers did not wholly understand the nature of the revelation mediated by the story they tell. They are "necessary intermediaries",[216] but "the Gospel text is somewhat like a password communicated by go-betweens who are not included in the secret."[217]

Those who try to follow Jesus may contribute to the subversive effect of the Gospel story.[218] This is especially true of the martyrs of whom Girard says, "Dying in the same way as Jesus died, for the same reasons as he did, the

---

[208] 1987a.186. Of course, this is true of predictions of divine vengeance in whatever religious system they may be found. 1979.307.
[209] 1987a.195.
[210] 1988a.227.
[211] 1987a.204-205.
[212] 1987a.224-262.
[213] 1987a.251.
[214] 1986a.Ch15; 1988a.227.
[215] 1986a.207.
[216] 1986a.163.
[217] 1986.164. Girard claims that their ignorance on this point "guarantees the authenticity of the message." 1986.164.
[218] 1987a.170-174.

martyrs multiply the revelation of the founding violence."[219] Furthermore,

> What the martyrs say has little importance because they are witnesses, not of a determined belief, as is imagined, but of man's terrible propensity, in a group, to spill innocent blood in order to restore the unity of their community. The persecutors force themselves to bury their dead in the tomb of their representation of persecution, but the more martyrs die the weaker the representation becomes and the more striking the testimony.[220]

The martyrs join Jesus in revealing the truth about all the innocent deaths *since the foundation of the world*.

Mimesis is inescapable and therefore humanity is confronted with a choice of models; we have been brought, led by mimesis and by the revelation of the mimetic mechanisms, to the point to which history has been heading. Ours is the eschatological moment when humanity must both face and make its final judgement and choose between the available models. The two models are incompatible. The first is the basis of all mythology and contemporary ideologies on which human cultures are founded. These are all discredited by the gospel revelation and can no longer preserve peace and order. Their arbitrary nature is plain. In fact, the end of human culture is already contained in the cross and resurrection of Jesus; which represents the vindication of the innocent victim. "Jesus's victory is thus, in principle, achieved immediately at the moment of the Passion, but for most men it only takes shape in the course of a long history secretly controlled by the revelation."[221] This end of culture is present wherever the Christian *kerygma*, the story of Jesus is represented. The second model is founded on the Gospels and these, when interpreted non-sacrificially, found a radically different form of community.[222] Those who imitate Jesus meet no rivals for he is without acquisitive desire;

> The Gospels and the New Testament do not preach a morality of spontaneous action. They do not claim that humans must get rid of imitation; they recommend imitating the sole model who never runs the danger-if we really imitate in the way that children imitate-of being transformed into a fascinating rival.[223]

The community built round the representation of the death of Jesus offers a contrast to the society built round the misrepresentation of the founding victim; a community founded on truth opposed to one founded upon a lie. However, the gospel community must use the framework and the language of the existing

---

[219] 1987a.173.
[220] 1986a.212.
[221] 1986a.207.
[222] 1987a.178.
[223] 1987a.430.

culture,[224] and so it can offer only indications and anticipations of the kingdom of God. Existing languages cannot articulate a social world in which violence is renounced; they are ultimately derived from the scapegoat mechanism and therefore any concept expressed in them will be tainted by sacrificial thinking and traditional ideas about the nature of the sacred. They can offer no privileged stance from which absolute truth can be discovered or stated, "That is why the Word that states itself to be absolutely true never speaks except from the position of a victim in the process of being expelled. There is no human explanation for his presence among us."[225] Therefore, language can offer only hints of what an alternative mimesis might be like. There can be no blueprint for the kingdom of God.

The eschaton to which mimesis drives humanity is open. It could be self-destruction in reciprocal violence, or it could be the kingdom of God. The present generation, and perhaps the next, have a choice between total destruction and the total renunciation of violence.[226] As Girard writes in the closing sentence of one of his books, "The time has come for us to forgive one another. If we wait any longer there will not be time enough."[227] Or, as the scripture puts it, "I call heaven and earth to witness against you today that I have set before you life and death, blessings and curses. Choose life so that you and your descendants may live".[228]

G. Conclusions

The five key ideas in the thought of Girard are therefore; mimesis as the foundational human drive; the scapegoat mechanism as the root of human culture and its representation as a means of social maintenance; the order - chaos - violent resolution - renewed order pattern of cultural phenomena; the exposure of the truth about that mechanism in the Judaeo-Christian Scriptures; and the consequences of that exposure for history.

Girard himself believes that the Revelation of John is "a text which is clearly less representative of the gospel inspiration than the apocalyptic chapters in the Gospels themselves".[229] Be that as it may, it is the contention of this thesis that Girard's thought can provide a helpful framework for interpreting Revelation. It is a text which understands itself as an apocalypse, an unveiling, and presents that unveiling in terms which appear to be violent. It therefore has certain parallels to and resonances with Girard's own ideas. The approach that will be taken will be formulated in the light of the discussion in the next chapter of the

---

[224] 1987a.191.
[225] 1987a.435.
[226] 1979.240.
[227] 1986.212.
[228] Deuteronomy 30:19. *NRSV*.
[229] 1987a.188.

reception of Girard's thought by theologians, biblical scholars, and representatives of other fields of discourse.

Chapter 3

Praise, Criticism and Interpretation: The Reception of Girard's Theory in Contemporary Thought

A. Introduction

The purpose of this chapter is to consider the work of some of the scholars who have engaged with Girard's work, especially those working in the disciplines of theology and of biblical studies. While his work is not that widely read in the United Kingdom, Girard is well known in France and increasingly influential in the United States of America.[1] He has been called "one of the most innovative and influential humanists of our age".[2] Nemoianu says Girard is "generally recognized to be one of the major thinkers of our century's last third".[3] Juilland points to the "universal influence of Girard's thought" and to the range of his theory's influence; "The fact that politicians, lawyers, economists, scientists, theologians, anthropologists, writers and experts from all horizons scrutinize and respond to Girard's insights, is in itself a recognition of it power."[4]

There is some dispute among Girard's readers as to the overall goal of his project. It has been suggested that his purpose is to vindicate Christianity.[5]

---

[1] While few abstracts of British theses refer to Girard (but see S.J. Taylor 1996), databases reveal that he is widely mentioned in North American abstracts; at least 23 abstracts in the period 1993-1995, 22 between 1988 and 1992, 12 between 1982 and 1987 and another 3 in the period prior to that. These are mostly in the field of literary criticism. More recent evidence suggests the numbers are increasing.

[2] Darr 1993.357.

[3] 1986.1.

[4] 1986c.330.

[5] This appears, e.g., to be the view of Alison 1993, 1996; Scubla 1988 and White 1978. Some accept Girard's anthropology without giving the Bible any privileged revelatory role. See Livingston 1988 who argues that the system created by the scapegoat mechanism is not necessarily closed; understanding of the system need not come through revelation but might arise from interaction between cultures. Scubla 1988 makes a similar point. Revelation is not needed to expose the mechanism because over the course of time ritual repetition of the mechanism becomes more and more distant from its origins. This makes it possible to see the roots of culture. However, even if this were the case, and it is doubtful that Girard will allow such insight to be decisive, it

However, Von Balthasar who states that "Girard's is surely the most dramatic project to be undertaken today in the field of soteriology and in theology generally",[6] claims that his "main campaign is to supersede and demolish psychoanalysis; his aim to overcome the structuralism of Lévi-Strauss, the Hegelian-Marxist dialectic, Heidegger and rationalist ethnology (Frazer) is only secondary."[7] A third possibility, hinted at by Girard, is that his purpose is to defend the possibility of meaning in discourse and the idea of truth.[8] Of course, his purpose may simply be to warn humanity of its need to renounce violence. However, Girard is probably best understood as having a desire to use texts to explain what it means to be human. To this end he has constructed a metanarrative derived from mythological, biblical, classical, medieval, literary, ethnological, psychological and theological texts.

Since his theory is a metanarrative, it inevitably has consequences for all fields of human discourse[9] and it has been used by scholars in many of them including politics,[10] economics,[11] law and criminology,[12] psychology,[13] the

---

offers no alternative to violence and would lead only to the repetition of the scapegoat mechanism and to a newly differentiated culture with its own myth and ritual.

[6] 1994.299.

[7] 1994.299.

[8] See the conclusion of 1987a, especially "our need is to escape from meaninglessness" 1987a.446. J.G. Williams writes that one of Girard's future projects will be a critique of Derrida and his technique of deconstructing texts. 1988.325-326, n2,4.

[9] Lascaris 1988 suggests Girard is contributing to the process through which the fragmentation of human knowledge into isolated specialist fields of discourse is being broken down.

[10] Dupuy 1986 examines the field of political economy, especially John Rawls's *A Theory of Justice* from a Girardian perspective. Palaver 1991 analyzes the political (and theological) thought of Thomas Hobbes using Girard's theory and concludes that Hobbes's thinking has its roots in the scapegoat mechanism. See also Dumouchel 1986. Reflections on Girard and Marxism may be found in Feenberg 1988 who links the idea of mimetic desire to the Marxist concept of commodity fetishism. Juilland acknowledges that it is possible to read *Violence and the Sacred* as "a defense of social hierarchy and therefore of a class system", (1986b.ii) and White 1978 suggests that the book promotes medievalism. However, the direction of Girard's subsequent work suggests that he does not wish to justify existing social structures but to demonstrate their nature and the need to develop cultures that are not based on violence or exclusion.

[11] Dumouchel examines the ambivalence of the concept of scarcity that is one of the presuppositions of economics. Both economic arrangements and violence are understood as responses to scarcity of goods and resources the supplies of which are limited and cannot meet the needs and desires of all. If Girard is correct and desire is mimetic, then scarcity may be a product of human relations rather than a natural phenomenon. 1979.137-254. Dupuy discusses the possibility that mimetic desire is the driving force behind the operation of the market. Dumouchel 1979.17-134. Girard is supportive of both these interpretations of his thought. Dumouchel 1979.257-265. Feenberg 1988 argues that Girard's theory challenges three traditional bases of

arts,[14] the human sciences and science generally.[15] Girard's thought has also been used to help understand the role of Martin Luther King II in North American culture before and after his assassination,[16] to discuss the strategy of terrorists,[17] and as a means to gain understanding into the conflict within Northern Ireland.[18] Some of his ideas have been taken up within feminist thought.[19] Given that Girard's first influential work was in literary criticism, it is not surprising that the greatest use of his theory has been in that field.[20] His thought has been used to give readings of myths,[21] non-Biblical texts from the

---

economic philosophy; that scarcity is natural, that people compete for goods rather than 'prestige', and that prices represent an hypostasized reality. Some of these points are also made by Lascaris 1987. Cazes 1986 looks at the relationship between mimetic desire, and the monetarist theory of inflation and the emergence of capitalism. Orléan 1986, 1988 uses Girard's theory to account for economic phenomena, including the development of money and currency speculation. See also Granstedt 1985, Lantz 1985, de Radkowski 1985.

[12] Gorringe 1996 uses Girard's theory in his study of the relationship between judicial systems and doctrines of atonement. Thomas 1986 examines law and judicial systems from a Girardian perspective. Girard discusses contemporary Western judicial systems. 1979.15-27.

[13] *Things Hidden from the Foundation of the World* is presented as a dialogue between Girard and two psychologists, Jean-Michel Oughourlian and Guy Lefort. Book 3 of this work is entitled "Interdividual Psychology" (283-447). Girard's interlocutors discuss psychotic structure in 1978. Livingston 1992 offers an analysis Girard's work from a psychological perspective. He is correct when he argues that Girard's understanding of mimesis makes it the foundational human drive, one shared with other animals. It is pre-cultural. Girard offers an account of the origins of representation but not of mimesis itself. It is the presupposition of his system. He doubts the move Girard makes from cultural imitative desire back to pre-cultural mimesis. He argues that Girard's system as a whole may be better regarded as descriptive rather than explanatory and concludes that Girard tells us something true about humans with respect to mimetic desire but that he can be followed in this without any commitment to his theories of human social origins. Girard's theory is related to issues of child development by Seibel 1985 and Morin 1985.

[14] Gans 1973 uses Girard's ideas on mimesis to examine aesthetic issues.

[15] Domenach 1988 discusses Girard's approach to the epistemology of Karl Popper and the way in which, he alleges, reason and faith sit together in the former's system. Élie 1985 also explores Girard's contribution to the debate between theology and the sciences.

[16] T.H. Smith 1994. Grimsrud 2000 discusses Girard and Christian pacifism.

[17] Kearney 1979 and 1982 where the debt to Girard is acknowledged at 706.n4.

[18] Kaptein 1993. Lascaris 1985 and 1993.

[19] Irigaray 1993 adopts Girard's language when she describes societies as 'sacrificial'. She and other feminists have been critical of aspects of Girard's work.

[20] The role of literature in Girard's work is discussed by Livingston 1986.

[21] In addition to Girard's own readings in 1979, 1986a, 1987a, a reading of a myth is offered by Bandera 1986.

Ancient Near East,[22] texts from classical Greece and Rome,[23] medieval texts,[24] and more recent literature.[25]

The reception of Girard's thought is significant in every field of discourse. However, it is of particular importance in those areas which he has used in order to establish his theory, for it is here that any fundamental weaknesses ought to be exposed. The crucial fields are therefore social and cultural anthropology, and structuralist and post-structuralist literary criticism. In addition, since his work provides a theory of culture, thinkers who take a non-conformist view of the dominant culture might be expected to provide insightful criticisms of Girard's theory. A number of feminists have written on Girard and so the results of their engagement with his ideas provide an example of such a critique and will be considered here. Given both the privileged status that Girard gives to the Christian Scriptures and the purpose of this thesis, his reception in biblical and theological work must also be discussed.

B. Social and Cultural Anthropology

Anthropology is one of the fields of discourse used by Girard to defend his theory. If it is safe to generalize in this area, it is fair to say that he has had less impact among anthropologists than might have been expected. This may be because the discipline has learned to distrust generic theories and has chosen to concentrate on the study of specific cultures. Authors of comparative studies do exist, including Mary Douglas[26] and Victor Turner,[27] but there is a sense in

---

[22] Keim 2000.
[23] Girard 1979 includes a reading of the Oedipus story, including the Sophocles version. Bailie 1994 offers a Girardian reading of Homer's *Iliad*. See also Segal 1990, Griffiths 1990, Pucci 1990, Joplin 1990.
[24] See the opening chapters of *The Scapegoat* and Bandera 1986.
[25] Bassoff 1986 looks at Kafka's *The Trial*. Hough 1994 examines Vietnam war poetry. Hensen 1993 compares Girard's thought with that of the Scandinavian novelist Askel Sandemose. Kirk-Duggan 1994 offers a reading of Alice Walker's *The Color Purple* and suggests that the text shows a resolution reached not through the death of a scapegoat as Girard would lead us to expect, but through "self-actualization nurtured by agape." 1994.266. In fact Girard expects myths to be resolved by the death of a scapegoat but the great novels to find resolution in experience of the transcendent. 1965.290-314, 1977. Koppisch 1986 looks at Molière's *Les femmes savantes* and shows that the author understands that rivalry derives not from difference but from sameness and that where there is rivalry, order cannot be permanent. Only the sacrifice of one of the characters keeps anarchy at bay but even this can be only a temporary measure. Morón-Arroyo 1994 reviews the work of Cervantes and Calderón. Strauss 1990 looks at Dostoievski and Ungar 1990 at Camus. Munk 1990 uses Girard to understand the dynamics of violence as they are represented in a number of literary texts.
[26] E.g. 1966, 1970, 1975, 1992. Her ideas have been influential on biblical studies and use is made of them by e.g. Malina 1986, Myers 1991 and Riches 1980.

which Girard has chosen to address issues that anthropologists have preferred to exclude from their discourse.[28] An exception is Yamaguchi, a structuralist anthropologist who suspects that Girard's theory about scapegoating may help to account for the fact that at a fundamental level human thought presupposes antithesis which means that some mechanism for exclusion, responsible for the generation of symbols, is foundational to all human cultures.[29] He acknowledges that since ethnology has abandoned the comparative work of Frazer and adopted a functionalism based on realist positivism and field experience, the work of thinkers, such as Girard and Eliade, who compare data from different cultures and develop totalizing theories, tends to be ignored within the discipline. However, there are examples of anthropologists apart from Yamaguchi who have reconsidered their work in the light of Girard's theory and these include Beattie,[30] Bureau[31], Muller,[32] and Rosaldo.[33]

Although Chilton's critique of Girard is included in a book that belongs to biblical studies, his discussion of Girard, apart from his adoption of Mack's argument,[34] is grounded in cultural theory.[35] Chilton argues that Girard is a

---

[27] E.g. 1969, 1978. Turner's positive comments about Girard 1979 are printed on its back cover. Biblical scholars who have interacted with Turner's ideas include Meeks 1983 and Niditch 1993a. Morgan 1988.133-166 discusses the use of social science in biblical interpretation.

[28] The comparative anthropologists are those who devise theories of culture and systems of cross-cultural classification. It is these theories that those engaged in biblical studies have tended to adopt. Dumouchel 1988b says that anthropologists resist the idea that sacrifice, incest taboos etc can be classified cross-culturally and therefore the discipline excludes general theories. He points out that these phenomena do share some features in different cultures, which can serve as a basis for comparative study.

[29] 1988.

[30] Beattie takes a functional view of sacrifice. He refers to scapegoating and regards Girard 1979 as "a stimulating treatment of this theme." 1980.44n1.

[31] 1988. Bureau reviews his own work among the Gabonese in the light of Girard's theory. He is not uncritical of Girard, adopting the critique made by Scubla 1988.

[32] Muller has applied Girard's work on sacrifice to the ritual killing of African kings. His work is cited and criticized by de Heusch 1985.100.

[33] In Hamerton-Kelly 1987.239-244. Rosaldo thinks the theory is subjective and Girard, in responding, does not disagree. He finds Girard's views on mimesis and rivalry helpful in evaluating the behaviour of young men involved in head hunting.

[34] See below.

[35] 1992. Pt1 is a discussion of sacrifice from the perspective of cultural theory. Chilton is not unsympathetic to the insight that sacrifice redirects violence (32), but criticizes Girard's rejection of the practice. The work's purpose is to argue that Jesus's primary concern was the efficacy of the sacrificial cult at the Jerusalem Temple. Chilton, to establish his case, tries to discredit both Girard's theory of culture and his reading of the Gospels. However, as R. Williams 1989 points out, Girard has identified an anti-sacrificial theme within the Gospels. It may not be as important as Girard implies but Chilton is forced to exclude it from his reconstruction. Gorringe takes the side of Girard

modernist who fails to allow the ancient world to be itself or to be understood in its own terms.[36] Girard objects to sacrifice because he is not an ancient and therefore does not belong to and cannot empathize with a society in which sacrifice had a central and accepted role. Chilton regards Girard's view of sacrifice as "ideological propaganda".[37] In other words, Chilton denies the legitimacy of the question of sacrifice's origin and purpose. The argument seems to be that a modern person cannot understand sacrifice because he or she is a modern person and not an ancient person; the attempt to understand and to explain is misguided. All that we may do, and what Chilton purports to do in his third chapter, is produce a typology of sacrifice, a description of its salient features. Of course, this is itself just another form of interpretation. However, this one claims to be ideologically neutral. Chilton's typology of sacrifice is helpful, but his reasons for rejecting Girard's hypothesis amount to a politically correct counsel of despair; we cannot understand and we should not try to do so. Yet the ubiquity of sacrificial acts and the variety of their stated motives are such that sacrifice may be regarded as both fundamental to culture and misunderstood by those who perform it. The issue therefore invites reflection. Girard may be wrong but he should not be criticized for posing the question. Chilton also attempts to read Girard against himself arguing that he makes ancient sacrifice the scapegoat for the modern experience of violence; Girard projects his own fear of violence onto sacrifice. However, that sacrifice, especially human sacrifice, is violent is hardly a point that needs to be defended, even if efforts are sometimes made to minimize the appearance of violence. Many of Chilton's criticisms are derived from those of the anthropologist de Heusch,[38] who accuses Girard of building a universal theory of sacrifice out of thin air and of a misuse of anthropology.[39] Girard's theory is founded on texts rather than anthropological fieldwork and to that extent it is

---

against Chilton when he follows Myers 1991 in reading the synoptic tradition of Jesus's action in the Temple as a rejection of sacrifice. 1996.60-68.

[36] Detienne, writing on the history of ancient Greek culture argues that the term *sacrifice* itself is an unwarranted Western modern imposition on other cultures. The centrality which sacrificial ritual is assumed to have in other cultures derives from its significance in the Judaeo-Christian world-view of the founders of the Western social sciences. Arbitrary elements from different parts of the culture are gathered and artificially labelled. 1989.20. He accuses Girard of perpetuating this approach. 1989.224.n85.

[37] 1992.25.

[38] 1985. De Heusch's work is a structuralist analysis of African sacrifice. As such it discusses sacrifice in a number of cultures and therefore acknowledges, as does Chilton, that there is a category of human behaviour, which has enough identifiable features, some or all of which are common to a number of different cultures, which may usefully be identified as *sacrifice*, implying either that the phenomenon is the same in each culture or that the various phenomena to which the designation sacrifice is given are in some way related.

[39] 1985.15-16.

founded on what might seem to be thin air. Girard is also accused of being reductionist in that he reduces the complex data on all forms of sacrifice to a theory about scapegoating.[40] This is to privilege one factor among many and there is no methodological warrant for doing so.[41] De Heusch, like Chilton, refuses to propose an overall theory but offers his own typology of sacrifice.[42] He thinks that all sacrifice is related to 'change of status',[43] to the payment of a debt of life,[44] and to establishing a medium of communication with the gods in order to ensure survival (or breaking that communication in order not to perish).[45] De Heusch rejects the idea that it is possible to articulate the want that sacrifice appears to satisfy;

> An unavoidable enigma remains...here the annihilation of life nourishes a phantasmagoria of want. A want that all the victims in the world would not fulfil...It is impossible to penetrate this existential emptiness (or to artificially fill it with violence as Girard does). We can only study sacrifice from the exterior, describe it as a symbolic work and analyse the systems of representations linked with the treatment of the victim.[46]

In fact, although the discussion in *Violence and the Sacred* begins with the issue of sacrifice, Girard's theory is not one of sacrifice but of the whole of human culture. The model is reductionistic but it does predict that while human cultures will all have sacrificial rituals, those rituals will vary a great deal from one another and will be explained in many and various different ways. De Heusch rejects the issues of the origin and cultural function of sacrifice on methodological grounds. This is perfectly comprehensible from the perspective of a field anthropologist who must at all costs avoid the imposition of a predetermined model on his or her observations of any given people. Nevertheless, this does not invalidate the question for other disciplines such as

---

[40] Gorringe, despite making extensive use of insights derived from his reading of Girard, says that his theory is "simplistic" because mimesis is not the only root of human conflict and because not all sacrifice can be understood as a rationalization of violence. 1996.45. Milbank makes a similar criticism arguing that rather than being a means of diverting violence and excluding scapegoats, sacrifices are sometimes understood as a re-enactment of the formation of divisions between gods and people and amongst people, "a re-affirmation of the cosmic order" 1996.48. This is certainly the case as has been argued by Eliade 1954, 1961. It is also predicted by Girard's theory, which regards sacrifice as a ritual representation of the murder that lies at the heart of human social life, and is the basis of all cultural differentiation; i.e. between gods and humans and between groups of humans.
[41] Similar points are made by C. Elliott 1995.180 and Moses 1992.65.
[42] 1985.213-216.
[43] 1985.16.
[44] 1985.215.
[45] 1985.215-216.
[46] 1985.215.

psychology or theology, and while anthropologists are in a privileged position with respect to the data gathered by their discipline, they are not entitled to impose their own necessary methodological constraints on the uses made of their data by other disciplines.[47]

It has been argued that Girard is mistaken to regard misrecognition as essential to the functioning of sacrificial mechanisms within a culture. Atlan, for example, accepts the idea that cultural differentiation derives from the scapegoat mechanism but does not think that the exposure of that mechanism, whether effected by Girard or, as Girard claims, by the Gospels, can prevent the mechanism from functioning.[48] Dupuy, writing from his perspective as a psychologist, takes a similar position. He concludes that "the recognition of a misrecognition is the recognition of a real object, not an illusion, so that the object is not destroyed by the knowledge of it which we acquire."[49] However, even if it were granted that any human cultural phenomenon could be designated as *real*, a recognized real object and a misrecognized real object within a culture will not function in precisely the same way. It is hard to conceive that persecution could serve a purpose to a culture which is aware that its chosen victims are blameless. It is true that the exposure of something's true nature need not render it ineffective. However, in Girard's theory, the effect of scapegoating and ritual sacrifice reconciles the community because the members of the community are unanimous in projecting their violence onto the victim. If some or all recognize that, according to the ideas of right and wrong which prevail in their culture and which the ritual process is designed to uphold, the victim is innocent, then the members can hardly participate in the same psychological state as they did when they believed the victim to be guilty and his or her expulsion essential to the survival of the community.

The issue of the origins of human culture is disputed. Some anthropologists, influenced by synchronic approaches, or because they regard their role as descriptive, deliberately bracket the question. Others favour evolutionary views while a few, like Girard, favour the view that an event generated symbolic thought. This discussion necessarily raises the question of what it means to be human. The answer might well be different depending upon the field of

---

[47] Davis does not rule out the possibility of constructing a comparative understanding of sacrifice but thinks it is doubtful that Girard has used a sufficiently broad database. 1989.311-328.

[48] 1988. Atlan regards the idea that to become conscious of something is to escape its influence as a product of Freudian psychoanalysis. Chilton 1992 makes a similar point when he accuses Girard of adopting the liberal argument that to be aware of something is to make an improvement. Of course, Girard says that the exposure of the mechanism offers the potential for either greater violence or for the renunciation of violence; it offers no automatic cure.

[49] 1988.100.

research being used.[50] A zoologist might give an answer based on the evolutionary acquisition of the characteristics associated with *homo sapiens*; walking upright, reversed thumb, large brain etc.. Social scientists look to characteristics associated with the social life of humans; the acquisition of language, of representation, of the incest taboo. Girard is not uninterested in the biological questions, particularly since he has related the extent of the human mimetic drive to the evolutionary growth of the brain,[51] but his primary interest is in the process which he calls hominization by which human communities acquire a social life characterized by the possession of cultural phenomena.[52]

Gans agrees that representation is the hallmark of humanity and that, "the origin of the specifically human category of formal representation cannot be understood as a gradual process but only as an *event*."[53] However, he suggests that Girard's account of the shift that makes participants in the mimetic crisis that precedes the operation of the scapegoat mechanism forget the desired object and concentrate on one another is inadequate.[54] A mimetic tendency strong enough to make a community forget the object of its desire and engage in violence must result from a prior collective representation; nothing else could account for it. The stage described by Girard and represented in ritual is already cultural. Girard offers an acceptable account of ritual but not of hominization.[55] However, this criticism is not well founded. Since, for Girard,

---

[50] Girard distinguishes between the 'life sciences' and the 'human and social sciences'. 1987a.3.

[51] 1987a.94-95.

[52] Defined as "the origin and genesis of signifying systems...the problem of what is called the process of hominization." 1987a.6-7.

[53] 1985.13.

[54] North 1985 also questions this shift from private hostility to unanimous violence.

[55] In his earlier work Gans accepts Girard's view that scapegoating lies at the origin of culture but posits a subsequent incomplete gesture of appropriation performed over the corpse as the first sign. 1981. He later proposes a new originary scene of representation in which members of a group surround an object for which they have an appetitive desire. Again each reaches for it but fails to complete the acquisition because they fear the conflict that it might provoke. The object is divided non-violently among the members. The abortive gesture of acquisition becomes the first representative gesture. Gans proposes that Girard's scenario relates to a subsequent stage in human culture not to the origin of representation. 1985, 1986, 1993. He posits an abortive gesture as the first sign because his reading of Derrida convinces him that an absence (the abortive gesture) lies at the heart of (Western) culture. However, it is difficult to understand why the scenario proposed by Gans should provide a different result from that which obtains among primates where the matter would be resolved through established dominance patterns. Furthermore, if culture has its origins in an *event* then such an event might be expected to be more memorable and emotionally charged than the one posited. Of course, in Girard's thought the corpse of the victim is the original sign; the scapegoat is dead but beliefs without grounding in reality about his or her influence before and after the murder become the basis of culture. The presence thought to be at the heart of

the attempt to acquire the disputed object is made only because another member of the social group is seeking to acquire it, the shift is not from object to human but from human to object and back to human; the whole process is social and the change in attention from model to object to rival requires no prior shared representation.

Occasionally the universalist claims of Girard's theory are challenged by scholars who wish to compare violent Western societies, which do operate in the way Girard describes, unfavourably with non-Western cultures.[56] These claims generally pass unsubstantiated. More apposite are the suggestions of a number of critics that other religious traditions also reveal the violent nature of human culture and call for an alternative.[57] Related to this are the suggestions

---

culture is really an absence. Incidentally, Chilton 1992.Appendix1 agrees with Gans's view that the shared meal is the prior event of human culture and of the emergence of sacrifice. Eating and hunting led to the development of ritual. This is conceivable but cannot account for the development of the realm we call the sacred. Milbank suggests that sacrifice has its origin in a desire to bring butchering, cooking and eating into the ritual domain. 1996.48. Again, this leaves open the issue of the origin of ritual and its relationship to the sacred and it is this that is Girard's primary concern. Such theories suggest that ethical behaviour, sharing and co-operation are foundational to society; they offer a much more positive view of culture or of its potential than that proposed by Girard. Gans also challenges Girard's view of myths suggesting that the variety of deaths that they portray demonstrates a non-unitary beginning of culture. However, Girard, unlike Freud, cannot be understood to argue for one unique murder at the root of one human culture.

[56] Irigaray 1993 implies that some Eastern cultures are non-sacrificial and conform to a cosmic temporality. Wink refers to "numerous surviving primitive societies that are remarkably nonviolent in their actual practice." 1992.154. Sykes cites J. Woodburn as authority for the view that some societies of hunter-gatherers (e.g. the Hadza) have no sacrificial rituals. 1980.82n2. This does not disprove Girard's theory for the ritualized hunt has the same social function as sacrifice. The claim that non-sacrificial cultures exist is related to the argument that Girard's theory is compiled on the basis of a limited ethnographic base and that scapegoating is not actually as widespread as he claims and that the ambivalence which he alleges to be a common characteristic of the *sacred* is only found in certain cultures, particularly that of ancient Rome. Milbank 1996.

[57] Orzech 1994 argues that non-violence lies at the heart of the Buddhist position and that the structuring power of sacrificial violence is not always and everywhere unobservable. Scubla 1988 suggests that Orpheus was lynched for advocating non-violence and for denouncing sacrificial rites and that the Orphic tradition 600 years before Jesus reproached the people for founding their *polis* on murder. Swanson 1994 claims that indigenous South American religions exposed the violence of the Conquistadors but as he hints himself (134-5) he may have shown only that the Inca people used Christian resources to demonstrate the sacrificial behaviour of the Spanish invaders. Wink makes the same points in a more general way. 1992.154. Delarge 1985 suggests that the difference between the Gospels and other sources of revelation about mimesis and the scapegoat mechanism is that only the former both expose the mechanisms and offer an alternative way of being.

that Girard and his followers are reintroducing Christian exclusivism. C. Davis says that in the name of non-violence, Girard advocates "the kind of exclusivism that has been an endless source of violence in Christian history.[58] Kearney's concern is that Girard is defining myth in such a way that his case is made for him. Having done this he can blame myths for causing all the evil in society.[59] However, Girard is not defining myths; he is arguing that all true myths bear certain marks. To challenge Girard one would need to cite examples of myths which do not have one or more of the marks he mentions.[60]

Girard's theory requires the primal killing(s) on theoretical grounds in order to account for mimetic phenomena. Mathews regards the case as proven. He writes

> That myths are the deluded narratives of a misapprehended process of arbitrary victimage, and that rituals uncritically mimic the compositional stages of that process in order to achieve the structural bounty that its climax triggers, are already, at least to persons of goodwill who are open to the magnitude of the evidence, incontestably established data...the demonstration had been accomplished in Violence and the Sacred.[61]

However, there can be no possibility of proof. As Wink points out, the origins of culture are not accessible to the kind of investigation that would provide conclusive evidence about the beginnings of systems of representation.[62] The only evidence we have is provided by archaeology, by texts (whether mythical, biblical, novelistic or ethnographic), and by observation of and participation in our own and other cultures. The most that may be said is that insights can be gained from reading texts and studying culture as though these things, or some of them, were true. Therefore, as Wink suggests, it may be wisest to regard Girard's theory as valuable for its analytical power and its usefulness in generating fresh understandings of the mechanisms of human relationships and of the texts that humans generate.

C. Literary Criticism and the Philosophy of Language

The normal and original effect of representational mimesis is, according to Girard, to structure the human experience of reality. The ontologically existing world is hidden behind the world as it is experienced through its mimetic representation. In this respect Girard has a great deal in common with post-

---

[58] 1989.327. Krondorfer describes leaving a meeting with Girard and his supporters and feeling as though he had attended "a revivalist meeting among academics" making "an academic attempt to salvage the superiority of the Christian Gospel." 1994.105-106.
[59] 1995.
[60] See Ch2.
[61] 1986.19.
[62] 1992.154-155.

structuralist writers like Jacques Derrida and Philippe Lacoue-Labarthe who believe that we are unable to escape from our systems of representation and into reality. Girard, however, believes that the step can be made.

Derrida criticizes Girard for betraying the essence of mimesis by seeking to confer an essence upon it, by seeing it as something that can be revealed.[63] For Derrida, there can be nothing without representation; referents exist but can be known only through the medium of mimesis.[64] Elsewhere, in *Plato's Pharmacy*,[65] a piece praised by Girard,[66] Derrida analyzes Plato's use of the term *pharmakon* and his use (and non-use) of its cognates in *Phaedrus*. He attempts to show that some aspects of Plato's thought undermine Plato's own 'Platonism', particularly its metaphysical binarity. The pharmakon may be remedy or poison, drug or recipe. The work describes writing as a pharmakon and Derrida claims that what they have in common is that neither is purely beneficent or maleficent, both can work for good or ill, they both open the possibility of differentiation and oppositions without being comprehended by them; they precede oppositions.[67]

Lacoue-Labarthe discusses Girard's theory and argues that Girard is wrong to regard mimesis as something that can be revealed.[68] Certainly, Girard claims to have exposed the effects and mechanisms of mimesis and to have understood the nature of representational mimesis. Lacoue-Labarthe, who uses the term mimesis for the latter concept, agrees that there was a stage before representation, a stage prior to the dualism of the present and without objective exhibition or secondary externalization but asserts that such a stage is inaccessible to perception. He argues that any primal act of violence must have been done in the name of a perceived difference and so this allegedly primary

---

[63] 1989.
[64] Johnson 1981 offers a helpful introduction to Derrida's thought.
[65] 1981.63-171.
[66] 1970.280, 1979.296, 1988a.220.
[67] Something similar might be said of mimesis in the sense in which Girard uses it. It is a pre-cultural phenomenon, standing beyond the original signifier and having potential for good or ill. Girard may claim to have traced human origins and the origins of representation but he has not really grasped mimesis as he himself understands it; it is the presupposition on which his system is based and whose existence his system seeks to prove. Wallace 1994b argues that violence is the pharmakon for Girard. This is true from the perspective of the operation of culture. However, violence in Girard's system is a consequence of mimesis (he calls it "an offspring of mimesis". 1988a.93) and only subsequently does violence generate a form of mimesis. Derrida and Girard are discussed by McKenna 1992. Siebers 1986 discusses Nietzsche's observation that violence generates metaphysics and relates them to Derrida's view that language generates violence and Girard's view that violence generates language. In the view of Eliade, symbolic thinking is consubstantial with human existence and is prior to language.
[68] 1989.

event takes place after difference already exists.[69] Mimesis (representational mimesis) cannot be revealed because it is itself the means by which representation functions so as to reveal. For Lacoue-Labarthe, it is representation that is primal. Therefore, he argues that Girard has no need to postulate any real act of founding violence which occurred prior to its religious and artistic repetition; its factuality cannot be known for representation is the beginning of all things that humans can know. For Lacoue-Labarthe, representation precedes mimesis; it is temporally and logically prior to mimesis and mimesis functions only through representational media: in Girard mimesis precedes representation for representation is a cultural manifestation of the human mimetic drive. One source of the disagreement between Lacoue-Labarthe and Girard may be the fact that each is using the term mimesis in a different way. The former is effectively accusing the latter of reducing the term to imitation. In fact, Girard's use of the term is polyvalent. Imitation, representation and the process by which reality is transmuted into perception through the medium of representation are all present in Girard's use of the term.[70] Lacoue-Labarthe, on the other hand, appears at times to collapse the distinction between representation and mimesis.

Lacoue-Labarthe argues that knowledge of the origins of mimesis can only have originated in some place neither comprised of nor compromised by the mimetic economy. He regards this as a faith claim and therefore as both unchallengeable and unprovable. Certainly, Girard cannot account for the origin of mimesis in its broadest sense and Lacoue-Labarthe is right to point to the part played by revelation in Girard's thought.

D. Feminism

The reception of Girard's ideas among feminists has not been straightforward. The theory appears to offer a useful critique of existing culture, explaining its violence. However, it does not necessarily hold out an acceptable prospect of liberation. Sometimes Girard's positions are simply at odds with feminist views about women. Kofman, for example, criticizes Girard because he argues that women use self-sufficiency as a strategy.[71] She points out that he believes the claim of women to be indifferent to male desire is a pretence. Kofman is

---

[69] This argument is repeated by Milbank 1996. However, whatever perceived difference may or may not have existed in the minds of those who participated in a founding murder, it is the representation of difference, rather than the 'natural' and pre-cultural differences inherent in animal dominance systems, which, according to Girard, derives from the scapegoat mechanism.

[70] For a comparison of Girard's understanding of mimesis with those of Gadamer and Ricoeur see Schweiker 1994. Schweiker 1987 includes a critical appraisal of Girard's understanding of mimesis.

[71] 1980.

committed to the liberation of women and regards the ability of women to choose to be indifferent to men as an essential step in the process. For Girard, of course, with his rejection of the idea of the Cartesian self, it is impossible for anyone to be indifferent to the desires of others who are a part of one's social context; any alleged self-sufficiency, whether male or female, is a lie.

Moi's argument gets closer to undermining Girard's position.[72] She claims that Girard has difficulty in acknowledging women as agents in the texts that he discusses because "Girard's theory of mimetic desire cannot account for feminine desire."[73] She points out that, if Girard is correct, a male child ought to imitate the desire of his mother for his father and the mother's desire ought to be paradigmatic of all desire and all men would therefore be homosexual. In fact, as Moi acknowledges, Girard regards heterosexuality as instinctive, a part of the apparatus that humans have inherited from animal life.[74] Moi finds this unacceptable. She believes that Girard has achieved an accurate description of male behaviour under patriarchy. However, his position represses the role of the mother in forming an infant's desires and as a consequence Girard has failed to account for the desire of women, and for that of those humans who have escaped patriarchal constraints.

The criticism of Shea, who argues that Girard neglects culture's victimage of women, is also astute.[75] It is true that in many cultures women are marked out by their sex as victims, as others are by their skin colour or their disabilities. This phenomenon is probably related to the one noticed by Scubla, that Girard's theory offers little prospect of accounting for the fact that religious hierarchies tend to be dominated by men while the role of women is secondary and marginal. He describes religion as a masculine privilege.[76] A similar point is made by Irigaray. She accepts, perhaps for the purposes of argument,[77] elements of Girard's theory, acknowledging that social space is created by immolation.[78] Women in such sacrificial societies are the victims hidden behind the sacrificial victims and are confronted by a conflict between cosmic temporality (the natural rhythms of the world) and other forms (cultural, ritual, symbolic, imposed) of temporality. She speculates that it might be possible to live without sacrifice if a society conformed to cosmic temporality alone for the imposition of sacrificial time onto cosmic time creates imprecisions that demand a catharsis.[79]

---

[72] 1982.
[73] 1982.21.
[74] 1987a.335-338.
[75] 1994.
[76] "un privilège masculin" 1982.106.
[77] In a note she suggests that the cultural patterns discerned by Girard are related to male sexuality; tension/discharge/homeostasis 1993.75-76.
[78] 1993.
[79] Women are, for Irigaray, by virtue of their bodily cycles, the sex that is equipped to mediate cosmic time.

Given that most of the texts Girard discusses are either written by men or are about the behaviour of men or both, and that the rituals he describes are dominated by men, it is hardly surprising that Girard's theory offers a helpful interpretation of the ways in which men behave and is less adequate at describing the experiences of women. Jay says that Girard, "grounds all community and culture on male control of male violence."[80] She claims that Girard's theory offers a legitimation of hierarchical distinctions by claiming that they are essential for social order, for the only alternative is chaos.[81] While *Violence and the Sacred* can and has been read in this way, Girard is not seeking to defend social hierarchy but to demonstrate its violent origins. His subsequent work makes this clear for it argues that such hierarchy can no longer be maintained and that an alternative model of human social life is available. Nevertheless, it is clear that the primary role in committing acts of violence and therefore in representing those acts in sacrifice, belongs to men. It is conceivable that biological factors make men more aggressive than women and that they play the leading roles in generating and resolving cultural crises and therefore in the rituals and texts which represent them. However, it is also possible that in describing the scapegoat mechanism, Girard is also describing the foundation of the patterns of cultural power relations which feminists call patriarchy. If that is the case then women are, as they are in so many rituals and as some of them were at the crucifixion of Jesus,[82] the innocent onlookers at the foolish games played by men. (That is, when they are not themselves the immediate victims.) It may be possible to interpret Girard as a critic of patriarchy. In any event, Girard is describing culture, he is certainly not defending it. One of his purposes, like that of feminists, is to offer a critique of existing cultural patterns and to advocate the adoption of an alternative.

E. Theology

A number of theologians have engaged with Girard's thought and some have taken up his ideas and have attempted to use them. C. Elliott, for example, uses them in formulating one aspect of his understanding of salvation, particularly Girard's "intuition that the internalization of the story of Jesus's life and death (and, rather neglected by Girard, resurrection) can deliver freedom from our

---

[80] 1992.130.

[81] 1992.131.

[82] Mark 15:40, Matthew 27:55, Luke 23:49, John 19:25-27. In Mark and Matthew only women are mentioned, in Luke their presence is specified, while in John the beloved disciple is outnumbered by the women at the cross. The non-participation of the women in the crucifixion and their witnessing of it and of the resurrection, make them the key intermediaries between the exposure of the scapegoat mechanism in the life and death of Jesus and its subsequent exposure in the Gospels. See Myers 1991.396-397.

inner compulsions to repeat the destructive games of the past."[83] Gorringe makes some use of his ideas,[84] regarding as proven the theory that sacrificial theories in all cultures are a rationalization of collective violence. Schwager,[85] Von Balthasar,[86] and Janowski[87] make use of Girard in their discussions of soteriology.[88] R. Williams uses Girard's work to give a theological perspective on the arms race.[89] Wink describes Girard's work as "a hypothesis still being tested, but possessed of such remarkable heuristic power that it deserves serious consideration",[90] and says of him that "I regard his treatment of violence as fundamentally correct."[91] He uses Girard in establishing his own theory of the dominance of contemporary Western society by what he calls "the myth of redemptive violence".[92]

Perhaps the warmest reception comes from M. Wallace who, while critical at a number of points, praises Girard claiming that his

> ability to link a metatheory of religion and culture with a particular vision of nonmimetic life based on the synoptics is freshly innovative. Herein lies the appeal and originality of Girard's project: by breaking the cycle of sacrificial violence through a recovery of Jesus' message of love, he has forged for our troubled times a healing life-ethic grounded on a comprehensive uncovering of the matrix of all religio-cultural production in the persecution of victims.[93]

He also says of Girard that with his unmasking of the mimetic origins of the culturally mediated structures of violence,

> and his use of the synoptics as a response to them, he has proposed a new antiviolent and antisacrificial biblical hermeneutic that rates the attention that has been given to other interpretative strategies - from Barth's and Bultmann's to Gutierrez's and Derrida's.[94]

---

[83] 1995.191.
[84] 1986.63-4, 1996.
[85] 1978, 1985, 1988.
[86] 1994.231-316, especially 297-309.
[87] 1995. A discussion of Isaiah 53 and the drama of representation.
[88] Girard is mentioned in a number of recent works on sacrifice and atonement (see below note 109). Articles that discuss atonement using Girard's ideas include Miller 2000, R. Collins 2000.
[89] 1989.
[90] 1992.144.
[91] 1992.152.
[92] 1992.13-31.
[93] 1989.
[94] 1989.323-324.

Few of these theologians have adopted Girard's work uncritically.[95] Despite his praise for the project, Von Balthasar regards Girard's synthesis as a closed system that makes no allowance for any natural concept of God.[96] This leads him to compare Girard's theology to that of Karl Barth.[97] Von Balthasar claims that the implication of Girard's position is that all human ideas about justice, the distinction between good and evil, and all positive ideas about family relationships do not arise directly from human nature,[98] as Roman Catholic social teaching insists, but are derived from the scapegoat mechanism and are essentially social constructs. For Girard these abstract ideas are not God-given concepts which were subsequently corrupted but things which, like all abstract ideas, have their roots in systems of differentiation which are fundamentally arbitrary.[99] Girard's position is clearly not compatible with the relatively positive view of natural human society and family structures that is one of the presuppositions of Catholic teaching in these areas. For Von Balthasar this necessarily means that Girard must be mistaken but this is not the only possible conclusion that can be drawn.[100]

In addition, Von Balthasar regards Girard's introduction of the concept of revelation, and hence of God, into his system as a contradiction which "explodes his allegedly pure scientism".[101] In fact Girard argues that revelation is the natural corollary of the fact that the scapegoat mechanism has been exposed; it seems to be Von Balthasar's own system which regards all talk of

---

[95] Sollers comes close. He accepts Girard's critique of 'sacrificial' Christianity as resistant to the true revelation of the Gospels and therefore as something that "nourishes a horizon of violence", and agrees that rightly understood it exposes the truth dissimulated in every culture. 1986.192.

[96] In fact, although Girard does not discuss natural religion, it is not impossible to fit it into his system. Humans have retained certain instincts that were possessed by their pre-cultural selves. It would be possible to argue that an awareness of God was one of these.

[97] A comparison also made by Swanson 1994. Parallels certainly exist. Barth speaks of a God who is manifested in times of crisis as absence. Humans exist in real darkness into which a light shines. 1933.42-54, 374-390. Girard, in comparing the *Logos* of Heraclitus with the *Logos* of John speaks of the God who is expelled from the world. 1987a.Bk2Ch4.

[98] In a similar way, Jay criticizes Girard for regarding as irrelevant "Everything that arises from the sociability of mothers and infants or from any other affectionate relationship". 1992.132

[99] Schweiker 1987 also points out that Girard's view contradicts the view of human sociality taken in Christian (and Jewish) tradition.

[100] Obviously, it is conceivable that Catholic social teaching is founded on a misconception. O'Donovan 1986b offers an alternative source for Christian ethics. Of course, while abstract concepts such as justice, good, evil, right, wrong etc., must, for Girard, be derived from the scapegoat mechanism, attention to the needs of sexual partners, siblings and other social group members could be an instinct retained from pre-cultural existence.

[101] 1994.309.

God as unscientific, but this is not so for Girard whose work posits the critical unavoidability of the transcendent.[102] Von Balthasar would prefer it if Girard offered a system in which an original, natural knowledge of God had been lost through the operation of the scapegoat mechanism and which was recovered through the Gospels.[103]

Girard's understanding of atonement in terms of revelation, which might be understood as knowledge (it is through awareness of the scapegoat mechanism that the cross has its effects) leads Von Balthasar to suggest that he is open to the charge of gnosticism.[104] Girard, of course, has little in common with the Gnostics of the early centuries of our era and the charge is merely an attempt to classify Girard's theory so that it can be rejected. In fact, for Girard, Christian conversion is not the acquisition of knowledge about the nature of human society but the rejection of the dominant cultural forms of mimesis in favour of a mimesis of Jesus.[105] It is therefore praxiological rather than intellectual. Furthermore, in Girard's thought, this knowledge has no necessary salvific effect. The exposure of the violent foundations of human culture may lead to increased violence or to the kingdom of God. The revelation itself does not necessarily produce a new kind of life, although it is a necessary condition of its possibility. It is rather the appropriation of the knowledge and its use as the basis of an alternative praxis, one based on a mimesis of renunciation (using Jesus as a model in a mimesis of external mediation) rather than the dominant mimesis of acquisition, which allows humans the possibility of a different way of being. Thus, Girard's system is not Gnostic.

Von Balthasar also reacts to Girard's implicit criticism of the traditional teaching about the Eucharist as a re-presentation of Christ's sacrifice to God on the cross. For Girard, Jesus's death, while the most likely consequence of his life, is something that a non-violent God cannot have wanted and in which such a God can have taken no pleasure. Von Balthasar prefers the use made of Girard by Schwager, who argues that God is the real scapegoat for sinful humanity and that the cross of Jesus is to be understood as the place humans transfer their hostility against God concretely to Jesus.[106] Furthermore, it is not just the punishment due to the sins which is transferred, but the sins themselves.[107] This move appears to require an understanding of sin and a metaphysics of sin which are not present or are undeveloped in Girard's system. Nevertheless, Von Balthasar makes use of Schwager's adaptation of Girard in the development of his own soteriological ideas. He rejects it because, he claims, humans must load their sins onto Jesus and therefore the initiative is

---

[102] See the discussion at the beginning of Milbank 1990.
[103] In this respect, Von Balthasar's position is not unlike that of Milbank 1990.
[104] A point also made by North 1985.
[105] 1993.348-50.
[106] 1978.210.
[107] 1978.210.

Praise, Criticism and Interpretation 113

with people rather than God; Girard and Schwager are therefore Pelagian (or Semi-Pelagian).[108] Christian theology has always struggled to explain the mechanism by which the cross of Jesus atones for human sin. If Girard is to be read for a doctrine of atonement,[109] his view is that both human sin (the basis of human culture and its proclivity to violence) and an alternative (love which renounces acquisitive mimesis) are revealed in the cross and in the representation of the cross in the gospel. The initiative is God's and without this action humans would remain trapped within cycles of violence. Humans may respond in different ways to this revelation and Girard does not speculate on the reasons only some appear to escape the existing culture's mimetic consensus and imitate Jesus while others remain within that consensus and do not seek to imitate him. This is not a doctrine of salvation by works for the initiative in the process lies with the action of God in Jesus. This, to use the language of theology,[110] is an act of God's grace which calls forth a human response of faith in Jesus which leads to the abandonment of sin (the mimetic consensus) in order to follow Jesus (*imitatio Christi*). The means of grace are mediated to Jesus's followers through communities organized around the representation of the story of his life, death and exaltation, in the reading, proclamation and living of the gospel and in the administration of the Lord's Supper which re-presents the last days of Jesus's earthly life. These communities which have the gospel as their founding story differ from and provide a contrast to the prevailing culture which is founded on myths and ideologies which conceal and justify human violence.[111] The gospel community is founded on the Logos who is rejected and cast out rather than the Logos of

---

[108] Scubla makes a similar point claiming that Girard is Pelagian because once revelation is accomplished, all that takes place is between humans and God no longer intervenes.

[109] Many publications on atonement and sacrifice demonstrate a limited awareness of Girard. Ashby's understanding is derived from a single article and he claims that Girard teaches that Christ channels all human violence onto himself and therefore removes it. Of course, this would make Jesus's death a sacrifice, the very understanding Girard is at pains to reject. 1988.18. Bradley calls Girard, "the French anthropologist". He explains Girard's theory but does not exploit the idea that Jesus's death reveals human complicity in victimization. 1995.215. Goldingay develops the view of sacrifice found in Girard 1979, and applies it to Jesus so that the cross becomes "God's once-for-all absorbing of human violence" and is thus the key to peace. 1995b.20. Hulmes 1991, Moses 1992.65 and Sykes 1991.1 all refer to Girard in passing. Gudorf 1992 discusses Girard but her critique demonstrates that her knowledge of Girard is limited to the two works cited in her bibliography, 1979, 1987b. Her understanding of Girard's theory appears to be wholly derived from the former.

[110] Although Girard does not refer much to the idea of grace, (nor to many of the terms used in systematic theology), he does speak of the work of the Paraclete in history. 1986a, 1993.

[111] Girard himself offers little discussion of these issues, including the Lord's Supper. Nor does he discuss what might be meant by the expression, "blood of the covenant".

violence.¹¹² As such it presents a threat to the social differentiation in which the wider culture is grounded.

In later works, Schwager treats Girard's ideas in other ways. In considering in what ways the death of Jesus can be regarded as a sacrifice, he argues that in his ministry Jesus offered forgiveness without antecedent conditions but with the consequent condition of a change in behaviour. This raises the question of the need for the cross. It is a consequence of Jesus's activities and is accepted because Jesus remains faithful to the command to love his enemies. On the cross Jesus identifies himself with victims rather than with sinners who therefore still need repentance, conversion and faith.¹¹³ In a subsequent article, Schwager offers a way in which a theology of the wrath of God might be constructed using Girard's thought. He points out that if the sacred is the externalization and transference of human violence onto a scapegoat, then divine violence is a projection of human violence. Human violence is generated by the exposure of the scapegoat mechanism and this exposure was a divine action. This unleashing of violence through the failure of the traditional mechanisms to contain violence is the wrath of God; it is God's because God's revelation provokes it even though the perpetrators are human. In the final analysis it is legitimate to say that the process which the Scriptures call the wrath of God was provoked by Christ.¹¹⁴

Other Catholic thinkers have found Girard's work constructive. James Alison makes Girard's theory the basis of a defence of Catholic Christianity. Jesus is one who demonstrates that God takes the side of the victims and who is unmoved by the violence of others. Israel, like all nations, built its structures on the basis of expulsion but faith in the expelled victim becomes the basis of a new and transnational community.¹¹⁵ The influence of Girard on the Dominican order can be demonstrated through Radcliffe's article in which he contrasts the culture of reciprocal, ultimately fruitful violence represented by the film *Jurassic Park* with the non-violent culture represented by the Last Supper in which Jesus shows himself prepared to bear the violence of others without passing it on.¹¹⁶ The article does not mention Girard, but his ideas are everywhere apparent. Nevertheless, Radcliffe, like some other Catholics, does not take sufficiently seriously the limited scope for natural religion in Girard's thought and so he writes of humans, "Deep down we are not nearly as nasty as our contemporaries would have us believe, because that for which we long is communion, the common good, God."¹¹⁷ And "The deepest truth of our human nature is not that we are greedy and selfish but that we hunger and thirst for

---

¹¹² Girard's use of the term *Logos* is discussed by Gans 1982.
¹¹³ 1985.
¹¹⁴ 1988.
¹¹⁵ 1993.
¹¹⁶ 1995.
¹¹⁷ 1995.760.

God."[118] While Girard might sympathize with the plea for communities of forgiveness built on a non-violent story, his system will not permit that their appeal is any more natural than the appeal of violence. The foundational human drive is mimesis and this may be for violence or non-violence. That which we call good and evil can have meaning only through being measured by the figure of Jesus presented in the Gospels. The traditional teaching that good and evil are accessible to human reason is denied.

A major attempt to engage theology and social theories has been made by Milbank.[119] Milbank's work begins with an examination of thinkers who reject the methodological atheism and/or agnosticism derived from Nietzsche and post-structuralism, and canvass the critical non-avoidability of the theological and the metaphysical. He discusses Girard as a writer whose work falls into this category and criticizes what he regards as Girard's positivism, in particular the view that religion can be explained in social terms.[120] Certainly, Girard offers a positivist account of the social origins of ideas of the sacred, indeed of all symbolic thought. However, he also explains the means by which the social origins of religion have been made accessible in terms of Christian revelation.[121] So, Milbank's suggestion that Girard projects a modern, liberal grid into traditional, hierarchical societies, really only tells the reader that Girard has a theory of human culture which he believes to be universally applicable.[122] While Girard's theory offers no legitimation for any form of hierarchy, except as a temporary brake on mimetic violence, Milbank claims that it is possible to envisage a primordial hierarchical society in which rivalry existed but was secondary and that expulsions took place as components of an already existing social order. So anarchy is not the state which produced humanity but coercive assertion of power. In other words, Milbank believes that power relationships within human society may be natural, legitimate and justifiable.[123] For Milbank, theology must reject the ontological priority of violence which characterizes the social sciences.[124] In fact, while violence has a

---

[118] 1995.763.

[119] 1990. It has been widely reviewed. See for example the collection of essays in *New Blackfriars* 73 (1992) and Roberts 1993.

[120] Kerr 1992 offers a helpful rebuttal of Milbank's main criticisms of Girard.

[121] As Domenach points out, this view represents "a decisive rupture with positivism". 1988.158.

[122] 1990.394.

[123] For Girard, the only structures that might be called natural are animal dominance patterns but these are pre-cultural and humans cannot return to them.

[124] A similar point is made by C. Davis 1989 when he argues that Girard claims that mimesis must always lead to violence and that since human nature is therefore evil, the God who made such creatures would necessarily also be evil. However, Girard has always allowed that externally mediated mimesis, of which *imitatio Dei* and *imitatio Christi* may be examples, need not lead to rivalry, conflict and violence. Lascaris 1989 has responded to Davis's main criticisms of Girard.

chronological and cultural priority in Girard's theory of culture it has no ontological priority because, while it is a characteristic of the normal human condition, it is not inevitable. Hypothetically, humans need not have formed cultures founded on lies about violence, but in practice no known group managed to avoid it. The non-violent love of God, revealed in Jesus and the Gospel, demonstrates the priority and possibility of peace. However, as far as humans are concerned, mimesis is prior; it is beyond good and evil.[125] It can and does lead to violence but it need not do so; a non-acquisitive, non-violent mimesis is possible although hard to conceive because all conceptual tools available have their root in scapegoating.[126]

Milbank also criticizes Girard for failure to develop in any detail the new practice to be derived from God's revelation in Jesus.[127] Certainly, Girard talks of mutual forgiveness and the Kingdom of God, but in practical terms the ideas have not been explicated.[128] There is some truth in all this.[129] However, if

---

[125] For Girard, "In the beginning there is *mimesis*". Domenach 1988.154. This implies that humans are social from their origin for the very idea of mimesis implies the existence of a model who can be imitated. I dare not speculate as to whether or not mimesis can be usefully spoken of as having an ontology.

[126] Of course, since all culture is founded on violence and repeats the lie of its violent origins, the only prospect of a non-violent mimesis lies in the imitation of Jesus.

[127] Milbank regards this as a Christological and ecclesiological objection to Girard.

[128] C. Davis 1989 claims that Girard needs to explicate how the imitation of Jesus will transform humans. Similarly, C. Elliott doubts that Girard's work offers much hope of redemption from the unconscious processes that it reveals. 1995.180.

[129] The criticism is also made by North 1985. A part of Milbank's argument, related to the accusations of Gnosticism some have made against Girard, is that revelation in his thought could be extrinsic to human life. However, for Girard, the revelation comes not through an account of human origins but through the incarnation of Jesus and his life within a specific human culture and the representation of that life in the narrative of the Gospels. Milbank's criticism can apply only where Girard's theory is used without being grounded in the gospel story. Then again, some theologians have accused Girard of being too concerned with ethical issues and have suggested that his theory is thus a version of liberal Protestantism. In a similar vein, Schweiker 1987 takes issue with Girard because his concentration on the problem of violence collapses God and the Kingdom of God into something that has social utility for ideology critique. However, as Von Balthasar suggests, Girard has much in common with "the 'theology' of the young Karl Barth". 1994.308. In Girard's thought revelation of the gospel comes from beyond human culture; in the Gospels themselves it begins in the wilderness. It is from the realm that transcends human social life. This is not a position normally associated with liberal Protestantism. For Girard, religion and human ideas about the transcendent sacred are the creations of the mimetically induced scapegoat mechanism. Only the Gospels offer access to a transcendence that is not a human construct. However, as McKenna has argued, revelation in Girard's thought is not a voice from above. Revelation comes through a voice from below; it is the voice of the excluded victim.

Girard is correct and all human symbolic thought is derived from the scapegoat mechanism then any practical suggestions which he made could be readily deconstructed. The existence of the church telling the gospel story to itself and to others can only be expected to hint at the possibility of other ways of being; just as the parables offer hints of the nature of the coming Kingdom of God. The idea that human language is insufficient to express the rule of God can be found in others.[130] On the other hand, attempts have been made to begin to construct practical proposals on the basis of Girard's thought. Kaptein, for example, writes out of the reflections of the Corrymeela community. Some of the conclusions about the roles of nurses and probation officers may be open to debate, but there is no doubt that Girard's work lies at the heart of an attempt to become a community in which Catholics and Protestants are reconciled.[131] T.H. Smith acknowledges that "as an analysis of social violence Girardian theory does not seem disposed to address pragmatic or 'praxiological' questions."[132] However, he advances a praxis of transformation as a means of advancing what he calls "Girard's underrepresented interests".[133] He uses Girard to analyze the role played by Martin Luther King II as a scapegoat within North American culture in the context of the Black religious quest to cure racism. The work of Wink is dependent on Girard and full of ideas about the ways in which a distinctively Christian praxis might develop.[134]

Wink has made extensive use of Girard in the construction of his theory that Western cultures (and some, though not all, other human cultures) are dominated by the myth of redemptive violence that he believes characterizes the majority of manifestations of popular culture.[135] He traces the myth to the story of the battle between Marduk and Tiamat celebrated in the New Year festival of the ancient Babylonian cult and he compares it with the domination-

---

1990, 1992. This is not the voice of the community, it is the voice of the other; the very thing against which the community originally defined itself.

[130] Prigent suggests that the Seer of Revelation finds he must confound the present and the future and contradict human logic in order to present the gospel. What is the new creation? "C'est la venue de l'Autre" (The coming of the Other).1980.244. See also Frye 1957.341-354. He writes, "Whenever we construct a system of thought to unite earth with heaven, the story of the Tower of Babel recurs: we find that after all we can't quite make it, and that what we have in the meantime is a plurality of languages." 1957.354. See also Frye 1981.

[131] 1993.

[132] 1994.244.

[133] 1994.244. Others share the task, e.g. Fodor 2000 and Swartley 2000a who both discuss Christian discipleship in the light of Girard's ideas. I have made limited attempts myself in Finamore 2000, 2004.

[134] 1992.

[135] 1992. Livingston 1992 regards many contemporary films as ritualistic fictional evocations of the resolution of a violent crisis by means of the heroic extermination of a monstrous scapegoat.

free order advocated by God in the Gospels. He does offer some objections to Girard. He argues that myths are not false as Girard insists, but are often true and straightforward depictions of actual power relations.[136] This misses the point. For Girard, such myths do describe power relations in society. They are false in that they purport to justify those power relations. Wink also claims that Girard leaves out of his theory those means other than scapegoating by which order is maintained.[137] However, this is not the case; Girard discusses a range of cultural institutions. He finds their origins in the scapegoat mechanism and his theory is thus reductionist.[138] Wink also questions the way in which Girard privileges Christianity and suggests that other religions are nonviolent. He makes a number of other criticisms but none of them is pertinent except his observation that the evidence of pre-historical human culture is very thin and that we do not have access to the truth about human origins. This cannot be denied. Wink may therefore be right to regard Girard's real value as the analytical power of his theory in explaining human violence.

R. Williams accepts that Girard has identified an important theme within the Gospels, that of opposition to sacrifice. He writes,

> there are other, perhaps contrary, themes in the Gospels...Girard's reading of the Gospel narrative is certainly selective, even cavalier at times; but all he needs to establish is that one novel and subversive theme is present, as the distinctive change wrought by Christ...Girard needs only to demonstrate that Christianity possesses the transforming critical principle he identifies: even if this may not be the prevailing voice in historical Christianity.[139]

Williams, while regretting Girard's failure or refusal to discuss the manner in which a community founded on the overthrow of sacral violence might actually function, finds himself in sympathy with his basic thesis and particularly with the idea that a transcendent God may inhabit a realm beyond and outside of mimesis.

In relation to his main theme, the arms race, Williams acknowledges the 'apocalyptic' dimension to Girard's thought by summarizing his position as, "Either we face uncontrollable mimetic escalation, which can be halted only temporarily by reciprocal threat, or we relapse into the 'displaced' sacral violence."[140] On this basis, Williams argues that humanity needs a community founded on the anti-sacrifice of Jesus, one which can offer an alternative foundational myth to that of sacred violence. The suggestion is that the church

---

[136] 1992.153.
[137] 1992.153.
[138] A similar point is made by C. Elliott who writes of Girard that "He does for scapegoating what Freud had done for Oedipus - discover a hugely important part of the human psyche and then seek to explain too much with it." 1995.177.
[139] 1989.7.
[140] 1989.10.

may be or may become such a community, an idea also found in the work of the Corrymeela community.[141] Williams's conclusion is that in our time "Girard's voice needs to be heard."[142]

Wieser offers a similar approach, interpreting Girard so that Jesus's proclamation of the kingdom of God is an offer of a radically new type of community. Human cultures use sacrifice to maintain differences and to define insiders and outsiders. Jesus builds a community in which these differences are not grounds for exclusion. Despite this, the disciples fail to understand and continue to have their rivalries. He concludes by attempting to draw some practical conclusions from his observations. He argues that where the identity of churches is dependent on exclusion, they find themselves at odds with the message they proclaim. However, where the church lives authentically, in accordance with its message, distinctions break down and a crisis results. Hence,

> We are approaching the moment in history - and the ecumenical movement can be seen as a signal for this moment - when it becomes <u>inescapably</u> clear that the <u>oikumene</u>, the whole inhabited world, must provide room for all, or else it will face over-all destruction. In this sense the ecumenical movement can be said to be truly apocalyptic.[143]

It is this 'apocalyptic' dimension to Girard's thought,[144] noted by Williams and Wieser, which suggests that his theory might provide a means of reading the Bible's apocalyptic passages.[145] Perhaps the most thorough discussion is by Bater who compares Girard's approach with that of North American fundamentalism. While both see the convergence of Scripture and history they are uneasy allies because fundamentalism understands a vengeful God to be the source of apocalyptic violence whereas Girard sees the violence of humans in a crisis of differentiation exacerbated by the revelation of the innocence of the

---

[141] This would, as Kerr suggests, conform to Hauerwas's dictum that the church is "the organized form of Jesus's story." Kerr 1992.397. Compare MacIntyre's call for the abandonment of the existing imperium and the construction of new local forms of community to sustain moral life. 1985.263. See Sacks 1991.19.

[142] 1989.11.

[143] 1985.95 (underlining is from the original).

[144] Perhaps the majority of those who discuss Girard neglect this aspect of his thought. Some deny that, with some exceptions, his ideas are apocalyptic, e.g. Nemoianu 1986. On the other hand, Domenach acknowledges that, for Girard, humanity faces an "apocalyptic glare". 1988.157. Dupuy summarizes this aspect of Girard's view of the contemporary world, "with Christian revelation working away at it to undermine it from within, it can only culminate in something radically *other*; either terminal violence or the Kingdom of Love." 1988.79. Scubla makes a similar point 1988.171.

[145] See Green 1995, Hauerwas 1996 review ideas for reading the Bible from the perspective of a Girardian understanding of social violence.

scapegoat.[146]

F. Biblical Studies

An important part of Girard's theory is based on his reading of the four canonical Gospels. His reception among biblical scholars is therefore of some significance. It is particularly important for the present study which will attempt to apply Girard's thought to the Book of Revelation. As in other fields, Girard has both his followers and his critics. The latter will be considered first so that their perspectives can be taken into account in reviewing the work of those who have attempted to read the Bible in the light of Girard's work.

Burton Mack has offered one of the most influential critiques of Girard's position.[147] He argues that the Gospels do not so much reveal the operation of the scapegoat mechanism but make that mechanism constitutive for early Christian practice. The Gospels are not written from the perspective of the victim but from that of the early Christian communities. Jesus was not innocent but was portrayed as such so that the Jews rather than the Romans could be blamed for his death.[148] The authors of the Gospels were persecutors and Girard has failed to see the difference between the time of Jesus and the time of the Gospels. The Jews are the scapegoats of the Gospel text. Girard would have known this if he had not chosen to ignore social historical and historical critical readings of the Gospels. In other words this is, as Mack acknowledges, a Girardian reading; one which reads Girard against Girard. Elsewhere he is critical but not unsympathetic to Girard's theory of culture.[149]

Clearly, while Mack's argument challenges Girard's reading of the Gospels, it actually supports rather than opposes the latter's understanding of culture.[150] In addition, the confidence of Mack and his followers in their reconstructions,

---

[146] 1994.

[147] 1985. He has been followed, e.g., by C. Davis 1989, C. Elliott 1995.178.

[148] See Mack 1988; he discusses this hypothesis with respect to Mark's Gospel. Mack argues that Jesus's innocence is an invention of the church. Girard's response must be that Jesus's active non-violence certainly promoted the crisis that led to his own death. However, he was not to blame for that violence which derived from the structures of the cultures concerned. The killing of Jesus was therefore not justified. Jesus was an arbitrary victim in that he was not responsible for the crisis that his killers hoped his death would resolve. It is in this sense that Jesus was innocent rather than whether or not he was technically responsible for the disturbance of public order.

[149] See his contribution to Hamerton-Kelly 1987.

[150] N. Elliott accepts this when he argues that the Gospels, in the aftermath of the Jewish War, shift the blame for Jesus's death onto the Jews. He writes, "This narrative scapegoating is readily accounted for by René Girard's theory of mimetic (i.e., imitative) conflict and victimage. That theory has won increasing acceptance from biblical scholars, for it proposes to explain how sacred narratives (myths) arise from the dynamics of social formation." 1995.103.

based on historical-critical methods, may be misplaced. The dating of the Gospels and the contexts in which they were written have not been definitively established. Work on the historical Jesus demonstrates the extent to which the ideology of the researcher influences the Jesus who is uncovered.[151] Attempts to gain access to the historical reality which lies 'behind the text' have produced such a variety of different results that the methodology itself must be open to doubt.[152] As a literary critic, Girard is entitled to offer a literary-critical reading of the text and to take the text as it stands rather than relying on unproven and unprovable assumptions about its original life-setting. Even if it were true that the Gospels scapegoat Jews, the fact remains that the texts tell the story from the perspective of the victim and this point is not challenged. To say that the texts tell the story from the perspective of subsequent Christian communities is an historical-critical assumption. They may have been written by and for such communities but they attempt to tell a victim's story and that this should be so is, if Girard is right, astonishing and unique; the more so if, at the time of his death, everyone had deserted the victim. What Mack's position amounts to, at most, is that even the Gospels are distorted by the mechanism. His sympathy for Girard's position is not always appreciated by those who reproduce his arguments about the Gospels. Mack himself would find Girard's position more acceptable if he, like Bultmann, would prefer a *kerygma* to the Gospel texts. In Girard's case this would mean the attribution to Jesus or to the earliest Christian communities of a core message concerned with the exposure of violence. Mack implies that he would find this acceptable even though the Gospel texts are, in his view, tainted.[153]

Other scholars have criticized Girard for failing to take seriously the results of critical study of the Bible,[154] and for failing to acknowledge the anti-

---

[151] Schweitzer 1926 and on Schweitzer's own interpretation see O'Neill 1991. 248-265.

[152] The variety of the different accounts of the historical Jesus can be observed from the differing conclusions reached by, e.g., Borg 1984, Chilton 1992, Crossan 1991, Harvey 1982, Horsley, 1987, Meyer 1979, Nolan 1977, E.P. Sanders 1985, Schüssler Fiorenza 1983, Theissen 1987, Vermes 1973, 1983, 1993, Wright 1992, 1996.

[153] 1988.20n9, 355.n1. North 1985 claims Girard is inclined to use the Sermon on the Mount as a canon within the canon. This is true where issues of praxis are concerned. However, the canon within the canon for Girard's hermeneutical purposes is the passion stories, stories Girard tends to conflate.

[154] E.g. C. Davis 1989. North 1985 notes that Girard takes little account of the differences between the Gospels and tends to concentrate on those parts of the Bible which can be interpreted in accordance with his theory. In particular, he questions whether the Gospels and the rest of the New Testament are as non-sacrificial as Girard claims, a point also made by Wink. 1992.153 and Scubla 1988. Scubla also questions Girard's assertion that the Gospels refuse to impute violence to God. Darr 1993 points out Girard's tendency to conflate stories and so to force the evidence to fit his theory. Darr also criticizes Girard for his lack of interest in historical reconstruction, which the

Semitism of the Gospels. Girard himself has responded to this.[155] His position is that, "If the Passion is only one example of a kind of murder that occurs all over the world, the Gospels are saying something about human culture as such."[156] The structural relationships between the Gospels and countless cults must be acknowledged. Christians have argued their position over against the Jews rather than seeing the relationship of the Gospel texts to universal religion. Christians have tended to stress the uniqueness of the Passion and hence exaggerate the ferocity of the Jews. The Gospels see Jesus's death as one among many (Matthew 21:33-46, 23:34-39 and parallels). Therefore, the uniqueness lies not in the way in which Jesus was killed but in the fact that after his death, the mimetic consensus is broken; the victim is seen to be innocent and vindicated. The Gospels are unique because

> Only the Gospels denounce the founding violence as an evil that should be renounced. Only the Gospels put the blame not on the victim, but on the violent perpetrators. Only the Gospels do not regard the violence as sacred and do not transfigure it. Only the Gospels portray this violence as the vulgar scapegoat phenomenon that it is, the fruit of mimetic contagion.[157]

Girard acknowledges that the Christian church has misread these texts so that they were understood to be anti-Semitic but he rejects the idea that today's Christians can exonerate themselves from their own anti-Semitism and that of their predecessors by scapegoating the Gospels.[158]

Thus, while he may at times overstate his case and twist material so that it conforms to his perspective, Girard has identified an important theme within the Bible. A number of scholars have attempted to make use of his insights in

---

former believes, is necessary for understanding the text. Nevertheless, he acknowledges the helpfulness of Girard's theory at a number of points.

[155] 1993.

[156] 1993.340.

[157] 1993.347-348.

[158] Dewey responds to Girard's argument by agreeing that while the Gospels may not be anti-Semitic themselves, such an interpretation became likely once the church became a powerful group within society. She also argues that to see the Jews as a cipher for human cultures in general is to make the Jews of the story invisible and to turn them into symbols of human violence. Therefore, whatever Girard's intention, his reading could lead to anti-Semitism. However, Girard's position requires a Jewish context because the revelation of the mechanism needed a culture that had been influenced by the progressive revelation of the roots of violence found in the Jewish Bible. The Jews of the story are therefore not rendered invisible. To acknowledge that all cultures are violent is to say that Christian cultures are violent and that Jewish cultures are violent and that Islamic cultures are violent and that Hindu cultures are violent and that pagan cultures are violent. The revelation of the scapegoat mechanism in a Jewish milieu is simply the corollary of the idea that the milieu had been prepared for that revelation by the Old Testament.

order to gain a better understanding of the Scriptures. In addition to the work of Schwager, Goodhart has applied Girard to the writings of the Old Testament, including Jonah[159] and Genesis.[160] Lasine discusses the association of the tribe of Levi with violence.[161] Niditch discusses Girard's theories in her account of the ban, the destruction for Yahweh of booty and prisoners taken in war.[162] Vigée examines traditions about Abraham's attempt to sacrifice his son Isaac in the light of Girard's thought.[163] Mabee looks at Deuteronomic texts[164] while Matties discusses Girard and the Book of Joshua[165]. Discussions of a number of Old Testament texts may be found in McMahon.[166]

A number of scholars have attempted to read the New Testament in the light of Girard's theories. These include Lascaris,[167] Mabee,[168] Hardin,[169] Johns[170] and Schwager. The latter's work is based on a series of readings of different texts in the Old and New Testaments and his main conclusions are discussed

---

[159] 1985. Jonah wishes to reserve salvation for Israelites alone and to this end makes an idol of the law against idolatry.

[160] 1988. He claims that the story of Joseph confronting his brothers in Egypt is a deconstruction of sacrificial thinking. It sees the victim identifying himself at the moment he has become the potential victimizer; this demonstrates that victims and victimizers are the same and therefore calls on all to recognize and give up their violent inclinations.

[161] In some strands of the Pentateuch traditions, the Levites stand as substitutes for the first-born redeemed from Yahweh. In Exodus 32 they kill their brothers and sons as a sacrifice to prevent the continuation of the divine wrath. Their action ends the spiralling collective violence of the community; the Levites channel and limit social violence by drawing it onto themselves.

[162] She writes, "Girard's theories of scapegoating...seem especially relevant to an ideology of the ban in which the enemy is portrayed as the poisonous, sinful and contagious other who must be cut off in order that the author's community survive." 1993b.25

[163] 1986.

[164] 2000.

[165] 2000.

[166] 1994.

[167] Lascaris 1993 uses Girard's thought to read a number of texts from both Testaments within the context of reconciliation between different communities in Northern Ireland. 1993.

[168] He suggests that the New Testament decontextualizes the term 'Messiah', for Jesus's life is presented as a challenge to the violent nature of kingship itself. The Gospels attempt to unmask the king as an innocent victim and so deconstruct the entire idea of Messiahship. 1994.116. He concludes that Christian scholarship must learn to separate Jesus from Jewish expectations of the Messiah.

[169] 2000.

[170] 2000.

above.[171] In one of his subsequent articles he discusses different Christian understanding of the wrath of God and points out the deficiencies in the positions which treat the wrath as allegorical and those which take it a God's just punishment for sin. He suggests that Girard's theories offer the prospect of progress on this issue.[172]

The most thorough attempt to use Girard to interpret the New Testament has been carried out by Hamerton-Kelly, firstly in his work on Paul[173] and more recently in his article and monograph on Mark.[174] He has also written on Girard's thought generally[175] and has edited a volume which compiles a variety of views about human beginnings and their relationship to violence.[176]

His work on Paul is based on the idea that the Apostle to the Gentiles rejected his ancestral religion because his experience of Jesus made him perceive the violence within it. The cross revealed to Paul the violent murder of the innocent victim; a distorted view of the law had killed Jesus and thus revealed the law's own violent basis. Paul's conversion experience showed him this, and, most importantly, showed him the violence within himself. It also revealed the possibility of a new order based on non-violent love. Humans needed to leave the world dominated by sin, that is by mimetic desire (covetousness) and an order based on violence, and enter a world based on Jesus. Paul saw that violence caused by the desire to be as God is the basis of the human problem. This fits to some extent with Schwager's idea that God is the true scapegoat of humanity. Paul found that the law, even though it included the command to love, had become distorted so that it could serve violent ends such as those demonstrated in the crucifixion of Christ and the exclusion of the Gentiles. In Hamerton-Kelly's hermeneutic, Judaism, being violent, can stand as representative of all human religions so that Paul's critique of Judaism is a critique of all religion. Paul remains tainted by certain aspects of sacrificial thinking, including the idea of election from which he was unable to free

---

[171] Girard himself draws attention to Schwager's work as an example of the interest, admittedly limited at that stage, his proposals on the interpretation of the Gospels had generated among biblical scholars. 1978b.48-49. Schwager is very supportive of Girard's proposal. He differs from Girard in that Schwager understands the New Testament to teach that Jesus's death was in some sense required. Girard's interpretation of the Gospels suggests that had the alternative mimesis offered by Jesus been adopted (had his offer of the kingdom been accepted), an eventuality which was possible even if highly unlikely, then Jesus would not have been killed nor need he have been killed. Later Schwager acknowledges that on the cross Jesus is identified with victims rather than with sinners and that in consequence sinners still require repentance, conversion and faith. 1985.
[172] 1988. See Section E.
[173] 1985, 1990a, 1990b, 1992a. See also Gans 1985b.
[174] 1992b, 1994a.
[175] 1994b.
[176] 1987.

himself.

Hamerton-Kelly has been subjected to severe criticism by Boyarin who accuses him of giving credence to anti-Semitism and to supporting Christian complacency.[177] This is far from being his intention. Neither the church, nor the power structures which the church has traditionally supported and defended, are regarded as being free from violence and they are, like Judaism, to be subjected to the critique of the Gospels. Nevertheless, this use of Girard does open the possibility that Hamerton-Kelly might be misinterpreted so as to offer support for anti-Jewish sentiments. It is debateable whether he can be held responsible for this. Boyarin's reading is excessively critical and depends on a view of biblical studies which would disallow any hermeneutic which permitted any criticism of other religions and cultures. Paul cannot be understood unless we are prepared to wrestle with his attitude towards the religion in which he was raised and which he perceived himself, in some sense at least, as having left or outgrown.[178] Certainly, there are points at which Paul appears to equate paganism and Judaism; both belong to the principle of this world.[179]

In his work on Mark, Hamerton-Kelly begins from Jesus's action in the Temple and works from there. He attempts to show in depth the truth of Girard's contention that the Gospel text reveals the truth about the scapegoat mechanism and the mimetic forces which cause it and which flow from it. The difficulty is that the exercise becomes reductionist. All other nuances and themes within Mark are co-opted for the sake of the imposed reading. So, while there are points where the analysis proves enlightening, there are others where the reading fails to convince. It is as though Hamerton-Kelly has regarded Girard's work as revelation and interpreted the Gospel text accordingly. He has used Girard's theory as though it were a grid which could be placed upon the text and has interpreted the text as though the grid were a perfect fit.[180]

Thus Hamerton-Kelly's work on Mark is less successful than his work on Paul. In the latter his view that Paul himself has not fully escaped sacrificial thinking allows him to explain the points, such as Romans 3:25, where Paul seems to resort to sacrificial language.[181] Even in his work on Paul though, Hamerton-Kelly treats Girard's theory, or his understanding of it, as revealed truth and Paul's writings are regarded as falling short of that standard. This may not be the best way in which to make use of Girard's work.

Perhaps the most ambitious attempt to read the whole Bible in the light of Girard's thought has been made by J.G. Williams.[182] He explores conflictual

---

[177] 1994.

[178] Galatians 1:13-14, Philippians 3:4-7.

[179] Galatians 4:1-11.

[180] See Ward 1994b.

[181] Even here, it may be possible that Paul has in mind an archetypal killing that renders all future killings/sacrifices redundant.

[182] 1991.

mimesis among the enemy brothers, Cain and Abel, Jacob and Esau, Joseph and his family; he discusses the way in which the Pharaoh attempts to resolve a crisis by scapegoating Hebrew children; the manner in which Israel, in contrast to other nations, emerges as a people in the wilderness rather than through sacred violence; the way in which the ten commandments forbid the mimesis of God, maintain social and temporal differentiation, prohibit inappropriate acquisition and violence, and, crucially, forbid mimetic desire, that is, covetousness, acquisitive envy; the role of the king as a creature of the crowd and as a sacred victim; the prophetic concern for the victims of violence; Job as the innocent victim whom his community attempts to scapegoat; the Gospels as the revelation of the innocent victim; and some reflections on the victim as the *locus* of truth. At the end, he touches on the crisis which confronts North American culture and sees in Girard's work the source of a positive mimesis which may yet prevail. He writes of the United States of America,

> Grounded first of all in individual commitment and participation in some sort of intentional or voluntary community, those who heed the voice of the victim through whom God is calling us will think, trust, and act on the promise that a good mimesis, the work of the Spirit, is expanding like leaven and will bring us to some good end, whether in this world or in the world to come.[183]

It is doubtful that Williams has sufficiently grasped the apocalyptic dimension of Girard's thought and it is interesting to note that in his foreword to the book Girard observes of Williams that "My general outlook is perhaps a little less optimistic that his."[184] Furthermore, Williams is inclined to treat Girard's theory uncritically and regard readings derived from it as privileged rather than as one possible reading among a number of others.[185]

Of more interest than his readings themselves are Williams's hermeneutical proposals. He compares sacrificial and non-sacrificial readings of the text and finds the key difference in the attitude towards violent acts of atonement.[186] More important is Williams's attempt to define his approach to the reading of the biblical text. He cites Girard on the idea that the Word of God speaks only from the position of a victim in the process of being expelled from a community and argues that the Gospels witness to this Word which is revealed only in its own death and expulsion.

---

[183] 1991.258.

[184] 1991.x.

[185] This criticism of Williams is articulated by Krondorfer 1994. He discusses Williams 1994b article on sacrifice and the beginnings of the Israelite monarchy and accuses him of treating the biblical text as though it were a straightforward historical document and imposing his model upon it. He acknowledges that Williams has offered a useful possible reading but rejects the idea of it as an illustration of a single unifying theory. Williams 2000 returns to the issue of Israelite kingship.

[186] 1994a.

G. Conclusions

Girard has amassed a formidable array of evidence in support of his ideas and there is every reason to take them seriously. There is little or nothing which could be said to directly contradict him. However, for a number of reasons many scholars are reluctant to use his theories as though they were proven.

Firstly, Girard's ideas about mimesis, while they may be a helpful means of interpreting a great deal of human and animal behaviour, are more descriptive than explanatory. Mimesis is treated as primordial and no account of its origins is offered. Since mimesis requires more than one person if it is to operate, the question of origins remains. Furthermore, there is reason to think that not all human behaviour can be accounted for in terms of mimesis; some actions are instinctive. These include feeding, procreating and nurturing; they are natural and yet they are, for humans, also highly cultural activities. It is not possible to say categorically which aspects are pre-cultural and which are cultural, which are instinctive and which are derived from scapegoating. Indeed the concept of mimesis inevitably raises the question of what the human experience of consciousness is and does and this question has not yet been fully addressed by Girard. It is therefore difficult to be sure, for example, that all human conflict is caused by mimesis. Nevertheless, the idea of mimesis does allow us to account for a great deal about human behaviour, both in texts and in observation of social life. There is no reason why the idea should not be used in the study of biblical texts.

Secondly, while Girard gathers a great deal of evidence in favour of his views on human origins, the academy simply does not have access to these events. Other species of primates have secure dominance patterns and, so far as is known, do not resort to scapegoating or, if they do, the scapegoating does not generate systems of representation. According to Girard's anthropology, the main difference between humans and other primates lies in the formers' greater mimetic drive. This is, at the pre-cultural stage, an issue of quantity rather than quality and as such may offer insufficient grounds for the differences which must be explained. The only feasible verdict on Girard's theory of human origins is 'not proven'. However, Girard's theory of hominization functions well as a founding narrative; it can function as a story that tells us what people are like, what motivates them, what their inclinations are when faced with a crisis and so on. In this sense, its historicity is not an issue; it is its usefulness as a means for understanding rituals, texts and, indeed, the present state of our own culture, which is important.

Next, Girard's reading of the Bible is problematic. He cannot conclusively demonstrate that the Gospels at no point regard Jesus's death as a sacrifice. Nor is he able to show that the whole of the text of all the Gospels is concerned with the exposure of founding violence and the offer of an alternative. There are other things happening in the text which must also be taken into account. Nevertheless, Girard has identified a theme within the Gospels and within the rest of Scripture which needs to be taken seriously and which might provide the basis for a hermeneutic.

Then, Girard's view that the exposure of the scapegoat mechanism in the Gospels is leading to a crisis of differentiation which will prove impossible to resolve other than by the renunciation of acquisitive mimesis rests on a number of challengeable suppositions. However, to deny that acquisition-inducing market economies are generating the potential for violence on a global scale is to ignore what is happening in the inner cities of the north and the outer-cities of the south. Existing cultural systems, so often an effective brake on violence, are disintegrating as evidenced by the levels of breakdown in family and community life and by accelerating rates of criminal activity. Ethnic scapegoating on a vast scale has occurred in Africa and in Europe.[187] Girard's diagnosis of these phenomena may not be wholly accurate but the potential for violence and disorder at levels hitherto unimagined now exists. Girard has attempted to relate these things to the Christian gospel and his theory predicts many of them. It is therefore appropriate for the discipline of biblical studies to assess his thought.

In addition, it is unclear whether Girard's theory is really open to falsification. He claims that it is and acknowledges that he would be forced to abandon his theory in the face of a single exception.[188] However, an acceptable exception is difficult to imagine. Girard's system is sufficiently flexible for him to be able to account for widely differing cultural phenomena. A ritual or a myth which had no chaos or violence within it would not necessarily be counted as a falsifying objection; Girard could argue that since cultural phenomena tend to develop in a way which slowly obscures their violent origins, such a myth or ritual should be regarded as being fully evolved. Perhaps a wholly non-violent and non-acquisitive culture (other than one founded on the gospel) would suffice, but even then the theory is probably flexible enough to cope. Only a cultural theory which accounted for the evidence more adequately, or some means of gaining access to the truth about hominization, or a categorical demonstration that Jesus advocated sacrifice or violence or both, or the long-term survival of a wholly peaceful market economy, would really serve to falsify Girard's position. Since none of these things is likely to happen, the theory is probably immune to demonstrable falsification for the foreseeable future. Human inability to state clearly, within the parameters of existing knowledge, the terms on which a theory must be declared falsified, need not be regarded as a weakness in the theory. For the time being, the theory may be used to see if it throws new light on human culture, its systems of differentiation and its systems of exchange.

Finally, and perhaps most significantly, Girard's theory is reductionistic. It

---

[187] On the problem of scapegoating in modern Europe see N. Cohn 1993b. Boxall 1992 applies Cohn's ideas to Revelation and claims that it 'demonizes' the Roman cult.
[188] 1973a.563.

seeks to explain everything about non-instinctive human behaviour in terms of mimesis; human origins and culture (including rites and ideas about the sacred) in terms of scapegoating and the diversion of social violence; the Gospels in terms of the revelation of mimesis and scapegoating; and the condition of the world in terms of the influence of the gospel. All these ideas are plausible but other factors may also play some part in each of them. Nevertheless, texts may be read in the light of Girard's theory to see if it enables us to understand the processes described in the text, without necessarily taking a position on the truth or otherwise of all or any of his assertions. Where such readings are helpful, that should not be taken to justify Girard's theory.[189]

Thus, none of the grounds for doubting Girard's theory prevent the critical use of his ideas in the study of cultural phenomena such as texts. Since his ideas deal with the nature of the chaos and order images in religious thought and the way in which order may be understood to be derived from chaos, his thought seems to be an appropriate means by which to study the imagery found in the Book of Revelation. While the difficulties of using Girard's work as a grid to be placed upon the text are apparent, there are two ways in which it may be used productively. These approaches will test Girard's own relatively negative assessment of Revelation's value.[190]

The first is as a heuristic device. This method acknowledges that themes other than those required by Girard's theory exist within Scripture and need make no attempt to exclude them or to force them to fit a Girardian mould. However, where there are themes which are amenable to a Girardian approach, such an analysis will make a contribution to the overall understanding of the text. Firstly, it may be possible to detect elements of mimetic rivalry between the characters within the text.[191] Then, the move from order to chaos and back to order via a violent resolution which is characteristic of human cultures and their representation in texts, may be apparent. Next, there may be evidence of scapegoating or of the apocalyptic effects of a revelation of the truth of scapegoating; or indeed both.[192]

The second method is through a hermeneutical proposal. There is within the Bible a thread of texts, many of which have been identified by Girard, which take the perspective of the victim for their own. If the peak of God's revelation of Godself to humanity is, as Christian theology has usually acknowledged, found in the story of Jesus of Nazareth and the peak of that peak has been found in the passion stories, then it may be reasonable to propose a canonical

---

[189] Dumouchel 1988c points out that while Girard is the privileged interpreter of his theory, all may use, adapt and test it.

[190] See page 107.

[191] See Ford 1995.

[192] Pippin 1992 finds evidence within the text of a scapegoating which produces catharsis. She suggests that the female symbols used by the writers are prone to being treated as scapegoats.

reading of Scripture which approaches every text from the position of the dying Jesus, on the understanding that this is where God's clearest Word to a violent humanity is spoken.[193] A hermeneutic of the victim becomes possible. This hermeneutic will be able to criticize the Gospels as well as any other Biblical text. It presents itself only as a possible reading, for to assert itself as a final or authoritative reading, and so attempt to expel other readings, would be a denial of itself. The victim in the process of expulsion declares himself or herself to be arbitrary and to be innocent and therefore speaks, even in death, in judgement on violent human culture, exposes that culture to the truth of itself and in consequence brings the circumstances in which its disintegration comes about. The victim in the process of exclusion criticizes every myth and ideology that legitimates violence. The primitive Christian confession, "Jesus is Lord" may be understood as the affirmation that the excluded victim is the exposer of falsehood, the judge of ideologies and the destroyer of cultures founded on violence. The belief in the exaltation of Jesus to God's right hand is a spatial representation of the same fundamental idea. These observations do not necessarily exhaust the meaning of the early kerygma or of the primitive belief in Jesus's exaltation, but they do fill these ideas with meaning and explanatory power.

The purpose of applying these methods to the Book of Revelation is not to impose a new interpretation onto the text to replace the existing interpretations whose shortcomings have been discussed in Chapter 1. The methods are literary-critical and are to be used to gain some insight into the pattern and structure of the text so that we are enabled to engage more sympathetically with it than our current reading methods incline us to do. Their purpose is not to interpret the book in a 'this is that' manner but to offer contemporary readers the opportunity to enter imaginatively into the world of the text itself and allow it to speak.

---

[193] Placher uses Girard to make a case for identifying the gospel with victims. 1994.118-120. See Girard citation 121n220.

Chapter 4

Revelation, Illumination and Liberation: The Results of Jesus's Ministry According to the Book of Revelation

A. Introduction

This chapter is concerned with the understanding of the effects of the life, death and resurrection of Jesus of Nazareth (the Christ event) found in the Book of Revelation. The word *atonement* is often used for these effects. The use of this term by Christians implies the belief that human existence is not all that it might be and that this lack is related to a flaw in the relationship between humanity and God. Atonement is the event or process by which the flaw is repaired and the lack remedied. It is a conviction of the church that the Christ event has effected, or played a key role in effecting, atonement.[1]

Over the centuries, theologians have offered a number of accounts of the ways in which Jesus has atoning significance. Different theories, analogies and metaphors have been used in attempts to explain or to illuminate the essential experience and principal testimony of the church; that God has acted in and through Jesus Christ to deal with the fundamental flaw in human existence. Different understandings of atonement have stressed either the incarnation of God in Jesus, the death of Jesus on the cross, the resurrection of Jesus from the dead, or some combination of these, as being the key atoning act or acts. Most theologians of the Western church have defined the flaw in the relationship between God and humanity in terms of sin and its consequences and have tended to offer accounts of atonement in which the crucifixion of Jesus is the central act and is understood as a sacrifice. One difficulty with many of these views is that they concentrate on the death of Jesus and pay relatively little attention to his life.[2] Furthermore, their tendency to hypostatize sin leads to considerable metaphysical difficulties; they rely on metaphors involving the payment of debts or the demands of judicial punishment or the idea of sin as a

---

[1] Many studies of atonement have been published e.g., Aulén 1931; Barry 1968; Dillistone 1968; Fiddes 1989; Forsyth 1909; Grayston 1990; Grey 1989; Gunton 1988; Hodges 1955; R.C. Moberly 1924; Rashdall 1919; Young 1975, 1982.

[2] See Macquarrie 1977.311-317.

barrier that can be removed by sacrifice.

Theological reflection upon the cross of Jesus has tended to be restricted to its atoning significance. However, the word atonement, at least as it has been conventionally understood, and as it has been defined above, covers but one aspect, albeit a most important one, of the effects of the crucifixion of Jesus. In fact, atonement does not exhaust the effects of the ministry of Jesus as it is understood in the New Testament, including Revelation. For instance, discussions of atonement tend to regard the consequences of Jesus's death as purely beneficial; they explain how the cross disposes of sin or changes the results of sin. It will be argued that the consequences of Jesus's ministry cannot be understood as being wholly beneficial in any straightforward way. In many respects they can have adverse consequences for humanity. These effects of Jesus's work are described in a number of places in the New Testament and are described in terms reminiscent of the experiences that Girard associates with societies experiencing the breakdown of their systems of differentiation.[3] These phenomena form a major theme of Revelation in which the Lamb of God, by virtue of being slain, is shown to reveal the truth about human culture, and to initiate the eschatological process.[4]

Traditional understandings of the effects of the Christ event fail to give an adequate account of the way in which it amounts to the victory of truth. The idea that one of the consequences of Jesus's ministry consists of revealing the truth is found in the New Testament, in the Patristic writings and in the work of some contemporary theologians.[5] Furthermore, the status of Jesus Christ as the eschatological judge of the world is generally accepted to be a New Testament teaching.[6] However, the link between the crucifixion, the revelation of truth and the eschatological process is rarely noted, and even when it is, scholars find it difficult to suggest any appropriate theory by which the connections may be understood.[7] The work of Girard offers one possible avenue for research for it

---

[3] E.g., Luke 12:49-53 and parallel. Compare Mark 13 and parallels. See Romans 1:18-32.

[4] The exegetical basis of this is presented in Ch5. Compare Shelley's *Mask of Anarchy* in which Murder, Fraud and Hypocrisy are unmasked and associated with the names of three leading government ministers. Anarchy (social chaos) follows them on a white horse splashed with blood ("like Death in the Apocalypse"). See Nicholls 1989.216.

[5] John 8:32, 18:37. Instances of Patristic references are given by H.E.W. Turner 1952.29-46, a chapter entitled *Christ the Illuminator*. This approach to the understanding atonement has been revived by Gorringe 1986 whose work is subtitled *Atonement through Education*.

[6] E.g. John 5:19-29, 2 Timothy 4:1, Revelation 1:12-18.

[7] A thorough exploration of the New Testament's eschatological interpretation of the Christ event has been made by Allison 1985. He does not discuss why the cross should be understood as the beginning of the end of the world, or why the expectations of the New Testament writers did not materialize or were subjected to a delay. On the last issue see Bauckham 1980. See also Pobee 1985.86-91.

provides a theory of culture in which the Christ event reveals the truth about humanity and in which that truth brings about the end of existing forms of human social life.

Girard challenges the traditional sacrificial understandings of the cross. The death of Jesus has the same pattern as the deaths represented in sacrificial rites but its consequences are wholly different. Where sacrifices re-present the event on which the social order is founded and therefore re-found and legitimize the existing power arrangements, the death of Jesus exposes the truth about cultural origins and leads to a crisis of differentiation. It does not provide a covering for sin; rather it uncovers sin. It reveals the non-violence of God and the violence of all human cultures.[8] Girard's hostility to the idea of sacrifice is derived from his own theories about its origins and its true socio-cultural purpose. He believes that the God of the Gospels is non-violent, and so there can be no place in them for sacrifice as Girard understands it; such a God does not need to have violent inclinations satisfied or re-directed and would not make the nature of relationships with and between humans dependent on the provision of sacrifice. If Jesus's death is regarded as a sacrifice elsewhere in the New Testament (Girard believes this is so in Hebrews),[9] then such an understanding represents a step backwards from the revelation contained in the Gospels.

As far as the Old Testament is concerned, Girard is aware that, for the most part, it simply takes for granted that God requires sacrifice and that humans have a duty to offer it; it provides no developed theory of sacrifice nor any deep theological reflection upon its purpose. Yet it does contain precise instructions

---

[8] Of course, Girard's own position, defined in later works, has not prevented other scholars from attempting to understand the death of Jesus on the basis of the theory of sacrifice outlined in *Violence and the Sacred*; Jesus becomes seen as a kind of all-purpose scapegoat. See, e.g., Goldingay 1995b. A similar position is independently suggested by Young. She discusses scapegoating rituals as a means of dealing with repressed violence and argues that it is possible to see Jesus as "one who was 'scapegoated', the one on whom the aggressions and frustrations of his contemporaries were focused...he brought insecurity and anxiety. He is cast out of the community." 1975.108-109. Young goes on to suggest that just as scapegoat rituals had two functions; to make people conscious of sin and to provide them with a means for dealing with it, the passion story can have similar effects for us. It "can make us conscious of our aggression and guilt, showing us up for what we really are", and at the same time it provides "a dramatic or ritual way of dealing with the emotions we would like to repress or deny...providing a symbolic way of dissolving the destructive effect of our emotions." Girard would agree with the first half of the argument but would regard the second as 'sacrificial'. It is not enough that humans should have an outlet for their violence; they must stop being violent and the gospel makes this a possibility.

[9] 1987a.192. In recent years Girard has adapted the position taken in his major works and is now prepared to allow that the death of Jesus may legitimately be called a sacrifice if that word is understood 'in a special sense'. Williams 1997.253.

on how and when sacrifices should be made.[10] However, as Girard points out, there are strands within the prophetic and other traditions of the Hebrew Bible that reject sacrifice or appear to reject it. He understands Jesus as part of a continuing prophetic tradition of hostility towards the sacrificial cult.[11]

Even if Girard's theory of the origins of sacrifice is correct, it remains important to note that by the time the Gospels were written, there were several ways of thinking about sacrifice, not all of which relied on the violence of a god. For example, some saw sacrifices as expressions of thanks or commitment to God.[12] Whatever the origins of sacrifice may have been and whatever its socio-cultural effects were, sacrifices were offered from a variety of different motives. It may be that it was on the basis of such motives that the writers of the New Testament used the metaphor of sacrifice as a means of understanding the effects of Jesus's work on the cross. Thus, evidence of sacrificial imagery in the New Testament is not necessarily fatal to Girard's theory. Nevertheless, Girard's work raises once again the question of the extent to which New Testament writers understand Jesus's death as a sacrifice for sin.

This thesis attempts to see if Girard's theories can facilitate a meaningful reading of a particular text. Such an approach is appropriate if it can be demonstrated that its understanding of the consequences of the Christ event is not incompatible with that found in the text concerned. Therefore consideration must be given to the understanding of the Christ event that is found in the New Testament in general and in the Book of Revelation in particular.

While most readers recognize that Revelation is very different from the

---

[10] Discussions of sacrifice in the Hebrew Bible may be found in G.A. Anderson 1987, who concentrates on the social function and significance of the Yahwistic cult in tribal Israel, Dussaud 1921 who examines the relationship of the Israelite cult to that of the Canaanites, Ringgren 1962, who attempts to classify the different types of sacrifice, de Vaux 1964 who suggests a theory of the historical development of sacrifice. See also Goldingay 1995b, Gray 1925, Oesterley 1937, Pedersen 1940.299-375, Rowley 1967. Rogerson 1980 is a presentation of the key features of Old Testament sacrifice and a discussion of the interpretative difficulties, delivered to a conference which brought together Christian theologians and social anthropologists. Carter 2003 is a collection of extracts from major works on sacrifice.

[11] E.g. Psalms 40:6, 51:16-17, Isaiah 1:10-17, Jeremiah 7:21-22, Hosea 6:6, Amos 5:21-25, Micah 6:6-8. See also 1 Samuel 15:22. In the synoptic Gospels Jesus cites Hosea 6 at Matthew 9:13, 12:7, and a part of the argument of Jeremiah 7 at Mark 11:17. This pericope can be read as a rejection of the sacrificial cult based in the Temple, as is done by Myers 1991 and Gorringe 1996. See also Mark 12:28-34. Matthew 12:6 appears to relativize the place of the Temple in the purposes of God while Jesus's offer of forgiveness without recourse to the prescribed sacrifices may be seen as a rejection of the Mosaic covenant as it was understood. E.P. Sanders 1985.271. See also John 2:12-22.

[12] There is a very helpful typological presentation of sacrifice in Young 1979, usefully summarized in Young 1975. (Young 1975 was written after Young 1979 but published before it.)

other books of the New Testament, it is nevertheless customary, indeed inevitable, that it is read as a part of the canon and therefore readers are predisposed to understanding the text in certain ways. This applies to the understanding of the death of Jesus found in exegesis of Revelation. One of the themes of the book concerns the meaningfulness of martyrdom. Since the term 'sacrifice' is one that is often used for deaths which have a purpose and have consequences for others, it is often assumed that Revelation's language about death, especially the death of Jesus, must be understood in sacrificial categories.[13] There is some reason to doubt whether the imagery is best understood in this way.

It will be argued that Revelation understands the death (and exaltation) of Jesus in four related ways. Firstly, as a testimony to truth which may be emulated by the hearers of the book. Secondly, as a means of exposing or unmasking the false ideology by means of which the world's current rulers justify their own violence and sustain their own authority. Next, as a means by which the followers of Jesus are liberated from their own subjection to such ideologies. And finally, as the means by which the eschatological plans of God are initiated. Girard's work suggests that these effects are present in the cross and exaltation of Jesus and are re-actualized whenever these events are re-presented in the gospel,[14] most especially when a believer maintains his or her testimony to the point of martyrdom. Such a person acquires aspects of Jesus's own status. As a part of the demonstration of this case, it will be necessary to argue that Revelation's understanding of the effects of the Christ event are best understood in *Christus Victor* categories.[15]

The key words for the proposed reading are μάρτυς (witness), νικάω (conquer) and their respective cognates. The former is quite common in the New Testament but is especially so in the Johannine literature, particularly the Gospel. The latter is more unusual; the verb is used 27 times in the New Testament and seventeen of these are in Revelation while another five are in 1 John.

B. Μάρτυς (Witness) and Νικάω (Conquer) and Cognates

1. Μάρτυς *(Witness) and Cognates*

At the very beginning of Revelation at 1:1-2, the hearer is introduced to John as Jesus's slave who ἐμαρτύρησεν (*emartyresen*, testified to, bore witness to) the word of God and the μαρτυρίαν (*martyrian*, testimony, witness) of Jesus

---

[13] E.g., Goldsworthy 1984.46.

[14] I.e., in the telling of the story of Jesus, in reading the Gospels, in preaching, in the lives of his followers, and in the rituals of baptism and the Lord's Supper.

[15] See Aulén 1931.

Christ.[16] It appears from this that Christian service is related to giving testimony as Jesus gave testimony; to being a witness as he was a witness. Jesus's role as a witness is reinforced in 1:5 where certain key titles of Jesus are listed. These titles are descriptions of Jesus's attributes all of which may be shared by his followers.[17] It is significant that the first title in the list, indeed the first of the many Christological titles found in the book, apart from the designation 'Christ' in 1:1, is ὁ μάρτυς (*martys*), ὁ πιστός (the witness, the faithful one, or the faithful witness). This is the first in a series of three titles and their order is diachronic; Jesus is first the faithful witness, then the first born from the dead and then the ruler of the kings of the earth. The implication is that the same is true for Christians. If they wish to share Jesus's reign, they must first be raised from the dead; and if they wish to be raised from the dead, they must first be faithful witnesses. The title is found again at 3:14 where the words καὶ ἀληθινός (and true, genuine, reliable) are added. The words πιστὸς καὶ ἀληθινός (faithful and true) are again used Christologically at 19:11. These observations suggest that being a faithful witness is linked to truth.[18]

The expression ἡ μαρτυρία Ἰησοῦ Χριστοῦ (the testimony of Jesus Christ) found at 1:2 occurs a number of times in the text.[19] It is often linked to the expression 'the word of God'[20] or to 'the commandments of God'.[21] Thus, Revelation stresses Jesus's role as one who gives testimony, one who is a witness and who declares the truth.

In Revelation, the word μάρτυς (witness) is linked to death.[22] The same applies to its cognates.[23] Thus the word μάρτυς carries connotations of the meaning of the English word derived from it; martyr, one who maintains his or her testimony to the truth even though it results in his or her own death. This is

---

[16] On the translation of μαρτυρίαν Ἰησοῦ (testimony of Jesus) in Revelation see Lampe 1981, 1984; Strathmann 1967; Sweet 1981; Vassiliadis 1985. The meanings of this word and its cognates are discussed by Dehandschutter 1980. I have transliterated the first use of cognates of related words to make clear their connections. The connection between the words often translated witness, testimony/testify is not always clear in English nor is their link to the English word *martyr*.

[17] Except of course for Jesus's temporal priority. See, e.g., 2:10-11, 2:13, 5:10.

[18] See also 3:7. Trites 1973 demonstrates that, in Revelation, the word πιστός (faithful) carries the idea of death in much the same way as the word μάρτυς.

[19] 1:9, 12:17, 19:10, 20:4 see also 6:9, 11:7, 12:11; note 17:6, 22:16.

[20] 1:9, 20:4; see 6:9.

[21] 12:17; see 14:12.

[22] A reference to the dead follows its use at 1:5, the witness Antipas has been killed at 2:13, the two witnesses of 11:3-13 are killed by the beast and at 17:6 the blood of the witnesses has been shed.

[23] The martyrs of 6:9 have been slaughtered for their testimony. The witnesses of 11:3-13 are killed once they have finished their testimony. At 12:11 testimony is linked to not loving life to the point of death. 12:17 suggests that testimony attracts the attention of the dragon. 20:4 speaks of those beheaded for their testimony.

related to ἡ ὑπομονή (patient endurance, steadfastness, perseverance) advocated by Revelation.[24] The word is sometimes mentioned in relation to testimony and to the word or the commands of God.[25] In Revelation, Jesus dies as a witness to the truth and his followers may do the same.[26]

Trites examines the concept of witness throughout the New Testament and concludes that it is part of the Bible's judicial terminology. In Revelation, the μαρτυρία (testimony) of Jesus is related to his death and to the need for his followers to share that testimony and in consequence provoke the persecution that culminates in death.[27] Elsewhere Trites traces five stages in the development of the term μάρτυς from its original reference to a witness in a court to its subsequent use to describe someone who dies on account of their beliefs.[28] With respect to Revelation she concludes that, while the term retains its forensic connotations, its meaning has developed to the point where death is regarded as a key part of any act of true witness and is at times moving towards the point where death is the primary idea and the judicial meaning is secondary.[29]

Scholars disagree about the extent to which the churches that first heard Revelation faced the possibility of persecution and martyrdom.[30] The text itself

---

[24] 1:9, 2:2, 2:3, 2:19, 3:10, 13:10, 14:12.

[25] 1:9, 14:12.

[26] Reddish 1988 suggests that Revelation contains a martyr Christology in which Christ is portrayed as a proto-martyr in order to encourage the hearers to endure in the face of persecution.

[27] 1977.Ch10.

[28] 1973.

[29] Frend argues that in Revelation the relevant term is used in the technical sense of 'blood-witness'. 1965.91. The relationship between apocalyptic and martyrology is discussed by Riddle 1927.

[30] The traditional view (see, e.g., Stauffer 1955.147-191) is that the church was experiencing official persecution at the time the text was written. This has been challenged by those who doubt that there is contemporary evidence of state persecution. L. Thompson 1986 and 1990.95-185 disputes the usual portrayal of Domitian as a megalomaniac and finds no evidence of economic or political crisis or of widespread persecution of Christians. He concludes that Revelation's language is rhetorical; the seer "encourages his audience to see themselves in conflict with society; such conflict is a part of his vision of the world." 1990.174. Yarbro Collins suggests that Revelation's language reflects a perceived crisis. 1984.Ch3, 1989a. Schüssler Fiorenza reminds those who argue on the basis of historical sources that there was no persecution and no political or economic crisis, that all the texts cited were written by the powerful and, unlike Revelation, do not present the perspective of the poor. Therefore, while there may have been no official persecution, oppression may have been widespread. 1985.8-9, 1991.Pt3. Of course, while most scholars follow Irenaeus and date Revelation to the reign of Domitian, alternative datings are often suggested. Lane Fox 1986.419-492 suggests that periods of crisis provoked a fear of the gods, which created a stress on the need for rituals that were unanimously observed. Therefore Christian refusal of sacrifice

hints at persecution in the case of the author[31] and mentions the martyrdom of Antipas.[32] There are a number of other general references but nothing specific. The text certainly encourages its hearers to anticipate persecution and to be prepared to face martyrdom as Jesus did. It is possible that the veneration of martyrs in the early church may have been encouraged by the reading of Revelation.[33]

The idea that the deaths of Jesus's followers might have similar significance to his own is found in the New Testament, particularly in the Pauline corpus.[34] This idea gained some currency within the early church. Origen states that the deaths of the apostles and of the martyrs have atoning significance.[35] Tertullian suggests the existence of similar ideas among those he addresses.[36] It is possible to trace this idea to 4 Maccabees,[37] a text used by Origen. This idea poses a problem for most systematic understandings of the atonement. However, it causes no particular difficulty for Girard's theory for the deaths of the martyrs are mimesis of the death of Jesus and would therefore be expected to have a similar effect; the deaths of innocent victims expose the truth about the nature of the prevailing culture and therefore bring about its demise. In such an understanding, the connection between death and witness is clear, and the parallel between the deaths of the martyrs and that of Jesus is apparent.

In Revelation the deaths of the martyrs are understood to have a similar effect to that of their model, Jesus. This idea is already present in the exegesis

---

provoked persecution. Price states that one of the major reasons for the persecution of Christians was their rejection of the sacrificial system. 1984.221. And see the essays collected in Horbury 1981.

[31] See 1:9. Most commentators, like J.N. Sanders 1962-1963, have argued that the text alludes to exile or banishment but this has been disputed by some including L. Thompson who thinks it refers to the author's view of life in Christ and suggests that he went to Patmos in order to preach. 1990.173.

[32] 2:13. He is called 'faithful witness'.

[33] Frend 1965.91. See, e.g. Tertullian's use of Revelation in his advocacy of the view that Christians should be prepared to die for their faith and honour those who had done so. *On the Soul* 55 suggests only the martyrs enter heaven at death; all other souls are detained in Hades until the day of judgement. He writes, "The sole key to enter paradise is your own life's blood." In *Antidote to the Scorpion's Bite* 12 he urges the reader not to fear persecution or death but to face them as the New Testament instructs. See Origen's *Exhortation to Martyrdom*. On martyrdom in the early church generally see Frend 1965 and Lane Fox 1986.419-492. For early evidence of the veneration of martyrs see *The Martyrdom of Polycarp* 17, an account of the desire to collect their relics.

[34] E.g. 2 Corinthians 1:6, Ephesians 3:13, Colossians 1:24, 2 Timothy 4:6.

[35] *On Numbers* 10.2. One of the texts cited is Revelation 6:9-11. He writes, "I fear lest it may be that since the time that the martyrdoms have ceased and the sacrifices of the saints are no longer being offered for our sins we may fail to win remission of our transgressions." Cited by Bettenson 1969.222. And see *Exhortation to Martyrdom* 50.

[36] *To the Martyrs* 1 and *On Modesty* 22. Cited by Bettenson 1969.155.

[37] 6:28-29, 17:21-22.

of a number of scholars whose work antedates or is independent of that of Girard. Sweet discusses the relationship between the testimony of Jesus and the sufferings and victory of Christ and his followers. He concludes that one aspect of the ministry of Jesus and of Christians is to witness to the truth of God's word and against τὸ ψεῦδος (the illusion, the lie) which grips the world and which is evidenced in idolatry and immorality. Such a witness provokes and torments the world, which is expected to respond with persecution. The faithful Christians would be victorious because God would ultimately vindicate them. The defeat of the dying Christians is apparent rather than real; the final victory of the truth over falsehood is grounded in the death of Christ. The mechanism by which this is achieved is unclear. "Here there is no explanation, only mystery."[38] In her study of Revelation's political perspective, Yarbro Collins argues that the martyrs play a part in bringing about the end of the world. She writes, "the deaths suffered by members of the community are thought to play a role in bringing about the turning point, the eschatological battle", and

> The faithful are to suffer persecution and death in the present. They expect a violent resolution of the conflict in which heavenly forces will defeat their adversaries. Their contribution to this outcome may be made in the form of a martyr's death, which hastens the end, because a fixed number of martyrs must die before the eschatological battle can be initiated. The value of the martyr's death is greatly enhanced by the example of Christ.

And, "martyrdom in Revelation is part of the eschatological process."[39] Bauckham makes a number of observations on this theme. He claims that the messianic army are followers of the Lamb "who participate in his victory by following his path to death." And he argues that when Christians "maintain their witness even to death and are seen to be vindicated as true witnesses, then their witness participates in the power of his (Christ's) witness to convert the nations". Elsewhere he notes "how it was possible for the death of Christ to be such a victory is not explained."[40] Of course, as Trites says, "the testimony of the martyrs in life and death is valued only in so far as it is a repetition or continuation of the testimony of Christ."[41] As such a continuation of Jesus's own work, the testimony of the martyrs contributes to its consequences; it witnesses to the truth and is an agent of the eschatological process. As Lampe puts it, "Christ's death is re-presented in each martyrdom."[42] Girard comments

---

[38] 1981.102.
[39] 1977b.256.
[40] 1993a.229, 281, 185.
[41] 1977.162.
[42] 1984.258. See Caird's remarks on the theology of Revelation. 1984. 289-301 and those of Schüssler Fiorenza 1985.50. Compare Boff 1987.117-128. He argues that Jesus's death is a testimony to justice and truth and claims that those who side with the poor will stir up conflict and division as they bring the dominant ideology into question.

on the Johannine Paraclete,

> When the Paraclete comes, Jesus says, he will bear witness to me, he will reveal the meaning of my innocent death and of every innocent death, from the beginning to the end of the world. Those who come after Christ will therefore bear witness as he did, less by their words or beliefs than by becoming martyrs and dying as Jesus died.[43]

These observations are reinforced by noting the role played by the two witnesses of 11:3-13. They prophesy, give testimony and are killed in a way that is linked to the death of Jesus.[44] As Giblin notes, the deaths of the witnesses at the hands of the beast gives their martyrdoms a cosmic dimension and therefore the witnesses should be understood to represent the church's prophetic ministry.[45] This perspective is shared by Bauckham who regards Revelation 11 as the content of the scroll of 5:1 (and 10:2) and as an encapsulation of the message of the book about the role of Jesus's followers.[46]

Thus, one of the key understandings of Jesus in Revelation is that he is the faithful witness. The term retains its forensic flavour but the giving of testimony is clearly related in the text to dying and so the word and its cognates carry some of the connotations of the English word *martyr*. The life, death and resurrection of Jesus bring testimony of God's truth to the world. His followers are expected to witness to the same truth in the same way as he did and their testimony will augment the consequences of his.

The suffering they will endure has the same meaning as that of the prophets and of Jesus; it exposes structural sin and therefore plays its part in the project of liberation. The violence worsens as the powerful go to greater and greater lengths to silence the subversive prophetic voice but the effect of this is to enhance the truth, "the closed systems grow more and more violent as they approach their inevitable end." 1987.125. The memories people have of the martyrs are subversive of the existing structures of power relations within society. The martyrs are thus identified in the passion of Jesus. Hence the title of the book; *Passion of Christ, Passion of the World*. Compare Lehmann's look at revolutionary movements of the twentieth century from a Northern, Protestant perspective; he argues that some, given their parallels to the gospel story, "have brought the established power and order of colonialism, imperialism, and racism under a divinely appointed judgement." 1975.237.

[43] 1986a.212.
[44] On prophecy's link with testimony see 19:10.
[45] 1984.
[46] 1993a.273-283. There have been numerous other attempts to understand Revelation 11 and to identify the witnesses. An account of the future conversion of the Jews; Beckwith 1919, Ladd 1972: a prophecy of the end-times; Lindsey 1974. An ancient tradition identifies the witnesses with specific Old Testament saints. See Bauckham 1976, 1985. Greve 1978 believes they are James the apostle and James the brother of Jesus. See Feuillet 1964b.240-250.

2. The Verb Νικάω (Conquer)

Towards the end of each of the seven letters of 2:1-3:22, promises are made to the one who conquers.[47] In each case the verb is used intransitively and so it is by no means clear what has been conquered nor is it apparent what the means of this conquering might be. An examination of the context suggests that the promises must be made to those who heed the advice offered in the letters, even if it means their death. However, there are other factors that may affect the way the word should be understood.[48]

a. Νικάω in Revelation 4-22

Firstly, there is the use of the word elsewhere in Revelation. It is used, intransitively, of the actions of Jesus at 5:5 where Jesus conquers in order to open the scroll, an action interpreted in 5:9 which says that Jesus's right to open the scroll is derived from the fact that he was murdered and ransomed a people for God. It is this act, faithful death, which constitutes the act of conquering. This implies that when Christians endure and keep faith with Jesus, they may be said to conquer and this is ultimately done in being faithful unto death.

The next use of the verb comes in 6:2 where it is used twice and the use is again intransitive. At the opening of the first seal, the first of the four riders appears. His is a white horse and he goes out conquering and to conquer. Then at 11:7 the beast, one of whose functions in Revelation is to imitate the acts of God's agents, is said to conquer and kill God's two witnesses. The verb here is clearly transitive having αὐτούς (them) as its object. This gives the verb a rather different flavour. The same applies at 13:7 where the beast is permitted to conquer the saints. In between these two references, the verb is again used transitively at 12:11 but this time of the conquest of Satan by Christians. However, the same verse spells out in clear terms the nature of that victory. The accuser is conquered by the death of Jesus (the blood if the Lamb), καὶ διὰ τὸν λόγον τῆς μαρτυρίας αὐτῶν (and by the word of their testimony) and because the Christians did not love their own lives, an expression which suggests martyrdom. The verse expressly links the two key concepts; the μάρτυς (witness) word group and νικάω (conquer). The nature of God's eschatological victory is hinted at in strands within the Old Testament and the Apocrypha where it is God's word, the truth, the Law, which has the decisive effect.[49] God's victory is the achievement of truth, not of force.

It is more difficult to say if the verb is transitive or intransitive at 15:2. Certainly, none of the relevant nouns are in the accusative, although the English translations treat the beast and its image and the number of its name as though they were the direct objects of the verb. However, perhaps the text's ἐκ (from)

---

[47] 2:7, 2:11, 2:17, 2:26, 3:5, 3:12, 3:21.
[48] Bauernfeind 1967 discusses the verb and its cognates.
[49] E.g., Isaiah 11:1-9 and 4 Ezra 13:1-57. Compare Revelation 1:16, 2:12 and 2:16, 19:15 and 19:21.

should be allowed its force so that the conquering is understood as being 'from' the beast etc.[50] In other words, for a Christian, to conquer is to die faithful to Jesus, an act which saves from the beast and its allies.

Of the final two uses of in Revelation, the last, at 21:7, readily fits the understanding so far discerned. It is intransitive and takes the form of a promise similar to those found in the letters to the seven churches. The penultimate reference is more problematic. At 17:14 we are told of kings who hand over their authority to the beast and who make war upon the Lamb. The Lamb is said to conquer them, the verb being transitive. This conquest has often been understood to be achieved through physical violence. However, this would contradict the clearly defined nature of Jesus's way of conquering as it is expressed elsewhere in Revelation.[51] Those with the Lamb, who are on his side in this war, are described, among other things, as πιστοί (faithful), perhaps suggesting that they remain true to the methods associated with the use of the word elsewhere (1:5, 2:13).[52]

In Revelation then, the use of νικάω (conquer) for the activities of Jesus and of Christians is defined in 5:9 (interpreting 5:5) and 12:11. It refers to the idea of maintaining faithfulness to the truth whatever the opposition and strongly suggests the idea that this faithfulness is to be maintained to the point of death. Where the word is used intransitively, it suggests the idea of a new and victorious way of life. Such a life is marked by persecution and endurance and the threat of martyrdom. It may be called victorious because it is patterned on Jesus who achieved his present status through his own trials and death. The intransitive use of νικάω is reserved by the text for Jesus and his followers. Where the enemies of God conquer the verb always takes an object.[53] Certainly, representatives of the early church believed that conquering was achieved through martyrdom. Tertullian discusses the use of the verb in Revelation and writes, "Who, pray, are these so blessed conquerors, but martyrs in the strict sense of the word?"[54] Augustine links the ideas of testimony and conquering when he writes of the martyrs "drawing upon themselves by their testimony the hatred of the world, and conquering the world not by resisting it, but by dying."[55] This understanding makes νικάω, especially when used without an object, almost a technical term for maintaining faith in Jesus in the face of martyrdom; this conclusion is resisted by most commentators but fits well with the theories of Girard.[56]

---

[50] See the discussion in Newport 1986.
[51] 5:5, interpreted by 5:9-12, and see 12:11
[52] The nature of the victory described in 19:11 onwards is discussed in Ch5.C.
[53] The only text where this view is disputed is 6:2, see Ch5.D.4.
[54] *Antidote to the Scorpion's Bite* 12
[55] *City of God* 22.9.
[56] See Bauernfeind 1967. Metzger insists it is a military term chosen because the Christian life involves a struggle. 1993.30. Wall follows the *NIV* and translates the term

b. Νικάω in the Rest of the New Testament

The verb is used only once in the Gospel according to John. At 16:33 Jesus assures his disciples that they should not fear even though in this world they will have persecution, for he has conquered the world. When he speaks these words Jesus is anticipating his own death and so the verb carries implications of martyrdom. This text has probably influenced the use of the verb in 1 John, especially at in 5:4-5. About half of the uses of the verb νικάω in the rest of the New Testament are found in this letter.[57] In every case the verb is used with an object. John speaks of Christians as conquering the evil one, false spirits and the world. All these references carry the suggestion that, having conquered, Christians have moved into a new kind of existence. Nothing, except the link to the use of the verb in the Gospel, suggests any necessary association of the idea with martyrdom.

There are four other uses in the New Testament. It, or a cognate, are included in citations of the Old Testament at Matthew 12:20, Romans 3:4, and 1 Corinthians 15:54-55. Luke's use of the verb at 11:22 of his Gospel is noteworthy because it is used in the context of a discussion about Jesus's own conflict with Satan. If this was a known part of traditions about the teachings of Jesus, it may have influenced the expressions found in 1 John and Revelation.

Finally, there is Paul's use of the term in Romans. He uses the verb twice in 12:21 to explain the correct response to evil; it should not conquer the Christians but rather should be conquered by good. This thought is close to the understanding of the verb which can be discerned in Revelation.[58]

c. Νικάω in the Old Testament and Other Jewish Writings

Although νικάω or its cognates turn up in three Old Testament citations in the New Testament, there is scarcely any trace of it in extant Greek translations.[59] However, it does occur in the Apocrypha. The verb is found in the Wisdom of Solomon and is common in the Maccabean literature where, in books 1-3, it is used of military victories. However, it is in 4 Maccabees that the closest parallels to the New Testament uses can be found.

There are two interesting uses of the verb in the Wisdom of Solomon. The writer compares the fate of the Egyptians and the Hebrews. The former were

---

differently depending on context, offering *overcome* for the believer at 2:7 and *triumph* for the Lion at 5:5. 1991:71,101.

[57] 2:14, 4:4, 5:4a, 5:4b and 5:5

[58] Before concluding this review it is worth noting that Paul uses the verb ὑπερνικάω (more than conquer, 'hyperconquer') at Romans 8:37. He is describing the Christian condition in the face of persecution and death. The Christian is more than a conqueror for not even these things can separate him or her from the love of God in Christ Jesus. Again, Paul's thought is close to that found in Revelation although the major commentaries do not make the connection.

[59] See Leivestad 1954.21-23.

killed by the bites of locusts and flies but not even the teeth of dragons/serpents ἐνίκησαν (conquered) God's children.[60] Then at 18:20-25 the writer discusses the action of Aaron in stopping the destroying angel in the wilderness.[61] Aaron ἐνικησεν (conquered, overcame) the wrath of God not by strength of arms but by his word; by appealing to oaths and covenants given to the ancestors.

4 Maccabees takes the form of a philosophical homily advocating the idea that reason is sovereign over the emotions. It does this by means of examples taken from Jewish history, particularly the martyrs of the Maccabean period who refused to compromise their obedience to the law in spite of hideous tortures and death. The book contains a number of ideas that may have influenced the author of Revelation. Firstly, there is the idea that the deaths of martyrs can have a significance for others. This is perhaps clearest at 6:28-29 and 17:21-22. Secondly, at 14:5-6, there is reference to belief in life after death without or before the resurrection of the body. At 17:11-12 this is clearly associated with the idea that immortality is the particular reward of the martyrs. Finally, and most importantly from the point of view of the present study, 4 Maccabees uses the verb νικάω of the martyrs. At 1:11 the author refers to the martyrs saying, νικήσαντες τὸν τύραννον τῇ ὑπομονῇ (they conquered the tyrant by endurance). Similar language is found at 6:10, 9:6, 9:30 and 11:20. However, the verb is always used transitively; there is no precedent in 4 Maccabees for the distinctive intransitive use of the verb found in Revelation. Nevertheless, the parallels are striking and reinforce the conviction that Revelation's use of νικάω is related to the idea of faithfulness to the point of death.[62]

Thus, the evidence from elsewhere suggests that the νικάω language of Revelation may carry the idea of conquering through endurance and martyrdom.[63] The conquering is one which takes Jesus's passion as its mode of operation and one which uses methods which are radically different from the ones used by those who oppose the Christians, although the same verb may be used for their activities (11:7, 13:7). Patient endurance and, ultimately, martyrdom is conquering but the one defeated is not readily identifiable and this may account for the distinctive intransitive use of the verb found in

---

[60] 16:10.
[61] See Numbers 16:41-50.
[62] Reinforced by the frequent advocacy of ὑπομονη (patient endurance) in Revelation. See Wengst 1987.132-134.
[63] Metzing 1984 traces the motif to a pre-Johannine tradition in Palestinian Christianity according to which Jesus overcame hostile Satanic powers in the supernatural world. The motif was independent of the passion narratives and only gained martyrological overtones in subsequent stages of its development; Revelation preserves the original meaning at some points but mostly reflects a development of the idea. The study is source and redaction-critical and relies on a number of questionable assumptions about the ways in which religious ideas evolve. Nevertheless, it reinforces the link between the motif and *Christus Victor* understandings of the work of Jesus.

Revelation.

d. Νικάω in Revelation 2-3

Such an understanding of νικάω is supported by the contexts in which it is used in Chapters 2 and 3. Some of the promises with which the use of the verb is associated suggest a participation in the new creation, described at the end of the book, while others look forward to a sharing in the status or achievements of Jesus. At 2:7 the promise to the one who conquers is related to the closing vision of the city of God and particularly to 22:2 with its reference to the tree of life. The promise makes the best sense if given to those who face the prospect of death. Similar considerations apply to 2:11 which follows closely on the promise in 2:10 that the one who is πιστὸς (faithful) unto death will be given τὸν στέφανον τῆς ζωῆς (the crown of life). The threat of τοῦ θανάτου τοῦ δευτέρου (the second death) is more closely defined at 20:14-15. Among the promises made at 2:17 is one that refers to the gift of manna. There may be an allusion to Psalm 78:23-25 and to the Exodus story,[64] implying that God's action in Jesus is a new Exodus, a fresh act of liberation. Another promise refers to the gift of a new name known by no one else. This may allude to Isaiah 62:2. In any event, we are told later in the book that Jesus has a name which no one knows but himself;[65] the Christian's victory is comparable with that of Jesus. At 2:26 the expression ὁ νικῶν (the one who conquers) is closely associated with ὁ τηρῶν ἄχρι τέλους τὰ ἔργα μου (the one who keeps my works to the end), implying that conquering is related to faithfulness to the point of death. The promise given of power over the nations is expressed in language drawn from Psalm 2. Elsewhere, at 1:5, Jesus is the ruler of the kings of the earth and his rule is discussed in terms of the same psalm at 12:6. A number of texts, including 3:21, 5:10 and 20:6, suggest that faithful Christians will be Jesus's co-regents, sharing his status. In 3:5 the one who conquers is offered three promises. The first refers to white garments, which are referred to in the visions of the attendants at God's throne at 4:4, the martyrs at 6:11, of the ones who come out of the great tribulation at 7:13-14, and of the armies of heaven at 19:14. In 3:4, the promise that some will walk in white is related to the fact that they are ἄξιοί (worthy), an attribute elsewhere ascribed to Jesus on account of his death and its ransoming effect.[66] The names of those who conquer will be in the Book of Life. This indicates that they will have a share in the new creation as suggested at 20:15 and 21:27. The idea that Jesus will confess the conqueror's name before God appears to be related to the saying found in the synoptic gospels at Mark 8:38 and parallels, though expressed in positive rather than negative terms. The promises at 3:12 refer specifically to the new Jerusalem, which is described at 21:1-22:5, and to the gift of Jesus's

---

[64] Exodus 16:4-5, Numbers 11:7-9.
[65] 19:12.
[66] 5:9, 5:12.

own new name, implying a participation in his status and attributes. In a sense, these ideas are all summed up in the promise to the conquerors in the last of the seven letters at 3:21. Here it is explicit that ὁ νικῶν (the one who conquers) will share Jesus's throne just as Jesus himself conquered and shares his Father's throne. To conquer is to be like Jesus; to keep his works, to maintain his testimony and to be faithful even to the point of death (or the eschaton). The reward for this will be to share aspects of Jesus's own reward; his status, attributes and authority. The hearers are being encouraged to adopt or to maintain a way of life that involves faithful testimony to the truth even though it will provoke persecution from the surrounding culture.

3. Conclusions

A number of conclusions can be drawn from the observations that have been made. Firstly, the work of Jesus as it is understood by Revelation is achieved by faithful witnessing to the truth to the point of death. This is what constitutes conquest over the forces opposed to God. As a result of the work of Jesus, a work augmented by his followers, the eschatological process is inaugurated,[67] the sovereignty of God and his Christ over the whole earth is acclaimed,[68] then actualized,[69] and then finalized.[70] The hearers of the book are urged to participate in Jesus's victory by adopting a lifestyle like Jesus's own. This is a *Christus Victor* understanding or 'classic' theory of the work of Jesus, the kind advocated by Gustaf Aulén.[71] This is the predominant understanding. Jesus's death is not a sacrifice nor is its meaning to be sought in ideas of propitiation or expiation. Jesus's work is an act of truth telling, which is understood as conquering and in which his followers may participate.

The link between testimony and the conquering of the devil is expressly made at 12:11. The devil, it should be noted, is described as the opponent of truth. He is ὁ πλανῶν τὴν οἰκουμένην ὅλην (the one who leads astray the whole world)[72] and ὁ κατήγωρ τῶν ἀδελφῶν ἡμῶν (the accuser of our brothers),[73] while one of its allies ἤνοιξεν τὸ στόμα αὐτοῦ εἰς βλασφημίας πρὸς τὸν θεόν (opened its mouth in blasphemies against God)[74], and the other πλανᾷ τοὺς κατοικοῦντας ἐπὶ τῆς γῆς (deceives the ones who dwell upon the earth).[75] At 16:13 foul spirits like frogs come from the mouths of all three

---

[67] 5:1-14.
[68] 11:15-18.
[69] 16:1-18:24.
[70] 19:11-22:5.
[71] Aulén refers briefly to Revelation and implies that it reflects the view of Christ's work which he believes dominates the New Testament and the Patristic period. 1931.90.
[72] 12:9. See also 20:3 and 20:8.
[73] 12:10.
[74] 13:6.
[75] 13:14.

and one is called the false prophet. The dragon has deceived the whole world and, as Sweet puts it, the world is "in the grip of 'false consciousness' (*pseudos*)".[76] Only the truth will liberate humans from this condition and it is the work of Jesus and his followers to witness to it. This understanding of the condition of the world is compatible with the view of Girard that all human cultures are founded on a lie; a lie which hides their violent nature.[77] His theories suggest that the revelation of the truth generates violence against those who witness to it and their deaths contribute to the exposure of the lie. The result is that the system of differentiation on which culture is based is undermined and this results in social disorder and the experience of cosmic chaos.

There are a number of references to the death of Jesus in Revelation that are amenable to a Girardian reading. For example, at Revelation 1:7 a reference from Zechariah is used to universalize responsibility for the murder of Jesus. The vindicated Jesus will be seen by all and all the tribes of the earth will wail. It has been argued that the death of Jesus and the representation of that death in the Gospels are eschatological events which expose the violence of every human social group and, whether the truth is faced or not, they unmask the arbitrary nature of the victims whose persecution, rationalized by mythology

---

[76] 1979.138.

[77] Girard regards the Satan language of the synoptics as, in part at least, an hypostatization of the illusion rooted in countless murders (this illusion is a social reality) around which human societies are organized. Aspects of this organic lie permeate all human thought. Jesus, and subsequently the Spirit at work in human history, reveals the nature of the illusion and so conquers Satan. 1986.Chs13-15, 1993. Girard's interpretation of this language may be seen as an example of demythologization. However, it does allow for the existence of an evil and deceitful force within human social worlds, a social reality to which the name Satan is given in the New Testament texts. Caird's view is not very different. He does not address the issue of Satan's ontology but says that his characteristics are "those of his earthly representatives". 1984.150. The Pauline language of 'principalities and powers' is similarly interpreted. (Romans 8:38-39; 1 Corinthians 2:8, 15:24-26; Ephesians 1:20-21, 2:1-2, 3:10, 6:12; Colossians 1:16, 2:15. See also Galatians 4:3, 4:9, Colossians 2:8, 2:20. These ideas have been interpreted in different ways but generally as cosmic forces inimical to human welfare. Caird understands them as "evil embedded in the structure of society or woven into the fabric of the universe"; their revelation is one of the means by which they are defeated. 1956.84. Elsewhere Caird argues that Paul and his followers use this language to refer to "the political, social, economic and religious structures of power, Jewish and pagan, of the old world order". 1980.242. See Berkhof 1962. Carr disagrees 1981.43. (He regards Ephesians 6:12 as a Gnostic interpolation.) Wink's trilogy is the most thorough study, 1984, 1986, 1992. He regards the powers as symbols of the 'withinness' of institutions, structures and systems, the 'life of their own' which collective human endeavours acquire. His later ideas on the nature of the problem of human social systems have been greatly influenced by Girard's thought. The positions of Caird and Wink are not incompatible with a Girardian understanding of this language.

and ideology, is necessary to the survival of the group. This exposure prevents the group from maintaining its structural differentiation in the normative way and leads to a crisis of differentiation experienced as chaos. These cultural mechanisms are universal, their exposure in the light of the Gospel is universal and the collapse of such cultures will be universal. Hence the wailing of every tribe when the exemplary victim is vindicated. This text makes the link between the death of Jesus and the eschaton and this reading of the text offers a mechanism to account for that link. In a similar way, the vision at 1:12-18 of the exalted Jesus who had been dead and now lives contains no sacrificial imagery. He is the judge of the world for the revelation of the truth in his crucifixion judges all human cultures. The agent of his judgement comes from his mouth; the sword is his word, the truth.

Of course, there are a number of texts that may be understood to tell against the non-sacrificial interpretation of Revelation which is being advocated. For example, 1:5b is often understood in sacrificial terms because of the reference to blood as an agency. The Received Text reads λούσαντι (*lousanti* – washed), suggesting that the blood washes while modern textual critics read λύσαντι (*lusanti* – freed), suggesting that it frees. Thus both Douai, following the Vulgate, and the Authorized Version read, "washed us from our sins in his own blood". However, the balance of the manuscript evidence favours the modern reading.[78] The text may well have been altered because the words concerned are little different and because the preposition ἐν fits more naturally with ideas of washing than of freeing. On balance, especially in the light of the similar idea expressed at 5:9, of the manuscript evidence, and of the fact that the change to λύσαντι can be explained and is grammatically the easier reading, it seems best to agree with the modern editors and read λύσαντι. Perhaps the statement is not to be understood sacrificially, as though the blood of Jesus were a sacrificial offering that expiated the sins of Christians. Instead, the blood may be understood as a means of referring to the death of Jesus; the event through which the faithful witness liberated them from their sins.[79] In the past they were held captive by ways of behaving which relied on their acceptance of and complicity in the prevailing myths and ideologies; the Christ event both reveals the truth about this and offers an alternative way of living; they are freed to be part of a new kingdom of priests to God.[80] The image fits well with *Christus Victor* understandings of the atonement. The Christians are liberated and are transferred into a new kind of existence. As Schüssler Fiorenza has suggested, this experience is expressed in socio-political categories.[81] The death of Jesus liberates from their sins those who believe and adopt Jesus's way of being. This

---

[78] Charles calls the latter "by far the best attested reading." 1920.15

[79] The use of the word *blood* underlines the personal cost to the victim, especially in this paradigmatic death and in other cases where the victim is scapegoated.

[80] On such motifs in Revelation see Schüssler Fiorenza 1972.

[81] 1974, 1985.68-81. This is even more apparent in the related formula found at 5:9-10.

transformation has not been achieved by a warrior who succeeds by killing others but by one who is himself the victim of violence.[82] This victim is vindicated by God in order to bear witness to the truth about humanity. Of course, the language used in this verse is derived from the Exodus story which is a common motif in Revelation and which suggests the ideas of liberation and of transfer to a new kind of existence.[83] Similar considerations apply to the language used at 5:9-10.[84]

7:14 offers another example. Its reference to robes being washed and made white in the blood of the Lamb has been understood as a sacrificial image.[85] 3:4, 3:18 and 19:8 suggest that in Revelation, garments are a metaphor for ways of life and this suggests that the death of Jesus is understood to bring about a changed way of life. The text does not refer to their sins or to their expiation through sacrifice. Rather, the old way of life, characterized by enslaving sin was abandoned because of Jesus's death and a new way of being adopted. The same points can be made with respect to 22:14, a beatitude for those who have washed their robes. A textual variant makes this point quite neatly for instead of a blessing on οἱ πλύνοντες τὰσ στολὰς αὐτῶν (those who wash their robes), it offers one to οἱ ποιοῦντες τὰς ἐντολάς αὐτοῦ (those who do his commandments). It is worth noting that Revelation nowhere speaks of the forgiveness of sin.

Finally, many have understood the Lamb, the most common Christological title within Revelation, in sacrificial terms.[86] The Lamb is introduced at 5:6 where the key verb is σφάζω (slay), one that is sometimes used for sacrificial killing,[87] but may also be used of murder, slaughter and killing generally. It is certainly used in such ways elsewhere in Revelation.[88] This must cast some doubt on the sacrificial understanding of the verb. Perhaps the most enigmatic reference to the Lamb is at 13:8 where the most natural reading of the text describes him as slain ἀπὸ καταβολῆς κόσμου (from the foundation of the world). Those who follow this reading explain the text in terms of the predestining purpose of God,[89] or God's faithfulness to the promises made in the past.[90]

---

[82] On 19:11 onwards see Ch5.C.
[83] Exodus 19:6. Of course the Exodus was commemorated in the Passover sacrifice, but there is no necessary allusion to that rite in this text. The institution of the Passover in Exodus 12:14 makes it a festival of remembrance of God's act of liberation. It is not an offering for sin (although it has been suggested that the rite subsequently became assimilated to sin offering).
[84] The interpretative options are discussed by Schüssler Fiorenza 1974.
[85] The textual variant is not especially helpful.
[86] The most common exegetical options are referred to in the discussion of Revelation 5.
[87] E.g., LXX of Leviticus 16:15.
[88] E.g., 6:4, and 13:3 where it applies to the beast.
[89] As, e.g., Caird 1984.168. Compare 1 Peter 1:20 where the preposition is πρὸ (before).
[90] Wall 1991.170.

The words could also be an allusion to a tradition preserved in the synoptic Gospels. Luke 11:50, a passage in the double tradition, records the words of Jesus which refer to the blood of all the prophets shed from the foundation of the world, from Abel to Zechariah, which is to be required of the contemporary generation.[91] Vos and Bauckham have both demonstrated that Revelation is dependent on traditions which are also preserved in the synoptic Gospels,[92] although neither of them refers to this possible allusion. In Luke the text refers to martyrs, to prophets and apostles sent from God and killed.[93] The deaths are not sacrificial; they have no beneficial effects. They certainly do not control or divert communal violence. The exposure of the truth about their deaths will bring violence upon a generation that denies its own violence.[94]

In Revelation, it is the Lamb who is slain from the foundation of the world.[95] It cannot be proven that Revelation 13:8 alludes to the tradition preserved by Luke. However, both speak of the killing of those sent by God to declare truth. Both use the same form of words (neither includes any definite articles), a form apparently not derived from the Septuagint. Both anticipate the vindication of the ones who have been killed and expect violence to come upon those responsible for their murders. It is possible that Revelation expects the reader to understand that Jesus stands at the end of a line of murdered prophets whose witness to the word of God is now vindicated. It may also suggest that the Lamb is to be seen as the archetypal victim, the one who represents all the silent and innocent victims killed and expelled by violent humanity. It is even possible that Jesus represents the primal victim who, according to Girard's understanding of human social life, lies dead at the beginning of every human culture. God, acting through Jesus has exposed the truth and the vindicated Lamb, slain from the foundation of the world, now stands in judgement over all the works of men and women. Girard claims that no society can long withstand the knowledge that its scapegoats are innocent and therefore the Lamb, vindicated by God, may be seen, along with his followers, as the agent of God's eschatological process. One possible understanding is that in Revelation the Lamb becomes the key to understanding ideas hinted at in a range of Old Testament texts about innocent victims.[96] Incidentally, Matthew 13:35 speaks

---

[91] The Matthean parallel does not refer to the foundation of the world but describes the blood shed as δίκαιον (righteous, just). The same adjective is ascribed to Abel (or to his blood). Girard discusses the Lucan text. 1987a.170.

[92] Vos 1965; Bauckham 1977, 1983, 1993a.92-117.

[93] The Matthean parallel also mentions sages and scribes.

[94] See the discussion in Girard 1987a.163-167.

[95] On Lamb as a symbol, see pages 227-231.

[96] Note the words of Origen, "We also know that what was said of Abel, when he was slain by the wicked murderer Cain, is suitable for all whose blood has been shed wickedly. For let us suppose that the verse 'The voice of your brother's blood is crying to me from the ground' is said, as well, for each of the martyrs, the voice of whose blood cries to God from the ground." *Exhortation to Martyrdom* 50.

of Jesus as one who will fulfil the words of the Old Testament promise to utter what has been hidden from the foundation of the world.[97]

It is not claimed that this review of the language of Revelation concerning the death of Jesus has conclusively demonstrated that the text contains no sacrificial language. However the review demonstrates that sacrifice is probably not the predominant understanding of Jesus's death, that sacrificial language is much rarer than is sometimes assumed, and that some of the texts which are most often understood sacrificially are open to other interpretations. It is important to bear in mind that the culture in which Revelation was written and was first heard, was saturated with the idea of sacrifice.[98] In such circumstances, it may have been almost impossible to reflect the idea of a meaningful death, one having an impact on individual lives and upon history itself, without some resort to language which was used, in other contexts, to describe sacrifices. It is possible that the traces of sacrificial terms and thinking that may be present in Revelation are best understood as an inevitable reflection of the stock of common terms and shared ideas to which the author had access. They do not reflect the core of its thinking about the meaning of the death of Jesus. Revelation's understanding of Jesus's life, death and resurrection is best characterized in *Christus Victor* terms. Jesus conquers through his testimony to the truth.

C. The Book of Revelation and *Christus Victor*

There are a probably a number of reasons why *Christus Victor* understandings fell into disfavour after the Patristic period. It has been argued that they demean God by suggesting that he has deceived or dealt with the Devil and that they rely on a mythological and dualistic world-view. And, of course, it is frequently pointed out that the world since the death and resurrection of Jesus shows little sign, if any, that evil has been defeated. Girard's version of the theory offers a plausible world-view and preserves the divine integrity. Revelation itself anticipates the last objection. It asserts that through Jesus the truth has entered the world but suggests that one of the consequences of this will be the experience of chaos by the world and the persecution of the church. Jesus has defeated the powers of evil, but one of the signs of the victory is the increased activity of the defeated powers. These things happen because human culture cannot survive the demonstration of the truth. Thus, the dragon, the source of

---

[97] The reference appears to be to Psalm 78:2 where LXX has ἀπ' ἀρχῆς (77:2). The Matthean text provides Girard with the title of 1987a.

[98] Young writes, "In the Ancient World, the offering of sacrifice was a universal practice of religion. The various tribes and nations that eventually made up the Roman Empire each had their traditional cults, in all of which sacrifice played a central part...It never occurred to anyone that explanation or definition was necessary. Sacrifice was assumed, and played an essential part in everything which was claimed to be a religion." 1979:7.

the false view of reality in which humanity is trapped, is cast out of heaven and his wrath is great for he knows that his time is short.[99]

A further, sociological and ecclesiological reason has been suggested for the demise of the classic theory.[100] It was a useful image for the pre-Constantinian Church which understood itself to be confronted by an unsympathetic surrounding culture, alien to its values. Even when there was no active persecution, the Church endured a general feeling of oppression and impending crisis. In such circumstances the classic theory was valuable for reinforcing group identity and providing a sense of assurance. However, after the conversion of Constantine, the church's relationship with the prevailing culture underwent a profound change. The state came to be seen as one of God's agents and the church became a supporter of the *status quo*.[101] Once the church came to regard the state as Christian, the social and cosmic dimensions of the classic theory seemed inappropriate and so individualistic, sacrificial, or debt-repayment interpretations, such as those associated with Anselm and Abelard, became prominent. The church saw itself as reinforcing rather than undermining the social order. The shift away from *Christus Victor* understandings of the atonement would have occurred alongside the church's abandonment of chiliasm noted in Chapter 1.

Revelation does not share the perspective of the Constantinian church. It celebrates a victory of Jesus who has unmasked the violent nature of the existing power structures of the world, and offers liberation from their influence to those who follow him. It is possible that it is the fact that we live in a post-Christian or post-Christendom age[102], in which the churches are learning to regard themselves as offering alternatives to the societies and cultures around them, that has led to the rediscovery of the relevance of the classic theory of atonement.[103] Weaver claims, "In short, the work of Christ - atonement - as described in this historical version of Christus Victor establishes a new social order which stands over against - in confrontation with - the structures of this world."[104] The means by which Jesus has effected this victory are those suggested by Gorringe who has argued that one aspect of the work of Jesus is the revelation of the truth. He describes the divine pedagogy as "a rescue of the human race from powers which are beyond the capacity of the individual to counter. The gospel 'conquers' in the sign of the cross which exposes every

---

[99] Revelation 12:10-12. Minear 1953 argues that it is the things described at 12:11 which inflict the wound of 13:12, 14; Jesus's death reveals the fatal weakness of the beast.
[100] Weaver 1989-90.
[101] See the discussion of Eusebius in Ch1.B.1 above.
[102] See Wright, N.G. 2000.
[103] Attempts to present the classic theory of the of the work of Christ in a contemporary, sometimes called demythologized, form include Gorringe 1986; Hodges 1955.22-24, 37-41; Macquarrie 1977.318-327; Myers 1991.396-397, 404-409; Weaver 1989-1990. And see the essays collected in Barrow and Bartley 2005.
[104] 1989-90.309.

false claim to ultimacy".[105] He also refers to God's activity as "This unmasking of demons, this work of exorcism...".[106] And in addition he points out that in the New Testament there is a link between the classic theory of atonement and the idea of atonement by revelation. He writes, "The theme of the battle with the powers and the theme of divine education are inexorably linked, for the powers are defeated, according to both John and Paul, by their *exposure*".[107]

Much of this might also be said of the understanding of the work of Jesus found in Revelation. However, in addition to the beneficial effects which might be regarded as having atoning value, the exposure of the truth has considerable maleficent effects which are no less the consequence of the work of Jesus. Neither God nor Jesus need do anything actively to generate these effects. They are the result of the human response to the revelation of truth when humans fail to act appropriately in response to it. The exegetical work which follows uses Girard's theory to suggest that the text represents the consequences for good or for ill of God's vindication of the Lamb, the innocent victim of violent humanity. Before this can be done, it is necessary to show that the proposed understanding of the work of Jesus is not incompatible with other texts found in the New Testament.

Excursus: Images of Atonement in the New Testament

Wink, in commenting on the work of Girard, asserts that, "The idea of the sacrificial, expiatory death of Jesus is far more pervasive in the New Testament than Girard acknowledges".[108] An examination of the thirty or so texts he lists raises the question of what is meant by a sacrifice and when a text can be understood to teach that Jesus's death was sacrificial.

The Synoptic Gospels

In the synoptic Gospels Jesus is widely recorded as offering the forgiveness of sin,[109] of instructing his disciples to pray directly to God for forgiveness,[110] and of telling them to forgive others.[111] All these things are done without any suggestion of sacrifice, much less recourse to it. If forgiveness is made conditional upon any acts, it is the forgiveness of others,[112] and on repentance.[113] This appears to be a rejection of sacrifice. There are few clear

---

[105] 1986.12.
[106] 1986.13.
[107] 1986.24.
[108] 1992.153. A similar point is made by Scubla 1988.
[109] Mark 2:5, 10 and parallels.
[110] Matthew 6:12 and parallels.
[111] Matthew 18:21-22 and parallel.
[112] Mk 11:25 and parallel. Luke 6:37.
[113] Mark 1:4 and parallel, 1:15 and parallel, 6:12 ; Luke 24:47.

references to Jewish sacrifices in the synoptics and little interest is shown in them; they are mentioned in passing or to confirm an action already done by Jesus.[114] Jesus's attitude to the Temple is at best ambivalent,[115] and could conceivably have been one of wholehearted opposition.[116] Sykes argues that Jesus's teaching in the synoptics draws attention away from the cult and onto God and the activity of God.[117]

Gorringe's assertion that there is, "little evidence for expiatory theology in the gospels"[118] is well-founded as is his conclusion that it is unlikely that the synoptics alone could have led to the understandings of atonement which have dominated Western theology since the thirteenth century.[119] In fact the synoptic Gospels see the ministry of Jesus as a victorious battle against Satan and maleficent spirits,[120] a view compatible with *Christus Victor* understandings of atonement.

Even the often-cited reference to Jesus's life as λύτρον ἀντὶ πολλῶν (a ransom for many)[121] may be read as an example of service for others or as the promise of liberation from the dominant culture, rather than through the אשם (sin offering) of Isaiah 53:10.[122] The only references to the synoptic Gospels in Wink's list of alleged sacrificial texts are the accounts of the Last Supper. These contain, especially in the Matthean version and in the longer text of Luke, sayings which can and have been understood to teach that Jesus's death is a sacrifice.[123] Of course, the word sacrifice is never mentioned and the presence of the idea is assumed on the basis of the rest of the language, particularly the references to the pouring out of blood, to the forgiveness of sins and to the separation of flesh and blood. In the case of Luke-Acts the lack of sacrificial imagery has long been recognized. Apart from the long version of the Last Supper, the only possible exception is the comment made by Paul at Acts 20:28. In fact, Luke's passion narrative describes the death of a righteous, innocent man and the centurion's declaration at 23:47 makes just this point.

The texts of the synoptic Gospels taken as a whole do not show that a sacrifice was needed before God could offer forgiveness to humans or to effect atonement in other ways. The predominant understanding of the work of Jesus

---

[114] Mark 1:44; Matthew 5:23-24; Matthew 23:18-19, Luke 2:24.
[115] Matthew 12:6, 17:24-27. Luke is more positive 1:5-23, 2:25-38. This includes Jesus's parents, 2:22-24, Jesus himself, 2:49, and Jesus's followers, 24:53. And see Acts 2:46.
[116] Mark 11:15-17 and parallels, 13:1-2 and parallels.
[117] 1980.
[118] 1996.67.
[119] 1996.60-68.
[120] Mark 1:12-13 and extended parallels; the numerous exorcisms; Luke 10:18.
[121] Mark 10:45
[122] See Hooker 1957.74-79, 1983.93-94. See D. Hill 1967.49-81.
[123] Mark 14:24 and parallels. Gorringe 1996.60-68 discusses the issue. Hooker makes the link with Passover and suggests that Jesus's death is seen as the redemptive act that brings God's new community into existence. 1991.343.

is best expressed in *Christus Victor* categories. Jesus's death is never explicitly called a sacrifice although some parts of the text may allude to such an understanding. Rather, it is seen as the continuation and climax of Jesus's ministry. It is a consequence of Jesus's refusal, in the face of opposition and misunderstanding, to compromise his teaching about the nature of the coming kingdom of God.[124]

The Fourth Gospel and the Johannine Letters

It has often been noted that the Gospel according to John offers little support to the traditional understanding of the death of Jesus as a vicarious and expiatory sacrifice for the forgiveness of sins. Instead, Jesus's function is understood in terms of revelation. Jesus's death is an integral part of that revelatory work. According to Forestell, Christ's work in John is "the revelation of the glory of God through his word...effective for...salvation...through faith",[125] and the cross is regarded as the culmination of the revelatory process. This process is understood as salvific but without the cross being understood as a sacrifice or as satisfaction. Forestell thinks that 1:29 may suggest that Jesus might be compared to a cultic victim but that this is secondary to the understanding of salvation found in the rest of the Gospel. The fact that John is careful to ensure that Jesus dies just as the Passover lambs are being slaughtered should not be taken to imply that he regarded Jesus's death as a vicarious sacrifice. Rather, he understood it as important to the means by which humans might take part in a new Exodus a liberation from death into life.

A number of texts in John suggest a classic understanding of atonement. At 16:33 Jesus tells his disciples that in the world they will know tribulation but that he has conquered the world. For John's Jesus, the path to this victory lies in refusing to emulate the methods of the world. Jesus tells the representative of the most powerful man on earth that the realm over which he rules is unlike Pilate's and he acts accordingly; "If my kingship were of this world, my servants would fight." In the realm ruled by Jesus things are done differently. This world and its methods have been overcome for Jesus has revealed the truth.[126] 12:31-36 links Jesus's death with the idea of the driving out of the ruler of this world, with his drawing of people to himself, and with his role as the bringer of light, a metaphor for truth.

As Forestell argues, the main thrust of John (and 1 John) is that "Birth from God transfers the believer from a form of existence characterized by sin and

---

[124] See Schwager 1985. This is also the argument of Boff who regards Jesus's death as the consequence of and climax to his life. 1987.
[125] 1974.191.
[126] 18:36-38a. The reader knows that Jesus has already said Εγώ εἰμὶ...ἡ ἀλήθεια (I am the truth). 14:6.

hatred to a new form of existence characterized by justice and love."[127] Elsewhere he states that "The Johannine presentation of salvation...is revelation in human form of a God who loves all men and who gives them eternal life through the self-devoting death of Jesus upon the cross. Faith in such a God is salvific because it opens man's heart to the life-giving power of God's Word."[128] The effect of this word

> delivers man from a world of darkness, alienation, hatred and death into a community of light, peace, love and life. The model of this love is the death of Jesus upon the cross. Such a life is already eternal life and is, therefore, filled with hope for the future...The life with Christ begun now in faith is victorious over the hatred of the world and over physical death.[129]

This is essentially a *Christus Victor* understanding of the atonement with the victory being accomplished by the enlightening effect of Jesus's ministry upon the lives of humans.[130] As such it is quite in accord with the ideas advocated by Girard; after all, John's Jesus says of his enemy, whose desires are done by those opposing him, that ἀνθρωποκτόνος ἦν ἀπ' ἀρχῆς (he was a murderer from the beginning) and ψεύστης ἐστὶν καὶ ὁ πατὴρ αὐτοῦ (he is a liar and the father of lies).[131]

The Pauline Corpus

The focal point of Paul's understanding of the achievement of Jesus is the idea that it enables humans to change. Those who have faith are transferred from the realm of death, sin, the flesh and Adam into the realm of life, faith, the Spirit and Christ; they become participants in a new kind of life.[132] Paul writes very

---

[127] 1974.195. In fact, Forestell's case is much stronger in respect of the Gospel than it is for the letters. 1 John 2:2, 4:10 describe Jesus as an ἱλασμός, usually understood as an atoning sacrifice. It must be acknowledged that this language represents a significant strand of the letter's understanding of Jesus's ministry.

[128] 1974.203.

[129] 1974.204.

[130] See Gorringe's assessment of the evidence. 1996.78-80.

[131] 8:44.

[132] Ziesler argues that the death of Jesus is essential for this transfer from the old life to the new. The death of Jesus is understood sacrificially but this is secondary to the idea of Jesus's death as "something in which believers participate so that his death because of sin is appropriated and shared in as their death to sin. (Romans 6:10-11). Perhaps the most telling passage for this understanding of the cross is 2 Corinthians 5:11-21, where Paul talks about reconciliation to God and about the new being, the new creation, all in one breath...Christ has not died *instead of* us, but to enable us to die, just as he rose to enable us to rise (1 Corinthians 15:22; 2 Corinthians 5:15)." 1990.102. Similarly E.P. Sanders argues that sacrificial thinking does not lie at the heart of Paul's understanding of the death of Jesus. He cites with approval (as does Gorringe in the course of his discussion of Paul 1996.71-77) the view of Davies that Paul fails to develop the idea of

little about forgiveness as the mechanism by which this is achieved.[133] As Sanders argues, Paul does not conceive of sin as transgression; "People are not just guilty, they are enslaved, and they need to escape." One can only escape by dying and those who become one with Christ share his death and so escape; then they share his life, a life free from the power of sin.[134] Paul may occasionally use sacrificial language but it is not at the heart of his thought about the death of Jesus.

Perhaps the text most widely discussed is Romans 3:25 where scholars debate the meaning of the word ἱλαστήριον (means of atonement). Dodd understands it in terms of expiation,[135] as do Büchsel and Hermann who point out that God is the subject rather than the object of the relevant verb.[136] Barth links it to the mercy seat on the Ark of the Covenant,[137] and Manson to the locality where acts of atonement occur.[138] These views have been criticized by Morris who argues that the word suggests a propitiatory sacrifice.[139] D. Hill links the text to 4 Maccabees 17:22 and a tradition of the atoning death of the righteous martyr. However, Caird points out that although the word is from the vocabulary of sacrifice, it occurs in a passage where the apostle uses a number of metaphors drawn from diverse spheres of life without indicating how they are related.[140] Furthermore, as N. Elliott's rhetorical study argues, the profusion of purpose clauses in the text show that the central idea is the vindication of God; the point being made is that the justification of sinners is the decisive demonstration (ἔνδειξιν) of the divine integrity.[141]

At the centre of Paul's thought is the idea of a change in ways of being. Jesus has not achieved this through a sacrifice which expiates sin or propitiates God, but by initiating the promised future age and making it present in the decaying remains of the old; παπάγει γὰρ τὸ σχῆμα τοῦ κόσμου τούτου (for the form of this world is passing away).[142] Girard's theory would suggest that sin or life in Adam may be Paul's way of speaking about the mimetic

---

Jesus's death as a sacrifice but leaves the sacrificial terms inchoate. (See Davies 1962.242, 259). 1991.78-80.

[133] The reference at Romans 4:7 is a citation. The other references in the corpus are Ephesians 1:7 and Colossians 1:14 and 3:13. Both are works whose authorship has been widely questioned. Even here, all the references to forgiveness are made in passing; its means is not worked out. On this issue see Stendahl 1976.23-40.

[134] Sanders 1991.79. He cites Romans 6:5-11, 7:4-6, 14:8-9.

[135] 1935.82-95.

[136] 1967.

[137] 1933.

[138] 1945.

[139] 1950-1951, 1955-1956. Followed by Cranfield 1975.

[140] 1994.152.

[141] 1990.

[142] 1 Corinthians 7:31. On Paul's eschatology and apocalyptic worldview see Beker 1980, Lincoln 1981.

consensus; ways of thinking derived from the founding violence and sustained by acquisitive mimesis and imitative desire or covetousness. The life and death of Jesus reveal the possibility of a different and contrasting way of being and the Spirit of Jesus mediated through the believing community enables believers to conform to this new way of life.[143] The apparently sacrificial language causes some difficulty,[144] but is not to be seen as an expression of Paul's primary understanding of the death of Jesus.

Colossians contains one of the key texts for the *Christus Victor* understanding of the work of Jesus.[145] His triumph enables those who believe to move from death to life. Ephesians contains a similar idea. The hearers had once walked in death after the pattern of the world but have now been made alive, brought into a new kind of life, a life of good works.[146] It is worth noting that the writer to the Ephesians believes that the church has a role in making known the wisdom of God to the powers in the heavenly places.[147] In Girardian terms, this may be taken to indicate that the proclamation of the gospel is expected to affect the cultural mechanisms and structures that control the ways in which human societies operate.[148]

Other New Testament Writings

The First Letter of Peter also understands the work of Jesus as effecting a transfer from one way of life to another. 1:18-19 is especially interesting. 1:18 suggests that that the way of life from which Christians are rescued is one inherited from parents; it is the culture that we learn as infants and that makes us a part of human society. The means by which God breaks our imprisonment to this way of being human is to ransom us through Jesus. Jesus opens to humanity the possibility of a different way of being. The following verse indicates that Jesus was destined for this role from the foundation of the world, which may suggest that he represents the primal victim. According to the letter, this act of liberation that Jesus has accomplished can be compared with being brought out of darkness and into light.[149] This fits well with the idea that Jesus's victory is achieved through the revelation of the truth.[150]

---

[143] Hamerton-Kelly has made the most thorough attempt to read Paul in the light of Girard's thought; see Ch3.F.

[144] Sanders cites 1 Corinthians 15:3, Romans 3:25, 4:25, 5:9, Galatians 3:13, 2 Corinthians 5:21. 1991.78. Exegetical alternatives exist in many cases but for these purposes it is acknowledged that Paul sometimes expressed his understanding of Jesus's death in sacrificial terms.

[145] 2:10-15.

[146] 2:1-10.

[147] 3:10.

[148] Ephesians 1:13 regards the gospel as the word of truth.

[149] 2:9. *Christus Victor* themes may also be present at 3:21.

[150] However, 2:24 suggests that Jesus carried up our sins in his body on the cross, thus freeing us from sins.

Finally, the Letter to the Hebrews must be discussed. Girard himself regards the book as offering a sacrificial understanding of the death of Jesus and as therefore being the fount of what he calls "sacrificial Christianity", the misinterpretation of the gospel stories which prevented the revelation within them from being rightly understood and from having its anticipated impact.[151] There is no doubt that the letter does describe Jesus's death as a sacrifice.[152] However, it should be noted that this is a new kind of sacrifice. The old sacrifices served to enable sins to be forgiven. The sacrifice of Jesus does something more; it purifies the conscience from dead works to serve the living God.[153] In other words, the death of Jesus has the effect of changing the human disposition, something which sacrifice as such could never claim to do; sacrifices repaired what had been broken. The death of Jesus does not have this effect. Rather it enables a new kind of existence to be lived.[154] The effect of this is to subvert the sacrificial system itself for Jesus has made it redundant. This sacrifice is an anti-sacrifice. Of course, this subversion of sacrifice depends on an image of sacrifice itself as an act which cleanses, but the nature of the cleansing is no longer to restore humans but to transform them. Jesus has broken the sacrificial system itself. There is no more possibility of repair; there is instead a new kind of life, with no place and no role for any sacrificial system.[155]

Concluding Remarks

As Schwager points out,[156] the debate about the nature and extent of the sacrificial language of the New Testament is based on prior decisions about the nature and purpose of sacrifice itself. In his major works Girard's understanding of what constitutes a sacrifice is quite restricted. It is a rite which has a particular social effect; that of diverting human violence generated by mimetic desire and rivalry within the community onto an arbitrary scapegoat and so enabling the community to unite. This ritual action is usually explained in terms which involve the attribution of violence or anger to a deity and the appeasement of that violent intent or wrath through sacrifice. Jesus's killers do what the participants in the scapegoat mechanism always do and so perhaps Jesus's death is best described as a failed sacrifice. It failed because Jesus refused to play the role of scapegoat, because God vindicated him and because

---

[151] 1987a.192.

[152] 7:27. Gorringe suggests that in Hebrews the blood of Jesus is a metaphor for his obedience. 1996.77-78.

[153] 9:14.

[154] The postscript to Isaacs 1992 suggests that in Hebrews the meaning of the term 'sacrifice' shifts from literal to metaphorical.

[155] 10:26-31. Hebrews is considered from a Girardian perspective by Hardin 2000 and Johns 2000.

[156] 1985.

the Christian *kerygma* declared him innocent so that the unanimity required for a successful scapegoating did not prevail; this message is preserved in the texts that tell the story of his death. On the question of the New Testament interpretation of Jesus's death, it is not understood as effecting unity among those responsible for the killing.[157] On the contrary, the text suggests that this death unleashes further upheaval,[158] rather than keeping violence controlled and channelled. Nor is Jesus's death explained in terms of the need to propitiate the wrath of a violent deity who requires this death. In these senses, which rely on his own definition of sacrifice, the indications are that Girard's case is well made. The New Testament does not suggest that God needed to inflict violence on humanity and that Jesus suffered that violence vicariously.[159]

However, sacrifice in the ancient world was understood in a number of other ways. One of these carried the idea of cleansing, a concept which could be interpreted in terms of liberation or of the offer of a fresh start to life. And in our own world sacrifice is a word that has been used for any death which has meaning for others. If this definition is adopted, there is no reason Jesus's death cannot be understood as a sacrificial event. The New Testament has a number of ways of understanding the work of Jesus. However, at the very least it can be argued that the classic theory is present in all the major sections of the New Testament. Indeed, it is possible to go further and to assert that if there is a dominant soteriological theme in the New Testament, it is *Christus Victor*.

---

[157] It does however bring reconciliation between Herod and Pilate. Luke 23:12.

[158] See Matthew 27:50-53.

[159] Boff writes, "The death of Christ was a crime, not a requirement of the will of a God eager for the reparation of outraged honor." 1987.3 There is a sense, however, in which Jesus's death may be understood to avert the wrath of God for those who follow Jesus. If the wrath is understood, as Girard and Schwager propose, in terms of the human violence which is the consequence of the revelation of the scapegoat mechanism, violence which causes a crisis of differentiation perceived as chaos by those involved, then there is a sense in which Christians escape. They do not escape the violence itself; they are among its likeliest victims. They do, however, avoid the experience of cosmic chaos associated with the crisis of differentiation for they have some understanding and expectation of the processes involved. In this sense their participation in Jesus protects them from this plague. The parallels with the Passover are apparent. See Exodus 12:13 and compare Revelation 7:2-3 and its allusion to Ezekiel 9:4.

Chapter 5

Outline, Interpretation and Exegesis: Reading Revelation in the Light of Girard's Thought

A. Introduction

This study of Revelation uses tools drawn from a number of disciplines. Historical-critical issues are not wholly neglected, but it is primarily an attempt to test the applicability of Girard's theories of human culture. These include theological and anthropological elements but are grounded in his understanding of texts. This means that the approach to be taken is, broadly speaking, literary-critical.

Apart from the questions of literary unity,[1] literary analyses of Revelation tend to address three issues; the language, genre and literary structure of the text. These issues are not the primary concern of this study but some observations are necessary. In particular, some remarks relevant to the third issue will be made in the course of a discussion of the outline and interpretation of the text as a whole.

1. Language

It is generally agreed that the Greek of Revelation is unusual.[2] For example, in the course of the visions the verbs tend to shift between the tenses in ways that appear to be arbitrary. In addition, there are points where the rules of grammar seem to be ignored.[3] However, there is no consensus on why the book was written in such distinctive language.[4]

The predominant view in recent scholarship is that the Greek of Revelation

---

[1] Discussed in Ch1.C.5.
[2] Charles claims "the linguistic character of the Apocalypse is absolutely unique." And that "No *literary* document of the Greek world exhibits such a vast multitude of solecisms." 1920.1.cxliii.
[3] E.g. 8:1 where ὅταν (when, whenever) is followed by an aorist indicative. See Charles 1920:1.cxvii-cxlix.
[4] The options are summarized by Court 1994.86-88.

is influenced by one or more Semitic languages.⁵ It is argued that the tenses reflect the grammatical rules of the other language. In the Semitic languages which are alleged to have influenced Revelation, the tense of a verb, perfect or imperfect, does not of itself indicate whether the action it relates to is past, present or future; this must be determined from the context. It is claimed that the verbs of Revelation follow these rules rather than those of orthodox Greek grammar.

The advocates of this view disagree about the nature of the influence and the identity of the language concerned. Some hold that part or all of Revelation is translated from Hebrew or Aramaic while others think that the author wrote in Greek, his second language, and that his expressions are influenced by the Semitic language of which he was a native speaker.⁶ Some claim that this underlying language is Classical Hebrew,⁷ others believe it is a later form of Hebrew and others that the author spoke Aramaic.⁸ S. Thompson, for example, claims to have found evidence of the influence of biblical Hebrew,⁹ and concludes that context should determine the tense that should be understood. Mussies, on the other hand, argues that the Semitic colour of the verbs is mainly a stylistic matter and that the underlying Semitic language is post-biblical and therefore more similar to the Greek verb than are the biblical Semitic languages. He concludes that the shifts in tense are the result of the narrative context of the visions being reported; the visions were seen by the seer in the past, can be vividly depicted using present indicatives and yet predict the future. Thus the verb tenses, though unusual, make sense as they stand.¹⁰ A variation on views of this kind denies that the author necessarily knew Hebrew or Aramaic and accounts for the text's unusual language in terms of the influence of Greek translations of the Hebrew Bible.¹¹ All these views claim to account for the number of alleged Semitisms in the text and to help to explain the unusual grammar and syntax found in Revelation.

Critics of these theories maintain that any given language develops over time and is used in different places and by different social groups. To idealize the linguistic rules of a given era is a methodological error. Thus, "Semitic interference in the language of the Apocalypse cannot be proved. The most that

---

⁵ See, e.g., Black 1976; Charles 1920:1.cxvii-cxlix; Lancellotti 1964; Mussies 1971, 1980; Newport 1986, 1987, 1988; S. Thompson 1985. Some of these opinions are reviewed by Porter 1989.

⁶ Charles says of the author that "while he writes in Greek, he thinks in Hebrew." 1920:1.cxliii.

⁷ Lancellotti. 1964.

⁸ See the introductions to Mussies 1971 and S. Thompson 1985.

⁹ Conclusions. 1985.

¹⁰ 1971.Ch12.

¹¹ Schmidt 1991, in discussing reviews of S. Thompson 1985, argues that some stylistic features of Revelation are better regarded as Septuagintalisms than as Semitisms. I.e., Revelation is written in a 'translation-Greek' style.

can be argued is Semitic enhancement at points."[12] If this is correct then Revelation's language may simply be one of many forms of vulgar Greek extant in the first century.

Hurtgen takes a different approach. He neither accepts nor denies the possibility of Semitic influence on Revelation but discusses the social function of the kind of language found in the text. He analyzes its purpose in terms of sociolinguistics and argues that it functions as *anti-language*, "a language displaying all kinds of verbal play that a group employs to register its opposition to a dominant group in the culture."[13] It is a means employed by a minority group to 'talk back' to the powerful.[14] In the case of Revelation, it promotes group solidarity among its users and so encourages them to keep the commands of God and maintain the testimony of Jesus.[15]

Decisions about the underlying language of the text influence exegesis. The disagreement among scholars as to the nature or even the existence of that language suggests that arguments based on hypothetical Semitic originals or thought patterns should be used with caution when making exegetical decisions. The sense and tense of the Greek should not normally be overruled.

2. Genre

The text known as the Ἀποκάλυψις Ἰωάννου (The Apocalypse of John)[16] has given its name to the genre of writings which scholars designate as *apocalypses* or *apocalyptic*, and the majority of commentators either accept or assume that it is an example of this type of literature.[17] Certainly, Revelation possesses a number of the characteristics associated with the genre,[18] but there is no

---

[12] Porter 1989.599.

[13] 1993.3. He compares it to the language used by the protagonists in Anthony Burgess's, *A Clockwork Orange*. Compare Charles's remark that "It would almost seem that the author of the Apocalypse deliberately set at defiance the grammarian and the ordinary rules of syntax." 1920:1.cxliii.

[14] He makes use of the grid/group analysis devised and developed by Mary Douglas 1970, 1992 to define the social location of the Christian communities.

[15] Other considerations of Revelation's historical, social, political and rhetorical settings include Aune 1981; Böcher 1983; Burnet 1946.Ch2; Court 1994.94-108; Gager 1975; Georgi 1986; Schüssler Fiorenza 1985:181-203; L. Thompson 1986, 1990.Ch1-2, 6-11, appendix; Yarbro Collins 1977b, 1984.Ch3-5, 1986a, 1988a, 1989a. D. Barr 1984 offers a critique of the influential positions of Gager and Yarbro Collins.

[16] 1:1 suggests that its original title is Ἀποκάλυψις Ἰησοῦ Χριστοῦ (Apocalypse of Jesus Christ).

[17] Other Jewish examples include all or part of Daniel, 1 Enoch, 2 Enoch, 3 Enoch, Jubilees, 2 Baruch, 3 Baruch, 4 Ezra, Apocalypse of Abraham, Testaments of Levi and Naphtali, Ascension of Isaiah.

[18] E.g., the interpreting angelic figures of 1:1, 5:5, 7:13, 17:1, 17:7-18, 21:9; the heavenly ascent and throne vision of 4:1-11; the types of symbols used; the debt to

consensus that the text really belongs to it. The defining feature or idea of the genre is disputed. The matter is further complicated by the observation that despite the popular sense of the word, not all the apocalypses are particularly concerned with eschatology and apocalyptic eschatology is hard to distinguish from the eschatologies of non-apocalyptic texts written around the same time.[19]

Scholars who deny that Revelation is an apocalypse do so on a number of grounds; its attitude to suffering,[20] the fact that it is not pseudonymous,[21] its description of itself as a prophecy,[22] its lack of secrecy,[23] the absence of key features such as historical review sections in the form of prophecy given *ex-eventu*,[24] of lists of revealed things and of descriptions of heavenly journeys,[25] and the epistolary framework of the book.[26]

Schüssler Fiorenza takes these objections seriously and argues that the text is both "prophetic-apocalyptic",[27] and in the form of a circular letter.[28] She also notes Revelation's affinity to Greek drama.[29] Such a position is articulated by

---

apocalyptic traditions: see Bauckham 1993.38-91. There are numerous histories, descriptions and definitions of apocalyptic and apocalypses in the literature. See, e.g., including discussions of the genre of Revelation, Aune 1986; Burkitt 1914; J.J. Collins 1979, 1984, 1986; Court 1994.78-84; Cross 1969; Georgi 1986; P.D. Hanson 1971, 1973, 1975; Hellholm 1986, 1991; Koch 1972:18-35; Ladd 1957a; Rowley 1946; Russell 1960.93-160, 1964:104-139, 1978, 1986.99-121, 1987, 1992:1-13, 1994; Schüssler Fiorenza 1980, 1985:164-170; Stone 1976, 1980; Vielhauer 1965; Von Rad 1962. 263-283; Yarbro Collins 1986b, c, 1988c 1992a; and see the articles in Hellholm 1989.329-637, in *Semeia* 14 (especially the influential definition at 4) and 36, in Collins 1991 and P.D. Hanson 1983. Delcor 1977a reviews some contemporary studies. On the influence of apocalyptic on Christian theology, see the articles of Käsemann 1969a, b and Rowland 1995. Note the critiques of Käsemann by Rollins 1970-1971 and Rowland 1979.

[19] See both Rowland 1982.9-72, implicitly rejecting J.J. Collins's 1974 suggestion that apocalyptic eschatology, when compared to other Jewish eschatologies, is characterized by the transcendence of death, and Rowland's 1986 review of J.J. Collins 1984.

[20] Kallas 1967.

[21] Jones 1968.

[22] See, e.g. 1:3 and 22:18-19. Mazzaferri claims Revelation has the genre of classical prophecy. 1989.259-378.

[23] Compare 22:10 with Daniel 12:9 and see Isaiah 8:16.

[24] This alleged absence is disputed by Hopkins 1965.

[25] Noted by Schüssler Fiorenza 1985.168. On the lists of things revealed in apocalypses, see Stone 1976.

[26] Aune claims this makes Revelation unique among Apocalypses. 1987.240. J.J. Collins 1977a addresses some of these issues in a defence of the traditional position.

[27] 1985.20. See Aune 1983a.274-288, 1987a.226-252; D. Hill 1971-1972; Ladd 1957b; Vawter 1960.

[28] 1985.35. See 1985.165-170. Boring 1989 regards Revelation as a pastoral letter. Karrer 1986 insists it is thoroughly epistolary.

[29] 1985.176. See Blevins 1980; Bowman 1955, 1962; Brewer 1952; Kepler 1957.Ch7.

Ashcraft who describes Revelation as, "a dramatic apocalyptic-prophecy with the formal characteristics of a pastoral letter."[30] While this may be an adequate description of the text, it is not a useful generic category for there are no other examples of this type of literature.[31] The work has affinities with other forms of literature but does not belong to any definite category.[32] Perhaps the text offers something new, a literary form which incorporates elements of different types and transcends them. The legitimacy of interpreting Revelation on the basis of arguments from genre is open to question.

These observations suggest that the form of Revelation conveys the idea that something new has taken place. The nature and consequences of this new thing provide the content of the text and might be expected to find some reflection in the work's literary structure.[33] Exegesis will seek to show that Revelation understands the work of God both to have achieved its ends already, and yet still to be awaiting its consummation. Cullmann's work suggests that the Christian experience of time as the scene of redemptive history has a twofold character of this kind.[34] This dual perspective finds expression in the structure of Revelation.[35]

3. Literary Structure

It has become common for scholars to observe that there are as many literary structures of Revelation as there are people who have written on the issue.[36] Vanni thinks that literary considerations should condition exegesis and writes that, "Inattention to this aspect is one of the reasons for the chaotic multiplicity of so many exegetical interpretations of the Apocalypse found in the history of

---

[30] 1972.253

[31] This point is reinforced when one adds Bauckham's observation that Revelation may be compared with the Qumran War Scroll. 1993a.210-213. Nevertheless, Bauckham regards Revelation as an apocalyptic prophecy with some epistolary features. 1993b.Ch1.

[32] Revelation has an epistolary form, including messages to seven distinct churches, uses imagery drawn from both apocalyptic and myth, contains prophetic oracles, and numerous hymns.

[33] Schüssler Fiorenza regards Revelation as "a unique fusion of content and form" 1985.159, with the text's message manifested in the structure of the text. 1985.159-177.

[34] 1951.

[35] Schüssler Fiorenza has argued that the tension between the 'already' and the 'not yet' of early Christian eschatology finds expression in the structure of Revelation. 1985.5.

[36] Surridge remarks, "there is very little consensus on the overall structure of the work and how that structure should be interpreted. There are almost as many outlines of the book as there are interpreters." 1989-90.231.

interpretation"[37] He may be right but the variety of proposed structures offered is approaching that of interpretations.[38] Few have been followed,[39] and Aune may be right to assert that the structure is more complex than that of any other Jewish or Christian apocalypse and that it has yet to be satisfactorily analyzed.[40] Lambrecht acknowledges the difficulty of demonstrating the objective nature of any pattern by calling his own proposal a *structuration*.[41]

If Schüssler Fiorenza is correct then the book's form might be open to at least two understandings, one which reflects the 'already' of God's achievement in Jesus, and another which corresponds to the 'not yet' of promises still to be fully realized. The former is characterized by chiastic patterns and repetitions, while the latter allows for the forward movement of the text from present experience to future hope. The text's structure may turn out to be too complex for it to be reduced to any one straightforward structural pattern.

B. Outline

Girard's theory suggests that culturally significant texts may be characterized by a particular pattern, although this need not rule out the existence of other patterns in the same text. The pattern suggested by Girard's work is one in which an initial order is ended by a specific event which causes a period of disorder; this chaos is eventually resolved by an act of violence which brings about a new period of order.[42] This is the structure of Girard's narratology.[43]

While the Girardian account of the origins of the underlying pattern of narrative is novel, the description of the pattern itself is not. In the course of his discussion of Freud's *fort-da* game, Eagleton writes, "even the most complex narratives can be read as variants on this model: the pattern of classical

---

[37] "La disattenzione a questo aspetto è una delle cause della molteplicità caotica di tante interpretazioni esegetiche dell'Apocalisse quali ce la mostra la storia dell'esegesi." 1988.29.

[38] Significant attempts to define the literary structure, in whole or part, excluding source critical theories discussed in Ch1.C.5, include Bauckham 1993a.1-37; Benson 1900; Bowman 1955; Boyd 1948; Farrer 1949; Giblin 1974, 1994; Lambrecht 1980b; Loenertz 1947; Lohmeyer 1926.1-3; Lohse 1960.7-8; Lund 1992.323-411; Lust 1980; Mazzaferri 1989.331-365; Muñoz-León 1985; Rowland 1982.413-423; Schüssler Fiorenza 1985.51-56, 170-177; W. Shea 1983; C. Smith 1994; Strand 1978, 1983, 1984b, 1987a, 1987b; L. Thompson 1990.Ch3; Vanni 1980a; Yarbro Collins 1976.Ch1.

[39] Court 1994.Ch3 follows Schüssler Fiorenza's chiastic structure. Rist 1957 follows Lohmeyer 1926.

[40] 1987a.241.

[41] 1980. The charts in M. Wilson 2007 offer a fresh, schematic approach to the issue.

[42] See Ch2. This is also the structure which Girard discerns in rituals. It may help account for the liturgical and cultic patterns discerned in Revelation. See Ch1.

[43] There is progress but also a chiasm; order, event, chaos, event, order.

narrative is that an original settlement is disrupted and ultimately restored."[44] A similar point is made by Todorov in the course of his work on fantasy literature. He discusses "the very nature of narrative", and concludes, "All narrative is a movement between two equilibriums which are similar but not identical." The beginning presents a stable situation. Then something happens which introduces disequilibrium, there is then a transition and at the end a new equilibrium is established. "Every narrative includes this fundamental schema".[45] Neither Eagleton nor Todorov refer to violence but otherwise the pattern is the same. Wink discerns a similar pattern, including the violent resolution, in both myths and contemporary cultural artefacts. He calls the pattern "the myth of redemptive violence".[46]

This pattern may be discerned in some important biblical texts such as those which refer to the Zion myth and the related *Chaoskampf* (struggle against chaos). The essence of the tradition is that Mount Zion is the dwelling place of Yahweh and is a place of stability and safety. Nevertheless, the forces of chaos, represented either in mythological terms by the sea and the sea monster, or in demythologised terms by the kings of the nations,[47] rise up against Zion in battle. At dawn Yahweh triumphs, forces the enemies to retreat and re-establishes order.[48] Psalm 2, a coronation psalm, appears to relate elements of the tradition to the succession of a new king. The transfer of sovereignty from the new king's predecessor is the moment chosen by the nations and their kings to conspire against the dynasty. The rebellion fails because of the decisive action of God and order is re-asserted.[49]

This treatment of the transfer of authority reflects the Zion myth but may also reflect historical experience. Throughout the world, changes of sovereignty are accompanied by periods of social disorder. In the ancient world the death of a monarch often provoked revolt as subject peoples saw an opportunity to assert their independence. In other instances ambitious men and their followers contended for the prize of sovereign power. Two particular instances of this phenomenon may have been of relevance to the first hearers of Revelation. The first is the period of uncertainty which occurred in Palestine on the death of Herod the Great,[50] and the second, perhaps more significant, concerns the disruption of the Roman Empire which occurred on the death of Nero.[51] It

---

[44] 1983.185.
[45] 1975.163-165.
[46] 1992.13-25. Compare Hooker's observation, in discussing Revelation and *Dr Who*, that adversaries are a necessary element of narrative; "Without evil, there cannot be a story - there cannot be history." 1982.55.
[47] See Psalms 46, 48 and 76. Note Isaiah 17:12-14.
[48] See Cross 1973, Day 1990.43, Mowinckel 1967 and the essays in Hooke 1933a, (especially 1933b), 1935a.
[49] See discussions in Craigie 1983.62-69, Eaton 1994, Hanson 1973.
[50] See Josephus *Wars of the Jews* 2.1-6 and *Antiquities of the Jews* 17.7-11.
[51] See Wellesley 1975.

seems likely that some unease about public order accompanied the news of the death of every king or emperor and so this hypothesis is not dependent on any particular dating of Revelation.[52]

Excursus on the Date of Revelation

On the issue of when the text was written, the majority of scholars follow the tradition preserved by Irenaeus and date it to around AD 95, towards the end of the reign of Domitian.[53] This position has been ably defended by Yarbro Collins[54] and Feuillet.[55] However, a significant minority of scholars argue that the text was written just before or just after the death of Nero, perhaps in the reign of Galba, and before the destruction of the Jerusalem Temple.[56] Bell suggests that Revelation was prompted by the crisis caused by the death of Nero, a "general political and social upheaval which led John to envision the end of the Roman Empire and the inauguration of God's Kingdom."[57] The internal evidence can be read so as to make either case, as may be seen from a comparison of Yarbro Collins with Rowland.[58] R.B. Moberly suggests the work was conceived in the aftermath of Nero's death and revised by the author early in the reign of Trajan.[59] The dating of Revelation to the crisis that followed the death of Nero and to the height of the Jewish War is plausible and might lend support to the argument being made in this study. However, the reading is not dependent on any view of the text's date and neither a Domitianic, nor a Trajanic, nor any other proposed date, would seriously affect the case. Similar considerations apply to the authorship of the text.[60]

This pattern of a movement from order to order via chaos and violent resolution may be discerned in Revelation. 4:2-11 presents a vision of initial order; it will be argued that this order is not wholly stable.[61] The order is

---

[52] The options are discussed by Court 1994.94-108. Note how William Blake makes events from the past the subject of the reflections of the prophetic imagination; see *Europe, a Prophecy*, in Keynes 1966.237-245.
[53] *A.H.* 5.30.3.
[54] 1981a,b; 1984.54-83; 1988a; 1992.
[55] 1964a.89-94.
[56] E.g., Newman 1963-1964; Robinson 1976.221-253. See also Hort 1908.
[57] 1979. See also J. Wilson 1993.
[58] 1982.403-413.
[59] 1992.
[60] Apart from the commentaries, discussions of this issue include Feuillet 1964a.95-108; Gunther 1981; J.N. Sanders 1962-1963; Yarbro Collins 1984.25-53.
[61] Chs 1-3 also depict an unstable initial order but seen from a rather different perspective. Disorder, in the form of persecution and tribulation, is assured; if this is endured then there will come a new and enduring type of order. The parallels listed below between these messages and 19:1-22.21, noted by Charles 1920.44, reflect Revelation's chiastic pattern.

brought to an end by the events described in 5:1-14, which are then followed by the chaos represented by the three series of plagues. The chaos is resolved by the action of the word of God at 19:11-21, an action which is depicted in violent terms. The resolution leads to the establishment of order in the form of the new Jerusalem presented in 21:10-22:5.

In the Bible this is the pattern of God's victory over forces hostile to God's rule. In human experience it is the pattern of the transfer of political sovereignty. In Girard's thought, it is the pattern of cultural formation and of narratives and rituals derived from that process. The whole of the movement of the text of Revelation depicts the victory of God over God's enemies in terms of the transfer of sovereignty over the earth from its present rulers to God and his Messiah,[62] a process which brings about the formation of a new culture, a wholly new form of human social existence.

C. Interpretation

Revelation's understanding of the work of Jesus is that he is a witness. The deaths of the martyrs make them witnesses too. These acts of witness have an eschatological dimension.[63] The exposure of truth undermines the initial order and leads to the chaos depicted in the series of plagues. With each successive series of plagues, God is represented as being less directly involved. There is textual evidence that suggests that as the plagues develop, they get more and more serious,[64] yet the more remote they are from God's initial action depicted in 5:1-14, the more indirect is the depiction of God's involvement in the series. In the first series, the Lamb opens the seals. In the second, trumpets are given to the seven angels and plagues are released when they are blown. In the third, one of the living beings hands the bowls to the angels and the plagues come when the bowls are poured out. The wrath of God is the consequence of God's action in Jesus and yet, as the narrative progresses, becomes less and less the direct result of God's initiative. God's revelation of truth generates periods of disorder which expose the nature of God's adversaries and of humans who live under their rule.[65] The truth revealed by God, the word of God, is ultimately victorious and leads to the founding of a new universe.

God's victory at 19:11-20:15 is depicted in violent terms. This causes some

---

[62] See Ch4. Bauckham 1993b suggests this. Boring presents it in terms of rightful sovereign making claims effective; "God has always and everywhere been de jure king of his own creation. At the eschaton, God acts to make his kingship de facto. But this is first celebrated and sung about before it is ever pictured." 1993.69.

[63] See Ch4.B.1.

[64] At 6:8 a fourth of the earth is affected, at 8:7-12 a third, and at 16.2-10 the effects are universal, at least so far as the followers of the beast are concerned.

[65] Compare the language of *unmasking* used by some commentators, e.g. Minear 1953.101; Rowland 1988b, 1993.107; and the similar ideas used by Schüssler Fiorenza 1993.63. See the title of Wink 1986.

difficulty to those commentators who have noticed that God's agents conquer through the endurance of suffering and death.[66] The proposed interpretation takes the violence seriously without attributing violence as such to God or his agents. Firstly, the violence is found in the Old Testament traditions of the Holy War and the Zion myth in which biblical accounts of God's ultimate victory are framed and which have influenced the language and structure of Revelation.[67] Holy War is one of the traditions which have formed the thought-world of the text. Revelation freely reinterprets the images it uses and one of these concerns the effects of the breath of God's mouth. There is no reason to follow Ford and Buchanan in insisting that the language of war be treated as though it were literal or to assume that the actions of God's agents are to be understood as violent. The victorious rider on the white horse of 19:11-21 appears to be a metaphor for Jesus as the word of God or as the revealer of truth.[68] The weapon with which he smites the nations and kills his enemies is the sword that comes from his mouth,[69] which again suggests that it is the speaking of truth which has the decisive effect.[70] In addition, the robe of the rider is described as being dipped in blood even before the fighting has begun. This is the rider's own blood,[71] and makes the link between Jesus's death and the revelation of truth; it alludes to martyrdom. Thus, the victory is achieved through exposure of the truth. As Mealy argues, "Christ's way of expressing his authority to judge and rule was to *expose* the state of things."[72] He claims Jesus's followers join Jesus in bearing witness to the truth about human nature and their martyrdom provides the ultimate proof of their case.

In terms of Girard's theories, Jesus's exposure of the violent basis of human cultural order undermines that order. It also prevents the re-establishment of the historical forms of human culture but makes possible the founding of a culture without mimetic rivalry and therefore capable of permanence. The process described in Revelation during which truth is revealed and sovereignty changes hands, and which takes the form of a move from initial order to restored order,

---

[66] See, e.g., Laws 1978, 1988.52-68. Minear speaks of the transformation of the Christian mode of warfare in the light of the cross. 1968.232-233.

[67] For discussions on the origins and nature of the idea of Holy War in the Hebrew Bible see Niditch 1993b; Von Rad 1959, 1965.2.124, 1991. On the use of Holy War as a motif in Revelation see Bauckham 1993a 210-237; Buchanan 1993; Ford 1975; Giblin 1991; Yarbro Collins 1976.

[68] Court cites Vermes on the Jewish apocalypses, "warlike imagery is part of the apocalyptic style, but it does not necessarily entail violent political action, any more than the bloody metaphors in the description of the rider on the white horse (Rev. 19) would suggest that the early church conceived of the returning Messiah as a cruel war-Lord." 1994.114.

[69] 19:15, 21. See 1:16; 2:12, 16.

[70] See D. Barr 1984.42-43.

[71] Caird 1984, Laws 1978, Rissi 1972.24. Charles 1920 disagrees.

[72] 1992.237.

is accompanied by representations of chaos, as the theories of Girard suggest. It has often been observed that the ethic promoted by Revelation is uncompromising.[73] The text suggests that the systems of economics and power relationships and the systems of public discourse which currently exist or which are about to come into being are wholly alien to God's will. The followers of Jesus are to have nothing to do with other cults or other understandings of the world. They are to provide a contrast to a corrupt culture. This fits a Girardian understanding of the gospel, which sees Christian conversion as a break with the mimetic consensus.

1. Transfer of Sovereignty

The exegesis that follows will try to show that the event described in 5:1-14 represents the exaltation of Jesus and is depicted in terms of his enthronement. The text returns to this scene at a number of points to show the transfer of sovereignty taking place. The first is at 7:9-17, which depicts the martyrs of the great tribulation.[74] By the end of the scene, the Lamb is described as being τὸ ἀνὰ μέσον τοῦ θρόνου (the one in the midst of the throne) implying that his exaltation in heaven has been completed.

A key point occurs at 11:15-19 with the sounding of the seventh trumpet and the announcement that the transfer of sovereignty over the world has been accomplished. The significant verbs are Ἐγένετο at 11:15 and ἐβασίλευσας at 11:17. The former has a perfective sense while the latter is an aorist inceptive giving the translations "has become" and "you have begun to reign" (or "you have become king") respectively. Neither translation is in any way unusual. The majority of English translations render them in similar ways, as does Charles.[75]

The grammar of Revelation offers difficulties to the interpreter and this is especially true of the verbs. The best guides are the Greek tense and the context, rather than any presumed underlying language. Reference might also

---

[73] E.g., Abrams 1984, Aune 1966, L. Thompson 1990.186-197, Yarbro Collins 1986a. See remarks on theology in Ch1.C.7.

[74] 7:14. The Great Tribulation in Jewish literature and the New Testament is discussed by Allison 1985; Bauckham 1974 discusses the use of the motif in the Shepherd of Hermas; L. Thompson 1986 examines the idea of tribulation in Revelation from a sociological perspective.

[75] E.g. *JB, NASB, NEB, NIV, NRSV, RSV. AV* is based on a text which has the relevant words in the plural and translates "are become" at 11:15. At 11:17 it offers "hast taken to thee thy great power and hast reigned". *RV* offers "is become" and "didst reign". *Douai*, following the Vulgate's "factum est...regnasti", has "is become...hast reigned". *TEV* paraphrases "The power to rule over the world belongs now to our Lord and his Messiah...begun to reign" which is similar to Phillips. Charles lists over ten examples of aorists which report an event that has just occurred and should be translated as perfects. 1920.cxvii-clix.

be made to the use of the verbs elsewhere in the book. The verb Ἐγένετο is an aorist. Its perfective nature may be discerned from the context and from the use of the verb at 12:10. There the kingdom of God is announced because Satan has been thrown from heaven. In both 12:10 and 11:15, it is a recent event that is being acclaimed. The alternatives are to take the verb as either a normal or a gnomic aorist. The effect would be to set the transfer of the kingdom in the past or to make it a timeless occurrence. Neither allows it to find a place in the context of a scene of enthronement. In the case of 11:15 such a view would make the future βασιλεύσει, found towards the end of the verse, rather incongruous. Thus the context requires that the verb in question be given a perfective sense, though this does not apply to the aorist plural form of the verb found in the earlier part of the verse.[76]

This uncontroversial understanding of the verbs in 11:15 prepares the ground for reading ἐβασίλευσας as an aorist inceptive. It is already clear to the reader from 4:1-11 that God reigns in heaven. Now God's sovereignty, God's right to rule over the earth, is asserted.[77] There are a number of reasons for taking the verb in this way. Firstly, it helps to make sense of the previous verb, the perfect εἴληφας (you have taken). One could hardly translate the phrase as "you have taken your great power and reigned". Secondly, reigning is not an activity which is readily expressed by means of a punctiliar aorist.[78] Given this, the only possible alternative solution would be to render the aorist as a present giving "you have taken your great power and are king". This is Thompson's solution and is viable only because his prior decision about the underlying Semitic language allows him to ignore the Greek tense. The aorist inceptive is a possible rendering of the Greek and fits the context well and is therefore to be preferred.

These conclusions can be reinforced by reference to the Old Testament traditions drawn upon by the text. The acclamation of 11:15-18 is derived from the declaration of the enthronement psalms. For example, in Psalm 47:8 the מלך אלהים (God is king, God has begun to reign) of the Hebrew text[79] is rendered ἐβασίλευσεν ὁ θεὸς in the Septuagint,[80] the same aorist form adopted in Revelation. Similarly, Psalms 97 and 99 begin with the words יהוה מלך (Yahweh is King, Yahweh has become King) and are rendered ὁ κύριος ἐβασίλευσεν in the Greek.[81] There is some dispute about the way in which the

---

[76] Latin has no aorist and the Vulgate renders with the perfect 'regnasti'.
[77] This may be an example of "illocutionary speech", speech that does not merely transmit disclosures but has transforming effects: speech performs the act. See the discussions in Thiselton 1992.16-19, 286-307 and Wolterstorff 1995.240-280. Barr proposes that oral enactment brings about God's kingdom. 1986.2.
[78] On the non-punctiliar nature of the aorist, see Stagg 1972.
[79] MT 47:9.
[80] LXX 46:9.
[81] LXX 96:1 and 98:1.

Hebrew is best translated. The traditional rendering is "the Lord reigneth",[82] while the Douai's "the Lord hath reigned" reflects the Vulgate's perfect. Mowinckel states that a more adequate translation would be "the Lord has become king" and Day argues persuasively in support of this contention. He discusses Revelation 11:17 and notes that "It is interesting that *ebasileusen* corresponds precisely to the Septuagint's rendering of *mâlak* in the enthronement psalms."[83] Furthermore, Revelation's assertion that God's reign has begun is followed by a statement of the conditions which preceded that moment; τὰ ἔθνη ὠργίσθησαν (the nations raged). A similar concept is found in the psalms, which include the Zion myth, and in the enthronement psalms. The same verb, albeit in a different tense and mood, is found at Psalm 99:1.[84]

The great majority of commentators and translators adopt the translation being proposed. Zerwick offers the translation "Thou hast assumed kingship".[85] Bauer proposes that the relevant part of 11:15 be rendered as "the kingdom of the world has come into the possession of our Lord".[86] Elsewhere he discusses the verb βασιλεύω and offers "*become king, obtain royal power,* so esp. in aor." He cites Revelation 11:17 with reference to this.[87] Mussies cites the same verb as an instance of an aorist which has perfective value. One of the few authorities who disagrees on this point is S. Thompson who argues that the verb in question corresponds to a Semitic stative perfect which should be rendered in the present tense. He refers to the Septuagint of Psalm 98:1 and offers the translation "You are reigning and the nations rage." In fact there is no reason, even on Thompson's own questionable suppositions, why the verb should not be taken as an inceptive with the underlying stative perfect being regarded as describing a new condition. The context, which Thompson agrees is a key factor for decisions about tense, calls for the verb to be taken in an inceptive sense.

The scene at 11:15-19 has the same context as those of 4:2-5:14 and continues the description of the process that began there. The authority of God and the Lamb to rule the earth is asserted. This announcement is repeated at 19:6 where the same verb is used. In this instance the majority of the translations follow the *Authorized Version* and render the verb as a present.[88] There is every reason to take the verb in the same sense as in 11:17. The

---

[82] *A.V. NRSV* offers "the Lord is King".
[83] 1990.75-82.
[84] LXX 98:1.
[85] 1988.759.
[86] 1979.159.
[87] 1979.136.
[88] Moffatt, *NIV, NRSV, RSV, RV, TEV,* But Zerwick suggests an aorist inceptive 1988.772. This is the case with *NEB* which offers "has entered on his reign"; Phillips, "has come into his kingdom"; Weymouth, "has become king". Douai takes the Vulgate's perfect seriously and translates "hath reigned" while Knox's translation of the same text offers "has claimed his kingdom".

announcement is of the commencement of the reign of God over the world.

2. The Unique Quality of the Renewed Creation

Thus, Revelation's account of the change of sovereignty achieved through the exposure of the truth and accompanied by manifestations of chaos, conforms to the narrative pattern suggested by Girard's ideas. However, in one most important sense Revelation fails to conform to the normal pattern of culture. The re-established order with which most narratives end is itself subject to being undermined: it is not a true order but an order of the same quality as the initial order; a system of relationships which masks existing mimetic rivalries and which purports, but fails, to provide a legitimate ordering of human social life. Such order is inevitably temporary. In Revelation, the order with which the narrative ends is final, the end of all the cycles of history; it is an order which has a different basis from all those which have preceded it.

According to Girard's theory, cultural order is only possible on the basis of arbitrary systems of differentiation and any such order is eventually undermined by mimetic rivalry. Yet in the new Jerusalem a new kind of human community life is envisaged. Firstly, arbitrary differences are not used as a basis for hierarchy. In fact even one of the differences between humans and God, that which is expressed in their different realms, is collapsed.[89]

Secondly, and crucially, the sources of mimetic rivalry have been overcome. Throughout Revelation the enemies of God are portrayed as parodies of God and God's agents. This has been noticed by a number of scholars. Laws speaks of God's adversaries as being a parody of God and God's co-workers.[90] Hurtgen sees the text as creating a system of parallel opposites which reflect the tension between the church and the empire.[91] Barnett calls it 'polemical parallelism'.[92] Georgi claims that Revelation teaches that the Roman state and cult ape the authentic eschatological conviction caused by Jesus.[93] Ford actually uses the idea of mimetic rivalry, deriving the language from her reading of Hamerton-Kelly. She argues that in Revelation this rivalry is at the root of idolatry, economic sanctions and murder.[94]

Of course, the human order which is undermined by the action of God is apparent rather than real. According to Girard, social structures mask, as well as control, mimetic rivalry. The text reveals mimetic rivalry on a cosmic level as it shows the ways in which the dragon and his followers imitate the ways of

---

[89] Boring notes that the difference between the sacred and the profane, at least within the new Jerusalem, is abolished in this vision. 1993.
[90] 1988, especially 36-46.
[91] 1993.
[92] 1989.
[93] 1986.124.
[94] 1995.

God and the Lamb. This can be demonstrated by comparing the two beasts of 13:1-18 with the Lamb. The beast from the sea of 13:1-8 has an apparently mortal wound which is healed. The Lamb is described as ὡς ἐσφαγμένον (as if it had been slaughtered) at 5:6 while at 13:3, one of the heads of the beast is ὡς ἐσφαγμένην εἰς θάνατον (as if it had been slaughtered to death). The parody is also found at 17:8 where the beast is described as being the ὅ...ἦν καὶ οὐκ ἔστιν καὶ μέλλει ἀναβαίνειν ἐκ τῆς ἀβύσσου (who was and is not and is going to come up from the abyss) which is designed to recall the titles of God found at 1:4, 1:8 and 4:8, while the shortened version found at 17:11 may recall 11:17 and 16:5. The beast from the earth of 13:11-18 also parodies God and God's agents. Firstly, at 13:11, it is said to have horns ὅμοια ἀρνίῳ (like a lamb). At 13:14 it produces fire as do God's witnesses at 11:5 and as God does at 20:9. At 13:14-15 it promotes idolatry in opposition to the worship of the true God. At 13:16-17 it marks its own with a χάραγμα (mark, seal) in imitation of the seal given to God's servants by God's agents at 7:3-8. In addition, as argued in Chapter 4, both God's agents and their enemies are said to conquer.[95] Next, both Jesus and the beast have mysterious names; Jesus's are mentioned at 19:12-13 while those of the beast and God's other adversaries are referred to at 13:1, 13:18, and 17:3. Finally, and significantly from the perspective of this survey, both claim the right to rule the world. Both share or delegate their rule: God reigns with his Messiah as indicated by 7:17, 11:15, 22:3 and the Messiah's followers may participate in that rule;[96] at 13:4 the dragon delegates power to the beast[97] who rules through the kings of the earth.[98]

The dragon and his agents are the mimetic rivals of God and his agents. As such they are the present rulers of human social life. The exposure of truth that is accomplished by the Lamb reveals both their true nature and the reality of the purported order of existing culture. The establishment of an order without mimetic rivalry is only possible if these forces are 'destroyed'.[99] This is finally accomplished by God, the Lamb and his followers, through their testimony to the truth, at 19:11-21 and 20:7-10. Only when this is done can the vision of the new Jerusalem be presented. As Gundry points out, the new Jerusalem symbolizes people; it is not a topographical concept. It is not the future dwelling place of God's people, but a representation of a future community.[100] The city has no temple and therefore, by implication, no sacrificial cult.[101] Even

---

[95] The intransitive use of the verb is reserved for those on God's side.
[96] 3:21, 5:10, 20:4-6, 22:5.
[97] See also 13:12.
[98] 17:9-14, 18:9.
[99] The use of the language of destruction in this context indicates the difficulty of addressing these issues without resorting to the language of violence and exclusion.
[100] 1987.
[101] 21:22.

the most foundational differences are abolished. God dwells among humans,[102] and shares his prerogatives with humans, his glory,[103] light,[104] and, perhaps most significantly, reign.[105] Furthermore, there is no longer day or night, the dead have been raised and there is no more death,[106] the gates of the city are never shut,[107] the nations freely enter the city,[108] and even the sea, that ancient source of forces inimical to humanity, has gone.[109] Of course, the text does exclude some from the new creation.[110] These are those whose activities would undermine order founded on the absence of mimetic desire. If Girard is correct, then the very structure of language and thought requires exclusion, and so the references to those outside and to the destruction of the forces opposed to God's reign, are both inevitable and necessary to any articulation of a new kind of human social existence.[111] Any utopia is inevitably open to deconstruction.

---

[102] 21:3.

[103] 21:23.

[104] 22:5.

[105] 22:5, the fulfilment of the promises of 3:21 and 5:10.

[106] 20:11-14, 21:4.

[107] 21:25.

[108] 21:24-26.

[109] 21:1. This undifferentiated condition is similar to the phenomenon which V. Turner calls *communitas*. This is a social phenomenon experienced in periods of *liminality*. These occur while people are between statuses in the course of a rite of passage. Participants find themselves outside existing social structures and experience a different quality of life. Many of the characteristics of communitas are also associated with millenarian movements and with pilgrimage. Turner believes that communitas has a valuable social function but that it cannot last and that attempts to maintain it are doomed to failure. Human societies need their ordered structures if they are to endure. Revelation suggests that the defeat of mimetic rivalry might lead to a society which experiences indefinitely the immediacy, spontaneity and equality of communitas. 1967.93-111, 1969.Ch3-4, 1978. See R. Cohn 1981.Ch2. Turner adopts the pattern discerned by Van Gennep 1960.

[110] 21:8, 21:7, 22:15. Boring suggests that Revelation does not close the question of universal and particular. 1993.

[111] Discussions of these chapters include Boring 1993 who argues that they offer an ending but refuse to offer a closure; i.e., they satisfy the human need for an ending to a narrative, but do not resolve every issue. (On the idea that the human sense of structure requires endings in order to allow things to make sense, see Kermode 1995.) Certainly, the ending of Revelation is 'open'. However, it is clearly intended to present creation renewed and at peace. If Girard is correct then it is not certain that human language could articulate an ultimate and undifferentiated order. A similar idea is suggested by Prigent 1980 and by Glasson who speaks of the Parousia as a symbol for "tremendous realities beyond the compass of human language", and refers to Calvin's ideas about the eschaton; "the traditional Last Things are 'images' adapted to our finite understanding." 1988.269. Bull 1995b discusses different categories of endings and views of history. Contemporary versions of apocalyptic thinking are also discussed by Kumar 1995; Norris 1995. And see Derrida who notes that an apocalyptic tone implies that "Truth

In discussing the visions of the defeat of God's enemies and the establishment of the new Jerusalem, it is worth noting how many of the details reflect points made in the opening three chapters of the book, especially the promises made in the messages to the churches. For example, the tree of life,[112] the second death,[113] the unknown name,[114] rule with a rod of iron,[115] the book of life,[116] the new Jerusalem from God,[117] and the rule of the followers of Jesus.[118] This suggests a link between the present experience of the followers of Jesus and their eschatological destiny.[119] The vision which begins at 4:1 represents the process by which that destiny is to be fulfilled.

3. Conclusions

These observations about the structural pattern of Revelation and the agents referred to in the text suggest that the whole book could be read as a representation of the transfer of sovereignty over the earth to God and God's agents from God's adversaries. The transfer is brought about in a process generated by God's revelation of truth achieved in Jesus and in which those who follow Jesus participate. The existing patterns of human social life slowly disintegrate in the light of their exposure to the truth of their own nature. The exposure of truth makes it impossible for traditional forms of human social order to re-establish themselves and no new form of order can be achieved without the 'destruction' of the forces of mimetic rivalry. Only when this is achieved can a form of order not based on existing systems of differentiation become possible. The process by which all this occurs is represented in terms

---

itself is the end, the destination, and that truth unveils itself in the advent of the end. Truth is the end and the instance of the last judgement." 1992.53. But the moment of truth is, as it must be, always deferred; "I shall come: the coming is always to come. The *Adôn*, named as the aleph and the tav, the alpha and the omega, is the one who has been, who is, and who comes, which is the present of a to-come (*à-venir*). *I am coming* means: I am going to come, I am to-come in the imminence of an 'I am going to come,' 'I am in the process of coming,' 'I am on the point of going to come'." 1992.54-55. The truth is ever promised, yet ever deferred; in the process of being attained and articulated, yet forever just beyond grasping. Andrews compares Derrida's views on apocalyptic with Barth's doctrine of salvation. 1996.232-243.

[112] 2:7 and 22:2.
[113] 2:11 and 20:14.
[114] 2:17 and 19:12 and see 19:16.
[115] 2:27 and 19:15 and see 7:17.
[116] 3:5 and 20:12, 20:15.
[117] 3:12 and 21:2, 21:10.
[118] 3:21 and 22:5 and see 20:4-6.
[119] It may also be evidence of the text's literary unity. Images which reappear in the closing scenes of the book are also found at found at 7:15-17. Compare 7:15 with 22:3, and 7:15-17 with 21:1-6.

drawn from the Holy War traditions of Israel and is the wrath of God. It is God's because God has acted to reveal the truth and so generate the process. The violence itself is human. However, since the existing forms of differentiation are undermined, the social chaos of the crisis is experienced by the participants as having a cosmic dimension. That, it is suggested, is the pattern and framework of the narrative of Revelation.

Having offered an outline and an interpretation of the Book of Revelation, it remains to offer an exegetical demonstration that the proposed reading is plausible. The sequences of plagues flow out of the visions of 4:2-5:14. The exegesis will therefore focus on these verses and on 6:1-17 to include most of the first series of plagues. This exercise will indicate the ways in which the other plague sequences, and parts of the rest of the book, might be interpreted. The guiding idea is that the plagues depict the deep and enduring cultural crisis which is triggered by the Christ event and by the representation of that event in the lives of the followers of Jesus.

D. Exegesis: Revelation 4:1-6.17

1. Introduction

Although scholars have offered many different analyses of the literary structure of Revelation, there is one point on which they are almost unanimous; a new section commences at 4:1.[120] The inaugural vision and the associated messages to the seven churches have been reported and the seer is now summoned into heaven through an open door.[121] Of course, this new vision is not unrelated to those which precede it. The voice of 1:10 which summons the seer to turn in order to see the book's inaugural vision of 1:12-16 (out of which flow the announcement, instructions and interpretation of 1:17-19, and the seven messages to the seven churches of 2:1-3:22) is the same voice which summons him into heaven at 4:1.

4:1-11 provides the context for the events described in 5:1-14. The commentators are agreed that the two belong together.[122] This is the scene from

---

[120] E.g. Charles, "with chap. iv. there is an entire change of scene and subject." 1920.1.102. Vögtle, "Das etwas Formeschafte 'Danach sah ich' makiert den Abschluss der einleitenden Christus-Vision und ihrer sieben Sendschreiben" (...'then I saw' marks the end of the introductory Christ vision and its seven letters). Rowland, "the new dimension to John's experience which is reached in 4:2." 1982.415. Ellul is an exception; he argues that 4:1-11 belong with the messages to the churches and that the next section begins at 5:1. 1977.36-64.

[121] On the idea of an open door to heaven see Rinaldi 1963. The image also provides the title for Grayston 1992.

[122] Some claim they form a single vision e.g. Prigent who regards them as "une liturgie juive adaptée au christianisme" (a Jewish liturgy adapted to Christianity) 1964.46.

Outline, Interpretation and Exegesis 179

which the narrative of the rest of Revelation, particularly the sequences of plagues, develops. The first sequence of plagues is released as a consequence of the opening of the seals on the scroll which is introduced at 5:1. The second series is interlocked or intercalated into the first.[123] The third series has parallels with the first two, especially the second, features agents to whom the reader is introduced in 4:1-5:14, assumes the location described there for its context, and refers to its plagues as τὰς ἐσχάτας (the last), implying that they are related to those which have preceded it. This suggests that all the plagues of Revelation are a consequence of the events described in this vision. Therefore, Beasley-Murray is correct to argue that these chapters "may be viewed as the fulcrum of the Revelation".[124] In a similar vein, Rowland regards the scene as "preparatory to the material which forms the core of the book, the sequence of seven seals, trumpets and bowls, all of which arise directly out of" the events it describes.[125] Minear claims "this vision serves to prepare for all the later visions. John viewed the material in Chapters 4 and 5 as basic to the understanding of his whole message."[126] If the rest of Revelation flows out of this scene, then its interpretation is of considerable importance. 4:2-5:14 describe an event or a series of events which launches chaos upon the world. It will be argued that 4:1-11 sees heaven prepared for these things and that 5:1-14 sees them take place.

2. Chapter 4:1-11

The vision of 4:1-11 is one of order and of expectancy. God is worshipped and his sovereignty is uncontested; there is order. Nevertheless, the situation is not timeless.[127] There are things that remain to be done. The heavenly community

---

Others see them as the two elements of a "doppelstuftigen Himmelvision" [double-stepped heavenly vision] (Vögtle 1981.48), or as the beginning of an extended vision which lasts until 8:5 e.g. Yarbro Collins 1976.Ch1. Some writers see the extended vision as lasting till 11:19 or 22:6 or some other point in the text.

[123] For the use of the technique of interlocking, intercalation or dovetailing of the scenes of Revelation see Loenertz 1948; Schüssler Fiorenza 1985.170-177; Yarbro Collins 1976.Ch1.

[124] 1974.108

[125] 1982.415. There is some agreement on this point. Achtemeier 1986 holds that 5:1-14 forms the climax to the book and that the rest of the narrative merely works out its implications. Ulfgard, in establishing the context for his analysis of 7:9-17, accepts that the plagues have their origin in the heavenly liturgy described in 4:2-5:14. 1989.21-27. Oman, however, disagrees and rearranges the text so that the plagues precede these visions. 1923, revised proposal 1928.

[126] 1968.67.

[127] This view is not uncontested. Many commentators see the chapter as reflecting God in creation e.g. C.A. Scott undated, Glasson 1965, and Prigent 1964.47-68 who regards it as an announcement of creation, a liturgy celebrating the creator God. Bock 1957 sees

is presented as anticipating an act which will bring profound change. This is reflected in a number of ways. Firstly, the words of the four living ones[128] at 4:8, in the course of which God is addressed as ὁ ἐρχόμενος (the coming one), suggest that God still has some future act to carry out. The fact that it is God who is described in this way implies that the coming of God remains future. The title is also used at 1:4 and 1:8 but in the present vision or series of visions it is not used once the events of 4:1-5:14 are reported. In fact at 11:17 and 16:5 the other parts of the formula of which this title is an element, (ὁ ἦν καὶ ὁ ὢν [who was and who is]) are used and the omission in those places of ὁ ἐρχόμενος is striking. It implies that the action of God anticipated at 4:8 has been carried out.[129]

Secondly, these words are followed by two verses in which the key verbs δώσουσιν [they will give] (4:9), πεσοῦνται [they will fall down], προσκυνήσουσιν [they will worship] and βαλοῦσιν [they will throw] (4:10) are in the future tense.[130] Nearly all the translations treat these verbs as present

---

it as a depiction of creation at rest in perpetuity. Others regard the scene as a future event e.g. Lohse 1960. Cho 1992, Lindsey 1974, Walvoord 1966 believe that the seer's ascent into heaven represents the future rapture of the true church. Hengstenberg 1851 regards the scene as depicting a future heavenly assembly convened to reach a decision on the ungodly world. Some combine these ideas and see 4:1-11 as a depiction of the future creation, e.g. Torrance 1960 who sees it as a vision of the future in which God is enthroned in a tamed and redeemed creation, beyond the chaos of the present age. There is thus a tendency for commentators to see the vision as representing the eternal state of heaven. Discussions include Beale 1984, who seeks to demonstrate reliance on the structure of Daniel 7; Yarbro Collins 1976.Ch5 who approaches the text from a history of religions perspective and suggests that the scene can be interpreted in terms of the assembly of the gods on the model found in Canaanite mythology and some strands of Old Testament religion (see also 1979); R. Davis 1992 who regards the vision as a judgement session of the divine council, an element of the covenant theme which, he argues, dominates Revelation as a whole; Grayston 1992 who finds symbols derived from Ezekiel 1 and Isaiah 6; and Mowry 1952 where the influence of the Old Testament, especially the Psalms, that of imperial and royal cults, and the liturgy of the synagogue and the early Christian eucharistic rites is emphasized.

[128] These figures seem to have been derived from Ezekiel 1, a text which was of great significance for the development of the apocalyptic tradition of visions of God's throne. Rowland 1979. The location of the living ones in relation to the throne is much discussed in the literature, see Brewer 1952 who has them between the throne and the elders, and Hall 1990 who claims they are a constituent part of God's throne.

[129] It will be argued that God's decisive act is the sending of his Messiah. It is worth noting the Gospels appear to use ὁ ἐρχόμενος as a Messianic title at Mark 11:9 and parallels and Matthew 11:3 and parallel. See Matthew 3:11, Acts 19:4. The title is derived from the Old Testament; LXX has ὁ ἐρχόμενος at Psalm 117:26 (ET 118:26), and note Daniel 7:13, 9:25-27, Malachi 3:1. See Mowinckel 1956.

[130] Textual variants exist for some of the verbs but the principle of *lectio dificilior* leads textual editors to adopt the future tense in each case.

continuous, giving the familiar translation, "whenever the living creatures give glory...the twenty-four elders fall...and worship...they cast their crowns before the throne, singing..."[131] Many commentators choose to follow the translators without drawing attention to the tense of the verbs.[132] Those who do discuss them in order to defend the traditional position are forced to resort to arguments about the context and the natural meaning of the text. Zerwick argues that the futures are used in place of the subjunctives which would be expected after ὅταν (when, whenever).[133] In fact, the grammatical grounds for reading these verbs as present continuous are limited.[134]

In his study of the grammar of Revelation,[135] Charles argues that the verb tenses found in Revelation are not arbitrary but reflect the Hebrew verb tenses. In the case of 4:9-10 he says that the verbs might be rendered either by a past tense or a present. He favours the latter, arguing that "The Greek futures represent Hebrew imperfects...*used in a frequentative sense* - a common usage in Hebrew."[136] Zerwick allows that this is a possibility.[137] However, Charles's case is undermined by the fact that he can cite no other instance of this use in Revelation.[138] Furthermore, Charles argues elsewhere that there is a contrast between 4:1-8 and the action of 9-11. The action in verse 8 is constant but that

---

[131] *NRSV*. *RV* is an exception; it translates the verbs as futures.

[132] E.g. Morris 1987.

[133] 1988.750. There are instances of futures in place of subjunctives in Revelation at 2:22, 25; 3:9; 6:4; 9:4; 9:20, 13:10, 12; 14:13. None of them occurs with ὅταν and in any case many of them, including, e.g. the first three, refer to future, or contingent future, events.

[134] Beckwith 1919 solves the problem by treating the future forms as grammatical errors. While one expects ὅταν to be followed by a verb in the subjunctive, it is occasionally followed by an indicative elsewhere in the New Testament. Porter cites Mark 3:11 (an imperfect), 11:19 (an aorist), and 11:25 (a present). He claims that the major semantic difference is between *asserting* where the indicative is used and *projecting* where the subjunctive is found. 1994.240-242. Moule 1953 suggests ὅταν attaches indefiniteness or contingency to temporal clauses but this is contradicted in Revelation by the use at 8:1 which he does not discuss.

[135] 1920.1.cxvii-clix.

[136] 1920.2.399.

[137] 1988.750.

[138] S. Thompson 1985.Chs3-4 argues that Greek future indicatives are used for Hebrew imperfects in the LXX at Psalm 103:6 and Numbers 17:25. He admits that the usage is very rare. It is a Semitism for there are no parallels in non-Biblical Greek. In fact the instances cited are arguable. The meaning of the latter is adequately rendered by a future for it clearly refers to a contingent future happening. The former occurs within a version of the *Chaoskampf* [struggle against chaos] (103:6-9. See Allen 1987.26). The translators of LXX have rendered many of the key verbs within the section as futures, perhaps because they held an eschatological understanding of the motif. Therefore, these examples give little support to Thompson's, and therefore Charles's, argument about the meaning of Revelation 4:9-10.

of 9-10 is not; it occurs at intervals. The elders do not prostrate themselves constantly but at key points in the narrative; 5:8, 5:14, 11:16 and 19:4. One of them at least has other functions at 5:5 and 7:13. In addition, the living ones are not occupied in continuous praise throughout the rest of the book, they give praise at 5:8, 5:14, and 19:4 for example, but they too have other tasks which they perform at 6:1, 6:3, 6:5, 6:7 and 15:7. Charles's point is that the situation described in 4:1-8 is different from that found in the rest of Revelation.[139] This is surely right, but the argument undermines Charles's case for refusing to read the verbs of 4:9-10 as futures. If 4:1-8 present a different situation from the rest of Revelation, then it may be best to read 4:9-11 as a promise of what is to happen in the future.[140]

This is the view of Corsini. He argues that the word ὅταν (4:9) is used in order to refer to a specific future moment which is described in 5:1-14.[141] He argues that the moment represents the end of the Old Economy which was brought about by the death of Christ who acquires the mediatory functions previously held by the angels.[142]

Corsini's belief that the move from Revelation 4 to Revelation 5 takes the reader from the Old Testament into the New is shared by Rowland who has pointed out that there is nothing in the vision of 4:2-11 which is distinctively

---

[139] 1920.1.127

[140] Mussies finds no grammatical grounds for rendering the verbs of 4:9-11 in the present or past tenses. He cites examples of iterative verbs elsewhere in the text. 1971.344. He argues that the decision as to tense is to be made on exegetical grounds. Since Mussies believes that the events of 4:2-11 lie in the future, he argues that the verbs refer to unique 'one-off' future events, not to reiterated actions. 1971.342-347. A few commentators, e.g. Krodel 1989 and Warner 1944 agree that the verbs should be translated as futures.

[141] The word ὅταν occurs in Revelation at 8:1, 10:7, 11:7, 12:4, 17:10, 18:9 and 20:7. Bauer suggests that ὅταν plus the future means whenever but Revelation 4:9 is the only instance cited. 1979.588. There are no other instances in Revelation where it is used to mean *whenever* but it is frequently used to mean *when*. There are no instances of its being followed by a verb that is iterative. On the contrary, the following verbs are often punctiliar as at 10:7 and 11:7. This is certainly the case at 8:1 where the following verb is an aorist indicative! Such evidence as there is in Revelation suggests that Corsini is correct and that ὅταν followed by a verb in the indicative is best rendered as *when* with the verb having a punctiliar sense. S. Thompson 1985.Ch3 suggests that a number of futures in Revelation which represent a Hebrew imperfect and which could legitimately be rendered in the present or past tenses. These are 5:10, 11:15, 17:8, 18:8, 21:3. None are preceded by ὅταν and all are arguable.

[142] 1983. Corsini believes that 4:2-11 gives a picture of creation and the Old Economy while redemption and the New Economy are pictured in 5:1-14. A similar view is advocated by Harrington 1993, Hopkins 1965. Preston 1949 suggests 4:2-11 depicts the heaven of the old dispensation.

Christian.[143] He claims,

> This chapter shows no evidence at all of Christian influence, and, treated in isolation, it is evident that it is entirely Jewish in its inspiration. Indeed, the author obviously intends a deliberate contrast between the description of the divine court in Revelation 4 and the transformation which takes place as the result of the exaltation of the Lamb.[144]

The seer describes "the situation in heaven before the advent of Christ."[145] Rowland argues that there is a clear tension established by the text between heaven, where God's sovereignty is universally recognized, and the earth where his dominion is acknowledged by few.

The argument that the verbs of 4:9-10 should be read as futures is supported by the fact that most of them are repeated in the past tense in the succeeding chapters. The living ones give glory to the one seated on the throne and/or to the Lamb at 5:13 and may be understood to do so at 5:8-10 and 19:4 and they

---

[143] Hurtado 1985 disagrees. He reviews Jewish apocalyptic analogies to 4:2-11 and concludes that there are no parallels to the twenty-four elders of 4:4. He discusses the views of the major commentators and concludes that the elders possess characteristics promised to Christians in 2:1-3:22, and that they therefore represent the Christian elect. In fact the elders do not have all the things promised. They lack food from the tree of life (2:7), the manna, white stone and new name (2:17), the morning star (2:28). None of the claimed correspondences are exact except for the white robes (3:5, 18). So, while it may be true that there is no clear parallel to the elders in the Jewish apocalypses, it is far from clear that they represent Christians. As Ladd 1972 points out, they are not among the redeemed of 7:9-11. The interpretative options are discussed by Feuillet 1958 who concludes that the elders are Old Testament saints. There is certainly insufficient evidence to use these figures to overturn Rowland's case that 4:2-11 shows heaven as it was before the Christ event. (Kiddle 1940 holds that humanity is absent from the scene). Prévost 1993 takes the view that while the vision is influenced by the Old Testament, (he agrees with Feuillet about the identity of the elders) it has Christian elements throughout. His arguments rely on the location of the passage between 2-3 and 5 which he regards as Christian, and on the voice of 4:1 which the text identifies with the voice of 1:10 and which Prévost assumes is the voice of the one like a son of man whom the seer turns to see (1:12-16). The first argument is not valid. Revelation 4 starts a new vision which does not take its context solely from the visions which precede it, although they are not irrelevant to its interpretation. The second relies on a presumption that may well be false. In 1:10 the seer may not have been summoned by the one he turned to see. The voice of 1:10 and 4:1 may well be an angelic being of the type that Charlesworth 1986 calls a hypostatic voice. Even if the voice is Christ's, it may be that the vision of Chapters 4-5 is best regarded as beginning at 4:2 when the seer announces that he became ἐν πνεύματι (in spirit).

[144] 1982.222. See also Rowland 1979 who discusses the relationship of 4:1-11 to visions of God in Jewish apocalyptic literature.

[145] 1982.462. Harrington also takes this view. He points out that, unlike 5:1-14, there is no specifically Christian content in the hymns of 4:2-11. 1969.109.

may well participate at 5:12 and 7:11-12. The elders fall down and worship at 5:8-10, 14; 11:16; and 19:4. The exception is the throwing down of crowns which is not reported elsewhere in the book. This is not likely to be a continuous or even a frequent practice. The image suggests an individual event of some significance. It may provide a clue as to the nature of the anticipated action of God. The image suggests the transfer of the sovereign power represented by the crown.[146] After all, each elder has his own throne and a golden crown (4:4) which suggests that each has a realm of sovereignty.[147]

Other reasons for regarding 4:2-11 as an anticipatory scene can be discerned from some of the details in 5:1-14. For example, at 5:9 the living ones and the elders sing a new song. Heaven has changed and a new song is required to express the praise which is now due. Sweet suggests that the new song connotes the dawning of a new age for within Judaism Psalm 98:1 was linked to Isaiah 42:9-10 and was thought to refer to the messianic era.[148]

A final reason is related to the genre of Revelation. The text makes use of motifs derived from apocalypses but does not use them in ways which those familiar with the tradition might expect. For example, Rowland has suggested that Jewish apocalypses contain two types of material; mystical ascents into the heavenly realms in which divine secrets are mediated to the seer through angelic intermediaries, and dream-visions which are subsequently interpreted and in which the objects seen are not thought to have any real existence in the heavenly world. Revelation 4 begins with an account of a mystical ascent which leads to a sight of the throne. However, in Chapter 5 we read of a lion and a lamb. These words belong to the language of symbolic visions.[149] The text shatters the distinction between the types of apocalyptic material and so suggests, in its form, that something new and decisive is being described. This transformation occurs between Chapters 4 and 5.

The covenant imagery within 4:2-11 should also be noted. Without denying

---

[146] Tacitus is often cited as support for this. He reports that Tiridates placed his diadem, an emblem of his royalty, before a statue of Nero as a pledge of his submission and acknowledgement of his vassal status. *Annals* 15.29

[147] If the scene depicts the heavenly council as suggested by Yarbro Collins 1976 and Davis 1992, it is possible that the elders should be understood as the angels who ruled the world as God's agents and who now hand over this responsibility to another. The LXX of Deuteronomy 32:8 suggests that angelic figures had different peoples or regions apportioned to them. A similar idea may lie behind the enigmatic statement of the angel at Daniel 10:13. Corsini suggests that the angelic court is shown renouncing the mediatorial role it enjoyed during the Old Economy.

[148] See also Psalms 33:3, 40:3, 96:1, 144:9, 149:1. Tate 1990.512-515, 524-525 suggests that in Psalms 96:1 and 98:1 as in Isaiah 42:10, the new songs celebrate new works of God. Both Psalms are said to be in praise of the kingship of Yahweh.

[149] 1981. Rowland claims there are few, if any, parallels to this in the relevant literature although Daniel 7 may be an instance.

the debt of the whole vision to Ezekiel 1,[150] the rainbow of 4:3 may recall that of Genesis 9:12-17 which symbolized God's covenant with all flesh. The lightning, sounds and thunder of 4:5 (repeated and augmented after each of the series of plagues at 8:5, 11:19 and 16:18-21) is probably derived from Exodus 19:16 where these phenomena are related to God's Sinai theophany and the establishment of the Mosaic covenant.[151] This imagery suggests that the action which is about to take place is linked to things promised by God in the past; divine initiatives ratified by covenant but as yet unfulfilled in whole or in part.

Thus, Revelation 4 pictures heaven on the verge of a new happening. Something decisive is about to take place. It will be God's coming and it will change the roles of the heavenly functionaries; the elders and the living ones. Bauckham believes that God's coming is related to the establishment of God's kingdom, God's sovereignty on earth as it is in heaven. The casting of crowns by the elders suggests such an idea. This would accord with the omission of the title ὁ ἐρχόμενος (the one to come) from the formula at 11:16 for there God's rule over the world has been announced. Therefore, Bauckham is on the right lines when he writes,

> Chapter 4 is primarily a revelation of God's sovereignty, as it is manifest and acknowledged in heaven. Only a little acquaintance with prophetic-apocalyptic literature is required for a reader to infer that this vision prepares for the implementation of God's sovereignty on earth, where it is presently hidden and contested by the powers of evil. In other words, the kingdom of heaven is to come on earth as it already exists in heaven.[152]

The scene is set. Heaven is about to witness something which will bring about what God has promised. It will be an event which will have a profound effect in heaven and, it is implied, will be decisive for the future of the earth; it will be the thing which brings about the rule of God over the earth. The means by which God's promise is to be fulfilled remains unclear at the end of Chapter 4. The next scene suggests the answer.

---

[150] See Rowland 1979.

[151] Similar thunderstorm imagery, plus that of earthquake found in the parallel passages at 8:5, 11:19, 16:18 is found in descriptions of theophany throughout the Old Testament, e.g. Judges 5:4-5, Psalms 18:7-15, 29:3-9, Habakkuk 3:3-15. See *Pseudo-Philo* 11.4, which links all the traditional signs of theophany with the establishment of the "eternal covenant" at Sinai. On the earthquake in Revelation see Bauckham 1977a, 1993a.199-209.

[152] 1993a.249. Elsewhere Bauckham suggests that Revelation should be understood as a description of the fulfilment of the first three petitions of the Lord's Prayer, 1993bCh2. This position was adopted in some medieval exegesis. See Matter 1992.49.

3. Chapter 5:1-14

A scroll sealed with seven seals is seen in the hand of God (5:1).[153] Its nature, contents and meaning are discussed and disputed at some length in the literature.[154] The correct interpretation will be one which fits the picture which has been built so far. It will be related to the execution of the event for which heaven is waiting. The scroll refers to the deed of God or of God's agents which inaugurates the action for which heaven has been waiting, the establishment of God's sovereignty over the earth.

Among the theologians of the early church, the scroll was generally understood as the Old Testament. It had been a closed book but now Christ has opened it so that its true meaning can be understood and taught by the church. This is the view of Victorinus who writes, "therefore He is called Apocalypse, Revelation. For now His book is unsealed - now the offered victims are perceived - now the fabrication of the priestly chrism; moreover the testimonies are openly understood." Hippolytus says of Christ, "He took the book, therefore, and loosed it, in order that the things spoken concerning Him of old in secret, might now be proclaimed with boldness upon the house-tops."[155]

Similar interpretations have been adopted by modern scholars. Mowry regards the scroll as the Torah which is unsealed, that is made comprehensible, through Jesus.[156] Sweet prefers the idea that the scroll is both the Law and the prophetic interpretation of the Law; "the total revelation of God's will and plan

---

[153] An interesting parallel is found in *The Odes of Solomon* 23:5-22 where the thought of the Lord is compared to a letter which many sought to read but no people were allowed to read for the power of its seal was greater than they. Aune 1982 discusses the relationship between the Odes and early Christian prophecy including Revelation.

[154] While it is agreed that the image is derived from Ezekiel 2:9-10, the type of scroll meant is disputed. See e.g. Bornkamm 1937, Ford 1971, Ramsay 1905, Roller 1937, Yarbro Collins 1976.Ch1. A related issue is whether it could be opened until all seven seals were broken. Bornkamm says not but Charles describes a scroll so constructed that to break the first seal allowed part of the scroll to be read while the remainder remained secure. The same applied to each succeeding sealed portion. 1920.1.137. For some, this leads to a debate about whether the events which occur at the seal-openings should be regarded as the contents of the scroll. Bornkamm says not; the scrolls contents are revealed from 8:1 onwards after the last seal is broken. This appears over-literal. There is also disagreement over which, if any, of the visions of the rest of the book should be regarded as the content of the scroll; just the events which occur at the loosing of the seals or the other series of plagues too? The relationship between the βιβλίον (scroll) of 5:1 and the βιβλαρίδιον (little scroll) of 10:2 is also disputed. Bauckham follows Mazzaferri in arguing that the two are the same. 1989.264-279. This leads Bauckham to suggest that the scroll's contents are to be sought in 11:1-13. 1993a243-283.

[155] *On Daniel* 20. Origen argues that the scene refers to the allegorical interpretation of scripture which he advocated. *The Philocalia* 2.1.5.5.

[156] 1952.

in scripture."[157] This is likely to be the correct solution. It is in accord with the observation that the words γεγραμμένον ἔσωθεν καὶ ὄπισθεν (written on the inside and the outside) at 5:1 allude to Ezekiel 2:10.[158] The scroll contains the promises of God, of both judgement and salvation, as they have been revealed to God's people and written in the Hebrew Bible. Another common view is that the scroll contains God's plan for the cosmos.[159] This view is not incompatible

---

[157] 1979.123. Prévost 1993, Prigent 1964 agree that the scroll is the Old Testament.

[158] See also Isaiah 29:11. Beale 1984 discusses the influence of the Old Testament, especially Daniel, upon this vision.

[159] Perhaps the most popular understanding is the one that sees the scroll as containing God's plan of redemption which has now been put into effect. This is the view of Allo 1921, Ashcraft 1972, Barclay 1976, Beckwith 1919, Caird 1984, Coffin 1951, Court 1994, Lilje 1957, Loenertz 1947, Mounce 1977, Scullion 1969. Rowland writes of "God's purposes for the restoration of the world which are set in train by the coming of the Messiah." 1993.74. Lohse combines this view with the view that the scroll is a legal document; "eine Urkunde" (a title deed). This legal document contains, "den endzeitlichen Geschichtsplan Gottes; denn mit der Lösung der sieben Siegel werden die Geschicke der letzten Zeit entbunden." (God's end time history plan; that with the opening of the seventh seal delivers the fates of the last times.) 1960.38. A variant on this view is held by Swete 1907 who, followed by Burnet 1946, argues that the scroll is the Book of Destiny. Yarbro Collins's history of religions approach leads her to the conclusion that the scroll represents the secret tablets of destiny associated with kingship in the relevant mythological literature. 1976.Ch1. A range of other interpretations has been offered. Niles 1962 suggests it is the Lamb's Scroll of Life which is referred to at 3:5; 13:8; 17:8; 20:12, 15; 21:27. He is supported by R. Davis 1992. However, this fails to address the link between the opening of the scroll and the sequences of plagues. Many scholars believe, as Davis argues, that Revelation 4-5 is a court scene and this influences their view of the scroll. Mealy believes that one of Christ's roles is as, "the witness whose testimony before God is instrumental in convicting the guilty." 1992.66. Grayston 1992 believes the scroll contains the facts which are to be used in God's indictment of humanity. The Lamb who opens the scroll is a victim who acts as a witness for the prosecution. Others share the view that the scroll is a legal document. Ford 1971 finds the background in the ritual described in Numbers 5:12-31. She believes the scroll is a bill of divorce that provides for disciplinary punishments which give the wife opportunity to repent. The Lamb is to divorce unfaithful Jerusalem and then marry the new Jerusalem. Roller 1937, followed by Mealy 1992, regards the scroll as a certificate of debenture recording the debt of one party to the other. The debt is owed to God and those who have failed to pay are liable to judgement. Krodel 1989 believes that the scroll is a document that transfers authority from God to the Son. Buchanan 1993 argues that it is the testament which enables Israel to inherit the Promised Land. Ramsey 1905 suggests that the scroll contains a record of the covenant between God and humanity. While these views give helpful insights into the role of the Lamb in bringing judgement, these proposals fail to connect the scroll to the Old Testament prophets. Some cast little light on the meaning of the sequences of plagues which follow. All rely on the idea that the scene is one of a court in session. This position cannot be readily demonstrated. Beasley-Murray 1974 argues that this is not a

with the view that the book is the Old Testament understood as a book full of promises of salvation and threats of judgement which have yet to find their ultimate fulfilment.

In Chapter 4 the reader finds a scene that represents heaven as it awaits the event which will herald the fulfilment of God's covenanted promises. The scene depicts the expectancy of heaven during the time of the Old Testament. Chapter 5 sees that Testament opened so that its promises can be fulfilled. The deed which was necessary to bring about the things which had been written has been accomplished; the promises of God are now made effective.

To take the scroll and break it open is to launch the process by which God's kingdom comes. Up until this point, nobody had proved able to accomplish this. God's plan for the end times, his eschatological purposes, remained sealed, awaiting the event which would put them into operation. This explains the tears of the seer when none could be found who could open the scroll (5:4). The expectancy of heaven described in Chapter 4 has raised his own sense that the beginning of the fulfilment of the promises of God is imminent. Now he thinks that nothing can put those promises into effect. This raises questions about the integrity of God and the purpose of his own faith and faithfulness.

It is at this point that one of the elders tells of the Lion of the tribe of Judah, the Root of David. This language suggests that the Jewish Messiah has accomplished that which needed to be done for God's eschatological activity to be initiated.[160] However, when the Seer actually looks, he sees not a lion but a lamb standing as though slaughtered. Caird stresses the contrast between the images of the lion and the lamb and suggests that the text gives the reader an indication of Revelation's method of Old Testament interpretation;

> It is almost as if John were saying to us..."Wherever the Old Testament says **'Lion'**, read **'Lamb'**." Wherever the Old Testament speaks of the victory of the Messiah or the overthrow of the enemies of God, we are to remember that the gospel recognizes no other way of achieving these ends than the way of the Cross.[161]

---

judgement scene but an exultant vision about the coming of the kingdom of God. Aune 1993 also doubts the alleged judicial context of these verses. Stefanovic 1995 believes the scroll is the book handed to the true Davidic king on his coronation.

[160] Most of the commentaries discuss the phrases ὁ λέων ὁ ἐκ τῆς φυλῆς Ἰούδα (the lion of the tribe of Judah) which is usually traced to Genesis 49:9, and ἡ ῥίζα Δαυίδ (the root of David) which is said to be derived from Isaiah 11:1. Both are said to be texts which were interpreted in terms of the expected Messiah. Krodel 1989 also cites Testament of Judah 24:5, 1 Maccabees 3:4, 4 Ezra 11:1-23, 46.

[161] 1984.75. Some years previously Burnet noted that "It is very hard to resist the idea that John is setting side by side here the Messiah as longing Israel envisaged Him, and the true Messiah as He was revealed in Christ." 1946.64. Caird's view has been

Caird's position has been adapted by Bauckham who offers other examples from Revelation of contrasts between that which is heard and that which is seen.[162] He resists some of the implications of Caird's position, insisting that Revelation's use of militaristic language, for example, is not without purpose: there is a battle to be fought even if war is to be waged in a different way; through martyrdom rather than armed conflict.[163] The study of Moyise into the use of the Old Testament in Revelation confirms Bauckham's perspective and adds that the effect of the militaristic language on the reader is intended; the text forces an interaction between military imagery and Christian ethics.[164]

Nearly all the commentators are agreed that the Lion and the Lamb are symbols for a messianic figure,[165] but some resist the idea of such a strong contrast between the two animal images. They reject Caird's assertion that "**The Lamb** is the symbol of self-sacrificing and redemptive love."[166] Barrett, who argues that Revelation was compiled over many years and from many sources, suggests that the word Lamb is "practically a technical term for the Messiah",[167] the imagery having been inherited from early Christianity and Jewish apocalyptic. Lindars proposes a misreading of a text in 1 Enoch as evidence for Lamb as a Jewish title for the expected Messiah.[168] Hooker agrees that the origin of the title should be sought in Jewish apocalyptic texts.[169] O'Neill discusses the evidence from The Testaments of the Twelve Patriarchs.[170] Ford agrees that the Lamb of Revelation is the apocalyptic ram; he is a military leader who was slain on the battlefield.[171] Buchanan suggests that the references to the death of the Lamb may be Christian emendations to the Jewish apocalyptic original. The source shared the traditional understanding that the Messiah was, "expected to overpower all ruling forces by his military

---

influential; the Lamb is regarded as a thoroughly Christian and pacific symbol by Laws 1988, Weber 1988 and M. Williams 1989.

[162] 1993a.179-180.
[163] He discusses Revelation as a "Christian War Scroll" in 1993a.210-237.
[164] 1995.108-138. See Harrington 1993.
[165] But see Gascoyne's 1875 anti-Catholic interpretation which understands heaven to refer to the visible church. He explicitly denies that the Lion and the Lamb are the same. The Lion stands for the sacramental elements which are falsely worshipped by the officiating priests while the Lamb represents a stage when the church was only nominally Christian.
[166] 1984.74. Many rely on the fact that while ἀρνίον technically a diminutive of ἀρήν, it had lost its diminutive force by the time of the New Testament (Bauer 1979.108).
[167] 1954-1955.
[168] 1976.
[169] 1959.126, following Dodd 1954.231-232.
[170] 1979. The key texts are Joseph 19:8 and Benjamin 3:1, 6-8.
[171] 1975. The seven horns on the Lamb suggest it may be a ram but these are stated to be the seven spirits of God sent out into all the world. Dix 1927 discusses the origin and development of this image. On the Spirit in Revelation see Waddell 2006.

strength and take control of the Promised Land, ruling there as king."[172] One difficulty with the reliance on The Testaments of the Twelve Patriarchs is that it is difficult to demonstrate that the texts are pre-Christian.[173] The ones usually cited have almost certainly been subjected to Christian interpolation. It should also be noted that there is little other evidence that Revelation cites or refers to the extant apocalyptic texts in the way in which it does to the Hebrew Bible.[174] Nevertheless, the writers who take this view are right to point out the paradoxical nature of the Lamb motif. This is a Lamb that leads a body of followers;[175] who is slain yet stands;[176] an apparently unclean thing at the centre of God's purposes.[177]

The commentators who accept the idea that the animal figures of Revelation 5 are designed to contrast with one another are divided over the source from which the symbol of the Lamb is derived. A number of alternatives are advocated and it is not uncommon for writers to suggest that the symbol combines motifs drawn from more than one source.[178] Writers who believe that Revelation and the Fourth Gospel share the same author, or that both are products of a Johannine School, frequently rely on the use of the Lamb image in both documents.[179] In fact the two texts use different terms when referring to the Messiah. The Gospel has ὁ ἀμνός (*ho amnos*)[180] while Revelation has τὸ ἀρνίον (*to arnion*).[181] Furthermore, the Lamb in Revelation is never described as τοῦ θεοῦ (of God). It therefore cannot be assumed that the imagery of Revelation has been influenced by that of the Fourth Gospel.

It is frequently suggested that the image is derived from Isaiah 53.[182] Inman finds overtones of dumbness, passivity and acceptance in the description in Chapter 5, which she believes relate to the Lamb's role as a servant.[183] At 5:6, the Lamb is described as ὡς ἐσφαγμένον (as having been slain or slaughtered). In Isaiah 53:7 there is reference to a lamb that is led to the

---

[172] 1993.147. He says that Caird "failed to notice how often the Lamb in the Book of Revelation behaved like a lion."
[173] Jonge 1975a.b: 1988.
[174] Bauckham 1993a. 38-91 shows no literary dependence of Revelation on Jewish apocalyptic texts but does demonstrate its distinctive use of traditional apocalyptic motifs. Charles 1920 discusses the influences.
[175] 14:1-5.
[176] 5:6. See Acts 7:55-56.
[177] Leviticus 11:39. (Unless the Lamb is regarded as having been ritually killed.)
[178] E.g. Bauckham 1993a.215, Hillyer 1967, Reddish 1988.
[179] On the issue of the existence of a Johannine School, see Schüssler Fiorenza 1977a, 1985.85-113.
[180] John 1:29, 36.
[181] The plural form of the latter is found in the Gospel at 21:15 but refers not to the Messiah but to members of the Christian community. See Whale 1987.
[182] E.g. Daalen 1986. This position is criticized by Hooker 1959.126 and see 1982.
[183] 1993.

slaughter and to a sheep which is silent before its shearers. The Septuagint offers the translations πρόβατον (sheep) and ἀμνὸς (lamb) in that order; not the words found in Revelation. However, the word used for slaughter is σφαγὴν, a cognate of the word found in Revelation. An allusion to Isaiah 53 is therefore possible but by no means certain. The related verb is used elsewhere in the text of Revelation. It is applied to the Lamb at 5:6, 9, 12, 13:8; it is applied to the martyrs at 6:9; to the behaviour of humans once peace has been taken away at 6:4 (the only active use); to the beast from the sea at 13:3; and all who have been slain on the earth at 18:24.

Other authors suggest that the image is related to the sacrificial cult, to the Aqedah,[184] or to the Passover Lamb of Exodus.[185] The latter idea gains support from the extensive use of Exodus imagery found elsewhere in Revelation[186] and from the understanding of atonement found in the book. At 5:10, one part of the Lamb's work is to make those whom he has purchased into a kingdom and priests who will reign upon the earth. This idea is probably derived from Exodus 19:6 where it describes the vocation of Israel. This link with the Exodus story suggests that the Lamb of Revelation has Passover implications. Casey suggests that Revelation regards the Exodus story as a paradigm for God's continuing activity.[187]

The proposed understandings of the Lamb motif are often reflections of prior decisions about the genre of Revelation, rarely on the role played by the Lamb in the text.[188] If, as has been suggested, the text uses many of the techniques associated with apocalyptic writings but deliberately abandons the literary conventions associated with the genre for polemical purposes, then it may be that the symbols used are being given new values.[189] Caird and

---

[184] The telling or re-telling of the story of the sacrifice of Isaac. See Bredin 1996. He acknowledges that no direct link can be established. It is an interesting conjecture but cannot be determinative for exegetical purposes.

[185] This is the view of Holtz 1962.39-47, Prigent 1964.69-76 and Schüssler Fiorenza 1985.95-96. Other proposals have been made. Grayston 1992 sees the Lamb as a representative victim reading the indictment against oppressors. Reddish 1988 sees the Lamb as a martyrological title. Kraft 1974 sees the Lamb as an innocent sufferer.

[186] E.g. 1:6, 5:10, 15:3 and the parallels between the plagues of Exodus and of Revelation. See Casey 1987, Hre Kio 1989 and Ulfgard 1989.35-41.

[187] "the redemption from among humankind of a people to become a kingdom and priests to God is effected by the sacrifice of the Lamb and is presented in a pattern moulded by the Exodus tradition of redemption." 1987.35-36. Daube shows that the Exodus pattern is linked to God's activity throughout the Bible. However, LXX does not use ἀρνίον of the Passover Lamb. Prigent believes the motif alludes to Isaiah 53, the Passover and to a military leader. 1981.97-98.

[188] A classification of the status and functions of the Lamb in Revelation may be found in Hasitschka 1994. And see the structural approaches of Calloud 1977 and Prigent 1979-1980.

[189] The image of a slain lamb standing is not found in the Jewish apocalypses.

Bauckham would then be right to speak of a contrast between what is heard and what is seen. It is in the contrast that the primary meaning should be sought. This endorses Farrer's view that Revelation represents a rebirth of traditional images,[190] Deutsch's understanding of it as a text which transforms existing religious and political symbols,[191] and D. Barr's argument that Revelation offers its hearers a symbolic transformation of the world through the radical transvaluation of images from traditional apocalyptic.[192] The expectations of Jewish apocalyptic are metamorphosed into the realities of Christian experience. The seer hears about the Lion, the anticipated warrior messiah, but sees the slain Lamb. He expects a warrior and sees a victim. The promise is fulfilled in an unexpected way. It is the slain Lamb who opens the scroll.

The right of the Messiah to open the scroll is achieved not by virtue of who he is but by virtue of what he has accomplished. In the case of the Lion, the achievement is unclear. The text says the lion ἐνίκησεν (has conquered), the verb being used without an object. In the case of the Lamb, the accomplishment is clarified when the living ones and the elders sing the new song of 5:9-10. This being was slaughtered and purchased a people for God. If the Lion and the Lamb are both images used for the Messiah then the act of conquering which the Messiah was expected to execute has been achieved through his being killed. Elsewhere in Revelation, the verb 'slaughter' or 'slay' is used of people killing one another at 6:4, of the martyrs of 6:9-11 and of victims generally at 18:24. 12:11 explicitly links conquering and dying. The verbs used to describe what the Lion has done and what the Lamb has done are, in Revelation, two ways of saying the same thing. The Lamb accomplishes God's promised action by being a victim.

The effect of the achievement of the Messiah is that the scroll can be opened. The scroll contains the Hebrew Scriptures, the promises of which await fulfilment. The Messiah has done what is necessary to initiate the process by which they will be fulfilled. This is the moment for which heaven as it is depicted in Chapter 4 has been waiting. The actions promised in 4:9-10 take place.[193] In a series of concentric circles, all creation acknowledges what has happened. First at 5:8-10 the elders and the living ones, those closest to the throne of God, fall down and acclaim. Then at 5:11-12 the myriads of angels join in. Finally, at 5:13, no creature in any part of the creation is excluded.

---

[190] 1949.13-22.

[191] 1987.

[192] 1984. Prigent claims "the Lamb represents the perfect reversal of values" (l'agneau représente l'inversion parfaite des valeurs.) 1979-1980.129.

[193] Other apocalyptic texts suggest that the exaltation of the Messiah in heaven brings about changes in that realm. See, e.g., The Ascension of Isaiah where the descent of the Messiah from the fifth heaven downwards goes unrecognized but his ascent is noticed at every level and culminates in his taking a seat at the right hand of God. (9:6-11:43) It is only when the Messiah ascends that the righteous receive their robes, thrones and crowns (9:17-18).

Everything joins in the praise. This can only be the eschaton for everything in heaven and earth is in agreement and acknowledges the rule of God and the Lamb.[194] The achievement of the Messiah and the eschaton are here represented in one scene. The latter is depicted as a consequence of the former. The process by which the promises of God are fulfilled culminates in the eschaton and, from the perspective of this scene, the beginning and the end of the process are almost simultaneous. From one perspective, the Christ event and the eschaton are one happening. It is all one and the same event and the eschaton is viewed as being already achieved.[195] At the eschaton, the elders fall and worship (5:14). The verbs are in the aorist. An event which was future in the old dispensation has become a fact of the new dispensation. From another perspective, the eschaton remains future; there is a process to be endured before it can be reached and this process is described in the rest of the book. The involvement of God's people in this process is suggested by the clue which the text gives to the meaning of the incense in the golden bowls which the elders hold as they prostrate themselves before the Lamb; it is the prayers of the saints.[196] The context in which this is acclaimed is one of worship. It suggests that worship is the context in which the reign of God is realized and experienced in the present, even as it awaits its future culmination.[197]

A number of scholars have attempted to find an analogy from human cultural life that would enable us to name the ritual which is described in Revelation 5. It is sometimes argued that the word ἄξιος (worthy) is derived from the acclamation of the emperor in the imperial cult.[198] This leads to the suggestion that an enthronement is taking place; the Lamb is being enthroned as king, or perhaps as God's co-regent, in heaven.[199]

---

[194] The cultic setting of realized eschatology in Revelation and other early Christian texts is discussed by Aune 1972. L. Thompson 1969 discusses the relationship between worship and eschatology in Revelation.

[195] Cullmann says of the cross and resurrection of Jesus that all God's plan for salvation history is "latently contained" within it. 1967.166.

[196] As Heil points out, the only prayer of supplication in Revelation is that found at 6:10. 1993.

[197] Aune suggests that worship in the Spirit is a proleptic experience of the promised eschatological existence, a provisional realization of the final goal. "In the Apocalypse of John...the final judgement is realized in the present within the context of worship." 1972.14. See D. Barr 1984; L. Thompson 1969.

[198] Schüssler Fiorenza 1991. The influence of the imperial cult on Revelation is discussed by Aune 1983b, Janzen 1994, Kraybill 1996, Moore 1995, Scherrer 1984. On the cult in Asia Minor see Price 1984.

[199] Van Unnik 1970 criticizes this position and traces the idea of worthiness to the possession of a right inner attitude, revealed through testing, which entitles its possessor to approach a magical or divine book. Beasley-Murray 1974 responds to the criticism and finds evidence of exaltation, presentation and authority which he regards as elements of an enthronement ceremony.

This view may be supported by the fact that the scene that is revealed at the sounding of the seventh trumpet at 11:15-19 takes place in the same location as 4:1-5:14. The elders appear again, falling down in worship of God. During this scene, the loud voices of heaven announce at 11:15 that sovereignty over the world has changed so that the kingdom of the world now pertains to God and his Messiah. God is worshipped but is no longer called ὁ ἐρχόμενος (the coming one); the promised intervention has taken place, God is no longer appropriately described as the one who is to come for he now reigns with his Messiah alongside him.[200]

The seer is witnessing the enthronement of the Lamb in heaven. The Messiah who was slain is being appointed king in heaven. In the final form of its text, Revelation is clearly a Christian document and Chapter 5 is best understood as a representation of the early Christian kerygma about Jesus who died and then ascended to the right hand of God.[201] It was believed that heavenly beings, angelic powers, became subject to Jesus at his exaltation.[202] This observation suggests, but does not require, that the elders of Revelation 4 should be regarded as angelic beings.[203] This is what is depicted in Revelation 5: the initiation and the culmination of the eschatological process;[204] God's vindication of the victim.

---

[200] This argument is reinforced by the observation that Revelation 11:15-19 contains allusions to Psalm 2 which depicts the enthronement of God's chosen king. See Craigie 1983.64-69.

[201] E.g. Acts 2:22-36, 5:28-32, 7:51-56, Romans 8:34, Ephesians 1:20, Hebrews 1:3, 10:12, 12:2. See Dodd 1963.9-42. The idea that the Messiah is to be found at the right hand of God appears to be ultimately derived from Psalm 110:1, the Old Testament text most frequently cited in the New Testament. See Court 1983. Attempts have been made to understand Revelation as an exposition of the verse, e.g. Craddock 1986 and see Caird 1984 78-79. The proposal has considerable appeal but must be considered speculative since the book contains no allusion to the verse.

[202] Ephesians 1:20-23, 1 Peter 3:22, Ascension of Isaiah, (all are examples of *Christus Victor* understandings of atonement). The parallels between Revelation 5 and Philippians 2:6-11 are particularly striking. In both the Messiah is exalted and his Lordship is acknowledged in every part of creation. Yet both Paul and Revelation appear to hold their universalism in tension with the view that all will not experience God's salvation. Martyn 1967 suggests that in Paul's thought the cross is the epistemological watershed between the old age and the age to come which are two different ways of knowing. See also 1985.

[203] This is the position of, e.g., Ladd 1972. Farrer 1964.89 points out that Judaism knew an order of angels known as 'thrones' being the highest order among those named at Colossians 1:16. These are probably to be understood as being among the powers over which Jesus triumphs by his cross according to Colossians 2:15.

[204] Schüssler Fiorenza argues that in Revelation the final time begins with the exaltation of Christ, which she finds described at 5:6 and again at 12:5. Everything after the cross is eschatological. 1985.42. Yarbro Collins 1976.Ch1 also regards the visions of Revelation 4-5 and 12 as parallel.

Therefore, 4:2-11 is a vision of heaven awaiting the work of the Messiah. The next chapter depicts the exaltation of the Messiah in heaven and the fulfilment of his work at the eschaton. The succeeding chapters which, as the best commentators agree, flow out of 5:14, may be read as a commentary on it; an account of the means by which the eschaton derives from the accomplished work of the Messiah; a more detailed version of what has already been described. We should anticipate an account of the transfer of sovereignty over the earth from its present ruler(s) to God and the Messiah. Since the key event described in 5:1-14, the exaltation of the Lamb, had already taken place at the time the text which represents it was written,[205] the process unleashed by that event and described in the following chapters is best understood as already being in process when the text was written. The things which occur with the breaking of the seals reveal the process that began with the death and exaltation of Jesus and which continues in the time of the first hearers of the book. The happenings associated with the end-times have therefore, from the perspective of the text, already begun.[206] The ages have turned and Chapters 4 and 5 are a representation of the events which have wrought this transformation.

A Girardian perspective suggests that one effect of Jesus's death is to witness to the truth. Jesus, the just and innocent witness who represents the victim who stands at the beginning of human culture, (for he is the lamb slain from the foundation of the world)[207] is now vindicated - shown to have been in the right. This event, the death and exaltation of Jesus, and its representation in the gospel, now has its influence on human cultures; it reveals their violence, the innocent blood on which they are founded and which sustains them; it summons them to a new way of being; it provokes a crisis of differentiation and yet prevents its resolution through existing methods. The sign of the slain Lamb stands over the world, judging it by exposing it to the truth of its own nature and the eschatological process is begun as a result. The death and exaltation of the Lamb have changed the world. They undermine cultural differentiation. The effects of non-differentiation and the cultural crisis it provokes can only be described in symbolic language. This is what the reader finds depicted once the vision of 5:1-14 is over. The effects of the death and vindication of the slain

---

[205] The enthronement of Jesus as king in heaven is accomplished by his death and resurrection. Revelation does not anticipate a future heavenly enthronement of Jesus. See Beale 1984 and Beasley-Murray 1974. Many futurist readings disagree with this position, preferring to regard Revelation 5 as a future event which will inaugurate the last days. Walvoord 1966.

[206] See Allison 1985, especially Chapters 1, 7, and 11-13, including the idea of an eschatological process inaugurated at the cross (152). Raber says that the "action of the Apocalypse is to be understood as being in process. Any notion that God, living and active, might be sitting about waiting for some predestined moment to commence the eschaton would have been unthinkable to the writer and of no consequence whatever to his first century readers". 1986.297.

[207] 13:8. See Ch4.

lamb are firstly, the representation of his story and the imitation of his way and secondly, the breakdown of culture in violence and disorder with futile attempts made to restore it through scapegoating; that is to say that the effects are the gospel and the wrath. These phenomena are described in Revelation beginning at 6:1.

4. Chapter 6:1-17

The seals are the first of the three plague septets found in Revelation. The first four seals are clearly related to one another for the opening of each introduces a rider upon a horse. These images may well have their origin in a traditional mythological motif. Gunkel has argued that the four riders ultimately derive from the idea of four world gods.[208] Baldensperger[209] cites Boll's suggestion that astrological signs lie behind the image.[210] Others, like Bousset, have claimed that other mythological ideas about the four winds, the messengers of the gods, underlie the motif.[211] Given the extent to which Revelation borrows from the Old Testament, it is probable that, whatever the origins of the image, the immediate prompting to use the motif came from the use of a similar one in Zechariah. At 1:8 the horses are red, red, sorrel and white; at 6:1 onwards they are red, black, white and dappled grey; and at 6:6 they are black, white and dappled.[212] In Zechariah 1:10 they are said to patrol the earth, and at 6:5 are called the four winds/spirits of heaven. The order of the horses is confused and the text may be corrupt.[213] One thing that is clear is that, unlike the riders of Revelation, the white horse never comes first.

Although most scholars insist that the four riders should be treated as a set,[214] there are grounds for regarding the white horse as distinct from the others.[215] Firstly, it comes first, a position that it never has in Zechariah. Secondly, the other three riders represent the elements of an existing threefold structure of woes which may be traced to Jeremiah 14:12 and 21:9 where sword, famine and pestilence are mentioned.[216] Then, the first is unlike the rest in that it offers no physical harm or danger. Next, the power of the last three is clearly limited but that of the first is not. Finally, the consequences of the last

---

[208] 1930.38-73.
[209] 1924.
[210] 1914.
[211] 1896. Winds are associated with judgements (and blessings) at 1 Enoch 76.
[212] *NRSV*.
[213] See Petersen 1985.263-264.
[214] Caird is particularly insistent about this. 1984.80-81.
[215] This case is made by Allo 1921, Bachmann 1986, Bousset 1896, Considine 1944, Ellul 1977, Feuillet 1966.
[216] Beckwith, who thinks the first rider symbolizes conquest, acknowledges that this is "not elsewhere with certainty mentioned in the list of God's punitive judgements." 1919.517.

three horses appear to be summarized at 6:8 while no reference is made to those of the first.[217]

While the interpretation of the first rider is widely debated in the literature,[218] there is some consensus about the meaning of the other three. There is argument about whether any specific historical references can or should be found, but it is generally agreed that the riders represent, or are derived from a schema in which they represented, warfare, famine, and pestilence respectively. The observation that the fifth seal speaks of martyrdom and the sixth of cosmic disturbances has led some commentators to suggest that Revelation 6:1-17 is based on the same pattern as that used by the synoptic evangelists in Mark 13 and parallels.

Charles argues that a sevenfold pattern of Messianic birth pangs or woes can be traced in the relevant Jewish literature.[219] These woes are the sufferings which herald the close of the present age and the dawn of the age to come. The seal-openings depict events taken from a list that existed in written or oral form within the tradition from which the text of Revelation emerged. Charles claims that sevenfold schemes may be traced to Leviticus 26:21 and that a developed scheme may be found at Sirach 40:9.[220] A further example may be found at Testament of Benjamin 7:2, "the sword is the mother of seven evils... moral corruption... destruction... oppression... captivity... want... turmoil... desolation".[221] Charles believes that the seven seals of Revelation and the synoptic apocalypses are based on a more developed version of such a sevenfold scheme. [222]

There are certainly a number of parallels between the texts. All refer to war, famine, earthquakes, persecutions and cosmic disorder. However, there is reason to doubt that the Synoptics provide evidence of a sevenfold scheme as such. Charles can define seven woes only in the case of Luke and in every case he distinguishes between war and international strife for reasons which are not justified and which appear to be related to his desire to link the former to the first rider of Revelation and the latter to the second. This effectively gives the first two riders the same meaning. Furthermore, Charles uses the text of

---

[217] Rissi, who suggests that the first horse represents demonic forces, links these to the wild beasts of 6:8. 1965.89-94.

[218] Feuillet claims, "The first horseman of the Apocalypse is one of this book's great enigmas" (Le prem. cav. de l'Ap. (6:2) est une des plus grandes énigmes de ce livre.) 1966.229.

[219] 1920.1.153-160.

[220] In fact LXX lists eight woes at this point although there is no καὶ (and) between ῥομφαία (sword) and ἐπαγωγαί (things brought upon one, calamities), nor between the latter and λιμὸς (famine).

[221] The contemporary 2 Baruch offers a twelve-fold scheme at 25-27.

[222] This implies that Charles must treat the various woes as having a symbolic meaning. However, he allows that they also have a secondary, historical referent, but this is surely inconsistent.

Revelation to impose a sevenfold pattern on the synoptic apocalypses, one which could not be constructed otherwise. So, while there is a strong case to be made for the suggestion that Revelation 6 is dependent on a tradition also found in the synoptic gospels,[223] and for the idea of sevenfold schemes of woes, it is not clear that the synoptic scheme is sevenfold. In addition, in the text of Revelation the first four seals form a group, while the next three do not; the last is separated from the fifth and sixth by the visions of Chapter 7. Charles's theory cannot account for the way in which the first four seal-openings are clearly differentiated from the others. In fact, the Old Testament tradition on which Revelation draws includes references to fourfold schemes of woes as well as the three and sevenfold patterns mentioned by Bousset and Charles. This can be seen at Ezekiel 14:21, "when I send upon Jerusalem my four deadly acts of judgement, sword, famine, wild animals and pestilence".[224] It may have influenced the pattern of four found in Revelation and may lie behind the effects of the fourth rider described at 6:8. Revelation shows signs of all three patterns.

Bousset's position is that while the last three riders are to be treated as general symbols, the first rider is set apart from the others because it is unique in having a contemporary-historical meaning. It is the sign which makes it possible to look for the rest of the signs. He argues that it represents either the Roman or the Parthian Empire, with the latter being the more likely. The rise of the Parthians leads to conflict with Rome and thus to the events symbolized by the subsequent riders. Bousset's position is not consistent. While there are grounds for treating the first rider as distinctive, there are none for using wholly different means of interpreting them. It would be wiser to interpret the first rider as a general symbol.

Nevertheless, Bousset's solution to the problem of the first rider has been widely followed. It is probably the most popular position among commentators, especially those who take a historical-critical approach. Metzger expresses this view most clearly when he says of the white horse,

> Its rider holds a bow and rides off on a career of conquest. The key to the meaning of this lies in the bow. It was the characteristic weapon of the mounted Parthian warriors, to whom also white was a sacred color...What is suggested here is a Parthian invasion that meets with success.[225]

---

[223] See the discussion in Vos 1965.181-192, D. Wenham 1984.205-210. Yarbro Collins 1992b reaches a similar conclusion with respect to Revelation's use of the Son of Man tradition; it is an independent development of an earlier tradition.
[224] *NRSV*. See also Ezekiel 5:15-17, 33:27-29.
[225] 1993. Similar views are shared by, e.g., Barclay 1976, Beckwith 1919, Boring 1989, Bruce 1979, Charles 1920, D'Arap... 1968, Harrington 1969, Hobbs 1971, Kepler 1957, Krodel 1989, Lilje, 1957, Quispel 1979, Schüssler Fiorenza 1991, Summers 1951; Swete 1907, Yarbro Collins 1979.

Other commentators, who believe that all four riders should be interpreted as more general symbols often regard the first rider as an image of warfare, conquest, invasion, or military victory.[226] Many, perhaps influenced by Charles,[227] combine the views finding a general symbol with a specific referent.

A number of other attempts have been made to interpret the first rider. Efird's contemporary-historical reading leads him to identify the figure with the Emperor Domitian.[228] Court, on the other hand, follows Gunkel in identifying the rider with the cult of Mithras that was spreading throughout the Empire.[229] Kerkeslager prefers to identify the rider with Apollo whom Revelation uses in a polemic against the false prophets of pagan society.[230] Feuillet suggests the white horse personifies the punishments effected by the riders that follow, "it personifies, not a particular calamity, but the divine judgement whose instruments will be the traditional trio of war, famine and plague."[231] Those who understand Revelation to tell the history of salvation or the spiritual history of humanity sometimes understand the first rider as the prelapsarian Adam or sinless human nature.[232] Finally, some interpreters, particularly those with a futurist perspective, understand the rider to represent the Antichrist or some other adversary of God.[233] This position has been ably defended by Vos and Rissi.[234] Both rely on the alleged link between Revelation 6 and the synoptic apocalypses and argue that the white horse stands for the false messiahs which are the first of the signs in the lists. In addition, Rissi suggests that the Antichrist is presented in a perverted imitation of Christ.

The difficulty with all these views is that they interpret the text by importing a framework from outside the text; they use the grid of contemporary history, or the human spiritual story, an alleged literary parallel, or a selected figure from the history of religions. None of them attempt to understand the figure in terms of the text of Revelation itself. An acceptable interpretation should take the context seriously. The rider is the first consequence of the turn of the ages depicted in Chapters 4 and 5. This is effected by the revelation of truth and the beginning of a process by which sovereignty over the earth is transferred. In addition, this rider is related to but distinct from those which follow it. Finally,

---

[226] E.g., Ashcraft 1972, Beasley-Murray 1974, Boesak 1987, Caird 1984, Carrington 1931, Lohse 1960, Niles 1962, Wall 1991, G. Wilson 1985.
[227] 1920.
[228] 1989.
[229] 1979.Ch3, 1994.3. See Gunkel 1930.53-54.n6. R.L. Gordon 1972 is a helpful introduction to Mithraism in Roman society.
[230] 1993.
[231] "il personnifie, non pas une calamité déterminée, mais le jugement divin dont les instruments seront le trio traditionnel de la guerre, de la famine et de la peste." 1966.247.
[232] Corsini 1983, Whitwell 1942.
[233] Bancroft 1994, Boxall 2006, Lindsey 1973, Torrance 1960, Walvoord 1966.
[234] 1965.181-192, 1964.

the ways in which the words used to describe the rider are used in the rest of the text must be taken into account. On this basis, it is argued that the rider of 6:2 represents the continuation of the work of Jesus by his followers; the representation of the life and death of Jesus in the proclamation and the activities of the churches.

While the majority of modern commentators reject this view,[235] a similar interpretation is found in the writings of the early church. The oldest extant commentary is that of Victorinus of Pettau. He argues that, as in Luke-Acts, the first act of the ascended Jesus is to send the Spirit so that the word about Jesus might be made known;

> after the Lord ascended into heaven and opened all things, He sent the Holy Spirit, whose words the preachers sent forth as arrows reaching to the human heart, that they might overcome unbelief. And the crown on the head is promised to the preachers by the Holy Spirit...Therefore the white horse is the word of preaching with the Holy Spirit sent into the world.[236]

Victorinus relates this interpretation to the promise of Jesus at Matthew 24:14 that the Gospel would be preached as a testimony[237] to the nations before the end. He relates the other horses to the predictions of Jesus about coming wars, famines and pestilences. The idea that this rider represented Christ, an angel, the Spirit or the Gospel, in other words that it stands for something positive, is scarcely challenged in the early church.

An examination of the text of Revelation reinforces this argument. The image at 6:2 is comparable with, although not identical to, the image at 19:11-16. The riders are not necessarily the same but the parallels in their descriptions suggest some similarity of purpose. Compare; καὶ εἶδον, καὶ ἰδοὺ ἵππος λευκός, καὶ ὁ καθήμενος ἐπ' αὐτὸν ἔχων τόξον καὶ ἐδόθη αὐτῷ στέφανος καὶ ἐξῆλθεν *νικῶν καὶ ἵνα νικήσῃ* (**And I looked, and behold a white horse, and the one seated upon it** had a bow and a crown was given to him and he went out *conquering and to conquer*) [6:2] with; Καὶ εἶδον τὸν οὐρανὸν ἠνεῳγμένον, καὶ ἰδοὺ ἵππος λευκός καὶ ὁ καθήμενος ἐπ' αὐτὸν καλούμενος πιστὸς καὶ ἀληθινός, καὶ ἐν δικαιοσύνῃ *κρίνει καὶ πολεμεῖ* (**And I saw heaven opened, and behold a white horse, and the one seated upon it** is called faithful and true, and in righteousness *he judges and makes war*.) [19:11]. The relationship is clear.[238] The implication is surely that that the

---

[235] Caird summarizes the majority position, see pages 244-247. There are exceptions, e.g. Allo 1921, Bachmann 1986, Bonsirven 1951, Buis 1974, Cullmann 1951.160-163; Ellul 1977, Farrer 1964; Hendriksen 1939, Hengstenberg 1851, Ladd 1972, Loernertz 1947, Prévost 1993, Sweet 1979, Walpole 1911, Warner 1944. Ford 1975 understands the rider as the angel of the Lord.
[236] The Latin is in Haussleiter 1916.68.
[237] The Greek text has μαρτύριον.
[238] Bold type shows where the same words are used. Italics indicate a parallel idea.

same or closely related persons are being described in the two verses.

In addition, the horse is white, the rider is crowned, carries a bow, and goes out conquering. These are, except for the bow, which does not appear elsewhere, positive images in Revelation. The word λευκός (white) is used some sixteen times in the text. In every other case it is indisputably associated with God, his agents and followers. It is the colour of Jesus's hair at 1:14, of the horses of 19:11, 14, of God's throne at 20:11, of the clothes of the redeemed at 3:4, 5, 18; 6:11; 7:9, 13, 14 (verbal form); 19:14 and those of the elders at 4:4. It is also the colour of the cloud at 14:14 and the stone at 2:17. Vos asserts that the colour should not influence exegesis unduly because it is derived from Zechariah.[239] But this ignores the fact that Revelation adapts images it adopts for its own purposes and Zechariah's order has been changed to put the white horse first. Evidence derived from outside the text should not overrule the internal evidence that white is always and everywhere in Revelation a colour associated with God and his servants.[240]

The word στέφανος (crown) is used some eight times in Revelation. The others who have such crowns are Christians at 2:10, 3:11; God's attendants at 4:4, 10; the woman of 12:1 and the one like a son of man at 14:14. The only occasion where the word relates to God's adversaries is at 9:7 where the headwear of the locusts is said to be ὡς στέφανοι (*like* crowns). All the true στέφανοι are positive images and it seems most unlikely that the rider of 6:2 should be the only exception.

As far as the bow is concerned, there is no other use of the word τόξον (bow) in the text to guide interpretation. In this instance external evidence may be sought but it should not be given priority over the internal evidence for the positive nature of the rider's other characteristics. While it cannot be demonstrated that Revelation contains any intentional references to specific contemporary historical phenomena, debt to the Hebrew Bible has frequently been shown.[241] Vos argues that in the Old Testament the bow is frequently the weapon of God's enemies[242] and that in Revelation Christ carries a sword. In fact the evidence is much more ambivalent than he allows. Psalm 45, for example, was subjected to messianic interpretations and the king fires arrows at verse 5.[243] One presumes he is to be pictured as carrying a bow.[244] The majority

---

[239] 1965.

[240] The Babylonian Talmud suggests this is a positive image. R. Papa says at Sanhedrin 93a "a white horse is a favourable omen in a dream." For comments on Revelation in the light of the Talmud and other Jewish texts see Strack 1926.

[241] See Ch1.C.5.

[242] 1965. He cites Psalms 11:2, 37:14, 46:9, 78:57; Hosea 7:16. Rissi 1964 mentions Ezekiel 39; 1966 refers to 2 Corinthians 11:14.

[243] See Craigie. 1983.340

[244] As Sweet points out, this Psalm certainly lies behind 19:11-16. 1979.139. Elsewhere in the Old Testament God is depicted as an archer, e.g. Habakkuk 3:5-9. In the covenant

of commentators make the bow the decisive factor in their exegetical decision. Since the text offers no guides to its meaning, this method must be challenged. The evidence is not decisive and such evidence as exists suggests the bow may be a positive image.

The rider's activity is described as νικῶν καὶ ἵνα νικήσῃ (conquering and to conquer). This is, in Considine's words, "the progressive and continuous effect of Christ".[245] The verbs are used without objects. Every other such use in Revelation clearly refers to the activity of God's agents and servants. Where the verbs are used of God's adversaries, they always take an object. The evidence from throughout the book therefore suggests that the key verbs in 6:2 refer to the activities of a divine agent or servant. Furthermore, the use of the verb νικάω up to this point in the text is always with reference to the action of God's agents. It has been applied to the actions of the followers of Jesus in the messages to the churches of Chapters 2-3, and of the Lion of Judah at 5:5. In Chapter 4 it was argued that the verb is to be understood in terms of witnessing to the truth in the face of death. From a Girardian perspective, this conquering is to be understood as the subversion of the dominant culture by the representation of the life and death of the Lamb.[246] It is the eschatological mission of the apostles and of the communities they founded.[247]

Finally, it is worth noting that the living one's word to the rider (as it is to the other riders) is Ἔρχου (come). The one who is to come is God who achieves this through the actions of the Messiah. This suggests that all the riders are linked to the decisive act of God anticipated in 4:1-11 and initiated in 5:1-10.[248]

Therefore, on the basis of the exegesis of the early church, the internal textual evidence, and the material set out in Chapter 4, the first rider is almost certainly a symbol for the activities of Jesus and his followers. It is the story of Jesus proclaimed and used as a pattern for life in the face of opposition, the gospel having its effect upon the world, the participation of Jesus's followers in the process that brings about the change of the ages. God's word is uttered through the excluded victim and those who follow him; the truth of their witness as they are expelled from culture goes forth conquering. This phenomenon leads out the other riders, the curses of war, famine and

---

scene of Genesis 9, God's weapon is a bow (τόξον in LXX). And see Psalm 7:12, Lamentations 3:12-13, Zechariah 9:13-14, 4 Ezra 16:13.

[245] 1944.421.

[246] Note Blake's assertion, "the bitter groan of a Martyr's woe Is an Arrow from the Almightie's Bow." *Jerusalem*. 52.25.

[247] Funk suggests that Paul thought of his own presence as bearing an eschatological power which might be life-enhancing or death-bringing. 1967. Cullmann relates eschatology and the apostolic missionary effort. 1936, 1956.

[248] Farrer links the word of the living ones to the *Maranatha*, the customary response to a doxology giving the kingdom and the glory to Christ. 1964.98. Bornkamm sees this word as a call to judgement included within a Eucharistic liturgy. 1969b.169-176.

pestilence; the gospel reveals or brings about the plagues which follow. This is a conclusion that many exegetes are anxious to avoid. They regard the effects of the Christ event and its representation in the gospel as salvific and beneficent. In the light of this a number of objections have been made to the interpretation being advocated here.

Commentators tend to assimilate arguments which identify the rider as Christ, the Spirit and the Gospel and objections to all such readings can only be handled together. Bousset and Charles both argue that the Messiah cannot be revealed before the Messianic birth pangs represented by the other seal openings; he is revealed at 19:11. In fact, it might be better to argue, in the light of the New Testament as a whole, that the Messiah is revealed at the cross, an event which was his initiation of and participation in the woes which precede and herald the eschaton.

Caird raises, appropriately enough, seven objections to the position adopted here, a view he regards as being "open to insurmountable objections."[249] Firstly, Luke 21, which provides the closest parallel to the woes brought about by the seals, does not mention, as do the Matthean and Marcan parallels, that the preaching of the gospel is to be a sign of the end. However, the position advocated here relies on internal evidence, not alleged dependence on an external tradition. Furthermore, Charles, who makes the most thorough case for the view that the seals follow the pattern of the synoptic apocalypses, acknowledges that they are probably dependent on a common tradition rather than on the version found in Luke; while they are, on the whole, closest to Luke, they are sometimes closer to the pattern found in the parallels. Wenham's examination of the evidence suggests that Revelation shows familiarity with traditions preserved in all three synoptic gospels and that therefore it may reflect a pre-synoptic tradition, perhaps one which included elements attested separately by Matthew, Mark and Luke.[250] Caird's second objection is that the similarity between the riders of 6:2 and 19:11 is illusory. Again, the argument made here does not depend on this link. Nevertheless, the shared language suggests the two are related and Caird fails to offer any account of the link. It is possible that the imagery of both is derived from Psalm 45 in which the king is depicted as both swordsman and archer. This is related to Caird's third argument; that the bow is not a symbol of the word of God. Certainly, the sword is a more usual symbol. Nevertheless, as has been argued, the idea that the bow is not traditionally associated with God is false. Next comes the claim that the relevant verb cannot be regarded as carrying a positive sense because the beast is also said to engage in conquering. But Caird fails to note that until this point the use of the verb has been positive and that the verb is never used intransitively of the action of God's enemies. Then he argues that that the fourth horseman is an epitome of the other three. But this is not correct. The

---

[249] 1984.80.
[250] Wenham 1984.205-212.

last rider epitomizes the preceding two but not the first. The description of the fourth contains no reference to the activity of the first. Sixthly, Caird argues that since the plagues of the last three riders are preliminary and carefully qualified, it makes little sense for the gospel to be ranked among them. Here Caird fails to acknowledge that the first rider is set apart from the others as well as connected to them. The sequence as a whole is a consequence of the death and exaltation of Jesus and a key element of that is the representation of the gospel. Finally, and claims Caird, fatally, is the use of the word ἐδόθη (was given). The word is used for the divine permission to do harm in the case of the fourth rider and to other powers hostile to God at 9:1, 13:5, and 13:14. However, it is also used of God's redemptive gifts at 6:11, 12:14, and 19:8. The use of the word for one of the riders who is an agent of harm need not mean that a prior rider of whom the verb is used is an adversary of God. Caird forgets to note what is given; the first rider is given a crown and in Revelation crowns belong only to the agents of God. Thus none of Caird's objections, nor their cumulative effect, is persuasive.

The argument that the first rider is a deceptive figure who has the trappings of the Messiah but is really a harbinger of doom and therefore an adversary of God causes more difficulty. However, the internal evidence is against it. It is true that the enemies of God imitate God's agents but in every other case it is clear to the reader that an adversary is being discussed. Furthermore, as Sweet points out, the text has yet to set up the Satanic parody on which the argument relies, and "The imagery, if interpreted by what has gone before rather than by what is yet to come, points unequivocally to something heavenly. This rider's function is simply *conquering*, which must be interpreted by the Lamb's conquest."[251]

In fact, the underlying objection to the position advocated here is not exegetical but theological. Indeed, it is the most common objection raised to the proposed interpretation. It is said that the gospel, being a message of good news, could never be grouped with symbols representing judgements such as war, death and pestilence. However, the evidence from the rest of the New Testament is not so decisive as this argument suggests. The gospel, the truth, the word of God, heralds both salvation and judgement. The metaphor of the two-edged sword for the word of God is a most apt one.[252] The Gospels show that the ministry and message of Jesus is divisive and is a sign of the end.[253] As Sweet says, "The gospel in the NT is not simply beneficent. It declared God's victory in Christ and warned of coming judgement".[254]

---

[251] 1979.138
[252] Revelation 1:16, 2:12, see Hebrews 4:12. One meaning of the Greek δίστομος is, appropriately enough, 'two-mouthed'
[253] Luke 12:49-53, Mark 13:10, and parallels.
[254] 1979.138.

Excursus: Romans 1:16-32 [255]

This point can be elucidated by reference to the ideas of the apostle Paul about the relationship between the gospel and the wrath of God. Commentators frequently argue that there is a parallel between the pattern of Revelation 4-6 and Romans 1:16-18.[256] In the case of both Revelation and Romans, the gospel is seen to bring the consequences which are predicted by Girard's theory. The purpose of this excursus is to understand Paul's language about the ὀργὴ θεοῦ (wrath of God) which is mentioned at 1:18 and described in Chapters 1-3 of his letter to the Christians in Rome. It concentrates on 1:16-32 and in particular on verses 17-18. It uses the theories of René Girard to try to gain fresh insights into the text.

It is generally accepted that Romans 1:1-15 forms an introductory section and that 1:16-17 states the theme of the letter; the gospel is the power of God for salvation to all who believe for God's δικαιοσύνη (righteousness) is revealed in it. The first major section is said to begin at 1:18 and is usually thought to end at 3:19-20 with the declarations that every mouth is silenced and the whole world (not just one group or another) accountable to God, for no flesh can be put right with God on the basis of the works of the Law. Having thus summed up the state of humanity, Paul can proceed to 3:21 and state how God's δικαιοσύνη has been revealed and the effects which this has on the human condition.

On this basis it is often argued that 1:18-3:20 states the problem and that 3:21 begins the account of God's solution. Within this structure, Romans 1:18-32 is taken to be a description of the state of all or a part (i.e. the gentiles) of humanity; it presents humanity under the wrath of God.

Broadly speaking, such a breakdown of the text is acceptable. However, a number of issues are raised and two of them are addressed here. Firstly, the very idea of the wrath of God raises theological questions while the description of its effects in 1:18-32 raises both theological and anthropological questions not the least of which concerns the mechanisms or means by which the wrath operates. And secondly, there is the issue of the connection which exists between the revelation and operation of the wrath of God and the revelation and operation of the δικαιοσύνη of God in and through the gospel. The two issues are related and discussion of one inevitably raises the other. The second is discussed first because it leads into a discussion of the text itself.

Before proceeding, a translation of δικαιοσύνη is required. The commentaries and translations offer righteousness, justice, faithfulness, covenant faithfulness and uprightness. And these are just the more popular options. There is no space to defend a new proposal but the translation 'integrity' is offered as a possible alternative. It carries the idea of uprightness

---

[255] A version of this excursus was published in Rowland and Fletcher-Louis 1998.137-154 and appears here with the kind permission of the publisher.
[256] E.g., A. Hanson 1957, Rowland 1993.86-87, Sweet 1979.123

and faithfulness, particularly in the sense of commitment to promises given. Furthermore, it carries the sense of a commitment to truth and to acting in ways that are in keeping with one's own character.

Romans 1:17-31

While our Greek texts quite rightly offer a new paragraph at 1:18, a number of commentators point out that verse 18 is closely related to the preceding verse. In verse 17 we read that, δικαιοσύνη γὰρ θεοῦ ἐν αὐτῷ ἀποκαλύπτεται (because in it (i.e. the gospel) the integrity of God is revealed), while in verse 18 we find, Ἀποκαλύπτεται γὰρ ὀργὴ θεοῦ ἀπ' οὐρανοῦ (because the wrath of God is revealed from heaven). It seems likely that the thoughts are intended to be in parallel with one another and if they are one must ask in what way the wrath of God is related to the gospel. The key words are ἀποκαλύπτεται (is revealed) and γὰρ (for, because).

Bockmuehl has carried out a very helpful study of Paul's use of revelation language and explores its past, present and future dimensions.[257] An examination of Paul's use of the verb ἀποκαλύπτω (reveal) shows that it nearly always has an eschatological context. Excluding Ephesians and the Pastorals from consideration, Paul uses the verb in the following places: Romans 8:18, "the coming glory to be revealed to us"; 1 Corinthians 2:10, "God has revealed to us that which he has prepared for those who love him"; 1 Corinthians 3:13, "the work of each will be manifest on that day because it will be revealed with fire"; 2 Thessalonians 2:3, "the man of lawlessness is revealed"; 2:6, "he may be revealed in his time"; 2:8, "and then the lawless one will be revealed". There are also two uses of the verb in Galatians, at 1:16 and 3:23, "But when...God was pleased to reveal his son in me" and "we were kept under restraint until faith should be revealed". These refer to past events yet, it might be argued, refer to the fulfilment of God's promises and purposes in Christ and so have an eschatological aspect to them. There are a couple of non-eschatological uses; these are Philippians 3:15, "if any of you are otherwise-minded, God will reveal this to you" and 1 Corinthians 14:30, "but if anything be revealed to another". Paul's use of cognates is extensive and these frequently have an eschatological aspect too. Therefore, it is likely that Paul's thought in Romans 1:17-18 has an eschatological dimension. His use of ἀποκαλύπτω in 1:18 may contrast with his use of φανερόω (make known) in the following verse.

The verb ἀποκαλύπτεται has the same form in both verses; it is present and passive. In verse 17 we might translate; "The integrity of God is being revealed in the gospel." Furthermore, since it is God who is responsible for this revelation, we should probably understand a divine passive allowing us to paraphrase the words as, "In the gospel God is causing his own integrity to be revealed".

---

[257] 1990.

Paul's gospel is a narrative that concerns the life, death and resurrection of Jesus (Romans 1:4). Paul's conviction is that these events, and the narrative which represents them, generate a process of the revelation of God's integrity. This belief is eschatological: firstly because this revelation is the promised and anticipated divine vindication of God's own character; and secondly because, while the revelation is operating in history, it will culminate in the day of judgement. God's integrity has always been in existence but is now revealed in such a way that it generates a process which is worked out in history and which will culminate in the eschaton.

Since it is a parallel thought, the verb ἀποκαλύπτεται in verse 18 probably has a similar meaning. This implies that the wrath of God is a process that is connected in some way to the gospel. It is, after all, revealed ἀπ' οὐρανοῦ (from heaven). In every other case, except one, where Paul uses the phrase 'from heaven', he is referring to Christ: 1 Corinthians 15:47, 'The second man is from heaven'; 1 Thessalonians 1:10, 'To wait for his son from heaven'; 1 Thessalonians 4:16, 'The Lord himself will descend from heaven'; and, 2 Thessalonians 1:7, 'When the Lord Jesus is revealed from heaven'. The exception is Galatians 1:8, which refers to the possibility of an angel from heaven preaching another gospel. In every case except for Galatians the reference is eschatological. This observation serves to support the contention that the wrath of God is, like the integrity of God, an eschatological phenomenon. It is, in some sense at least, a new or newly revealed phenomenon and this implies that it is in some way related to the gospel.

As to the word γὰρ, while it is conceivable that it could carry an adversative sense, it is, according to Bauer, usually used to express cause, inference, continuation or to explain.[258] It is therefore normally translated by the word 'for' or the word 'because'. It seems that the revelation of God's wrath is, so far as the text is concerned, closely related to the revelation of God's δικαιοσύνη in the gospel. Most commentators touch on these issues when discussing the words γὰρ and ἀποκαλύπτεται and they arrive at a remarkable number of remarkably different conclusions. Many are uncomfortable with the idea of the wrath of God and are resistant to the idea that it is closely related to the gospel. It is worth examining some of the exegetical positions which have been adopted.

The Views of Some Exegetes

Bornkamm accepts that the gospel heralds both salvation and judgement.[259] The two are related in Paul's thought at 2 Corinthians 2:15, "For we are the aroma of Christ to God among those who are being saved and among those who are perishing". He also cites 2 Corinthians 4:3 and 1 Corinthians 1:23. However, in his view, the wrath of God is not a part of the gospel as such. He summarizes

---

[258] 1979.151-152.
[259] 1969a.47-70.

the available views on the connection between the wrath of God and the gospel as juxtaposition and succession. In the former, the ἀποκαλύπτεται is regarded as timeless; a description of the way of the world. The revelation of God's wrath is not related to the content or to the effects of the gospel. On this view, in its pure form, the wrath of God is not really related to the final judgement; the eschatological dimension is lost and Paul is thought to be speaking of a process which occurs entirely within history.

C.H. Dodd is associated with a position of this kind and his views about God's wrath have proved influential and are discussed by almost all the commentators. He writes that "there is something impersonal about the 'Wrath of God'" and that "Wrath is the effect of human sin", the term being used "not to describe the attitude of God to man, but the inevitable process of cause and effect in a moral universe." For Dodd, this is something that is the case and has always been the case; there is nothing new that has happened in the gospel as far as the operation of God's wrath is concerned.[260] Dodd is often accused of allowing his exegesis to be influenced by his theological concern to avoid ascribing the emotion of anger to God. Nevertheless, his reasons for this are understandable and his position has influenced the view taken in this study. He is, for example, correct to point to human responsibility for, and involvement in, the phenomenon Paul calls the wrath of God, and he is right to be concerned that God should be understood to act in ways that are consistent with his own character as it is revealed in Jesus. However, Dodd's view is inadequate because it loses the eschatological dimensions of God's wrath; it also fails to acknowledge God's involvement in initiating the wrath or the connection between the wrath and the gospel; finally, Dodd does not discuss the anthropology which would enable a process of the kind he envisages to operate. His may be an accurate observation about the effects of certain kinds of behaviour but it is hardly of great explanatory value.

Hanson takes Dodd's understanding of the wrath of God in Paul and develops it, applying it to the whole of the New Testament. In the process, it ceases to fit Bornkamm's category 'juxtaposition'; it is discussed here because of its relationship to Dodd's view. Hanson regards the wrath of God as something impersonal that has always been operating within history. However, he attempts to deal with one of the objections which have been raised to Dodd's view by linking God's wrath to the gospel. He does this by arguing that although it, like God's δικαιοσύνη, existed before the Christ event, its operation is fully revealed in Christ. He develops his argument with reference to the wrath of the Lamb in Revelation. He believes that the author has a similar view to Paul's. The judgements recorded in Revelation 6, for example, are precipitated by the cross of Jesus and by the martyrdoms of his followers. These judgements take place in history and anticipate those of the eschaton. He argues that "The wrath here is not purely eschatological; it is a process,

---

[260] 1932.20-24. See also 1978.66-70.

stretching from the Cross to the Parousia." and "The crucifixion and its consequences in history are the means by which...wrath is manifested."[261] There is a great deal to be said for this perspective. Hanson has brought out the connection between the wrath and the gospel and the link between the cross and the eschaton. However, it is unclear why the impersonal laws of the universe should function in such a way. Furthermore, it is not clear why the process should be ascribed to God or to the Lamb.

Caird has an approach similar to Dodd's although he tries to avoid overstating the impersonal nature of God's wrath; he regards God as being actively involved in the process described in Romans 1:18-32. However, he seeks to qualify the link between verses 17 and 18 by arguing that ἀποκαλύπτεται has different meanings in the two verses; in 17 the δικαιοσύνη is not a disclosure of God's character but a process which has broken in; to be revealed is to come into operation. Caird argues that it cannot have this meaning in 18 because the wrath of God came into operation at the fall. The wrath of God was invisibly operative before Christ but now has become visible to faith. The righteousness of God only becomes operative in the gospel.[262]

Certainly, those who advocate a 'juxtaposition' view have to find some way to break the link between verses 17 and 18 and so to deny that they are in any way parallel. Dodd, whose commentary is based on the Moffatt translation of the Bible, found his job already done for him.[263] Moffatt translates the γὰρ of verse 18 as "but" and Dodd adopts this translation without question, regarding the word as an "adversative conjunction" and thus allowing the two verses to stand in contrast to one another.[264] He regards it as unthinkable that God's wrath and God's righteousness should be in any way identified. Fitzmyer's solution is to translate 'for' but to agree that the righteousness or 'uprightness' of God and the wrath of God stand in contrast to one another. The former saves humans from the latter.[265] As already indicated, if this were Paul's meaning, it would be an unusual use of the word γὰρ. Such a rendering should only be adopted if no other option is available.

The view which Bornkamm calls "succession" is based on a salvation-historical understanding of Paul's thought. According to this view, the wrath of God characterizes the epoch that has ended with the dawn of the age of the gospel. Until this point only God's wrath was being revealed. Now his righteousness is also being revealed or is being revealed instead. However, this view does not take sufficiently seriously the fact that the verbs in verses 17 and 18 are exactly the same. Nor can it deal with the fact that the period prior to

---

[261] 1957.172.
[262] 1994.85.
[263] Moffatt 1934.
[264] 1932.18.
[265] 1993.

God's revelation in Christ is elsewhere described by Paul not as the time of God's wrath but as the time in which sins were passed over ἐν τῇ ἀνοχῇ τοῦ θεοῦ, (in the forbearance of God) [Romans 3:26].

Bornkamm's own understanding is that the existence of God's revelation in the world is the rightful basis for the revelation of God's wrath, God's judgement on humanity. The wrath process has occurred before and has been recognizable. What is new is the eschatological dimension. Only now, in the gospel, is the world put in the light of the event, that is the judgement of God, to which history is directing it. This could not be discerned on the basis of revelation in creation. He writes, "In the light of the previous revelation of God in creation and law, the world cannot announce that its time has come. The possibility for this is disclosed only through the 'now' that has dawned over the world in the revelation of God's 'righteousness' in Jesus Christ." This is the eschatological 'now' of salvation history that ushers in the new age. Hence the revelations of δικαιοσύνη and wrath belong together and the γάρ explicitly establishes the link.

There is a great deal to be said for interpretations of this kind. Käsemann speaks of the revelations of God's wrath and of God's righteousness as being two different aspects of one and the same act of revelation, verses 17 and 18 being regarded as "deliberate antithetical parallels". The wrath of God was already present in the world but was unrecognized and only comes to light along with the gospel;

> the eschatological present implicitly illuminates the past which was previously concealed. This is not the result nor is it the true point of the gospel, but its reverse side. It is not merely something of which man now becomes conscious from within but an event which encounters him from without and which is therefore characterized as eschatological revelation.

Justification delivers some of us from the wrath to which the whole world is subject. God hands others of us over to the wrath; God is at work in this process in what Käsemann calls "a hidden way".[266]

Both Robinson and Dunn take similar positions.[267] They regard the two revelations as two different sides of the same coin, as one revelation having two different kinds of effects. Robinson argues that God is involved in both processes. The process called the wrath of God appears impersonal but this is because of the depersonalizing effects of sin. In fact everything exists by virtue of its relationship to God.

Cranfield argues that the wrath of God is, like the righteousness of God, revealed in the ongoing proclamation of the Gospel. The two revelations are two aspects of the same process. Behind the revelation of wrath in the

---

[266] 1980.35.
[267] 1979 and 1988.

proclamation of the gospel lies the revelation of the wrath of God in the gospel events themselves for the reality of the wrath of God is revealed in Gethsemane and at Golgotha.[268]

Here Cranfield is close to the thought of Barth. The gospel is the revelation of the divine verdict and one aspect of the verdict is God's wrath. The death of Christ is at the heart of the gospel and is the revelation of wrath. The times of ignorance have been overlooked in the forbearance of God, but now the gospel is being proclaimed and all humanity is being brought to the point of decision. In his commentary on Romans Barth writes, "The wrath of God is the righteousness of God - apart from and without Christ."[269]

This approach is on the right lines. Käsemann may be right to say that the wrath of God is not one of the results of the gospel, but it is one of its side effects. The wrath of God may have been operative before the gospel but its operation becomes recognizable and becomes more accentuated and more thoroughgoing as a result of the gospel. To ignore or to reject the gospel will leave humans caught up in the process which Paul calls the wrath of God. Those who accept the gospel and conform their lives to it will be saved from that process or kept safe through it. Bockmuehl arrives at a similar conclusion and states that both God's righteousness and God's wrath are being revealed in the gospel events and in the gospel proclamation. He writes,

> No doubt God has from time to time manifested his wrath in the past: but now in particular with the historical inauguration of the gospel, and apparently with its subsequent proclamation, the heavenly wrath of God has begun to come to its eschatological realization.[270]

Thus, the best interpretation of Paul's thought at this point takes seriously the parallel between verses 17 and 18 and therefore accepts that the revelations of God's wrath and δικαιοσύνη are closely related to one another and that both are eschatological processes which have roots in the gospel events and in the oral proclamation of those events by the church. The events have a once and for all nature but their re-presentation in the proclamation of the church allow them to have a continuing effect. This effect either brings humans to salvation or it produces the effects described by Paul in 1:18-32. These processes anticipate, and culminate in, the last judgement; they are a foretaste of the future. Any adequate account of the processes which are involved must allow God's actions to reflect his character and still take seriously the genitive θεοῦ; the wrath process is in some way God's.

---

[268] 1975.
[269] 1933.43.
[270] 1990.141.

Girard's Ideas as an Interpretative Grid for Romans 1:18-32

Girard's theories offer an understanding of why all this should be so by providing an account of the social and cultural mechanisms that underlie the operations of these processes in history. He provides an interpretative framework for understanding human society, culture and history and offers us a meaningful way to appropriate the eschatological language of the New Testament. His views provide a grid by which the historical processes that Paul describes in Romans 1:18-32 may be interpreted. Let me make it clear that this argument is not an attempt to demonstrate that the apostle had a Girardian view of society. Rather it suggests that Paul understands that the proclamation of the Christ event is an eschatological phenomenon because it must herald the close of the existing world order. It has two parallel effects; one which has the potential to transform the world, to produce a new world with a new way of being human, and the other which will see humanity launched on a cycle of violence which ends in self-destruction. The gospel offers to the whole of humanity its final choice between these two effects.

Paul calls one of these effects the revelation of God's integrity. God has revealed what is right and true of himself and has shown humans what they are like. Those who grasp these truths and live accordingly will, Paul believes, be saved. The other effect, the one with which the passage is primarily concerned, Paul calls the revelation of the wrath of God. This is the process of cultural disintegration which the revelation of the gospel generates or accelerates. This is a process that has always been present in the world. However, this time there can be no resolution of the kind there has been in the past; this time it is final; the gospel heralds the *eschatological* wrath of God. It is because the process is one which has always been present in culture that Paul's description has parallels with descriptions of human decline found elsewhere. The difference is that this time, when human culture descends into chaos, it will be unable to emerge.

Certainly, the effects described by Paul are those that a Girardian understanding would lead us to expect.[271] Furthermore, as Hooker (followed by Dunn) has pointed out, although her findings have been challenged by Fitzmyer, Romans 1 reflects the events described in the opening chapters of Genesis.[272] This could be because Paul had Genesis in mind or it could be that both are attempts to describe the same cultural phenomenon.

In verse 18 Paul demonstrates his intuitive understanding of the human dilemma; humans have lived in accordance with a lie and suppress the truth. This is the root of the problem. The fact of a transcendent creator can be known but is in practice suppressed in favour of the gods who are served in the violent rituals of paganism; the gods of the realm called 'the sacred'; the gods of violence. These are the idolatrous religions of which Paul speaks in verse 21,

---

[271] See the brief discussion in Alison 1990.
[272] 1959-60.

with which the revealed truth of the gospel is to be contrasted. These are, "the god of this world (who) has blinded the minds of the unbelievers" (2 Corinthians 4:4). The unbelievers are those whose minds have been darkened and who, like Adam, have exchanged and will again exchange the glory of the immortal God for images (Romans 1:21-23). Paul elsewhere urges us to exchange the Adamic, old way of being human for Christ's new way. Girard offers us an understanding of the lie which Paul claims lies at the heart of our cultures, our ways of being human.

In addition, Girard argues, and it certainly would have been true in Paul's context, that all idolatry is linked to sacrifice and thus to the gods of violence. It is certainly the case that sacrifice is a very common social phenomenon and is linked to nearly every pagan religion of which we have knowledge. Its practice was widespread in the Roman Empire and it was, of course, vital in the form of Judaism known to Paul. It is usually said that Paul regards idolatry as the root of human problems. This is very close to being true; it is a primary consequence of cultural acceptance of the primal lie. Paul is aware of the misrepresentation that lies behind idolatry and of which all humans are vaguely aware but which most choose to suppress, probably because to collude in the lie makes social life easier (or even possible or conceivable). Idolatry is linked to mimesis. The invisible God is (mis)represented in the form of a creature. Humans choose to render worship to the representation and accept the false religious rationale for worship that goes with it. The god is thought to demand victims and the effects of mimesis ensure that a violent god will have violent worshippers. Humans are trapped in idolatry and thus in sacrificial thinking and hence in violence.

Human cultural order founded on violence is unstable. Mimesis induces people to break prohibitions and the system of differentiation which is the basis of culture is undermined. Furthermore, since God has acted in the gospel to reveal the founding lie of culture, it may be said that God gives humans up (1:26) to the next stage of the cycle, for the awareness of the truth about cultural victims, a truth for whose revelation God is responsible, undermines the effectiveness of a culture's attempts to renew itself. As cultural differentiation breaks down, the cultural prohibitions against incest, adultery etc. become perceived to be purely cultural, and hence arbitrary, phenomena. There is no divine sanction to enforce them and no apparent likelihood of retribution. Therefore, people do not fear the consequences of breaching them; they feel able to act on desires which were previously kept in check. These prohibitions are vital to the survival of the culture and once they are breached, mimetic rivalry and hence violence must become more and more common. This is the next stage to which humans are given up (1:28) as the society of which they are a part disintegrates and murder, strife, ruthless behaviour etc become common. There remain no cultural values by which behaviour can be assessed and so the cultural crisis gets worse and worse. This process has happened in the past and will be repeated in the future. The future process will, because of the gospel, be worse and will be impossible to resolve in the normal way. This is because people are no longer able to convince themselves of the guilt of their victims.

Paul's account of the downward spiral of humanity caught up in the wrath of God is a good description of a crisis of differentiation. There is reason to believe that Paul and Girard have similar phenomena in mind. Or perhaps it would be better to say that Girard offers us a helpful, contemporary, interpretative grid for understanding Paul. In either case, there is reason to believe that the proclamation of the gospel would contribute to such a process. Since the process could not be resolved it would be eschatological. Thus the revelation of the gospel is linked to the eschaton.

There are, apart from the gospel, two possible responses to this process. One is to be involved in the process as described in Romans 1. The other position is found in Romans 2. This is the self-righteous position to which so many of us are prone. It is an attempt to exclude and to scapegoat the sinners; this amounts to an attempt to revert to the founding lie. The gospel offers a third alternative; it is revealed by God and stands over against the alternatives offered by human culture. Paul refers to the gospel at 1:16-17 and discusses it in more detail in 3:21 onwards.

The wrath of God is God's in the sense that it is initiated by the revelation of the gospel which breaks into human culture and exposes the violence on which it is based. The violence, however, is not God's but humanity's; the responsibility for the violent effects of the process lies with humans rather than with God. However, it is God's process in that it is God who has acted in a way which generates the process and prevents its resolution. God has acted so that humans are liberated from their endless cycles of cultures founded on violence and lies. God's own action is non-violent and exposes violence and untruth in human society. However, the result of this is that human violence has the potential to be greater than ever and to be resolved only by complete self-destruction.

The process can be escaped only insofar as humans recognize the lie which has deceived them in the past and embrace the truth manifested in the death of Jesus and re-presented in the gospel. Mimesis cannot be escaped in either of its forms. In the first, literary critical sense of the word, the mimetic representation of the founding lie must be replaced by mimetic representation of the gospel. In the second, imitative sense, the mimesis of the desires and acquisitions of others must be replaced by a mimesis of Jesus. In such a way the wrath of God will be averted and the expected new world will dawn.

Thus, the best interpretation of Romans 1:17-18 understands the gospel to be an agent for the revelation of God's wrath and of God's integrity; the two are related for both are processes set in train by the Christ event and its representation in the gospel. This twin process is eschatological because it presents humanity with a final crisis in which the choices are the gospel or destruction. Romans 1:18-32 describe the cultural effects of the eschatological wrath of God. Girard's theories offer a plausible and appropriate contemporary explanation of the process and the cultural mechanisms which underlie it.

The white horse of Revelation 6:2 symbolizes the primary consequence of the events depicted in Revelation 4 and 5; the witness to the truth in the face of death carried out by those who follow Jesus. This conclusion is required by the narrative, by exegesis and by theology. In one sense the first rider stands apart from the others, but in another it is a part of a fourfold and a sevenfold pattern both of which have precursors in the Old Testament. The three following riders are part of a threefold, a fourfold and a sevenfold pattern. They are related to the first rider for they too are in some sense consequences of the Christ event.

The opening of the seals shows things brought to light and processes set in motion by the Christ event. They are, as Minear puts it, "various descriptions of a single set of consequences released by the Lamb's victory."[273] Schüssler Fiorenza claims that the four riders reveal and highlight the true nature of Roman imperial power; "Revelation's visionary rhetoric reveals the true nature of the reality and power of Babylon/Rome in its inevitable collapse."[274] In a similar way Rowland claims,

> Just as the Lamb embodies injustice perpetrated which so disfigures the world, so its exaltation issues in a recognition of the extent of that injustice; there can be no proper triumph of the Lamb without a revelation of the reality of the disorder of the world.[275]

In other words, there is an exposure of the truth about existing power relations within the culture. The claims about order and peace are shown to be false and the nature of disorder and the extent of violence are revealed.[276] The role of the four riders is usually said to be different in Revelation and Zechariah. In the former they bring judgement in the latter they patrol the earth and report their findings. One advantage of the present approach is that it is closer to the use made of the motif in the Old Testament. Of course, the things revealed are not new but their existence was previously hidden in false claims about order, peace and justice. However, exposing the truth has additional consequences; it does not give only an intellectual knowledge of the world, it changes the way in which people and institutions behave. Attempts may be made to suppress the truth. This takes the form of the persecution of the witnesses. This action proves counterproductive because each innocent death is a further revelation of the truth. This accelerates the cultural breakdown and worsens the effects of the things symbolized by the last three riders.

The four riders belong together as part of an existing scheme which has been

---

[273] 1968.74.
[274] 1991.63.
[275] 1993.80.
[276] See Wengst 1987, especially 118-135.

arranged in order to place the white horse, representing the most significant phenomenon, at the head of the series. The first, as Bousset says, is the one which enables the others to be discerned. The second rider represents violence in one or more of its forms. It is a consequence of declining cultural differentiation. The third is famine or an acute shortage of food, so often a result of extensive violence. The last is usually stated to be pestilence. However, this rider also recapitulates the two that precede it and refers to wild beasts in addition to pestilence. Bousset argues that the colours of the horses have their own meaning and that this would have been clear to the hearers. The bodies of those killed by pestilence, depending of course on their original skin colour, have this pale green or pale yellow colour which is signified by the word χλωρός. Perhaps the fourth horse originally had such a meaning. However, its rider is now clearly identified as death and it achieves its ends by a number of means. While the order of the riders is not chronological, it is logical; each is a result of the one which precedes it.

The scene changes at 6:9-11 on the opening of the fifth seal.[277] The souls under the altar are revealed. Most commentators assume that these are Christian martyrs.[278] This is certainly a possible interpretation. However, the fact that their testimony is not specifically related to Jesus has suggested to some authors that they may be Jewish.[279] Bancroft uses such a reading to account for the nature of the martyrs' prayer,[280] which he and others regard as Jewish or sub-Christian.[281] The prayer is staunchly defended as a cry for vindication by Boesak and Schüssler Fiorenza.[282] Another interpretation links the martyrs to the story of Abel whose blood cried out to God from the ground.[283] Carrington finds a reference to the innocent dead in general,[284] while Giblin, alluding to Luke 11:49-52 and parallel, suggests that all the martyrs from Abel onwards are to be understood.[285] Torrance recognizes that the innocent dead were killed as scapegoats. The powers of the world, "try to disown the fact that they are the cause of all the evil and commotion and so they turn upon God's people and vent their rage upon them as scapegoats."[286] Whether Jewish or Christian or

---

[277] The scene is important but Heil 1993 overstates his case when he makes it the key to the whole book.

[278] E.g. Allo 1921, Beasley-Murray 1974, Charles 1920, Kepler 1957, Krodel 1989.

[279] E.g. Feuillet 1977; Ford 1975; Mealy 1992.85n1. Corsini regards them as the saints of the Old Economy. 1983.

[280] 1994.

[281] E.g. Ashcraft 1972, Beckwith 1919. Glasson 1965. Bousset 1896 speaks of a Jewish atmosphere.

[282] 1987, 1991.

[283] Genesis 4:10. See 1 Enoch 22:5-8.

[284] 1931.

[285] 1991. Swete 1907 also finds a reference to Abel. In T.Ab 13:2-8 Abel is one of the three witnesses who will judge the whole creation.

[286] 1960.55.

both, or even neither, and whether they lived before or after the time of Jesus, the martyrs are those killed on the basis of false accusations. They, like the phenomena symbolized by the other seal openings, are revealed by the death and exaltation of Jesus. This is because the death of Jesus exposes the truth about the victims of culture.[287]

The idea found in these verses that the full number of martyrs must be killed before God's rule on earth can be established is also found in some Jewish apocalypses.[288] As shown in Chapter 4, Revelation understands the martyrs to play a role in bringing about the eschatological process.[289] In terms of Girard's theory, they do this by reinforcing awareness of the exposure of the scapegoat mechanism achieved by Jesus. The persecutors become increasingly aware of the innocence of their victims until their violence loses its culturally acceptable outlet and becomes redirected in ways which provoke vengeance and other forms of reciprocal violence. This process, or the conversion to the way of Jesus of their victimizers, is the vindication for which the martyrs pray.[290] The moment the persecutors recognize that the grounds for their actions are baseless, lies in the future. The deaths of others will be necessary before the cultural crisis which has been generated reaches the stage where participants are forced to abandon their belief in the guilt of their victims.[291] When they do they will be forced to choose between the way of Jesus and uncontrolled violence. The victims sit in judgement over the culture which sought to silence their witness to the truth.[292]

The sixth seal opening causes considerable difficulty to commentators. The language appears to describe the end of the world but the book is far from over. The problem is resolved in a number of ways. Some argue that an underlying apocalypse ended at this point,[293] others that the statements are proleptic.[294] The images have been regarded as figurative,[295] or as metaphors for a social or

---

[287] Note final clause of Revelation 18:24.
[288] 1 Enoch 47:1-4, 4 Ezra 4:35-37. And see 1 Enoch 97:1-5, 99:3, 104:3.
[289] Caird claims, "the death of the martyrs is the means by which God is to win his victory over the powers of evil". 1984.87.
[290] Sweet 1979.142 proposes the translation *vindicate* for the Greek verb ἐδικέω, as at Luke 18:8, in place of the more usual *avenge*. The martyrs long to have their innocence made known to their killers.
[291] The extent to which such deaths should be seen as 'sacrificial', as Beasley-Murray 1974 and Charles 1920 believe to be implied by the position of the souls under the altar, depends, as shown in Chapter 4, on what is meant by the word sacrifice; certainly the deaths are meaningful and participate in the effects of the death of Jesus.
[292] Wisdom 2-3 suggests that the just will be victimized by the wicked but will become their judges.
[293] E.g. Bousset 1896.
[294] E.g. Charles 1920.
[295] E.g. Hengstenberg 1851, Boring 1989.

political event.[296] Some of these solutions raise the question of the nature of the language which is usually designated *eschatological*.[297] One of the difficulties of such approaches is that they offer no limit to the range of possible understandings. Bruce suspects that the language alludes to traditions about the passion of Jesus of the kind found in Matthew 27:45, 51 and parallels;[298] Corsini thinks that the verses are a representation of the death of Christ.[299] On the other hand, the literalistic approaches of Cho[300] and Walvoord[301] cause other difficulties. A number of scholars have attempted to resolve the difficulty by proposing a solution based on a view of Revelation's literary structure. The view that the three series of plagues recapitulate one another implies that the end can be described more than once. A solution which takes account of the progression of the series suggests that the second and third are contained within part of the first, and the third within the second. On this basis, the things revealed at the opening of the sixth seal are the phenomena which are depicted in more detail and from other perspectives in the rest of the book.[302] There is no reason in principle why this should not be the case. It was argued earlier that the eschaton is already depicted at 5:13. So, these verses represent both the threshold of the end,[303] and the beginning of the drama of the end.[304] Such an understanding would make a certain impression upon the hearer. The text raises the expectation that the end is close but does not meet that expectation. Perhaps the text reflects a part of Christian experience; the end is always imminent and yet always deferred.[305] Thus, where the reader has been led to expect a representation of the end, the opening of the seventh seal brings only a period of silence into which is intercalated the launch of a further series of plagues.[306]

The language is derived from Old Testament images of Holy War and the

---

[296] E.g. Boesak 1987, Caird 1984, Carrington 1931.

[297] See Caird 1980.243-271. Buchanan insists that the language refers to some anticipated historical event such as a new Exodus. There is no expectation of the end of the cosmos; "The notion that biblical authors expected the end of the cosmos and time was invented in the nineteenth century in Europe." 1993.179.

[298] 1979.

[299] 1983. And see Harrington 1993.

[300] 1992.

[301] 1966.

[302] Walvoord suggests that contained within the seventh seal, "are all the subsequent developments leading to the second coming of Christ, including the seven trumpets and the seven bowls of the wrath of God." These underlie and proceed from the sixth seal. 1966.150. A similar position is taken by Ladd 1972.

[303] Ladd 1972.

[304] Lohse 1960.

[305] Perhaps the experience is more universal. See Derrida 1992. And see Blake's *Europe, a Prophecy*, in Keynes 1966.237-245.

[306] 8:1-5.

Day of Yahweh.[307] The origins of this language are disputed,[308] but Sweet notes its nature; it is expressed, "in terms of God undoing his work of creation: bringing back chaos".[309] One of the biblical understandings of creation sees it in terms of differentiation; the process by which order emerges from chaos.[310] On the Day of Yahweh this process is undone and creation reverts to its primeval state. Evidence of this is found at the opening of the sixth seal. The changes to the sun, moon and stars mean that the difference between night and day is abolished. When the sky rolls up as a scroll, the difference between heaven and earth is lost and the one lies fully exposed to the other.[311] The removal of mountains and islands mean that all the principal means of orienting oneself on land and sea are lost. Verse 15 suggests that all seven types of human are not only equally affected but reduced to the same condition; all cultural hierarchy and difference is gone.[312] In other words, humans find themselves disoriented both physically and culturally. All this is brought about by the great earthquake which, as Bauckham has demonstrated, is traditionally the herald of God's coming in judgement.[313] And of course, like the preceding seal openings, this is a consequence of the exaltation of Jesus.

A Girardian approach to language of this kind offers a new way of interpreting it.[314] It avoids the difficulties of literalism and those associated with treating it as an intentional metaphor. It reads the eschatological language as a representation of the experience of participants in a crisis of cultural differentiation. Cosmogonies tell the story of the origins of culture in terms of the origins of the cosmos. The cosmic chaos is an expression of the social chaos which is perceived by those involved in cosmic terms and articulated after the event in myths of cosmic origin. The threat of a future crisis finds expression in the same language but this time the process is reversed and order breaks down into chaos. The renewal of chaos is a necessary precursor to the re-establishment of a renewed cultural order. This chaos, brought about by the exposure of human culture to the truth, is, according to the Girardian reading, the phenomenon which the Bible calls the wrath of God.[315]

While the ontologically existing cosmos beyond the earth is not affected

---

[307] See Isaiah 34:4, 8; Joel 2:11, 20-21; Amos 8:9; Nahum 1:6; Malachi 3:2.
[308] See Von Rad 1959, 1991.
[309] 1979.143.
[310] See Gunkel 1921.
[311] Here the loss of differentiation results in anguish. In the closing chapters, after the destruction of the forces of negative mimesis, the loss of differentiation is a part of the new Jerusalem.
[312] Harrington 1969 agrees that the text depicts the abolition of all forms of social difference.
[313] 1993a.199-209. See Bousset 1896.
[314] See Ch2.E, F and Schwager 1988.
[315] See the excursus on Romans 1. For a study of the Greek word ὀργή (wrath) see Kleinknecht 1964.

greatly by human behaviour, the same is not necessarily true for the cosmos as it is experienced by humans. A number of studies suggest that what is perceived as reality is a social construct.[316] Human perception of reality may therefore be affected by human behaviour; social chaos could be perceived as cosmic chaos. In the ancient world the link was often made between social disorder and cosmic chaos.[317] This idea is found in the Old Testament; Psalm 74 links the destruction of the Temple with the chaos that preceded creation and Psalm 72 links the fertility of the land to the justice done by the king. These themes are explored by R. Murray who suggests that the link between the state of the cosmos and justice in human society is the subject of a cosmic covenant.[318] Human disobedience fractures the cosmic order and chaos is come again.

On this basis this text may be understood to offer an insight into the perceptions of those who are involved in the final cultural crisis; the one which is a consequence of the exaltation of the Lamb, the one brought about by the ministry of Jesus and the representation of that ministry by his followers. During the crisis of differentiation, the perception of the cosmos by those involved is affected. In one sense the events are not literal; the stars do not fall out of the sky. In another sense, this language is the closest that human speech can come to articulating the experience of those who go through the trauma of such a crisis. Past crises of this kind have always been resolved by the operation of what Girard calls the surrogate victim mechanism; the killing of a scapegoat. In the final crisis, there can be no such resolution. The revelation of the truth of the innocence of the victim means that the mechanism cannot operate for the participants can no longer be deceived by the process. They murder the martyrs but their action is to no avail. All are aware that the crisis and their inability to resolve it are related to Jesus. It is in this sense that the process described can be called "the wrath of the Lamb". The sixth seal opening is a part of the response to the plea of the martyrs at 6:10.[319] The action of Jesus in revealing the truth and the ministry of his followers in witnessing to the truth have provoked the crisis. These followers are also the victims of the violence generated by the crisis. The word of God spoken in the exclusion of victims brings the wrath of God upon the human world. The violence is human but it has been brought about by God and the Lamb because the human mimetic consensus constrains people to engage in reciprocal violence unless and until they respond to the gospel's offer of an alternative.

---

[316] See Bellah 1970; Berger 1970, 1973, 1979; Geertz 1973. Douglas suggests that perspectives on the state of the earth's ecology are dependent on the social context of their holders. 1992.Ch14. Georgi argues that Revelation calls into question the claims of 'official' reality. 1986.123.

[317] See Cohn 1993.Ch1-2.

[318] 1992.

[319] Quispel says that in 6:12-17 the Lamb stands up for the martyrs.

The visions of Chapter 7 stand alongside these scenes of crisis, depicting the state of those who follow the way of Jesus. These are the victims of the violence of the crisis but, paradoxically, are also, in one way, those who avoid it; they do not participate in the violence generated by the cultural crisis for they have understood the true nature of human society and have chosen a different way of being. They escape from the wrath and enjoy the presence of the Lamb. As has been argued, their experience foreshadows that of the new Jerusalem.

E. Conclusions

In Chapter 5 Jesus, the innocent victim, is vindicated. The series of plagues which afflict humanity flow from this; they are the consequence of the exaltation of the Lamb. They could be avoided if humans changed their way of being and abandoned the mimetic consensus derived from acquisitive mimesis and embraced the mimesis of renunciation at the heart of Jesus's teaching about the Kingdom of God. In other words, the wrath would be avoided if humans repented.[320] The series of plagues describe the process by which humans enter a crisis of differentiation from which they prove unable to emerge by the usual means. The whole of creation is affected and the cosmos itself is experienced as being affected. Yet Revelation offers the possibility of hope. Whether its message holds out the prospect of a universal salvation may be doubted,[321] but the promise is made that the crisis will be resolved by the victory of truth over the one who deceives the whole world. The final vision is of a world in which the forces which generate human violence, mimetic rivalry and mimetic desire, are defeated and a new human way of social being is envisaged. The old language of the Day of the Lord is reappropriated in order to convey a sense of what is being achieved.

The day of the Lord begins with the opening of the sixth seal and its consequences are depicted in terms of cosmic and social chaos in the subsequent sequences of plagues. The plagues do not refer to specific historical events nor are they literal future events. The text uses traditional material to depict the sensations of humans caught up in the extended and final cultural crisis which the exaltation of the Lamb is bringing upon the world. The crisis will bring about the transfer of sovereignty over the earth to God from God's adversaries. The process begins at Calvary, it continues in the representation of the life and death of Jesus in the words and lives of his followers, and culminates in a new kind of human social life. The agency which achieves this change is God's ἀποκάλυψις (apocalypse, revelation, disclosure), the truth, the word of God, living and active, the sharpest of two-edged swords; it brings things into being and accomplishes the things of which it speaks. It breaks into

---

[320] See 9:20-21, 16:10.
[321] See Bauckham 1993a.238-337 for a discussion of the issue.

the human world and promises judgement and salvation, the end of the present age and the life of the age to come, the destruction of the existing human social world and a new type of human community.

Chapter 6

Conclusions

This book has attempted to show that the Book of Revelation can be read in a way which is both true to the text and meaningful today. It argues that understanding Revelation as an account of the change of sovereignty over the earth brought about by Jesus's exposure of the truth about human culture enables the plague sequences to find a natural place in the story told by the text. They flow out of a scene which depicts the vindication of Jesus as the fulfilment of God's promises and they are necessary steps on the way to the new way of being human depicted in the closing chapters of the book. They are visions of chaos, of un-creation, entering the human world. The visions are a reflection of the undoing of a human construct masquerading as creation and opposed to God. As such they need have no determined historical referent; the reading simply offers a framework for engaging with them. The images are then able to create their own impact on the reader.

The use of Girard's thought as an heuristic device has thrown light on the nature of the adversaries of God, on the structure of the text and the cycle which it depicts, and on the quality of the renewed creation which the book anticipates. In addition, the hermeneutic of the victim derived from Girard allows the reader to identify the word of God with Jesus, the excluded victim, and with those who share his testimony. This word offers both judgement and salvation; the chaos of the cultural crisis and the promise of a new form of human social life, a form which should already be anticipated in the experience of the church. This hermeneutic encourages the reader to identify with the excluded and sees their vindication, the demonstration that they were wrongly accused, as a part of the process which undermines the form of social life which led to their oppression and by which the kingdom of God is to come on earth. Thus, the deaths of the marginalized are not without meaning or effect. They provoke a crisis among those who persecute them. The sword which destroys the enemies of God and brings in the reign of the saints, is the truth of the excluded victim.

Revelation is prophecy and this hermeneutic understands prophecy as language which offers a glimpse of reality as it is perceived from the perspective of the transcendent. To read Revelation is therefore not primarily to get information about history but to enable one's view of reality, one's understanding of what is true, to be changed. Revelation offers an alternative means of seeing the world, one which contrasts with the prevailing means of understanding it and engaging with it. The use of Girard's theories in reading this prophecy opens the perspective of the reader to the violence of the world and to the true nature of that violence. The escalation of violence and the unleashing of chaos are, like the salvation of those who conquer, a consequence of the Christ event: ἃ δεῖ γενέσθαι (those things which must happen) [1:1, 4:1]. Revelation holds out to humanity the futures of the world; both the consequences of our carrying on as we are, and also the possibility of another way of existence.

The approach to the text offered here does not see every detail of Revelation's text as necessarily having a specific historical referent. It is a pattern or a process which is depicted. Nevertheless, this reading makes no attempt to exclude the valid insights of other interpretations, nor can it claim to have resolved every difficulty or clarify every detail. For example, there are some texts which appear to understand Jesus's death in sacrificial terms; some people are apparently excluded from the new Jerusalem; the victory of God is sometimes depicted in violent terms. The enemies of God described in the text are understood as a *social* reality. The lake of fire is a metaphor for the 'defeat' of mimetic rivalry achieved by the exposure of the truth.

If Girard is correct and language and symbolic thought are based on principles of difference and exclusion, then ultimate inclusivity and the victory of God over the negative consequences of mimesis may be difficult to fully articulate. It would certainly be impossible to do so in terms drawn from the religious traditions which influenced Revelation. Thus, this thesis cannot fully account for every detail of the text: what it can do is offer a lens through which the overall pattern of the text can be interpreted. Some sense can be made of the difficulties that remain but it is acknowledged that certain aspects do not fit readily into the reading. Nevertheless, it is argued that Girard's thought has provided a number of insights into Revelation. The thesis suggests that Girard's own relatively negative assessment of the book is open to question.

Of course, books of this kind, while they may offer some answers, inevitably raise further questions. Firstly, the overall issue of Revelation's literary structure remains to be resolved. The evidence suggests that there may be a twofold pattern; a chiasm and a pattern based on progression with later visions in some sense enclosed within or anticipated by those which precede. This double pattern may reflect the experience of Christians and the tension between realized and future eschatology. The tension is closely related to the practice of worship for it is the experience of the reign of God experienced in worship which contrasts with the present reality of the rule of the beast. The function of Revelation's worship scenes in generating and resolving the tensions of Christian experience needs further investigation.

Next, exegesis has been offered of only one of the plague sequences. It has been suggested that the others are to be understood in terms of a social crisis generated by the work of Jesus and its representation in the gospel story. More detailed work on these visions is necessary in order to fully validate the proposed reading.

Thirdly, there is clearly room for further research on the language of New Testament soteriology. In particular, the language of sacrifice must be examined and the differences explored between sacrifices and the death of Jesus. For example, as the writer to the Hebrews points out, sacrifices have to be repeated regularly if they are to be effective, but the death of Jesus is a once and for all event.[1] If it is a sacrifice, it is of a wholly different order of sacrifice to those to which the term originally applied. This has implications for the practice of the church. Girard is himself a Catholic as are most of his British followers. Yet Girard is critical of historical Christianity, calling it 'sacrificial' and claiming that it has misunderstood the teaching of the Gospels about the death of Jesus.[2] This suggests that some discussion of the sacrificial nature of the Mass, and the relationship between the death of Jesus and the Eucharist, may be necessary.

The book also raises the question of the relationship between the death of Jesus and the end of the world. Schweitzer claims that the death of Jesus destroys the eschatological conditions which he and the Baptist had set in motion.[3] Yet Schweitzer finds that Jesus's words, based on an eschatological worldview, are appropriate to any world view and address all prepared to meet their challenge and learn for themselves who Jesus is.[4] However, Allison argues that the New Testament understands the death and resurrection of Jesus as eschatological events.[5] Girard's theory suggests why this might be so. There is a case for examining the material discussed by Schweitzer and Allison from a Girardian perspective.

In the course of church history, many different ways of understanding Revelation have been advocated. Generally speaking, most existing readings have proved unhelpful insofar as they discourage readers from engaging with the text itself and have encouraged them to struggle instead with a reconstructed social-historical background, or the supposed patterns of history or the spiritual life. Some of these approaches have served the church well. They have enabled the book to be used in Christian devotion and teaching; some have enabled people to understand their own place in history and give meaning to their lives and experience. The argument of the book has sought to produce a reading of Revelation which allows the text to speak and which will be of use to the church today. It has shown it is possible to read the Apocalypse in a meaningful way without insisting on a hermeneutic which defines the

---

[1] 10.11-12.
[2] This idea is anticipated in Blake's *Jerusalem* (Keynes 620-747) which speaks of the "dread spectre" which had corrupted true Christianity.
[3] 1926.369.
[4] 1926.400-401.
[5] 1985.

meaning of every detail in the text. The use of Girard's theories enables the reader to wrestle with the text's problematic ideas and images in ways which are theologically fruitful and which cast light on the overall pattern of the book.

In the mean time, the struggles of the Peruvian people continue but the anticipated full-scale civil war has not materialized. Their catharsis has been postponed. If Girard is right then the young historians referred to in the introduction had reason to feel as they did; in the past, renewed human order has emerged from chaos. However, his work also suggests that any peace or order gained in such a way can never be final and that there is reason to doubt that the relevant mechanism can function at all in the contemporary world. Of course, the war may still come but the winners will no longer be able to silence the voices of their dead and dying victims. Therefore, other ways must be found to promote the longed-for new Peru.

The Book of Revelation read in the light of Girard indicates that a lasting, just and peaceful order will only come to Peru, indeed to any part of the world, when the existing mimetic consensus, with its urge to acquisition and rivalry, is renounced and a contrasting mimesis adopted in its place, an imitation of the Jesus of the Gospels. The churches of Peru, especially those associated with evangelicalism and Pentecostalism, are experiencing unparalleled growth. The Roman Catholic Church is responding to the challenge this presents to their historical position in creative ways. There are signs of the beginning of an ecumenical cooperation. Perhaps there is some prospect that the gospel will be not only believed but obeyed. Of course, any fundamental change may not happen without an unparalleled social and cultural crisis. Revelation suggests that God has told the truth and that humans are responsible for the consequences.

Bibliography

ABIR, Peter Antonysamy 1995, *The Cosmic Conflict of the Church; an Exegetico-Theological Study of Revelation 12, 7-12*, European University Studies 23.547, Peter Lang, Frankfurt
ABRAMS, M.H. 1984, "Apocalypse; Theme and Variations" in Patrides 1984a.342-368
ACHTEMEIER, Paul J. 1986, "Revelation 5.1-14", *Int* 40.283-288
ALISON, James 1990, "Justification and the Constitution of Consciousness; a new look at Romans and Galatians", *New Blackfriars* 71.17-26
ALISON, James 1993, *Knowing Jesus*, SPCK, London
ALISON, James 1996, "Girard's Breakthrough", *The Tablet* 29 June 1996
ALLEN, Leslie C. 1987, *Psalms 101-150*, WBC 21, Word, Milton Keynes
ALLISON, Dale C. 1985, *The End of the Ages Has Come; an Early Interpretation of the Passion and Resurrection of Jesus*, Fortress Press, Philadelphia
ALLO, E.-B. 1921, *L'Apocalypse*, Librarie Victor Lecoffre, Paris
ANDERSON, Bernhard W. 1987, *Creation versus Chaos; the Reinterpretation of Mythical Symbolism in the Bible*, Fortress Press, Philadelphia
ANDERSON, Gary A. 1987, *Sacrifices and Offerings in Ancient Israel; Studies in Their Social and Political Importance*, Scholars Press, Harvard Semitic Museum Harvard Semitic Monographs 41, Atlanta
ANDREWS, Isolde 1996, *Deconstructing Barth; a Study of the Complementary Methods in Karl Barth and Jacques Derrida*, Studies in the Intercultural History of Christianity 99, Peter Lang, Frankfurt
ARGYRIOU, Asterios 1982, *Les exégèses Greques de l'Apocalypse à l'époque Turque (1453-1821); esquisse d'une histoire des courants idéologiques au sein de peuple Grec asseni*, ΕΤΑΙΡΕΙΑ ΜΑΚΕΔΟΝΙΚΩΝ ΕΠΟΥΔΩΝ ΕΠΙΣΤΗΜΟΝΙΚΑΙ ΠΡΑΓΜΑΤΕΙΑΙ ΣΕΙΡΑ ΦΙΛΟΛΟΓΙΚΗ ΚΑΙ ΘΕΟΛΟΓΙΚΗ, Θεσσαλονικη
ARMERDING, Carl E., and GASQUE, W. Ward (editors) 1977, *Handbook of Biblical Prophecy*, Baker, Grand Rapids
ASHBY, Godfrey 1988, *Sacrifice; its Nature and Purpose*, SCM Press, London
ASHCRAFT, Morris 1972, "Revelation", Broadman Bible Commentary, Broadman Press, Nashville. 1972.12.240-361
ATLAN, Henri 1988, "Founding Violence and Divine Referent" in Dumouchel 1988a.192-208
AUERBACH, Erich 1968, *Mimesis; the Representation of Reality in Western Literature*, Princeton University Press
AULÉN, Gustaf 1931, *Christus Victor; an Historical Study of the Three Main Types of the Idea of the Atonement*, SPCK, London
AUNE, David E. 1966, "St. John's Portrait of the Church in the Apocalypse", *EQ* 38.131-149
AUNE, David E. 1972, *The Cultic Setting of Realized Eschatology in Early*

Christianity, NovTSup 28, E.J. Brill, Leiden
AUNE, David E. 1981, "The Social Matrix of the Apocalypse of John", *BR* 26.16-32
AUNE, David E. 1982, "The Odes of Solomon and Early Christian Prophecy", *NTS* 28.435-460
AUNE, David E. 1983a, *Prophecy in Early Christianity and the Ancient Mediterranean World*, Eerdmans, Grand Rapids
AUNE, David E. 1983b, "The Influence of Roman Imperial Court Ceremonial on the Apocalypse of John", *BR* 28.5-26
AUNE, David E. 1986, "The Apocalypse of John and the Problem of Genre", *Semeia* 36.65-96
AUNE, David E. 1987a, *The New Testament in Its Literary Environment*, Westminster Press, Philadelphia
AUNE, David E. 1987b, "The Apocalypse of John and Graeco-Roman Revelatory Magic", *NTS* 33.481-501
AUNE, David E. 1990, "The Form and Function of the Proclamations to the Seven Churches (Revelation 2-3)", *NTS* 36.182-204
AUNE, David E. 1993, Review of R. Dean Davis 1992, *CBQ* 55.804-805
AUNE, David E. 1997-1998, *Revelation* (3 volumes), Word, Dallas
BACHMANN, Theodore, E. (Editor) 1960, *Luther's Works*, Volume 35, Word and Sacrament I, Fortress Press, Philiadelphia
BACHMANN, Michael 1986, "Die erste apokalyptische Reiter und die Anlage des letzten Buches der Bibel", *Bib* 67.240-275
BAILEY, J.W. 1934, "The Temporary Messianic Reign in the Literature of Early Judaism", *JBL* 53.170-187
BAILIE, Gil 1994, "Sacrificial Violence in Homer's *Iliad*", in Wallace 1994a.45-70
BAILIE, Gil 1997, *Violence Unveiled; Humanity at the Crossroads*, Crossroad, New York
BAINTON, Roland 1983, *Here I Stand; Martin Luther*, Lion, Tring
BAKER, John Austin 1983, "Theology and Nuclear Weapons", *KTR* 6.1-4
BALDENSPERGER, G. 1924, "Les cavaliers de l'Apocalypse. Apoc. VI, 1-8", *RHPR*.1-31
BALE, John 1973, *The Image of bothe Churches*, Theatrum Orbis Terrarum, Amsterdam
BALTHASAR, Hans Urs Von 1994, *Theo-Drama; Theological Dramatic Theory*, 4; "The Action", Ignatius Press, San Francisco
BANCROFT, Sam 1994, *Revelation of Jesus Christ; through Revelation Verse by Verse*, Petorlan Publications, Peterlee
BANDERA, Cesáreo 1986 and 1988, "From Mythical Bees to Medieval Antisemitism", in Juilland 1986a.29-49 and Dumouchel 1988a.209-226
BARCLAY, William 1976, *The Revelation of John*, Daily Study Bible 21, St. Andrew Press, Edinburgh
BARKER, Margaret 1987, *The Older Testament; the Survival of Themes from the Ancient Royal Cult in Sectarian Judaism and Early Christianity*, SPCK, London
BARKER, Margaret 2000, *The Revelation of Jesus Christ; Which God Gave to Him to Show to His Servants What Must Soon Take Place (Revelation 1.1)*,

T&T Clark, Edinburgh

BARNETT, Paul 1989, "Polemical Parallelism; some Further Reflections on the Apocalypse" *JSNT* 35.111-120

BARNWELL, F. Aster 1992, *Meditations on the Apocalypse; a Psychospiritual Perspective on the Book of Revelation*, Element, Rockport

BARR, David L. 1984, "The Apocalypse as a Symbolic Transformation of the World; a Literary Analysis", *Int* 38.39-50

BARR, David L. 1986a, "The Apocalypse of John as Oral Enactment", *Int* 40.243-256

BARR, David L. 1986b, "Elephants and Holograms; from Metaphor to Methodology in the Study of John's Apocalypse", SBL Seminar Papers 1986.400-411

BARR, David L. 2001, "Waiting for the End that Never Comes; the Narrative Logic of John's Story" in Moyise 2001, 101-112

BARR, James 1961, *The Semantics of Biblical Language*, Oxford University Press

BARRETT, C.K. 1954-1955, "The Lamb of God", *NTS* 1.210-218

BARRETT, C.K. 1956, "The Eschatology of the Epistle to the Hebrews", in W.D. Davies 1956.363-393

BARROW, Simon and BARTLEY, Jonathan (eds) 2005, *Consuming Passion; Why the Killing of Jesus Really Matters*, Darton, Longman and Todd, London

BARRY, F.R. 1968, *The Atonement*, Hodder and Stoughton, London

BARTH, Karl 1933, *The Epistle to the Romans*, Sixth Edition, Oxford University Press, London

BASSOFF, Bruce 1986, "The Model as Obstacle: Kafka's *The Trial*", in Juilland 1986a.299-315

BATER, B. Robert 1994, "Apocalyptic Religion in Christian Fundamentalism", in Wallace 1994a. 287-304

BAUCKHAM, Richard 1974, "The Great Tribulation in the Shepherd of Hermas", *JTS* 25.27-40

BAUCKHAM, Richard 1976, "The Martyrdom of Enoch and Elijah; Jewish or Christian?", *JBL* 95.447-458

BAUCKHAM, Richard 1977a, "The Eschatological Earthquake in the Apocalypse of John", *NovT* 19.224-233

BAUCKHAM, Richard 1977b, "Synoptic Parousia Parables and the Apocalypse", *NTS* 23.162-176

BAUCKHAM, Richard 1978, *Tudor Apocalypse; Sixteenth Century Apocalypticism, Millenarianism and the English Reformation: from John Bale to John Foxe and Thomas Brightman*, The Sutton Courtney Press, Courtney Library of Reformation Classics, Appleford

BAUCKHAM, Richard 1980, "The Delay of the Parousia", *TynB* 31.3-36

BAUCKHAM, Richard 1983, "Synoptic Parousia Parables Again", *NTS* 29.129-134

BAUCKHAM, Richard 1985, "Enoch and Elijah in the Coptic Apocalypse of Elijah", in *Studia Patristica* 16.69-76

BAUCKHAM, Richard 1993a, *The Climax of Prophecy; Studies on the Book of Revelation*, T & T Clark, Edinburgh

BAUCKHAM, Richard 1993b, *The Theology of the Book of Revelation*, New Testament Theology, Cambridge University Press
BAUER, Walter 1979, *A Greek-English Lexicon of the New Testament and Other Early Christian Literature*, translated and adapted by Arndt, William F. and Gingrich, F. Wilbur, University of Chicago Press, Second Edition
BAUERNFEIND, O. 1967, "Νικάω, νίκη, νῖκος, ὑπερνικάω", in *TDNT* 4.942-945
BEAGLEY, Alan James 1987, *The 'Sitz im Leben' of the Apocalypse with Particular Reference to the Role of the Church's Enemies*, BZNW 50, Walter de Gruyter, Berlin
BEALE, Gregory K. 1980, "The Danielic Background for Revelation 13:18 and 17:9", *TynB* 31.163-170
BEALE, Gregory K. 1984, *The Use of Daniel in Jewish Apocalyptic Literature and in the Revelation of St. John*, University Press of America, Lanham
BEALE, Gregory K. 1985, "The Origin of the Title 'King of Kings and Lord of Lords' in Revelation 17.14", *NTS* 31.618-620
BEALE, Gregory K. 1988, "Revelation", in Carson, D.A. and Williamson, H.G.M. (editors), *It Is Written: Scripture Citing Scripture. Essays in Honour of Barnabas Lindars*, Cambridge University Press, 1988.318-336
BEALE, Gregory K. 1992, "The Interpretative Problem of Rev. 1:19", *NovT* 34.360-387
BEALE, Gregory K. 1996, "The Old Testament Background of Rev. 3:14", *NTS* 42.133-152
BEALE, Gregory K. 1999, *The Book of Revelation*, NIGTC, Paternoster, Carlisle
BEASLEY-MURRAY, George R. 1948, "Biblical Eschatology; II Apocalyptic Literature and the Book of Revelation, *EQ* 20.272-282
BEASLEY-MURRAY, George R. 1963, "Commentaries on the Book of Revelation", *Theology* 66.52-56
BEASLEY-MURRAY, George R. 1974a, *The Book of Revelation*, NCB, Oliphants, London
BEASLEY-MURRAY, George R. 1974b, "How Christian is the Book of Revelation", in Banks, Robert (editor), *Reconciliation and Hope: New Testament Essays in Atonement and Eschatology; presented to L.L. Morris on his 60th Birthday*, Eerdmans, Grand Rapids, 1974.275-284
BEASLEY-MURRAY, George R., HOBBS, Herschel H., ROBBINS, Ray Frank, GEORGE, David C. 1977, *Revelation; Three Viewpoints*, Broadman Press, Nashville
BEATTIE, J.H.M. 1980, "On Understanding Sacrifice", in Bourdillon 1980.29-44
BECKWITH, ISBON T. 1919, *The Apocalypse of John; Studies in Introduction with a Critical and Exegetical Commentary*, Baker, Grand Rapids
BEKER, J.C. 1980, *Paul the Apostle; the Triumph of God in Life and Thought*, T & T Clark, Edinburgh
BELL, Albert A. 1979, "The Date of John's Apocalypse; the Evidence of some Roman Historians Reconsidered", *NTS* 25.93-102
BELLAH, R. 1976, *Beyond Belief; Essays on Religion in a Post-traditional World*, Harper and Row, New York

BENSON, Edward White 1900, *The Apocalypse; an Introductory Study of St. John the Divine*, Macmillan, London

BERGER, Peter L. 1970, *A Rumour of Angels; Modern Society and the Rediscovery of the Supernatural*, Allen Lane, London

BERGER, Peter L. 1973, *The Social Reality of Religion*, Penguin, Harmondsworth

BERGER, Peter L. and LUCKMANN, Thomas 1979, *The Social Construction of Reality; a Treatise on the Sociology of Knowledge*, Penguin, Harmondsworth 1979

BERKHOF, Hendrik 1977, *Christ and the Powers*, Herald Press, Scottdale

BETTENSON, Henry (editor) 1969, *The Early Christian Fathers; a Selection from the Writings of the Fathers from St. Clement of Rome to St. Athanasius*, Oxford University Press, paperback edition

BETZ, Hans Dieter 1969, "On the Problem of the Religio-Historical Understanding of Apocalypticism" *JTC* 6.134-156

BIETENHARD, Hans 1953, "The Millenial Hope in the Early Church", *SJT* 6.12-30

BLACK, Matthew 1976, "Some Greek Words with 'Hebrew' Meanings in the Epistles and Apocalypse" in Johnston McKay 1976.135-146

BLEVINS, James L. 1980, "The Genre of Revelation", *RevExp* 77.393-408

BLEVINS, James L. 1984, *Revelation*, John Knox Press, Knox Preaching Guides, Atlanta

BÖCHER, Otto 1983, *Kirche in Zeit und Endzeit: Aufsätze zur Offenbarung des Johannes*, Neukirchener Verlag, Neukirchen-Vluyn

BÖCHER, Otto 1988, "Die Johannes-Apokalypse in der neueren Forschung", *ANRW* 2.25.5.3850-3893

BOCK, Emil 1957, *The Apocalypse of Saint John*, Floris Books, Edinburgh

BOCKMUEHL, Markus N.A. 1990, *Revelation and Mystery in Ancient Judaism and Pauline Christianity*, Wissenschaftliche Untersuchungen zum Neuen Testament 2.36, J.C.B. Mohr (Paul Siebeck), Tübingen

BOESAK, Allan A. 1987, *Comfort and Protest; Reflections on the Apocalypse of John of Patmos*, The Saint Andrew Press, Edinburgh

BOFF, Leonardo 1987, *Passion of Christ, Passion of the World; the Facts, Their Interpretation, and Their Meaning Yesterday and Today*, Orbis Books, Maryknoll

BOISMARD, M.-E. 1949, "'L'Apocalypse', ou 'Les Apocalypses' de S. Jean", *RB* 56.507-541

BOISMARD, M.-E. 1959, "L'Apocalypse" in A. Robert and A. Feuillet (editors), *Introduction à la Bible*, Tome 2 Nouveau Testament, Desclée, Tournai, 1959.709-742

BOISMARD, M.-E. 1966, "Introduction to the Book of Revelation", *JB*, Darton, Longman and Todd, London

BOLL, Franz 1914, *Aus der Offenbarung Johannis. Hellenistische Studien zum Weltbild der Apokalypse*, Stoiceia 1, Druck & Verlag B.G. Teubner, Leipzig

BONNER, Gerald 1993, "Augustine's Thoughts on this World and Hope for the Next" in *Hope for the Kingdom and Responsibility for the* Word, Princeton Seminary Bulletin Supplementary Issues 3.85-103

BONSIRVEN, Joseph 1951, *L'Apocalypse de Saint Jean, traduction et commentaire*, Verbum Salutis 16, Beauchesne, Paris

BORG, Marcus J. 1984, *Conflict, Holiness and Politics in the Teachings of Jesus*, Edwin Mellen Press, New York

BORING, M. Eugene 1986, "The Theology of Revelation; 'The Lord Our God the Almighty Reigns'", *Int* 40.257-269

BORING, M. Eugene 1989, *Revelation*, John Knox Press, IC, Louisville

BORING, M. Eugene 1993, "Revelation 19-21; End without Closure", Princeton Seminary Bulletin Supplementary Issues 3, *Hope for the Kingdom and Responsibility for the World*, 1993.57-84

BORNKAMM, Günther 1937, "Die Komposition der apokalyptischen Visionen in der Offenbarung Johannis", *ZNW* 36.132-149

BORNKAMM, Günther 1969a, "The Revelation of God's Wrath; Romans 1-3", in *Early Christian Experience*, New Testament Library, SCM Press, London, 1969.47-70

BORNKAMM, Günther, 1969b, "On the Understanding of Worship", in *Early Christian Experience*, New Testament Library, SCM Press, London, 1969.161-179

BOURDILLON, M.F.C. and FORTES, Meyer (editors) 1980, *Sacrifice*, Academic Press for the Royal Anthropological Institute of Great Britain and Ireland, London

BOUSSET, Wilhelm 1896a, *Die Offenbarung Johannis*, Vandenhoeck & Ruprecht, Göttingen

BOUSSET, Wilhelm 1896b, *The Antichrist Legend; a Chapter in Christian and Jewish Folklore*, Hutchinson, London

BOWMAN, John W. 1955 "The Revelation to John; Its Dramatic Structure and Message", *Int* 9.436-453

BOWMAN, John W. 1962, "Revelation, Book of", *IDB* 4.58-71

BOXALL, Ian 1992, *On the Side of the Lamb? A Socio-Psychological Perspective on the Theme of Martyrdom and Persecution in the Book of Revelation*, A thesis submitted for the degree of Master of Philosophy, University of Oxford

BOXALL, Ian 2002, *Revelation: Vision and Insight: An Introduction to the Apocalypse*, SPCK, London

BOXALL, Ian 2006, *The Revelation of St John*, Black's New Testament Commentaries, Continuum, London

BOYARIN, Daniel 1994, *A Radical Jew; Paul and the Politics of Identity*, University of California Press, Berkeley

BOYD, Robert 1948, "The Book of Revelation", *Int* 2.467-482

BRADLEY, Ian 1995, *The Power of Sacrifice*, Darton, Longman and Todd, London

BRADY, David 1979, "1666; the Year of the Beast", *Bulletin of the John Rylands University Library of Manchester* 61.314-336

BRADY, David 1983, *The Contribution of British Writers between 1560 and 1830 to the Interpretation of Revelation 13.16-18: (the Number of the Beast); a Study in the History of Exegesis*, BGBE 27, J.C.B. Mohr (Paul Siebeck), Tübingen

BREDIN, M.R.J. 1996, "The Influence of the Aqedah on Revelation 5.6-9", *IBS* 18.26-43

BREWER, Raymond R. 1952, "Revelation 4.6 and Translations thereof", *JBL* 71.227-231
BRIGHTMAN, F.E. 1915, *The English Rite; Being a Synopsis of the Sources and Revisions of the Book of Common Prayer*, Volume 1, Rivington, London
BROGAN, J.R. 1990, *Twentieth Century Light on the End of the Age; an Assessment of the Protestant Continuing Historicist Interpretation of the Books of Daniel and the Apocalypse brought through to the Year 2,000A.D.*, 2nd Edition, published by the author, Southampton
BROOKS, Terry 1988, *Revelation; Meaningful Mysteries for Today*, Harvestime, Bradford
BRUCE, F.F. 1938, "The Earliest Latin Commentary on the Apocalypse", *EQ* 10.352-366
BRUCE, F.F. 1979, "The Revelation to John", in Howley, G.C.D. (editor), *A Bible Commentary for Today*, Pickering and Inglis, London
BRÜTSCH, Charles 1966, *La Clarté de l'Apocalypse*, Fifth Edition, Éditions Labor et Fides, Geneva
BUCHANAN, George Wesley 1978, "The Word of God and the Apocalyptic Vision", *SBL Seminar Papers* 2.183-192
BUCHANAN, George Wesley 1993, *The Book of Revelation; Its Introduction and Prophecy*, Mellen Biblical Commentary 22, Mellen Biblical Press, Lewiston
BÜCHSEL and HERMANN 1967, "ἵλεως, ἱλάσκομαι, ἱλασμός, ἱλαστήριον", *TDNT* 3.300-323
BUIS, Harry 1974, *The Book of Revelation; a Simplified Commentary*, Presbyterian and Reformed Publishing, Philadelphia
BULL, Malcolm (editor) 1995a, *Apocalypse Theory and the Ends of the World*, Blackwell, Oxford
BULL, Malcom 1995b, "On Making Ends Meet", in Bull 1995a.1-16
BULTMANN, Rudolf 1955, *Theology of the New Testament* Volume 2, SCM Press, London
BURCH, V. 1939, *Anthropology and the Apocalypse; an Interpretation of "The Book of the Revelation" in Relation to the Archaeology, Folklore, and Religious Literature and Ritual of the Near East*, Macmillan, London
BURDON, C. 1997, *The Apocalypse in England 1700-1839; the Apocalypse Unveiling*, Abingdon, Nashville
BUREAU, René 1988, "A Gabonese Myth", in Dumouchel 1988a.27-43
BURGESS, Anthony 1972, *A Clockwork Orange*, Penguin, Harmondsworth
BURKITT, F. Crawford 1914, *Jewish and Christian Apocalypses*, The British Academy
BURNET, Adam W. 1946, *The Lord Reigneth; the Russell Lectures for 1944 on the Book of Revelation*, Hodder and Stoughton, London
BURR, David 1976, *The Persecution of Peter Olivi*, TAPSNS 66.5, The American Philosophical Society, Philadelphia
BURR, David 1989, *Olivi and Franciscan Poverty; the Origins of the Usus Pauper Controversy*, UPPMAS, University of Pennsylvania Press, Philadelphia
BURR, David 1992, "Mendicant Readings of the Apocalypse", in Emmerson 1992a.89-102

BURR, David 1993, *Olivi's Peaceable Kingdom; a Reading of the Apocalypse Commentary*, UPPMAS, University of Pennsylvania Press, Philadelphia

BUTLER, Judith 1987, *Subjects of Desire; Hegelian Reflections in Twentieth Century France*, Columbia University Press, New York

CABANISS, Allen 1953, "A Note on the Liturgy of the Apocalypse", *Int* 7.78-86

CAINES, G.A. 1960, *The Mystery of God*, Arthur H. Stockwell, Ilfracombe

CAIRD, G.B. 1956, *Principalities and Powers; a Study in Pauline Theology*, Clarendon Press, Oxford

CAIRD, G.B. 1980, *The Language and Imagery of the Bible*, Duckworth, London

CAIRD, G.B. 1984, *A Commentary on the Revelation of St. John the Divine*, Second Edition, BNTC, A & C Black, London

CAIRD, G.B. 1994, *New Testament Theology*, edited by L.D. Hurst, Clarendon Press, Oxford

CALLOUD, Jean, DELORNE, Jean and DUPLANTIER, Jean-Pierre 1977, "L'Apocalypse de Jean; propositions pour une analyse structurale", in Monloubou 1977.351-381

CAMILLE, Michael 1992, "Visionary Perception and Images of the Apocalypse in the Later Middle Ages", in Emmerson 1992a.276-289

CAPEL, Evelyn Francis 1989, *Pictures from the Apocalypse*, Temple Lodge Press, London

CAPP, Bernard 1984, "The Political Dimension of Apocalyptic Thought", in Patrides 1984a.93-124

CARNEGIE, David R. 1982, "Worthy is the Lamb; the Hymns of Revelation", in Harold H. Rowdon (editor), *Christ the Lord; Studies in Christology Presented to Donald Guthrie*, Inter-Varsity Press, Leicester

CARR, Wesley 1981, *Angels and Principalities; the Background, Meaning and Development of the Pauline Phrase hai archai kai hai exousiai*, SNTSMS 42, Cambridge University Press

CARRINGTON, Philip 1931, *The Meaning of the Revelation*, SPCK, London

CARTER, Jeffrey (editor) 2003, *Understanding Religious Sacrifice*; A Reader, Continuum, London

CASEY, Jay 1987, "The Exodus Theme in the Book of Revelation against the Background of the New Testament", *Concilium* 189.34-43

CAZELLES, Brigitte et GIRARD, René (editors) 1987, *Alphone Juilland; d'une passion l'autre*, Stanford French and Italian Studies 53

CAZES, Bernard 1986, "Fragile Désacrilisation", in Juilland 1986a.113-119

CHARLES, R.H. 1913, *Studies in the Apocalypse*, T & T Clark, Edinburgh

CHARLES, R.H. 1920, *A Critical and Exegetical Commentary on the Revelation of St. John*, ICC 46, T & T Clark, Edinburgh

CHARLES, R.H. 1922, *Lectures on the Apocalypse*, British Academy, London

CHARLESWORTH, James H. 1986, "The Jewish Roots of Christology; the Discovery of the Hypostatic Voice", *SJT* 39.19-41

CHARLESWORTH, James H. (editor) 1992, *The Messiah; Developments in Earliest Judaism and Christianity*, Fortress Press, Minneapolis

CHILDS, Brevard S. 1984, *The New Testament as Canon; an Introduction*, SCM Press, London

CHILTON, Bruce 1992, *The Temple of Jesus; his Sacrificial Program within a Cultural History of Sacrifice*, Pennsylvania State University Press, Pennsylvania
CHO, Paul Yonggi 1992, *Revelation; Visions of Our Ultimate Victory in Christ*, Word, Milton Keynes
CHRISTE, Yves 1992, "The Apocalypse in the Monumental Art of the Eleventh through Thirteenth Centuries", in Emmerson 1992a.234-258
CLOUSE, Robert G. (editor) 1977, *The Meaning of the Millenium; Four Views*, InterVarsity Press, Downers Grove
COFFIN, Henry Sloane 1951, "'To Him That Overcometh'; a Meditation", *Int* 5.40-45
COHN, Norman 1993a, *The Pursuit of the Millenium; Revolutionary Millenarians and Mystical Anarchists in the Middle Ages*, Pimlico Edition, London
COHN, Norman 1993b, *Europe's Inner Demons; the Demonization of Christians in Medieval Christendom*, Revised Edition, Pimlico, London
COHN, Norman 1993c, *Cosmos, Chaos and the World to Come; the Ancient Roots of Apocalyptic Faith*, Yale University Press, New Haven
COHN, Robert L. 1981, *The Shape of Sacred Space; Four Biblical Studies*, AARSR 23, Scholars Press, Chico
COLLINS, John J. 1974, "Apocalyptic Eschatology as the Transcendence of Death", *CBQ* 36.21-43
COLLINS, John J. 1977a, "Pseudonymity, Historical Reviews and the Genre of the Revelation of John", *CBQ* 39.329-343
COLLINS, John J. 1977b, "The Meaning of Sacrifice; a Contrast of Methods", *BR* 22.19-31
COLLINS, John J. 1979, "Towards the Morphology of a Genre", *Semeia* 14.1-20
COLLINS, John J. 1984, *The Apocalyptic Imagination; an Introduction to the Jewish Matrix of Christianity*, Crossroad, New York
COLLINS, John J. 1986, "Apocalyptic Literature", in Robert A. Kraft and George W.E. Nickelsburg (editors), *Early Judaism and Its Modern Interpreters*, Fortress Press, Philadelphia
COLLINS, John J. and CHARLESWORTH, James H. 1991, *Mysteries and Revelations; Apocalyptic Studies since the Uppsala Colloquium*, JSPSS 9, JSOT Press, Sheffield
COLLINS, Robin. 2000, "Girard and Atonement: An Incarnational Theory of Mimetic Participation" in Swartley 2000, 132-153
COMBLIN, J. 1953, "La Liturgie de la nouvelle Jérusalem" (Apoc., XXI,1-XXII,5), *ETL* 29.5-40
CONGAR, Yves M.-J. 1962, *The Mystery of the Temple or the Manner of God's Presence to His Creatures from Genesis to the Apocalypse*, Burns and Oates, London
CONSIDINE, J.S. 1944, "The Rider on the White Horse; Apocalypse 6:1-8", *CBQ* 6.406-422
CORSINI, Eugenio 1983, *The Apocalypse; the Perennial Revelation of Jesus Christ*, GNS 5, Veritas Publications, Dublin
COUCHARD, Paul Louis 1932, *The Book of Revelation; a Key to Christian*

Origins, Watts, London
COURT, John M. 1979, *Myth and History in the Book of Revelation*, SPCK, London
COURT, John M. 1983, "Risen, Ascended, Glorified", *King's Theological Review* 6.39-42
COURT, John M. 1994, *Revelation*, New Testament Guides, JSOT Press, Sheffield
COWLEY, Roger W. 1983, *The Traditional Interpretation of the Apocalypse of St. John in the Ethiopian Orthodox Church*, Cambridge University Press
CRADDOCK, Fred B. 1986, "Preaching the Book of Revelation", *Int* 40.270-282
CRAIGIE, Peter C. 1983, *Psalms 1-50*, WBC 19, Word, Waco
CRANFIELD, C.E.B. 1975, *A Critical and Exegetical Commentary on the Epistle to the Romans*, ICC, T & T Clark, Edinburgh
CROSS, Frank Moore 1969, "New Directions in the Study of Apocalyptic", *JTC* 6.157-165
CROSS, Frank Moore 1973, *Canaanite Myth and Hebrew Epic; Essays in the History of the Religion Israel*, Harvard University Press, Cambridge Mass.
CROSSAN, John Dominic 1991, *The Historical Jesus; the Life of a Mediterranean Peasant*, T & T Clark, Edinburgh
CULLER, Jonathan 1975, *Structuralist Poetics; Structuralism, Lingusitics and the Study of Literature*, Routledge, London
CULLMANN, Oscar 1936, "Le Caractère eschatologique du devoir missionaire et de la conscience apostolique de S. Paul; étude sur le katšcon (-wn) de 2. Thess. 2:6-7", *RHPR* 1936.210-245
CULLMANN, Oscar 1951, *Christ and Time; the Primitive Christian Conception of Time and History*, SCM Press, London
CULLMANN, Oscar 1956, "Eschatology and Missions in the New Testament", in W.D. Davies 1956.409-421
CULLMANN, Oscar 1967, *Salvation in History*, New Testament Library, SCM Press, London
DAALEN, David H. van 1986, *A Guide to the Revelation*, Theological Education Fund Study Guide 20, SPCK, London
DALEY, Brian E. 1991, *The Hope of the Early Church; a Handbook of Patristic Theology*, Cambridge University Press
DANIEL, R. Randolph 1992, "Joachim of Fiore; Patterns of History in the Apocalypse", in Emmerson 1992a.72-88
D'ARAGON, Jean-Louis 1968, "The Apocalypse", in Raymond Brown and others (editors), *The Jerome Bible Commentary*, Geoffrey Chapman, London
DARR, John A. 1993, "Mimetic Desire, the Gospels, and Early Christianity: a Response to René Girard", *Biblical Interpretation* 1, 357-367
DAUBE, David 1963, *The Exodus Pattern in the Bible*, Faber & Faber, London
DAVIES, W.D. and DAUBE, David 1956, *The Background of the New Testament and Its Eschatology; in Honour of Charles Harold Dodd*, Cambridge University Press
DAVIES, W.D. 1962, *Paul and Rabbinic Judaism*, SPCK, London
DAVIS, Charles 1989, "Sacrifices and Violence; New Perspectives in the Theory of Religion from René Girard", *New Blackfriars* 70, 311-328

DAVIS, R. Dean 1992, *The Heavenly Court Judgement of Revelation 4-5*, University Press of America, Lanham

DAY, John 1985, *God's Conflict with the Dragon and the Sea; Echoes of a Canaanite Myth in the Old Testament*, UCOP 35, Cambridge University Press

DAY, John 1990, *Psalms*, Old Testament Guides, JSOT Press, Sheffield

DAY, John 1994, "The Origin of Armageddon; Revelation 16.16 as an Interpretation of Zechariah 12:11", in Stanley E. Porter 1994.315-326

DEGUY, Michel and DUPUY, Jean-Pierre 1982, *René Girard et le problème du mal; textes rassemblés par Michel Deguy et Jean-Pierre Dupuy*, Bernard Grasset, Paris

DEHANDSCHUTTER, B. 1980, "The Meaning of Witness in the Apocalypse", in Lambrecht 1980a.283-288

DEICHGRÄBER, Reinhard 1967, *Gotteshymnus und Christushymnus in der frühen Christenheit: Untersuchungen zu Form, Sprache und Stil der frühchristlichen Hymnen*, SUNT 5, Vandenhoeck & Ruprecht, Göttingen

DELARGE, Frédéric 1985, "Statut de l'Évangile dans l'oeuvre de René Girard", in Dumouchel 1985.221-225

DELCOR, Matthias 1977a, "Bilan des études sur l'apocalyptique", in Monloubou 1977.27-42

DELCOR, Matthias 1977b, "Mythologie et Apocalyptique", in Monloubou 1977.143-177

DELLING, Gerhard 1959, "Zum Gottesdienstlichen Stil der Johannes-Apokalypse", *NovT* 3.107-137

DERRIDA, Jacques 1981, "Plato's Pharmacy", in *Dissemination*, Athlone Press, London, 63-171

DERRIDA, Jacques 1989, "Desistance", in Lacoue-Labarthe 1989.1-42

DERRIDA, Jacques 1992, "Of an Apocalyptic Tone Newly Adopted in Philosophy", in Harold Coward and Tobay Foshay, *Derrida and Negative Theology*, State University of New York Press, 25-71

DESCOMBES, Vincent 1980, *Modern French Philosophy*, Cambridge University Press, 1980

DETIENNE, Marcel and VERNANT, Jean-Pierre (Editors), 1989a, *The Cuisine of Sacrifice among the Greeks*, University of Chicago Press

DETIENNE, Marcel 1989b, "Culinary Practices and the Spirit of Sacrifice", in Detienne and Vernant, 1-20

DEUTSCH, Celia 1987, "Transformation of Symbols; the New Jerusalem in Rv 211-225", *ZNW* 78.106-126

DEWEY, Joanna 1993, "A Response to René Girard's 'Is There Anti-Semitisn in the Gospels?'", *Biblical Interpretation* 1, 353-356

DILLISTONE, F.W. 1968, *The Christian Understanding of Atonement*, James Nisbet, Welwyn

D'IRIBANE, Philippe 1985, "René Girard et l'amour évangelique", in Dumouchel 1985.227-234

DIX, G.H. 1927, "The Seven Archangels and the Seven Spirits; a Study of the Origin, Development, and Messianic Associations of the Two Themes", *JTS*, 28.233-250

DODD, C.H. 1932, *The Epistle to the Romans*, MNTC, Hodder and Stoughton,

London
DODD, C.H. 1935, *The Bible and the Greeks*, Hodder and Stoughton, London
DODD, C.H. 1954, *The Interpretation of the Fourth Gospel*, Cambridge University Press
DODD, C.H. 1960, *The Authority of the Bible*, Fontana, London
DODD, C.H. 1961, *The Parables of the Kingdom*, Collins Fount Paperbacks, Glasgow
DODD, C.H. 1963, *The Apostolic Preaching and Its Developments*, Hodder and Stoughton, London
DODD, C.H. 1978, *The Meaning of Paul for Today*, Collins Fount Paperbacks, Glasgow
DOMENACH, Jean-Marie 1988, "Voyage to the End of the Sciences of Man", in Dumouchel 1988a.152-159
DOUGLAS, Mary 1966. *Purity and Danger; an Analysis of Concepts of Pollution and Taboo*, Routledge and Kegan Paul, London
DOUGLAS, Mary 1967, "The Meaning of Myth", in Edmund Leach (editor), *The Structural Study of Myth and Totemism*, Association of Social Anthropologists of the Commonwealth Monographs 5, Tavistock Publications, London
DOUGLAS, Mary 1970, *Natural Symbols; Explorations in Cosmology*, Cresset Press, London
DOUGLAS, Mary 1975, *Implicit Meanings; Essays in Anthropology*, Routledge, London
DOUGLAS, Mary 1992, *Risk and Blame; Essays in Cultural Theory*, Routledge, London
DRAPER, J.A. 1983, "The Heavenly Feast of Tabernacles: Revelation 7.1-17", *JSNT* 19.133-147
DUMÉZIL, Georges 1980, *Camillus; a Study of Indo-European Religion as Roman History*, University of California Press, Berkeley
DUMÉZIL, Georges 1983, *The Stakes of a Warrior*, University of California Press, Berkeley
DUMOUCHEL, Paul and DUPUY, Jean-Pierre 1979, *L'enfer des choses; René Girard et la logique de l'économie*, Éditions du Seuil, Paris
DUMOUCHEL, Paul 1982 "Différences et paradoxes: réflexions sur l'amour et la violence dans l'oeuvre de Girard", in Deguy 1982.215-223
DUMOUCHEL, Paul (editor) 1985, *Violence et Vérité; autour de René Girard*, Bernard Grasset, Paris
DUMOUCHEL, Paul 1986, "Hobbes; la Course à la souveraintée" in Juilland 1986a.153-176
DUMOUCHEL, Paul (editor) 1988a, *Violence and Truth: on the Work of René Girard*, The Athlone Press, London, (partial ET of Dumouchel 1985)
DUMOUCHEL, Paul 1988b, "Introduction", in Dumouchel 1988a, 1-21
DUMOUCHEL, Paul 1988c, "Ouverture", in Dumouchel 1988a, 23-26
DUNN, James D.G. 1988, *Romans 1-8*, WBC 38a, Word, Milton Keynes, 1988
DUPUY, Jean-Pierre 1986, "John Rawls et la question du sacrifice", in Juilland 1986a.135-152
DUPUY, Jean-Pierre 1988, "Totalization and Misrecognition", in Dumouchel 1988a.75-100

DUROUSSEA, Cliff 1984, "The Commentary of Oecumenius on the Apocalypse of John; a Lost Chapter in the History of Interpretation", *BR* 29.21-34
DUSSAUD, René 1921, *Les origines Cananéennes du sacrifice Israélite*, Ernest Leroux, Paris
EAGLETON, Terry 1983, *Literary Theory; an Introduction*, Blackwell, Oxford
EATON, J.H. 1994, "'A Bloodless Compromise?' The Question of an Eschatological Ritual in Ancient Israel" in Stanley E. Porter 1994.69-82
ECO, Umberto 1984, *The Name of the Rose*, Picador, London
EFIRD, James H. 1989, *Revelation for Today; an Apocalyptic Approach*, Abingdon Press, Nashville
ELIADE, Mircea 1954, *The Myth of the Eternal Return*, BS 46, Pantheon Books, New York
ELIADE, Mircea 1958, *Birth and Rebirth; the Religious Meanings of Initiation in Human Culture*, Hamill Press, London
ELIADE, Mircea 1961, *The Sacred and the Profane; the Nature of Religion*, Harper Torchbooks, Harper and Row, New York
ELIADE, Mircea 1963, *Myth and Reality*, George Allen, London
ÉLIE, Bernard-Weil, 1985, "Théologie et systémique", in Dumouchel 1985.93-109
ELLIOTT, Charles 1995, *Memory and Salvation*, Darton, Longman and Todd, London
ELLIOTT, E.B. 1862, *Horae Apocalypticae; or, a Commentary on the Apocalypse, Critical and Historical; Including also an Examination of the Chief Prophecies of Daniel*, Fifth Edition in 4 Volumes, Seeley, Jackson and Halliday, London
ELLIOTT, Neil 1990, *The Rhetoric of Romans; Argumentative Constraint and Strategy and Pauls 'Dialogue with Judaism*, JSNTSS 45, JSOT Press, Sheffield
ELLIOTT, Neil 1994, *Liberating Paul; The Justice of God and the Politics of the Apostle*, Orbis Books, Maryknoll
ELLUL, Jacques 1977, *Apocalypse; the Book of Revelation*, Seabury Press, New York
EMMERSON, Richard K. and McGINN, Bernard 1992a, *The Apocalypse in the Middle Ages*, Cornell University Press, Ithaca
EMMERSON, Richard K. 1992b, "Introduction; the Apocalypse in Medieval Culture", in Emmerson 1992a.291-332
ENROTH, Anne-Marit 1990, "The Hearing Formula in the Book of Revelation", *NTS* 36.598-608
FANON, Frantz 1967, *The Wretched of the Earth*, Penguin, Harmondsworth
FARMER, W.R., MOULE, C.F.D. and NIEBUHR, R.R. (editors) 1967, *Christian History and Interpretation; Studies Presented to John Knox*, Cambridge University Press
FARRER, Austin 1949, *A Rebirth of Images; the Making of St. John's Apocalypse*, Dacre Press, Westminster
FARRER, Austin, 1964, *The Revelation of St. John the Divine; Commentary on the English Text*, Clarendon Press, Oxford
FEENBERG, Andrew 1988, "Fetishism and Form; Erotic and Economic

Disorder in Literature", in Dumouchel 1988a.134-151
FEKKES, Jan 1994, *Isaiah and Prophetic Traditions in the Book of Revelation; Visionary Antecedents and Their Development*, JSNTSS 93, JSOT, Sheffield
FÉRET, H.M. 1958, *The Apocalypse of St. John*, Blackfriars, London
FEUILLET, André 1958, "Les vingt-quatre viellards de l'Apocalypse", *RB* 65.5-32
FEUILLET, André 1963, *L'Apocalypse; l'état de la question*, Desclée de Brouwer, Paris
FEUILLET, André 1964a, *The Apocalypse*, Alba House, Staten Island, ET of 1963
FEUILLET, André 1964b, *Johannine Studies*, Alba House, Staten Island
FEUILLET, André 1966, "Le premier cavalier de l'Apocalypse", *ZNW* 57.229-259
FEUILLET, André 1977, "Les martyrs de l'humanité et l'agneau égorgé; une interprétation nouvelle de la prière des égorgés en Ap 6,9-11", *NRT* 99.189-207
FIDDES, Paul S. 1989, *Past Event and Present Salvation; the Christian Idea of Atonement*, Darton, Longman and Todd, London
FINAMORE, Steve 2000, *The Bible, Violence and the End of the World*, Whitley, Oxford
FINAMORE, Stephen 2004, "Violence and Covetousness: Nor anything Else that Belongs to Thy Neighbour" in Clarke, Anthony (editor), *Expecting Justice but Seeing Bloodshed: Some Baptist Contributions to Following Jesus in a Violent World*, Whitley, Oxford, 9-23
FIREBRACE, Aylmer 1963, *The Revelation to John: "...as Clear as Crystal..."; a Spiritually Scientific Interpretation*, Peter Owen, London
FIRTH, Katharine R. 1979, *The Apocalyptic Tradition in Reformation Britain 1530-1645*, OHM, Oxford University Press
FITZMYER, Joseph A. 1960-1961, "The Use of Explicit Old Testament Quotations in Qumran Literature and in the New Testament", *NTS* 7.297-333
FITZMYER, Joseph A. 1993, *Romans: A New Translation with Introduction and Commentary,* AB 33, Geoffrey Chapman, London
FLANIGAN, C. Clifford 1992, "The Apocalypse and the Medieval Liturgy", in Emmerson 1992a.333-351
FODOR, Jim 2000, "Christian Discipleship as Participative Imitation: Theological Reflections on Girardian Themes" in Swartley 2000, 246-276
FORD, J. Massyngberde 1971, "The Divorce Bill of the Lamb and the Scroll of the Suspected Adulteress; a Note on Apoc. 5,1 and 10,8-11", *JSJ* 2.136-143
FORD, J. Massyngberde 1975, *Revelation*, AB 38, Doubleday, Garden City
FORD, J. Massyngberde 1986-1987, "The Structure and Meaning of Revelation 16", *ExpT* 98.327-331
FORD, J. Massyngberde 1995, "The Construction of the Other: the Antichrist", *AUSS* 33, 203-230
FORESTELL, J. Terence 1974, *The Word of the Cross; Salvation as Revelation in the Fourth Gospel*, Biblical Institute Press, Rome
FORSTER, James W. 1853, *The Apocalypse its own Interpreter by the Application of a Sound and Ancient Rule for the Interpreting of Holy Scripture: to which is Added a Short Series of Dissertations on Symbolic

Prophecy, its Nature and Design, Richard Bentley, London
FORSYTH, P.T. 1909, *The Cruciality of the Cross*, Hodder and Stoughton, London
FORTNA, Robert T. and GAVENTA, Beverley R. 1990, (editors), *The Conversation Continues; Studies in Paul and John*, Abingdon Press, Nashville, 1990
FOXE, John 1563, *Actes and Monumentes of these Latter and Perillous Dayes, Touching Matters of the Church, wherein ar Comprehended and Described the Great Persecutions and Horrible Troubles, that have been Wrought and Practised by the Romanishe Prelates, Speciallye in this Realme of England and Scotlande. From the Yeare of our Lorde a thousande, unto the Tyme now Present*, First Edition.
FRAZER, James George 1922, *The Golden Bough; a Study in Magic and Religion*, Abridged Edition, Macmillan, London
FREDRIKSEN, Paula 1991, "Apocalypse and Redemption in Early Christianity; from John of Patmos to Augustine of Hippo", *Vigiliae Christianae* 45.151-183
FREDRIKSEN, Paula 1992, "Tyconius and Augustine on the Apocalypse", in Emmerson 1992a.20-37
FRÉMONT, Christiane 1986, "De la croyance et du savoir", in Juilland 1986a.197-201
FRENCH, S.H. 1968, *The Unsealed Book; an Exposition of the Book of Revelation*, Prophetic Light Publications, London
FREND, W.H.C. 1965, *Martyrdom and Persecution in the Early Church; a Study of a Conflict from the Maccabees to Donatus*, Basil Blackwell, Oxford
FREUD, Sigmund 1950, *Totem and Taboo; some Points of Agreement between the Mental Lives of Savages and Neurotics*, Routledge and Kegan Paul, London
FREUD, Sigmund 1939, *Moses and Monotheism*, Hogarth Press, London
FRIESEN, Steven J. 1995, "Revelation, Realia and Religion; Archaeology in the Interpretation of the Apocalypse", *HTR* 88.291-314
FRYE, Northrop 1957, *Anatomy of Criticism; Four Essays*, Princeton University Press
FRYE, Northrop 1981, *The Great Code; the Bible and Literature*, Routledge, London
FUNK, Robert W. 1967, "The Apostolic *Parousia*; Form and Significance", in W.R. Farmer 1967.249-268
FURCHA, E.J. 1984, *Selected Writings of Huldrych Zwingli*, Volume 1, *The Defense of the Reformed Faith*, Pittsburg Theological Monographs 12, Pickwick Publications, Allison Park
GAGER, John 1975, *Kingdom and Community; the Social World of Early Christianity*, Prentice-Hall, Prentice-Hall Studies in Religion Series, Englewood Cliffs
GANS, Eric 1973, "Pour une esthétique triangulaire", *Esprit* 41, 564-581
GANS, Eric 1981, *The Origin of Language; a Formal Theory of Representation*, University of California Press, Berkeley
GANS, Eric 1982 "Le *Logos* de René Girard", in Deguy 1982.179-213
GANS, Eric 1985, *The End of Culture; towards a Generative Anthropology*,

University of California Press, Berkeley
GANS, Eric 1985b, "Christian Morality and the Pauline Revelation", *Semeia* 33.97-108
GANS, Eric 1986, "Sacred Text in Secular Culture", in Juilland 1986a.51-64
GANS, Eric 1993, *Originary Thinking; Elements of a Generative Anthropology*, Stanford University Press
GARROW, A.J.P. 1997, *Revelation*, Routledge, London
GASCOYNE, R. 1875, *A New Solution in Part of John's Revelation, Showing that Chapters I.-XI. Chiefly Describe the Apostasy, and Chapters XII.-XXII. the True Church*, 3rd Edition, James Nisbet, London
GEERTZ, Clifford 1993, "Religion as a Cultural System", in *The Interpretation of Cultures; Selected Essays*, Fontana Press, London, 1993.87-125
GENNEP, Arnold van 1960, *The Rites of Passage*, Routledge and Kegan Paul, London
GEORGI, Dieter 1986, "Who Is the True Prophet?", *HTR* 79.100-126
GIBLIN, Charles Homer 1974, "Structural and Thematic Correlations in the Theology of Revelation 16-22", *Bib* 55.487-504
GIBLIN, Charles Homer 1984, "Revelation 11.1-13; Its Form, Function and Contextual Integration", *NTS*, 30.433-459
GIBLIN, Charles Homer 1991, *The Book of Revelation; the Open Book of Prophecy*, The Liturgical Press, *GNS* 34, Collegeville
GIBLIN, Charles Homer 1994, "Recapitulation and the Literary Coherence of John's Apocalypse", *CBQ* 56.81-95
GIET, Stanislas 1957, *L'Apocalypse et l'histoire; étude historique sur l'Apocalypse johannique*, Presses Universitaires de France, Paris
GIRARD, René 1961, *Mensonge romantique et vérité romanesque*, Grasset, Paris
GIRARD, René 1965, *Deceit, Desire and the Novel; Self and Other in Literary Structure*, The Johns Hopkins University Press, Baltimore, ET of 1961
GIRARD, René 1970, "Dionysos et la genèse violente du sacré", *Poétique* 1, 266-281
GIRARD, René 1973a, "Discussion avec René Girard", *Esprit* 41, 528-563
GIRARD, René 1973b, "Lévi-Strauss, Frye, Derrida and Shakespearian Criticism", *Diacritics* 3, 34-38
GIRARD, René 1976a, *Critiques dans un souterrain*, Grasset, Paris
GIRARD, René 1976b, "Superman in the Underground; Strategies of Madness - Nietzsche, Wagner and Dostoevsky", *MLN* 91.1161-1185
GIRARD, René (editor), 1977a, *Proust; a Collection of Critical Essays*, Greenwood Press, Westport
GIRARD, René 1977b, "Introduction", in Girard 1977a.1-12
GIRARD, René 1978a, "Interview with René Girard", *Diacritics* 8.31-54
GIRARD, René 1978b, "Quand ces choses commenceront...", *Tel Quel* 78.37-57
GIRARD, René 1979, *Violence and the Sacred*, The Johns Hopkins University Press, Baltimore and London, paperback edition.
GIRARD, René 1984, "Dionysus versus the Crucified", *MLN* 99, 816-835
GIRARD, René 1985, "The Ancient Trail Trodden by the Wicked", *Semeia* 33.13-41

GIRARD, René 1986a, *The Scapegoat*, The Athlone Press, London
GIRARD, René 1986b, "Nietzsche and Contradiction", *Stanford Italian Review* 6.53-65
GIRARD, René 1987a, *Things Hidden Since the Foundation of the World*, with Jean-Michel Oughoulian and Guy Lefort, The Athlone Press, London.
GIRARD, René 1987b, *Job: The Victim of His People*, Stanford University Press. 1985
GIRARD, René 1987c, "Generative Scapegoating" in Hamerton-Kelly 1987.73-105
GIRARD, René 1987d, "Jealousy in *The Winter's Tale*", in Cazelles 1987.39-62
GIRARD, René 1988a, *"To Double Business Bound": Essays on Literature, Mimesis, and Anthropology*, The Athlone Press, London
GIRARD, René 1988b, "The Founding Murder in the Philosophy of Nietzsche", in Dumouchel 1988a.227-246
GIRARD, René 1990, "Do You Love Him because I Do! Mimetic Interaction in Shakespeare's Comedies", *Helios* 17.1.89-107
GIRARD, René 1991, *A Theater of Envy; William Shakespeare*, Oxford University Press, New York
GIRARD, René 1993, "Is There Anti-Semitism in the Gospels?", *Biblical Interpretation* 1, 339-356
GIRARD, René 2001, *I See Satan Fall like Lightning*, Gracewing, Leominster
GLASSON, T. Francis 1961, *Greek Influence in Jewish Eschatology*, Biblical Monographs 1, SPCK, London
GLASSON, T. Francis 1965, *The Revelation of John*, CBC, Cambridge University Press
GLASSON, T. Francis 1988, "Theophany and Parousia", *NTS* 34.259-270
GOERTZ, Hans-Jürgen 1993, *Thomas Müntzer; Apocalyptic, Mystic and Revolutionary*, T & T Clark, Edinburgh
GOLDINGAY, John 1995a, *Atonement Today*, SPCK, London
GOLDINGAY, John 1995b, "Old Testament Sacrifice and the Death of Christ", in Goldingay 1995a.3-20
GOLDSWORTHY, Graeme 1984, *The Gospel in Revelation; Gospel and Apocalypse*, Paternoster Press, Exeter
GONZÁLEZ, Catherine Gunsalus and GONZÁLEZ Justo L. 1997, *Revelation*, Westminster Bible Companion, Westminster John Knox Press, Louisville
GOODHART, Sandor 1985, "Prophecy, Sacrifice and Repentance in the Story of Jonah", in *Semeia* 33.43-63
GOODHART, Sandor 1988, "'I am Joseph'; René Girard and the Prophetic Law", in Dumouchel 1988a.53-74
GORDON, R.L. 1972, "Mithraism and Roman Society; Social Factors in the Explanation of Religious Change in the Roman Empire", *Religion* 2.92-121
GORDON, Robert P. 1983, "Loricate Locusts in the Targum to Nahum III 17 and Revelation IX 9", *VT* 33.338-339
GORRINGE, Timothy 1986, *Redeeming Time; Atonement through Education*, Darton, Longman and Todd, London
GORRINGE, Timothy 1996, *God's Just Vengeance; Crime, Violence and the Rhetoric of Salvation*, CSIR 9, Cambridge University Press

GOULDER, Michael D. 1980-1981, "The Apocalypse as an Annual Cycle of Prophecies", *NTS* 27.342-367
GRANSTEDT, Ingmar 1985, "L'épilogue violent de la mimésis technoéconomique", in Dumouchel 1985.275-280
GRAY, George Buchanan 1925, *Sacrifice in the Old Testament; Its Theory and Practice*, Clarendon Press, Oxford
GRAYSTON, Kenneth 1990, *Dying, We Live; a New Enquiry into the Death of Christ in the New Testament*, Darton, Longman and Todd, London
GRAYSTON, Kenneth 1992, "Heaven and Hell; a Door Opened in Heaven", *Epworth Review* 19.19-26
GREEN, Kelly M. 1995, Review of Gil Bailie, *Violence Unveiled; Humanity at the Crossroads*, Crossroad, New York, 1995, *Sojourners* November-December 1995.80-83
GREVE, A. 1978, "'Mine to vidner'. Et forsøg på at identifecere de to jerusalemitiske vidner (Apok 11,2-13)", reported in *NTA* 22.53
GREY, Mary 1989, *Redeeming the Dream; Feminism, Redemption and Christian Tradition*, SPCK, London
GRIER, W.J. 1970, *The Momentous Event; a Discussion of Scripture Teaching on the Second Advent*, Banner of Truth, Edinburgh
GRIFFITHS, Frederick T. 1990, "Murder, Purification, and Cultural Formation in Aeschylus and Apollonius Rhodius", *Helios* 17.1.25-39
GRIMSRUD, Ted 2000, "Scapegoating No More: Christian Pacifism and New Testament Views of Jesus' Death" in Swartley 2000, 49-69
GUDORF, Christine E. 1992, *Victimization; Examining Christian Complicity*, Trinity Press International, Philadelphia
GUNDRY, Robert H. 1987, "The New Jerusalem; People as Place, not Place for People", *NovT* 29.254-264
GUNKEL, Hermann J.F. 1921, *Schöpfung und Chaos in Urzeit und Endzeit; eine Religionsgeschichtliche Untersuchung über Gen 1 und Ap Joh 12*, Vandenhoeck & Ruprecht, Göttingen.
GUNKEL, Hermann J.F. 1930, *Zum religiongeschichtlichen Verständnis des Neuen Testaments*, 3rd Edition, Forschungen zur Religion und Literatur des Alten und Neuen Testaments 1, Vandenhoeck & Ruprecht
GUNTHER, John J. 1981, "The Elder John, Author of Revelation", *JSNT* 11.3-20
GUNTON, Colin E. 1988, *The Actuality of Atonement; a Study of Metaphor, Rationality and the Christian Tradition*, T&T Clark, Edinburgh
HADORN, D.W. 1928, *Die Offenbarung des Johannes*, Theologischer Handkommentar zum Neuen Testament mit Text und Paraphrase, A. Deichertsche Verlagsbuchhandlung D. Werner Scholl, Leipzig
HALL, Robert G. 1990, "Living Creatures in the Midst of the Throne; Another Look at Revelation 4.6", *NTS* 36.609-613
HAMERTON-KELLY, Robert G. 1985, "A Girardian Interpretation of Paul: Rivalry, Mimesis and Victimage in the Corinthian Correspondence", *Semeia* 33.65-81
HAMERTON-KELLY, Robert G. (editor) 1987, BURKETT, Walter, GIRARD, René and SMITH, Jonathan Z., *Violent Origins; Ritual Killing and Cultural Formation*, Stanford University Press, Stanford California

HAMERTON-KELLY, Robert G. 1990, "Sacred Violence and Sinful Desire; Paul's Interpretation of Adam's Sin in the Letter to the Romans", in Robert T. Fortna and Beverly R. Gaventa (editors), *The Conversation Continues; Studies in Paul and John*, Abingdon Press, Nashville, 1990.35-54

HAMERTON-KELLY, Robert G. 1990, "Sacred Violence and the Curse of the Law (Galatians 3.13); the Death of Christ as a Sacrificial Travesty", *NTS* 36.98-118

HAMERTON-KELLY, Robert G. 1992a, *Sacred Violence; Paul's Hermeneutic of the Cross*, Fortress Press, Minneapolis

HAMERTON-KELLY, Robert G. 1992b, "Sacred Violence and the Messiah; the Markan Passion Narrative as a Redefinition of Messianology", in Charlesworth 1992.461-493

HAMERTON-KELLY, Robert G. 1994a, *The Gospel and the Sacred; Poetics of Violence in Mark*, Fortress Press, Minneapolis

HAMERTON-KELLY, Robert G. 1994b, "Religion and the Thought of René Girard; an Introduction", in Wallace 1994a.3-24

HANSON, Anthony Tyrrell 1957, *The Wrath of the Lamb*, SPCK, London

HANSON, Paul D. 1971, "Jewish Apocalyptic against Its Near Eastern Environment", *RB* 78.31-58

HANSON, Paul D. 1973, "Zechariah 9 and the Recapitulation of an Ancient Ritual", *JBL* 92.37-59

HANSON, Paul D. 1975, *The Dawn of Apocalyptic* Fortress Press, Philadelphia

HANSON, Paul D. 1983, *Visionaries and Their Apocalypses*, SPCK, Issues in Religion and Theology 2, 1983

HARDIN, Michael 2000, "Sacrificial Language in Hebrews: Reappraising René Girard" in Swartley 2000.103-119

HARRINGTON, Wilfred J. 1969, *The Apocalypse of St. John; a Commentary*, Geoffrey Chapman, London

HARRINGTON, Wilfred J. 1993, *Revelation*, Liturgical Press, SP 16, Collegeville

HARVEY, Anthony E. 1982, *Jesus and the Constraints of History*, Duckworth, London

HASITSCHKA, Martin 1994, "'Überwunden hat der Löwe aus dem Stamm Juda' (Offb 5,5): Funktion und Herkunft des Bildes vom Lamm in der Offenbarung des Johannes", *ZKTh* 116.487-493

HAUERWAS, Stanley 1996, Review of Gil Bailie, *Violence Unveiled; Humanity at the Crossroads*, Crossroad, New York, 1995, *Modern Theology* 12.115-117

HAUSSLEITER, Johannis 1916, *Victorini Episcopi Petauionensis Opera*, CSEL 49, Leipzig

HAYES, T. Wilson 1979, *Winstanley the Digger; a Literary Analysis of Radical Ideas in the English Revolution*, Harvard University Press, Cambridge Mass.

HEGEL, G.W.F. 1977, *Phenomenonology of Spirit*, Oxford University Press, Oxford

HEIL, John Paul 1993, "The Fifth Seal (Rev 6,9-11) as a Key to the Book of Revelation", *Bib* 74.220-243

HELLHOLM, David 1986, "The Problem of Apocalyptic Genre and the

Apocalypse of John", *Semeia* 36.13-64
HELLHOLM, David (editor) 1989, *Apocalypticism in the Mediterranean World and the Near East*, Second Edition, J.C.B. Mohr (Paul Siebeck), Tübingen
HELLHOLM, David 1991, "Methodological Reflections on the Problem of Definition of Generic Texts", in J.J. Collins 1991.135-163
HELMS, Charles Robert 1991, *The Apocalypse in the Early Church; Christ, Eschaton and Millenium*, D. Phil (c10291), University of Oxford
HEMER, Colin J. 1986, *The Letters to the Seven Churches of Asia in Their Local Setting*, JSOT Press, JSNTSS 11, Sheffield
HENDRIKSEN, William 1939, *More than Conquerors; an Interpretation of the Book of Revelation*, Baker, Grand Rapids
HENDRIKSEN, William 1971, *The Bible on the Life Hereafter*, Baker, Grand Rapids
HENGEL, Martin 1974, *Judaism and Hellenism; Studies in their Encounter in Palestine during the Early Hellenistic Period*, SCM Press, London
HENGSTENBERG, E.W. 1851, *The Revelation of St. John; Expounded for Those Who Search the Scriptures*, T&T Clark, Edinburgh
HENSEN, Hans J.L. 1993, "René Girard and Askel Sandemose; the Question of Salvation from Mimetic Double-Binds", *Journal of Literature and Theology* 7.66-77
HERZMAN, Ronald B. 1992, "Dante and the Apocalypse", in Emmerson 1992a.398-413
HEUSCH, Luc de 1985, *Sacrifice in Africa; a Structuralist Approach*, Manchester University Press
HILL, Christopher 1975, *The World Turned upside down; Radical Ideas during the English Revolution*, Penguin, Harmondsworth
HILL, David 1967, *Greek Words and Hebrew Meanings; Studies in the Semantics of Soteriological Terms*, SNTSMS 5, Cambridge University Press
HILL, David 1971-1972, "Prophecy and Prophets in the Revelation of St. John", *NTS* 18.401-418
HILLYER, Norman 1967, "'The Lamb' in the Apocalypse", *EQ* 39.228-236
HOBBS, Herschel H. 1971, *The Cosmic Drama; an Exposition of the Book of Revelation*, Word, Waco
HODGES, H.A. 1955, *The Pattern of Atonement*, SCM Press, London
HOLTZ, Traugott 1962, *Die Christologie der Apokalypse des Johannes*, Texte und Untersuchungen zur Geschichte der Altchristlichen Literatur 85, Akademie-Verlag, Berlin
HOOKE, S.H. (editor) 1933a, *Myth and Ritual; Essays on the Myth and Ritual of the Hebrews in Relation to the Culture Pattern of the Ancient East*, Oxford University Press, London
HOOKE, S.H. 1933b, "The Myth and Ritual Pattern of the Ancient East", in Hooke 1933a.1-14
HOOKE, S.H. (editor) 1935a, *The Labyrinth; Further Studies in the Relation between Myth and Ritual in the Ancient World*, SPCK, London
HOOKE, S.H. 1935b, "The Myth and Ritual Pattern in Jewish and Christian Apocalyptic", in Hooke 1935a.211-233
HOOKER, Morna D. 1959, *Jesus and the Servant; the Influence of the Servant*

Concept of Deutero-Isaiah in the New Testament, SPCK, London
HOOKER, Morna D. 1959-1960, "Adam in Romans 1", *NTS* 6.297-306
HOOKER, Morna D. 1982, "Myth, Imagination and History", *Epworth Review* 9.50-56
HOOKER, Morna D. 1983, *The Message of Mark*, Epworth Press, London
HOOKER, Morna D. 1991, *A Commentary on the Gospel According to Mark*, BNTC, A&C Black, London
HOPKINS, Martin 1965, "The Historical Perspective of Apocalypse 1-11", *CBQ* 27.42-47
HORBURY, William and McNEILL, Brian 1981, *Suffering and Martyrdom in the New Testament; Studies Presented to G.M. Styler by the Cambridge New Testament Seminar*, Cambridge University Press
HORSLEY, R.A. 1987, *Jesus and the Spiral of Violence; Popular Jewish Resistance in Roman Palestine*, Harper and Row, San Francisco
HORT, F.J.A, 1908, *The Apocalypse of John I-III; the Greek Text with Introduction, Commentary and Additional Notes*, Macmillan, London
HOUGH, Robert W. 1994, "You Will Reap Just What You Sow", in Wallace 1994a.161-181
HOWARD-BROOK, Wes and GWYTHER Anthony 2001, *Unveiling Empire - Reading Revelation Then and Now*, Orbis Books, New York
HRE KIO, Stephen 1989, "The Exodus Symbol of Liberation in the Apocalypse and Its Relevance for some Aspects of Translation", *Biblical Translator* 40.120-135
HULMES, Edward 1991, "The Semantics of Sacrifice", in Sykes 1991.265-281
HURST, L.D. 1990, *The Epistle to the Hebrews; Its Background of Thought*, SNTSMS 65, Cambridge University Press
HURTADO, L. W. 1985, "Revelation 4-5 in the Light of Jewish Apocalyptic Analogies", *JSNT* 25.105-124
HURTGEN, John E. 1993, *Anti-Language in the Apocalypse of John*, Mellen Biblical Press, Lewiston
INMAN, Anne 1993, "This is the Lamb of God", *New Blackfriars* 74.191-197
IRIGARAY, Luce 1993, "Women, the Sacred, Money", in *Sexes and Genealogies*, Columbia University Press, New York, 1993.73-88
ISAACS, Marie E. 1992, *Sacred Space: An Approach to the Theology of the Epistle to the Hebrews*, JSNTSS 73, Sheffield Academic Press
ISAAK, Helmut 1992, "Menno's Vision of the Anticipation of the Kingdom of God", in Gerald R. Brunk (editor), *Menno Simons: a Reappraisal; Essays in Honor of Irvin B. Horst on the 450th Anniversary of the Fundamentboek*, Eastern Mennonite College, Harrisonburg, 1992.57-82
JANOWSKI, Bernd 1993, "Er trug unsere Sünden. Jesaja 53 und die Dramatik der Stellvertretung", *ZTK* 90, 1-24
JANZEN, Ernest P. 1994, "The Jesus of the Apocalypse Wears the Emperor's Clothes", *SBL Papers* 1994.637-651
JAY, Nancy 1992, *Throughout Your Generations Forever; Sacrifice, Religion, and Paternity*, University of Chicago Press
JOHNS, Loren L. 2000, "'A Better sacrifice' or 'Better than Sacrifice'? Response to Hardin's 'Sacrificial Language in Hebrews'" in Swartley 2000.120-131

JOHNSON, Alan 1981, "Revelation", in *The Expositor's Bible Commentary* Volume 12, Zondervan, Grand Rapids
JOHNSON, Aubrey R. 1967, *Sacral Kingship in Ancient Israel*, Second Edition, University of Wales Press, Cardiff
JOHNSON, Barbara 1981, "Introduction", in Derrida 1981.vii-xxxiii
JOHNSTON, Robert M. 1987, "The Eschatological Sabbath in John's Apocalypse; a Reconsideration", *AUSS* 25.39-50
JONES, Bruce W. 1968, "More about the Apocalypse as Apocalyptic", *JBL* 87.325-327
JONGE, M. de (editor) 1975a, *Studies on the Testaments of the Twelve Patriarchs*, Studia in Veteris Testamenti Pseudepigrapha 13, E.J. Brill, Leiden
JONGE, M de 1975b, "Christian Influence in the Testaments of the Twelve Patriarchs", in de Jonge 1975a.193-246
JONGE, M. de 1988, "The Testaments of the Twelve Patriarchs; Central Problems and Essential Viewpoints", *ANRW* 2.20.1.359-420
JOPLIN, Patricia Klindienst 1990, "Ritual Work on Human Flesh; Livy's Lucretia and the Rape of the Body Politic", *Helios* 17.1.51-70
JUILLAND, Alphonse (editor) 1986a, *To Honor René Girard*, Stanford French and Italian Studies No 34, Department of French and Italian Studies, Stanford University
JUILLAND, Alphonse 1986b, "Preface; the Achievement of René Girard", in Juilland 1986a.i-ii
JUILLAND, Alphonse 1986c, "Postface; the Influence of René Girard", in Juilland 1986a.329-330
KALLAS, James 1967, "The Apocalypse - an Apocalyptic Book?", *JBL* 86.69-80
KAPTEIN, Roel, with the co-operation of MORROW, Duncan 1993, *On the Way of Freedom*, The Columba Press, Blackrock
KARRER, M. 1986 *Die Johannesoffenbarung als Brief. Studien zu ihrem literischen, historischen und theologischen Ort*, Vandenhoeck & Ruprecht. Cited *NTA* 31 (1987) 241
KÄSEMANN, Ernst 1969a, "The Beginnings of Christian Theology", *JTC* 6.17-46
KÄSEMANN, Ernst 1969b, "On the Topic of Primitive Christian Apocalyptic", *JTC* 6.99-133
KÄSEMANN, Ernst 1980, *Commentary on Romans*, SCM Press, London
KEARNEY, Richard, 1979 "Terrorisme et sacrifice, la cas de l'Irlande du Nord", *Esprit* 1979.4.29-55
KEARNEY, Richard 1982, "The IRA's Strategy of Failure", in HEDERMAN, Mark Patrick and KEARNEY. Richard (Editors), *The Crane Bay Book of Irish Studies (1977-1981)*, Blackwater Press, Dublin, 1982.699-707
KEARNEY, Richard 1985, "Le mythe chez Girard; un nouveau bouc émissaire?", in Dumouchel 1985.35-49
KEE, Alistair 1982, *Constantine versus Christ; the Triumph of Ideology*, SCM Press, London
KEIM, Paul 2000, "Reading Ancient Near Eastern Literature from the Perspective of René Girard's Scapegoat Theory" in Swartley 2000.157-177

KELLY, J.N.D. 1977, *Early Christian Doctrines*, 5th Edition, A & C Black, London
KEPLER, Thomas S. 1957, *The Book of Revelation; a Commentary for Laymen*, Oxford University Press, New York
KERKESLAGER, Allen 1993, "Apollo, Greco-Roman Prophecy and the Rider on the White Horse in Rev 6:2", *JBL* 112.116-121
KERMODE, Frank 1995, "Waiting for the End", in Bull 1995a.250-263
KERR, Fergus 1992, "Rescuing Girard's Argument?", *Modern Theology* 8, 385-399
KEYNES, Geoffrey (editor) 1966, *Blake; Complete Writings*, Oxford University Press
KIDDLE, Martin assisted by ROSS, M.K. 1940, *The Revelation of St. John*, MNTC, Hodder and Stoughton, London
KIRBY, John T. 1988, "The Rhetorical Situations of Revelation 1-3", *NTS* 34.197-207
KIRK-DUGGAN, Cheryl A. 1994, "Gender, Violence and Transformation in *The Color Purple*", in Wallace 1994a, 266-286
KIRWAN, Michael 2005, *Discovering Girard*, Darton, Longman and Todd, London
KLASSEN, William 1966, "Vengeance in the Apocalypse of John", *CBQ* 28.300-311
KLEIN, Peter K. 1992, "Introduction; the Apocalypse in Medieval Art", in Emmerson 1992a.159-199
KLEINKNECHT, H., FICHTNER, J. STÄHLIN, G. and others 1964, *Wrath*, A & C Black, London (from *TWNT*)
KNAPPEN, M.M. 1939, *Tudor Puritanism; a Chapter in the History of Idealism*, University of Chicago Press
KNIGHT, Jonathan 1999, *Revelation*, Sheffield Academic Press, Sheffield
KNOX, Ronald A., *The New Testament of Our Lord and Saviour Jesus Christ; Newly Translated from the Latin Vulgate and Authorized by the Archbishops and Bishops of England and Wales*, Burns, Oates and Washbourne, 1948
KOCH, Klaus 1972, *The Rediscovery of Apocalyptic; a Polemical Work on a Neglected Area of Biblical Studies and Its Damaging Effects on Theology and Philosophy*, SBT Second Series 22, SCM Press, London
KOESTER, Craig R. 2001, *Revelation and the End of All Things*, Eerdmans, Grand Rapids
KOFMAN, Sarah 1980, "The Narcissistic Woman; Freud and Girard", *Diacritics* 10, 36-45 and in Toril Moi (editor), *French Feminist Thought; a Reader*, Blackwell, Oxford, 1987.210-226
KOPPISCH, Michael S. 1986, "'Beau Soupe' or 'Beau Langage'; Difference and Sameness in *Les Femmes Savantes*", in Juilland 1986a.281-297
KORSHIN, Paul J. 1984, "Queuing and Waiting; the Apocalypse in England, 1660-1750", in Patrides 1984a.240-265
KOVACS, Judith L. and ROWLAND, Christopher 2004, *Revelation*, Blackwell, Oxford
KRAFT, Heinrich 1974, *Die Offenbarung des Johannes*, Hanbuch zum Neuen Testament 16a, J.C.B. Mohr (Paul Siebeck), Tübingen
KRAYBILL, J. Nelson 1996, *Imperial Cult and Commerce in John's*

Apocalypse, JSNTSS 132, Sheffield Academic Press
KREITZER, Larry Joseph 1987, *Jesus and God in Paul's Eschatology*, JSNTS 19, JSOT Press, Sheffield
KREITZER, Larry Joseph 1988, "Hadrian and the Nero *Redivivus* Myth", *ZNW* 79.92-115
KRODEL, Gerhard A. 1989, *Revelation*, Augsburg Commentary on the New Testament, Augsburg Publishing House, Minneapolis
KRONDORFER, Björn 1994, "Re-mythologizing Scriptural Authority; on Reading 'Sacrifice and the Beginning of Kingship'", *Semeia* 67.93-107
KUMAR, Krishan 1995, "Apocalypse, Millennium and Utopia Today", in Bull 1995a.200-224
KÜMMEL, Werner Georg 1975, *Introduction to the New Testament*, Revised Edition, SCM Press, London
LACOUE-LABARTHE, Philippe 1978, "Mimesis and Truth", *Diacritics* 8.10-23
LACOUE-LABARTHE, Philippe 1989, *Typography; Mimesis, Philosophy, Politics*, Harvard University Press, Cambridge Mass
LADD, George Eldon 1957a, "The Revelation and Jewish Apocalyptic", *EQ* 29.95-100
LADD, George Eldon 1957b, "Why Not Prophetic-Apocalyptic?", *JBL* 76.192-200
LADD, George Eldon 1972, *A Commentary on the Revelation of John*, Eerdmans, Grand Rapids
LAMBRECHT, J. (editor) 1980a, *L'Apocalypse johannique et l'Apocalyptique dans le Nouveau Testament*, Leuven University Press Éditions Ducolot, BETL 53, Paris-Gembloux
LAMBRECHT, J. 1980b, "A Structuration of Revelation 4,1-22,5" in Lambrecht 1980a.77-104
LAMPE, G.W.H. 1981, "Martyrdom and Inspiration", in Horbury 1981.118-135
LAMPE, G.W.H. 1984, "The Testimony of Jesus is the Spirit of Prophecy", in William Weinrich (editor), *The New Testament Age; Essays in Honor of Bo Reicke*, Mercer University Press, Macon, 1984.1.245-258
LANCELLOTTI, Angelo 1964, *Sintassi ebraica nel Greco dell'Apocalisse; 1. Uso delle forme verbali*, Collectio Assisiensis 1, Studio Teologico "Porziuncola", Assisi
LANE FOX, Robin 1986, *Pagans and Christians*, Viking, London
LANTZ, Pierre, 1985 "Monnaie archaïque, monnaie moderne", in Dumouchel 1985.159-181
LASCARIS, Andrew 1985, "The Likely Price of Peace; René Girard's Hypothesis", *New Blackfriars* 6.517-524
LASCARIS, Andrew 1987, "Economics and Human Desire" *New Blackfriars* 68.115-124
LASCARIS, Andrew 1988, "Girard against Fragmentation", *New Blackfriars* 69.156-163
LASCARIS, Andrew 1989, "Charles Davis *versus* René Girard", *New Blackfriars* 70.416-422

LASCARIS, André 1993, *To Do the Unexpected; Reading Scripture in Northern Ireland*, The Corrymeela Press
LASINE, Stuart 1994, "Levite Violence, Fratricide, and Sacrifice in the Bible and Later Revolutionary Rhetoric", in Wallace 1994a.204-229
LAWRENCE, D.H. 1932, *Apocalypse*, Martin Secker, London
LAWS, Sophie 1978, "The Blood-Stained Horseman; Revelation 19.11-13", *Studia Biblica* 1978.3.245-248
LAWS, Sophie 1988, *In the Light of the Lamb; Imagery, Parody, and Theology in the Apocalypse of John*, GNS 31, Michael Glazier, Wilmington
LE GRYS, Alan 1992, "Conflict and Vengeance in the Book of Revelation", *ExpT* 104.76-80
LEE, Harold, REEVES, Marjorie, SILANO, Giulio 1989, *Western Mediterranean Prophecy; the School of Joachim of Fiore and the Fourteenth Century Breviloquium*, Studies and Texts 88, Pontifical Institute of Medieval Studies, Toronto
LEHMANN, Paul 1975, *The Transfiguration of Politics*, SCM Press, London
LEIVESTAD, Ragnar 1954, *Christ the Conqueror; Ideas of Conflict and Victory in the New Testament*, SPCK, London
LERNER, Robert E. 1992, "The Medieval Return of the Thousand-Year Sabbath", in Emmerson 1992a.51-71
LÉVI-STRAUSS, Claude 1963, *Structural Anthropology*, Volume 1, Penguin, London
LÉVI-STRAUSS, Claude 1973, *Structural Anthropology* Volume 2, Penguin, London
LEVINE, Baruch 1985, "René Girard on Job; the Question of the Scapegoat", *Semeia* 33.125-133
LEWIS, Suzanne 1992, "Exegesis and Illustration in Thirteenth-Century English Apocalypses", in Emmerson 1992a.259-275
LILJE, Hanns 1957, *The Last Book of the Bible; the Meaning of the Revelation of St. John*, Muhlenberg Press, Philadelphia
LINCOLN, Andrew T. 1981, *Paradise Now and Not Yet; Studies in the Role of the Heavenly Dimension in Paul's Thought with Special Reference to His Eschatology*, SNTSMS 43, Cambridge University Press
LINDARS, Barnabas 1976, "A Bull, a Lamb and a Word; 1 Enoch XC.38", *NTS* 22.483-486
LINDSEY, Hal 1973, *The Late Great Planet Earth*, Bantam, New York
LINDSEY, Hal 1974, *There's a New World Coming; "a Prophetic Odyssey"*, Coverdale, London
LITTLETON, C. Scott 1982, *The New Comparative Mythology; an Anthropological Assessment of the Theories of Georges Dumézil*, Third Edition, University of California Press, Berkeley
LIVINGSTON, Paisley 1986, "Girard and Literary Knowledge", in Juilland 1986a.221-235
LIVINGSTON, Paisley 1988, "Demystification and History in Girard and Durkheim", in Dumouchel 1988a.113-133
LIVINGSTONE, Paisley 1992, *Models of Desire; René Girard and the Psychology of Mimesis*, The Johns Hopkins University Press, Baltimore
LO BUE, Francesco and WILLIS, G.G. 1963, *The Turin Fragments of*

Tyconius' Commentary on Revelation, Texts and Studies; Contributions to Biblical and Patristic Literature 7, Cambridge University Press

LOENERTZ, R.J. 1947, *The Apocalypse of Saint John*, Sheed and Ward, London

LOHMEYER, Ernst, *Die Offenbarung des Johannes*, Handbuch zum Neuen Testament, J.C.B. Mohr (Paul Siebeck), Tübingen, 1926

LOHSE, Eduard 1960, *Die Offenbarung des Johannes*, Das Neue Testament Deutsch 11, Vandenhoed & Ruprecht, Göttingen

LORIE, Peter 1995, *Revelation: St. John the Divine; Prophecis for the Apocalypse and Beyond*, Boxtree, London

LUND, Nils Wilhelm 1992, *Chiasmus in the New Testament; a Study in the Form and Content of Chiastic Structures*, Hendrickson, Peabody

LUPIERI, Edmondo F. 2006, *A Commentary on the Apocalypse of John*, Eerdmans, Cambridge

LUST, J. 1980, "The Order of the Final Events in Revelation and Ezekiel", in Lambrecht 1980a.179-183

LYON, David 1994, *Postmodernity*, Concepts in the Social Sciences, Open University Press, Buckingham

MABEE, Charles 1994, "Un/rivaling the Old Testament; before the Law", in Wallace 1994a.100-117

MABEE, Charles 2000, "Text as Peacemaker: Deuteronomic Innovations in Violence Detoxification" in Swartley 2000.70-84

MACINTYRE, Alasdair 1985, *After Virtue; a Study in Moral Theory*, Second Edition, Duckworth, London

MACK, Burton L. 1985, "The Innocent Transgressor; Jesus in Early Christian Myth and History", *Semeia* 33.135-165

MACK, Burton L. 1988, *A Myth of Innocence; Mark and Christian Origins*, Fortress Press, Philadelphia

MACKAY, T.W. 1978, "Early Christian Exegesis of the Apocalypse", *Studia Biblica* 3.257-263

MACQUARRIE, John 1977, *Principles of Christian Theology*, Revised Edition, SCM Press, London

MALINA, Bruce J. 1986, *Christian Origins and Cultural Anthropology; Practical Models for Biblical Interpretation*, John Know Press, Atlanta

MANSON, T.W. 1945, "ΙΛΑΣΤΗΡΙΟΝ", *JTS* 46.1-10

MARTYN, J. Louis 1967, "Epistemology at the Turn of the Ages; 2 Corinthians 5:16", in W.R. Farmer 1967.269-287

MARTYN, J. Louis 1985, "Apocalyptic Antinomies in Paul's Letter to the Galatians", *NTS* 31.410-424

MARX, Karl and ENGELS, Frederick 1977, *The German Ideology; Critique of Modern German Philosophy according to Its Representatives Feuerbach, Bruno Bauer and Stirner, and of German Socialism according to Its Various Prophets*, Progree Publishers, Moscow

MASON, John R. 1993, *Reading and Responding to Eliade's* History of Religious Ideas; *the Lure of the Late Eliade*, Edwin Mellen Press, Lewiston

MATHESON, Peter (Editor) 1988, *The Collected Works of Thomas Müntzer*, T&T Clark, Edinburgh

MATHEWS, Aidan Carl 1986, "Knowledge of Good and Evil; the Work of

René Girard", in Juilland 1986a.17-28
MATTER, E. Ann 1992, "The Apocalypse in Early Medieval Exegesis", in Emmerson 1992.38-50
MATTIES, Gordon H. 2000, "Can Girard Help Us to Read Joshua?" in Swartley 2000.85-102
MAURICE, Frederick Denison 1861, *Lectures on the Apocalypse; or, Book of Revelation of St. John the Divine*, Macmillan, Cambridge
MAZZAFERRI, Frederick David 1989, *The Genre of the Book of Revelation from a Source-Critical Perspective*, BNZW 54
McGINN, Bernard 1979, *Visions of the End; Apocalyptic Traditions in the Middle Ages*, Columbia University Press, New York
McGINN, Bernard 1984, "Early Apocalypticism; the Ongoing Debate", in Patrides 1984a.2-39
McGINN, Bernard 1985, *The Calabrian Abbot; Joachim of Fiore in the History of Western Thought*, Macmillan, New York
McGINN, Bernard 1994, *Apocalypticism in the Western Tradition*, Variorum Collected Studies Series 430, Ashgate, Aldershot
McGINN, Bernard 1995, "The End of the World and the Beginning of Christendom", in Bull 1995a.58-89
McHUGH, John 1975, *The Mother of Jesus in the New Testament*, Darton, Longman and Todd, London
McKAY, John 1994, *Visions of the End-Times; a Guide to Reading the Book of Revelation*, Revised Edition, Kingdom Faith Ministries, Horsham
McKAY, Johnston R. and MILLER, James F. 1976, *Biblical Studies; Essays in Honour of William Barclay*, Collins, London
McKENNA, Andrew J. 1985, "Introduction", in *Semeia* 33.1-11
McKENNA, Andrew J. 1990, "Biblical Structuralism; Testing the Victimary Hypothesis", *Helios* 17.1.71-87
McKENNA, Andrew J. 1992, *Violence and Difference; Girard, Derrida and Deconstruction*, University of Illinois Press, Urbana
McMAHON, Edward 1994, "Violence - Religion - Law; a Girardian Analysis" in Wallace 1994a.182-203
MEALY, J. Webb 1992, *After the Thousand Years; Resurrection and Judgement in Revelation 20*, JSNTSS 70, JSOT, Sheffield
MEEKS, Wayne 1983, *The First Urban Christians; the Social World of the Apostle Paul*, Yale University Press, New Haven
MEGIVERN, James J. 1978, "Wrestling with Revelation", *BTB* 8.147-154
MEGIVERN, James J. 1981, "Jacques Ellul's *Apocalypse*", *BTB* 11.125-128
METZGER, Bruce M. 1993, *Breaking the Code; Understanding the Book of Revelation*, Abingdon Press, Nashville
METZING, Erich Helmut 1984, *The Nikan Motif and Related Subjects in Johannine Literature*, PhD. disseration submitted to the University of Cambridge, PhD 13071
MEYER, Ben F. 1979, *The Aims of Jesus*, SCM Press, London
MILBANK, John 1990, *Theology and Social Theory; Beyond Secular Reason*, Blackwells, Oxford
MILBANK, John 1996, "Stories of Sacrifice", *Modern Theology* 12, 27-56
MILLER, Marlin E. 2000, "Girardian Perspectives and Christian Atonement",

in Swartley 2000, 31-48
MILNE, Bruce 1979, *I Want to Know what the Bible Says about the End of the World; the Doctrine of the Last Things*, Kingsway, Eastbourne
MINEAR, Paul S. 1953, "The Wounded Beast", *JBL* 72.93-101
MINEAR, Paul S. 1968, *I Saw a New Earth; an Introduction to the Visions of the Apocalypse*, Corpus, Washington
MOBERLY, R.C. 1911, *Atonement and Personality*, John Murray, London
MOBERLY, Robert B. 1992, "When Was Revelation Conceived?", *Bib* 73.376-393
MOFFATT, James 1934, *A New Translation of the Bible Containing the Old and New Testaments*, Hodder and Stoughton, London
MOI, Toril 1982, "The Missing Mother; the Oedipal Rivalries of René Girard", *Diacritics* 12.21-31
MONLOUBOU, Louis (editor) 1977, *Apocalypses et théologie de l'espérance*, Lectio Divina 95, Les Éditions du Cerf, Paris
MOORE, Stephen D. 1995, "The Beatific Vision as a Posing Exhibition; Revelation's Hypermasculine Deity", *JSNT* 60.27-55
MORGAN, Robert with BARTON, John 1988, *Biblical Interpretation*, Oxford Bible Series, Oxford University Press
MORIN, Lucien 1985, "Le désir mimétique chez l'enfant; René Girard et Jean Piaget", in Dumouchel 1985.299-317
MORÓN-ARROYO, Ciriaco 1978, "Co-operative Mimesis; Don Quixote and Sancho Panza", *Diacritics* 8.75-86
MORRICE, W.G. 1985-1986, "John the Seer; Narrative Exegesis and the Book of Revelation", *ExpT* 97.43-46
MORRIS, Leon 1950-1951, "The Use of ἱλάσκεσθαι etc. in Biblical Greek", *ExpT* 62.227-233
MORRIS, Leon 1955-1956, "The Meaning of ἹΛΑΣΤΗΡΙΟΝ in Romans III.25", *NTS* 2.33-43
MORRIS, Leon 1987, *The Book of Revelation; an Introduction and Commentary*, Second Edition, Tyndale New Testament Commentaries, Inter-Varsity Press, Leicester
MORRISON, Karl F. 1992, "The Exercise of Thoughtful Minds; the Apocalypse in some German Historical Writings", in Emmerson 1992a.352-373
MOSES, John 1992, *The Sacrifice of God; a Holistic Theory of Atonement*, Canterbury Press, Norwich
MOULE, C.F.D. 1953, *An Idiom Book of New Testament Greek*, Cambridge University Press
MOUNCE, Robert H. 1977, *The Book of Revelation*, NICNT, Eerdmans, Grand Rapids
MOWINCKEL, S. 1956, *He that Cometh*, Basil Blackwell, Oxford
MOWINCKEL, S. 1967, *The Psalms in Israel's Worship*, Abingdon, Nashville
MOWRY, Lucetta 1952, "Revelation 4-5 and Early Christian Liturgical Usage", *JBL* 71.75-84
MOYISE, Steve 1992-1993, "Intertextuality and the Book of Revelation", *ExpT* 104.295-298
MOYISE, Steve 1995, *The Old Testament in the Book of Revelation*, Sheffield

Academic Press, JSNTSS 115
MOYISE, Steve (Editor) 2001, *Studies in the Book of Revelation*, T&T Clark, Edinburgh
MOYISE, Steve 2001, "Does the Lion Lie down with the Lamb" in Moyise 2001.181-194
MÜLLER, Hans-Peter 1960, "Die Plagen der Apokalypse; eine formgeschichtliche Untersuchung", *ZNW* 51.268-278
MUNK, Linda 1990, "The Design of Violence", *Journal of Literature and Theology* 4.251-262
MUÑOZ LEÓN, Domingo 1985, "La estructura del Apocalipsis de Juan. Una aproximación a la luz de la composición del 4.° de Esdras y del 2.° de Baruc", *EstBib* 43.125-172
MURRAY, Iain H. 1971, *The Puritan Hope; a Study in Revival and the Interpretation of Prophecy*, Banner of Truth, Edinburgh
MURRAY, Robert 1992, *The Cosmic Covenant; Biblical Themes of Justice, Peace and the Integrity of Creation*, Heythrop Monographs 7, Sheed and Ward, London
MURRIN, Michael 1984, "Revelation and Two Seventeenth Century Commentators", in Patrides 1984a.125-147
MUSSIES, G. 1971, *The Morphology of Koine Greek as Used in the Apocalypse of St. John; a Study in Bilingualism*, NovTSup 28, E.J. Brill, Leiden
MUSSIES, G. 1980, "The Greek of the Book of Revelation", in Lambrecht 1980a.167-177
MYERS, Ched 1991, *Binding the Strong Man; a Political Reading of Mark's Story of Jesus*, Orbis, Maryknoll
NELSON, Ronald R. 1981, "Apocalyptic Speculation and the French Revolution", *EQ* 53.194-206
NEMOIANU, Virgil 1986, "René Girard and the Dialectics of Imperfection", in Juilland 1986a.1-16
NEWBOLT, M.R. 1952, *The Book of Unveiling; a Study of the Revelation of St. John*, SPCK, London
NEWMAN, Barclay 1963-1964, "The Fallacy of the Domitian Hypothesis. Critique of the Irenaeus Source as a Witness for the Contemporary-Historical Approach to the Interpretation of the Apocalypse", *NTS* 10.133-139
NEWPORT, Kenneth G.C. 1986, "The Use of ἐκ in Revelation; Evidence of Semitic Influence", *AUSS* 24.223-230
NEWPORT, Kenneth G.C. 1987, "Semitic Influence in Revelation; some Further Evidence", *AUSS* 25.249-256
NEWPORT, Kenneth G.C. 1988, "Some Greek Words with Hebrew Meanings in the Book of Revelation", *AUSS* 26.25-31
NICHOLLS, David 1989, *Deity and Domination; Images of God and State in the Nineteenth and Twentieth Centuries*, Routledge, London
NIDITCH, Susan 1985, *Chaos to Cosmos; Studies in Biblical Patterns of Creation*, Scholars Press Studies in the Humanities 6, Scholars Press, Chico
NIDITCH, Susan 1993a, *Folklore and the Hebrew Bible*, Guides to Biblical Scholarship Old Testament Series, Fortress Press, Minneapolis

NIDITCH, Susan 1993b, *War in the Hebrew Bible; a Study in the Ethics of Violence*, Oxford University Press
NILES, D.T. 1962, *As Seeing the Invisible*, SCM Press, London
NOLAN, Albert 1977, *Jesus before Christianity; the Gospel of Liberation*, Darton, Longman and Todd, London
NORRIS, Christopher 1995, "Versions of Apocalypse; Kant, Derrida, Foucault" in Bull 1995a.227-249
NORTH, Robert 1985, "Violence and the Bible; the Girard Connection", *CBQ* 47, 1-27
OBERWEIS, Michael 1995, "Erwägungen zur apokalyptischen Ortsbezeichung 'Harmagedon'", *Bib* 76.305-324
ODEN, Robert A. 1992, "Cosmogony, Cosmology", in David Noel Freedman (editor), *Anchor Bible Dictionary*, Doubleday, New York, 1992.
O'DONOVAN, Oliver 1986a, "The Political Thought of the Book of Revelation", *TynB* 37.61-94
O'DONOVAN, Oliver 1986b, *Resurrection and Moral Order; an Outline for Evangelical Ethics*, Inter-Varsity Press, Leicester
OESTERLEY, W.O.E. 1937, *Sacrifices in Ancient Israel; Their Origin, Purposes and Development*, Hodder and Stoughton, London
O'LEARY, 1994, *Arguing the Apocalypse*
OLSEN, Carl 1992, *The Theology and Philosophy of Eliade; a Search for the Centre*, Macmillan, Basingstoke
OMAN, John 1923, *Book of Revelation. Theory of the Text: Rearranged Text and Translation; Commentary*, Cambridge University Press
OMAN, John 1928, *The Text of Revelation; a Revised Theory*, Cambridge University Press
O'NEILL, J.C. 1979, "The Lamb of God in the Testaments of the Twelve Patriarchs", *JSNT* 2.2-30
O'NEILL, J.C. 1991, *The Authority of the Bible; a Portrait Gallery of Thinkers from Lessing to Bultmann*, T & T Clark, Edinburgh
ORLÉAN, André 1986, "La théorie mimétique face aux phénomènes économiques" in Juilland 1986a.121-133
ORLÉAN, André 1988, "Money and Mimetic Speculation", in Dumouchel 1988a.101-112
O'ROURKE, John J. 1968, "The Hymns of the Apocalypse", *CBQ* 30.399-409
OSBORNE, Grant R. 2002, *Revelation*, Baker, Grand Rapids
ORSINI, Christine 1982, "Introduction à la lecture de René Girard" in Deguy 1982.11-59
ORSINI, Christine 1985, "Girard et Platon", in Dumouchel 1985.323-329
ORZECH, Charles D. 1994, "'Provoked Suicide' and the Victim's Behaviour", in Wallace 1994a.137-160
OUGHOULIAN, Jean-Michel and LEFORT, Guy 1978, "Psychotic Structure and Girard's Doubles", *Diacritics* 8.72-74
PALAVER, Wolfgang 1991, *Politik und Religion bei Thomas Hobbes; eine Kritik aus der Sicht der Theorie René Girard*, Innsbrucker theologische Studien 33, Tyrolia-Verlag
PARKER, T.H.L. 1987, *John Calvin*, Lion, Tring

PATRIDES, C.A. and WITTREICH, Joseph (editors) 1984a, *The Apocalypse in English Renaissance Thought and Literature; Patterns, Antecedents and Repurcussions*, Manchester University Press

PATRIDES, C.A. 1984b, "'Something Like a Prophetick Strain'; Apocalyptic Configurations in Milton", in Patrides 1984.207-237

PAULIEN, Jon 1988, "Recent Developments in the Study of the Book of Revelation", *AUSS* 26.159-170

PAULIEN, Jon 1995, "The Role of the Hebrew Cultus, Sanctuary and Temple in the Plot and Structure of the Book of Revelation", *AUSS* 33.245-264

PAVEL, Thomas G. 1989, *The Feud of Language; a History of Structuralist Thought*, Blackwell, Oxford

PEDERSEN, Johs. 1940, *Israel; Its Life and Culture*, Oxford University Press, London

PELIKAN, Jaroslav 1984, "Some Uses of Apocalypse in the Magisterial Reformers" in Patrides 1984a.74-92

PETERSEN, David L. 1985, *Haggai and Zechariah 1-8; a Commentary*, Old Testament Library, SCM Press, London

PHILLIPS, J.B. 1957, *The Book of Revelation; a New Translation of the Apocalypse*, Geoffrey Bles, London

PIPER, Otto A. 1951, "The Apocalypse of John and the Liturgy of the Ancient Church", *CH* 20.10-22

PIPPIN, Tina 1992a, *Death and Desire; the Rhetoric of Gender in the Apocalypse of John*, Westminster/John Knox Press, Literary Currents in Biblical Interpretation, Louisville

PIPPIN, Tina 1992b, "Eros and the End; Reading for Gender in the Apocalypse of John", *Semeia* 59.193-210

PIPPIN, Tina 1992c, "The Heroine and the Whore; Fantasy and the Female in the Apocalypse of John", *Semeia* 60.67-82

PLACHER, William C. 1994, *Narratives of a Vulnerable God; Christ, Theology and Scripture*, Westminster John Knox Press, Louisville

POBEE, John S. 1985, *Persecution and Martyrdom in the Theology of Paul*, JSNTSS 6, JSOT Press, Sheffield

POPKIN, Richard 1995, "Seventeenth-Century Millenarianism", in Bull 1995a.112-134

PORTER, Stanley E. 1989, "The Language of the Apocalypse in Recent Discussion", *NTS* 35.582-603

PORTER, Stanley E. 1994a, *Idioms of the Greek New Testament*, (Second Edition), JSOT Press, Sheffield

PORTER, Stanley E., JOYCE, Paul M. And Orton, David E. 1994b, *Crossing the Boundaries; Essays in Biblical Interpretation in Honour of Michael Goulder*, Biblical Interpretation Series 8, E.J. Brill, Leiden

POULTON, Edward Bagnall 1929, "Mimicry" in *The Encyclopaedia Britannica*, Fourteenth Edition, The Encyclopaedia Britannica Company, London

PRESTON, Ronald H. and HANSON, Anthony T. 1949, *The Revelation of Saint John the Divine*, Torch Commentaries, SCM Press, London

PRÉVOST, Jean-Pierre 1993, *How to Read the Apocalypse*, SCM Press, London

PRICE, S.R.F. 1984, *Rituals and Power; the Roman Imperial Cult in Asia Minor*, Cambridge University Press
PRIGENT, Pierre 1959, *Apocalypse 12; Histoire de l'exégèse*, BGBE 2, J.C.B. Mohr (Paul Siebeck), Tübingen
PRIGENT, Pierre 1964, *Apocalypse et liturgie*, Cahiers Théologique 52, Delachaux et Niestlé, Neuchatel
PRIGENT, Pierre 1979-1980, "L'Apocalypse; exégèse historique et analyse structurale", *NTS* 26.127-137
PRIGENT, Pierre 1980, "Le temps et le royaume dans l'Apocalypse", in Lambrecht 1980a.231-245
PRIGENT, Pierre 1981, *L'Apocalypse de Saint Jean*, Commentaire du Nouveau Testament 14, Second Series, Delachaux and Niestlé, Lausanne
PUCCI, Pietro 1990, "The Tragic *pharmakos* of the *Oedipus Rex*", *Helios* 17.1.41-49
QUISPEL, Gilles 1979, *The Secret Book of Revelation; the Last Book of the Bible*, Collins, London
RABER, Rudolp W. 1986, "Revelation 21.1-8", *Int* 40.296-301
RAD, Gerhard von 1959. "The Origin of the Concept of the Day of Yahweh", *JSS* 4.97-108
RAD, Gerhard von 1962, *Wisdom in Israel*, SCM Press, London
RAD, Gerhard von 1965, *Old Testament Theology*, Oliver and Boyd, Edinburgh
RAD, Gerhard von 1991, *Holy War in Ancient Israel*, Eerdmans, Grand Rapids
RADCLIFFE, Timothy 1994, "*Jurassic Park* or Last Supper", *The Tablet* 248.760-763
RADKOWSKI, de 1985, "Le règne du signe; richesse et rivalité mimétique", in Dumouchel 1985.267-274
RAMSEY, W.M. 1904, *The Letters to the Seven Churches of Asia and Their Place in the Plan of the Apocalypse*, Hodder and Stoughton, London
RAMSEY, W.M. 1905, "The Early Christian Symbol of the Open Book", *Expositor*, 6.2.294-306
RASHDALL, Hastings 1919, *The Idea of Atonement in Christian Theology*, Macmillan, London
REDDISH, Mitchell G. 1988, "Martyr Christology in the Apocalypse", *JSNT* 33.85-95
REEVES, Marjorie and Hirsch-Reich, B. 1954, "The Seven Seals of Joachim of Fiore", *Recherches de Théologie ancienne et médiévale* 21.211-247
REEVES, Marjorie 1969, *The Influence of Prophecy in the Later Middle Ages; a Study in Joachimism*, Clarendon Press, Oxford
REEVES, Marjorie and Hirsch-Reich B. 1972, *The Figurae of Joachim of Fiore*, Clarendon Press, Oxford
REEVES, Marjorie 1976, *Joachim of Fiore and the Prophetic Future*, SPCK, London
REEVES, Marjorie 1984, "The Development of Apocalyptic Thought; Medieval Attitudes", in Patrides 1984a.40-72
REEVES, Marjorie 1995, "Pattern and Purpose in History in the Later Medieval and Renaissance Periods", in Bull 1995a.90-111
REIMAN, Donald H. and POWERS, Sharon B. (editors) 1977, *Shelley's Poetry*

and Prose: Authoritative Texts; Criticism, Norton Critical Edition, W.W. Norton, New York

RESSEGUIE, J.L. 1998, *Revelation Unsealed; a Narrative Critical Approach to John's Apocalypse*, Brill, Leiden

RICHARD, Pablo 1994, *Apocalipsis; reconstrucción de la esperanza*, Departamento Ecuménico de Investigaciones, San José

RICHES, John 1980, *Jesus and the Transformation of Judaism*, Darton, Longman and Todd, London

RICOEUR, Paul 1984, *Time and Narrative*, Volume 1, University of Chicago Press

RIDDLE, Donald W. 1927, "From Apocalypse to Martyrology", *Anglican Theological Review* 9.260-280

RINALDI, G. 1963, "La porta aperta nel cielo (Ap 4,1)", *CBQ* 25.336-347

RINGGREN, H. 1962, *Sacrifice in the Bible*, World Christian Books, United Society for Christian Literature, Lutterworth Press, London

RISSI, Mathias 1964, "The Rider on the White Horse; a Study of Revelation 6.1-8", *Int* 18.407-418

RISSI, Mathias 1965, *Was ist und was geschehen soll danach: die Zeit- und Geschichtsauffassung der Offenbarung des Johannes. Zweite, stark veränderte Auflage von «Zeit und Geschichte in der Offenbarung des Johannes»*, ATANT 46, Zwingli Verlag, Zürich

RISSI, Mathias 1966, *Alpha und Omega: eine Deutung der Johannesoffenbarung*, Freidrich Reinhardt Verlag, Berlin

RISSI, Mathias 1972, *The Future of the World; an Exegetical Study of Revelation 19.11-22.15*, SBT Second Series, SCM Press, London

RIST, Martin 1957 and HOUGH, Lynn Harold, "The Revelation of St. John the Divine; Introduction and Exegesis", *Interpreter's Bible* 12.347-613

ROBBINS, Ray Frank 1977, in Beasley-Murray 1977.147-222

ROBERTS, Richard H. 1993, "Transcendental Sociology? A Critique of John Milbank's *Theology and Social Theory; beyond Secular Reason*", *SJT* 46, 527-535

ROBINSON, John A.T. 1976, *Redating the New Testament*, SCM Press, London

ROBINSON, John A.T. 1979, *Wrestling with Romans*, SCM Press, London

ROGERSON, J.W. 1980, "Sacrifice in the Old Testament; Problems of Method and Approach", in Bourdillon 1980.45-59

ROLLER, Otto 1937, "Das Buch mit sieben Siegeln", *ZNW* 36.98-113

ROLLINS, Wayne G. 1970-1971, "The New Testament and Apocalyptic", *NTS* 17.454-476

ROSS, James Robert 1977, "Evangelical Alternatives" in Armerding 1977.117-129

ROWLAND, Christopher C. 1979, "The Visions of God in Apocalyptic Literature", *JSJ* 10.137-154

ROWLAND, Christopher C. 1981, "Theology and Personality 3. Through a Glass Darkly", *Epworth Review* 8.50-55

ROWLAND, Christopher C. 1982, *The Open Heaven; a Study of Apocalyptic in Judaism and Early Christianity*, SPCK, London

ROWLAND, Christopher C. 1986, Review of J.J. Collins 1984, *JTS* 37.484-

490
ROWLAND, Christopher C. 1988a, *Radical Christianity; a Reading of Recovery*, Polity Press, Oxford
ROWLAND, Christopher C. 1988b, "Keeping Alive the Dangerous Vision of a World of Peace and Justice", *Concilium* 200.75-86
ROWLAND, Christopher C. 1993, *Revelation*, Epworth Commentaries, Epworth Press, London
ROWLAND, Christopher C. 1995, "'Upon Whom the Ends of the Ages Have Come'; Apocalyptic and the Interpretation of the New Testament", in Bull 1995.38-57
ROWLAND, Christopher C. and Fletcher-Louis, Crispin H.T. 1998, *Understanding Studying and Reading; New Testament Essays in Honour of John Ashton*, JSNTS Supplement Series 153, Sheffield Academic Press, Sheffield
ROWLEY, H.H. 1946, *The Relevance of Apocalyptic; a Study of Jewish and Christian Apocalypses from Daniel to the Revelation*, Second Edition, Lutterworth Press, London
ROWLEY, H.H. 1967, "The Forms and Meaning of Sacrifice", in *Worship in Israel; Its Forms and Meaning*, SPCK, London, 1967.111-143
RUIZ, Jean-Pierre 1994, "The Apocalypse of John and Contemporary Roman Catholic Liturgy", *Worship* 68.482-504
RUSSELL, David S. 1960, *Between the Testaments*, SCM Press, London
RUSSELL, David S. 1964, *The Method and Message of Jewish Apocalyptic 220 BC - AD 100*, Old Testament Library, The Westminster Press, Philadelphia
RUSSELL, David S. 1978, *Apocalyptic; Ancient and Modern*, SCM Press 1978
RUSSELL, David S. 1986, *From Early Judaism to Early Church*, SCM Press, London
RUSSELL, David S, *The Old Testament Pseudepigrapha; Patriarchs and Prophets in Early Judaism*, SCM Press 1987
RUSSELL, David S. 1992, *Divine Disclosure; an Introduction to Jewish Apocalyptic*, SCM Press, London
RUSSELL, David S. 1994, *Prophecy and the Apocalyptic Dream; Protest and Promise*, Hendrickson, Peabody
SACKS, Jonathan 1991, *The Persistence of Faith; Religion, Morality and Society in a Secular Age*, Wiedenfeld and Nicholson, London
SANDERS, E.P. 1985, *Jesus and Judaism*, SCM Press, London
SANDERS, E.P. 1991, *Paul*, Past Masters, Oxford University Press
SANDERS, J.N. 1962-1963, "St. John on Patmos", *NTS* 9.75-85
SANDLER, Florence 1984, "*The Faerie Queen*; an Elizabethan Apocalypse", in Patrides 1984a.148-174
SARUP, Madan 1993, *An Introductory Guide to Post-Structuralism and Postmodernism*, (Second Edition), Harvester Wheatsheaf, New York
SCHERRER, Steven J. 1984, "Signs and Wonders in the Imperial Cult; a New Look at a Roman Religious Institution in the Light of Rev. 13:13-15", *JBL* 103.599-610
SCHMIDT, Daryl D. 1991, "Semitisms and Septuagintalisms in the Book of Revelation", *NTS* 37.592-603

SCHÜSSLER FIORENZA, Elisabeth 1968, "The Eschatology and Composition of the Apocalypse", *CBQ* 30.537-569
SCHÜSSLER FIORENZA, Elisabeth 1972, *Priester für Gott: Studien zum Herrschafts- und Priestermotiv in der Apokalypse*, Neutestamentliche Abhandlungen Neue Folge 7, Verlag Aschendorff, Münster
SCHÜSSLER FIORENZA, Elisabeth 1973, "Apocalyptic Gnosis in the Book of Revelation and in Paul", *JBL* 92.565-581
SCHÜSSLER FIORENZA, Elisabeth 1974, "Redemption as Liberation: Rev. 1:5-6 and 5:9-10", *CBQ* 36.220-232
SCHÜSSLER FIORENZA, Elisabeth 1977a, "The Quest for the Johannine School; the Fourth Gospel and the Apocalypse", *NTS* 23.402-427
SCHÜSSLER FIORENZA, Elisabeth 1977b, "Composition and Structure of the Apocalypse", *CBQ* 39.344-366
SCHÜSSLER FIORENZA, Elisabeth 1980, "Apokalypsis and Propheteia; the Book of Revelation in the Context of Early Christian Prophecy", in Lambrecht 1980a.105-128
SCHÜSSLER FIORENZA, Elisabeth 1983, *In Memory of Her; a Feminist Theological Reconstruction of Christian Origins*, SCM Press, London
SCHÜSSLER FIORENZA, Elisabeth 1985, *The Book of Revelation; Justice and Judgement*, Fortress Press, Philadelphia
SCHÜSSLER FIORENZA, Elisabeth 1991, *Revelation; Vision of a Just World*, Proclamation Commentaries, Fortress Press, Minneapolis
SCHWAGER, Raymund 1978, *Brauchen wir einen Sündenbock; Gewalt und Erlösung in den biblischen Schriften*, Kösel-Verlag, München
SCHWAGER, Raymund 1985, "Christ's Death and the Prophetic Critique of Sacrifice", *Semeia* 33.109-123
SCHWAGER, Raymund 1988, "The Theory of the Wrath of God", in Dumouchel 1988a.44-52
SCHWEIKER, William 1987, "Sacrifice, Interpretation, and the Sacred; the Import of Gadamer and Girard for Religious Studies", *Journal of the American Academy of Religion* 55.789-810
SCHWEIKER, William 1994, "Religion and the Philosophers of Mimesis", in Wallace 1994a.25-42
SCHWEITZER, Albert 1926, *The Quest of the Historical Jesus; a Critical Study of its Progress from Reimarus to Wrede*, Second English Edition, A & C Black, London
SCOBIE, Charles H.H. 1993, "Local References in the Letters to the Seven Churches", *NTS* 39.606-624
SCOFIELD, C.I. and others 1967, *Holy Bible; New Scofield Reference Edition*, Oxford University Press
SCOTT, C. Anderson Undated; *Revelation*, Century Bible, T.C. and E.C. Jack, Edinburgh
SCUBLA, Lucien 1982, "Contribution à la théorie du sacrifice", in Deguy 1982.103-167
SCUBLA, Lucien 1988, "The Christianity of René Girard and the Nature of Religion", in Dumouchel 1988a.160-178
SCULLION, John J. 1969, "Revelation (the Apocalypse)" in Fuller, R.C. and others (editors), *A New Catholic Commentary on Holy Scripture*, Revised

Edition, Nelson, London
SEEL, Thomas Allen 1995, *A Theology of Music for Worship Derived from the Book of Revelation*, Studies in Liturgical Musicology 3, The Scarecrow Press, Metuchen
SEGAL, Charles 1990, "Sacrifice and Violence in the Myth of Meleager and Heracles; Homer, Bacchylides, Sophocles", *Helios* 17.1.7-24
SEIBEL, Claude 1985, "Désir mimétique et échec scolaire; transpositions des hypothèses de René Girard à la situation pédagogique dans une classe", in Dumouchel 1985.288-298
SHAFFER, Elinor 1995, "Secular Apocalypse; Prophets and Apocalypses at the End of the Eighteenth Century", in Bull 1995a.138-158
SHEA, Chris 1994, "Victims on Violence; 'Different Voices' and Girard", in Wallace 1994a.252-265
SHEA, William H. 1983, "The Covenantal Form of the Letters to the Seven Churches". *AUSS* 21.71-84
SHEPHERD, Massey H. 1960, *The Paschal Liturgy and the Apocalypse*, Ecumenical Studies in Worship, Lutterworth Press, London
SIEBERS, Tobin 1986, "Language, Violence, and the Sacred; a Polemical Survey of Critical Theories", in Juilland 1986a.203-219
SIEGMAN, E.F. 1967, "Apocalypse, Book of", in *New Catholic Encyclopaedia*, McGraw-Hill, New York, 1967.654-659
SIMONETTI, Manlio 1994, *Biblical Interpretation in the Early Church*, T & T Clark, Edinburgh
SMALLEY, Stephen S. 1994, *Thunder and Love, John's Revelation and John's Community*, Nelson Word Ltd , Milton Keynes
SMALLEY, Stephen S. 2005, *The Revelation to John: A Commentary on the Greek Text of the Apocalypse*, SPCK, London
SMITH, Christopher R. 1994, "The Structure of the Book of Revelation in the Light of Apocalyptic Literary Conventions", *NovT* 36.373-393
SMITH, Theophilus Harold 1994, "King and the Black Religious Quest to Cure Racism", in Wallace 1994a.230-251
SOLLERS, Philippe 1986, "Is God Dead? 'The Purloined Letter' of the Gospel", in Juilland 1986a.191-196
SOUTHERN, R.W. 1970, *Western Society and the Church in the Middle Ages*, The Pelican History of the Church 2, Penguin, Harmondsworth
STAGG, Frank 1972, "The Abused Aorist", *JBL* 91.222-231
STANLEY, John E. 1986, "The Apocalypse and Contemporary Sect Analysis", *SBL Seminar Papers* 1986.412-421
STAPLES, Peter 1972, "Rev. XVI 4-6 and its Vindication Formula", *NovT* 14.280-293
STAUFFER, Ethelbert 1955, *Christ and the Caesars; Historical Sketches*, SCM Press, London
STEFANOVIC, Ranko 1995, "The Background and Meaning of the Sealed Book of Revelation 5", dissertation abstract, *AUSS* 34.95
STEIN, Stephen J. 1984, "Transatlantic Extensions; Apocalyptic in Early New England", in Patrides 1984a.266-298
STEINHAUSER, Kenneth B. 1987, *The Apocalypse Commentary of Tyconius; a History of its Reception and Influence*, European University Studies

23.301, Peter Lang, Frankfurt
STENDAHL, Krister 1976, *Paul among Jews and Gentiles and Other Essays*, Fortress Press, Philadelphia
STETKEVYCH, Suzanne Pinckney 1986a, "The Rithâ of Ta'abbata Sharra; a Study of Blood-Vengeance in Early Arabic Poetry", *JSS* 31.27-45
STETKEVYCH, Suzanne Pinckney 1986b, "Ritual and Sacrificial Elements in the Poetry of Blood-Vengeance; Two Poems by Durayd Ibn Al-Simmah and Muhalhil Ibn Rabî'ah", *JNES* 45.31-43
STONE, Michael Edward 1976, "Lists of Things Revealed in the Apocalyptic Literature", in Cross, F.M. and others (editors), *Magnalia Dei: the Mighty Acts of God; Essays on the Bible and Archaeology in Memory of G. Ernest Wright*, Doubleday, Garden City, 1976.414-452
STONE, Michael Edward 1980, *Scriptures, Sects and Visions; a Profile of Judaism from Ezra to the Jewish Revolts*, Fortress Press, Philadelphia
STRACK, Hermann L. and BILLERBECK, Paul 1926, "Die Offenbarung Johannis", in *Kommentar zum Neuen Testament aus Talmud und Midrasch*, C.H. Beck'sche Verlagsbuchhandlung, Oscar Beck, Munich, 3.788-857
STRAND, Kenneth A. 1978, "Chiastic Structure and some Motifs in the Book of Revelation", *AUSS* 16.401-408
STRAND, Kenneth A. 1983, "A Further Note on the Covenantal Form in the Book of Revelation", *AUSS* 21.251-264
STRAND, Kenneth A. 1984a, "An Overlooked Old Testament Background to Revelation 11:1", *AUSS* 22.317-325
STRAND, Kenneth A. 1984b, "Revelation 5 and 19 as Literary Reciprocals", *AUSS* 22.249-257
STRAND, Kenneth A. 1987a, "The Eight Basic Visions in the Book of Revelation", *AUSS* 25.107-121
STRAND, Kenneth A. 1987b, "The 'Victorious Introduction' Scenes in the Visions in the Book of Revelation", *AUSS* 25.267-288
STRATHMANN, H. 1967, "Μάρτυς, μαρτυρέω, μαρτυρία, μαρτύριον", *TDNT* 4.474-514
STRAUSS, Walter A. 1990, "Dostoevsky; the 'Double' Precursor", *Helios* 17.1.121-128
STRENSKI, Ivan 1987, *Four Theories of Myth in Twentieth Century History*, Macmillan Press, Basingstoke
SUMMERS, Ray 1951, *Worthy is the Lamb; an Interpretation of Revelation*, Broadman Press, Nashville
SURRIDGE, R. 1989-1990, "Redemption in the Structure of Revelation", *ExpT* 101.231-235
SWANSON, Ted 1994, "Colonial Violence and Inca Analogies to Christianity", in Wallace 1994a.121-136
SWARTLEY, Willard M. (editor) 2000, *Violence Renounced; René Girard, Biblical Studies and Peacemaking*, Pandora, Pennsylvania
SWARTLEY, Willard M. 2000a, "Discipleship and Imitation of Jesus/Suffering Servant: The Mimesis of New Creation", 218-245
SWEET, John P.M. 1979, *Revelation*, SCM Pelican Commentaries, SCM Press, London
SWEET, John P.M. 1981, "Maintaining the Testimony of Jesus; the Suffering

of Christians in the Revelation of John", in Horbury 1981.101-117
SWETE, Henry Barclay 1907, *The Apocalypse of St. John; the Greek Text with Introduction, Notes and Indices*, Second Edition, Macmillan, London
SYKES, S.W. 1980, "Sacrifice in the New Testament and Christian Theology", in Bourdillon 1980.61-83
SYKES, S.W. 1991, *Sacrifice and Redemption; Durham Essays in Theology*, Cambridge University Press
SZITTYA, Penn 1992, "Domesday Bokes; the Apocalypse in Medieval English Literary Culture", in Emmerson 1992a.374-377
TANNENBAUM, Leslie 1982, *Biblical Tradition in Blake's Early Prophecies; the Great Code of Art*, Princeton University Press
TATE, Marvin E. 1990, *Psalms 51-100*, WBC 20, Word, Dallas
TATFORD, Frederick A. 1969, *Prophecy's Last Word; an Exposition of the Revelation*, Bible and Advent Testimony Movement, Eastbourne
TAYLOR, Simon J. 1996, *Sacrifice, Revelation and Salvation in the Thought of René Girard*, a thesis submitted for the degree of Master of Philosophy, Oxford University
TAYLOR, W.S. 1930, "The Seven Seals in the Revelation of John", *JTS* 31.266-271
THEISSEN, Gerd 1987, *The Shadow of the Galilean; the Quest of the Historical Jesus in Narrative Form*, SCM Press, London
THISELTON, Anthony C. 1992, *New Horizons in Hermeneutics*, HarperCollins, London
THOMAS, Konrad 1986, "On Law, Religion, and Custom", in Juilland 1986a.177-190
THOMPSON, Leonard 1969, "Cult and Eschatology in the Apocalypse of John", *Journal of Religion* 49.330-350
THOMPSON, Leonard 1985, "The Mythic Unity of the Apocalypse", SBL *Seminar Papers* 1985.14-28
THOMPSON, Leonard 1986, "A Sociological Analysis of Tribulation in the Apocalypse of John", *Semeia* 36.147-174
THOMPSON, Leonard 1990, *The Book of Revelation; Apocalypse and Empire*, Oxford University Press
THOMPSON, Steven 1985, *The Apocalypse and Semitic Syntax*, SNTSMS 52, Cambridge University Press
TODOROV, Tzvetan 1975, *The Fantastic; a Structural Approach to a Literary Genre*, Cornell University Press, Ithaca
TORRANCE, T.F. 1960, *The Apocalypse Today*, James Clarke, London
TOUT Charles A. 1992, *The Apocalypse and Last Days Prophecies*, Arthur H. Stockwell, Ilfracombe
TRITES, Allison A. 1973, "Μάρτυς and Martyrdom in the Apocalypse; a Semantic Study", *NovT* 15.72-80
TRITES, Allison A. 1977, *The New Testament Concept of Witness*, Cambridge University Press
TRUDINGER, L. Paul 1966, "Some Observations Concerning the Text of the Old Testament in the Book of Revelation", *JTS* 17.82-88
TURNER, H.E.W. 1952, *The Patristic Doctrine of Redemption; a Study of the Development of Doctrine during the First Five Centuries*, A.R. Mowbray,

London
TURNER, Victor W. 1967, *The Forest of Symbols; Aspects of Ndembu Ritual*, Cornell University Press, Ithaca
TURNER, Victor W. 1969, *The Ritual Process: Structure and Anti-Structure*, Routledge, London
TURNER, Victor W. and TURNER, Edith 1978, *Image and Pilgrimage in Christian Culture; Anthropological Perspectives*, Columbia University Press, New York
TUVESON, Ernest L. 1984, "The Millenarian Structure of *The Communist Manifesto*", in Patrides 1984a.323-341
ULFGARD, Håkan 1989, *Feast and Future; Revelation 7:9-17 and the Feast of Tabernacles*, ConB New Testament Series 22, Almqvist and Wiksell, Stockholm
ULRICH, Simon 1984, "Regarding the Apocalypse", *King's Theological Review* 7.21-22
UNGAR, Steve 1990, "The Appeal of History; Reading Girard on Camus", *Helios* 17.1.145-155
UNNIK, W.C. van 1962-1963, "A Formula Describing Prophecy", *NTS* 9.86-94
UNNIK, W.C. van 1970, "'Worthy is the Lamb'; the Background of Apoc. 5", in Albert Descamps and André de Halleux (editors) *Mélanges Bibliques en hommage au R.P. Béda Rigaux*, Duculot, Gembloux
VANHOYE, Albert 1963, "L'utilisation du livre d'Ezéchiel dans l'Apocalypse", *Bib* 43.436-476
VANNI, Ugo 1976, "Un esempio di dialogo liturgico in Ap 1,4-8", *Bib* 57.453-467
VANNI, Ugo 1980a, *La struttura letteraria dell'Apocalisse*, Second Edition, Aloisiana Pubblicazioni della Pontificia Facoltà Teologica dell' Italia, Meridionale-Sezione S. Luigi, Naples
VANNI, Ugo 1980b, "L'Apocalypse johannique; état de la question", in Lambrecht 1980a.21-46
VANNI, Ugo 1988, *L'Apocalisse; ermeneutica, esegesi, teologia*, Supplementi alla Rivista Biblica 17, Edizioni Dehoniane, Bologna
VANNI, Ugo 1991, "Liturgical Dialogue as a Literary Form in the Book of Revelation", *NTS* 37.348-372
VASSALIADIS, Petros 1985, "The Translation of *Martyria Iêsou* in Revelation", *Bible Translator* 36.129-134
VAUX, Ronald de 1964, *Studies in Old Testament Sacrifice*, University of Wales Press, Cardiff
VAWTER, Bruce 1960, "Apocalyptic; Its Relation to Prophecy", *CBQ* 22.33-46
VERMES, Geza 1973, *Jesus the Jew; a Historian's Reading of the Gospels*, Collins, London
VERMES, Geza 1983, *Jesus and the World of Judaism*, SCM Press, London
VERMES, Geza 1993, *The Religion of Jesus the Jew*, SCM Press, London
VIELHAUER, P. 1965, "Apocalypses and Related Subjects, Introduction", in E. Hennecke, *New Testament Apocrypha*, Lutterworth Press, London, 1965.2.579-607

VIGÉE, Claude 1986, "Le Parfum d'Isaac", in Juilland 1986a.65-84
VÖGTLE, Anton 1981, *Das Buch mit den sieben Siegeln: die Offenbarung des Johannes in Auswahl gedeutet*, Herder, Freiburg
VOLLMANN, Herbert 1987, *The Apocalypse Today*, Stiftung Gralbotschaft, Stuttgart
VOS, Louis Arthur 1965, *The Synoptic Traditions in the Apocalypse*, J.H. Kok, Kampen
WADDELL, Robby 2006, *The Spirit in the Book of Revelation*, Journal of Pentecostal Theology Supplement Series, vol. 30, Deo Publishing, Blandford Forum
WADDY, Stacy 1935, *The Drama of the Eucharist; as Set forth in the Book of Revelation of St. John the Divine*, Society for the Propagation of the Gospel/SPCK, London
WAINWRIGHT, Arthur W. 1993, *Mysterious Apocalypse*, Abingdon, Nashville
WAKEMAN, Mary K. 1973, *God's Battle with the Monster; a Study in Biblical Imagery*, E.J. Brill, Leiden
WALL, Robert W. 1995, *Revelation*, Paternoster Press, New International Bible Commentary 18, Carlisle
WALLACE, Howard 1948, "Leviathan and the Beast in Revelation", *BA* 11.61-68
WALLACE, Mark I. 1989, "Postmodern Biblicism; the Challenge of René Girard for Contemporary Theology", *Modern Theology* 5.309-325
WALLACE, Mark I. and SMITH, Theophilus H. (Editors) 1994a, *Curing Violence*, Polebridge Press, Sonoma
WALLACE, Mark I. and SMITH, Theophilus H. 1994b, "Religion as Cure or Religion as Structure of Violence", in Wallace 1994a.xvii-xxvi
WALLIS, N.H. (Editor) 1938, *New Testament Translated by William Tyndale, 1534 Edition*, Cambridge University Press
WALPOLE, G.H.S. 1911, *The Revelation of Saint John the Divine*, Revised Edition, Cambridge University Press
WALVOORD, John F. 1966, *The Revelation of Jesus Christ*, Marshall, Morgan and Scott, London
WARD, Graham 1994, "Mimesis; the Measure of Mark's Christology", *Journal of Literature and Theology* 8, 1-29
WARD, Graham 1994, Review of Hamerton-Kelly 1992a, *Reviews in Religion and Theology* 1,50-52
WARNER, S.M. 1944, *"The Best is yet to Be"; Studies in the Book of Revelation*, Marshall, Morgan and Scott, London
WATSON, Francis 1994, *Church, Text and World; Biblical Interpretation in Theological Perspective*, T & T Clark, Edinburgh
WEAVER, J. Denny 1989-1990, "Atonement for the Nonconstantinian Church", *Modern Theology* 6.307-323
WEBER, Hans-Ruedi 1988, *The Way of the Lamb: Christ in the Apocalypse; Lenten Meditations*, Risk Book Series 36, WCC Publications, Geneva
WEIZSÄCKER, Carl von 1895, *The Apostolic Age of the Christian Church*, volume 2, Theological Translation Library 5, Williams and Norgate, London
WELLESLEY, Kenneth 1975, *The Long Year AD 69*, Paul Elek, London

WENGER, John Christian (Editor) 1956, *The Complete Writings of Menno Simons (1496-1561)*, Herald Press, Scottdale
WENHAM, David 1984, *The Rediscovery of Jesus' Eschatological Discourse*, Gospel Perspectives 4, JSOT Press, Sheffield
WENHAM, Gordon J. 1991, *Genesis 1-15*, WBC 1, Word, Milton Keynes
WENGST, Klaus 1987, *Pax Romana and the Peace of Jesus Christ*, SCM Press, London
WEST, Morris 1982, *The Clowns of God*, Coronet, London
WHALE, Peter 1987, "The Lamb of God; some Myths about the Vocabulary of the Johannine Literature", *JBL* 106.289-295
WHEALON, J.F. 1981, "New Patches on an Old Garment; The Book of Revelation", *BTB* 11.54-59
WHITE, Hayden 1978, "Ethnological 'Lie' and Mythical 'Truth'", *Diacritics* 8.2-9
WHITWELL, Richard 1942, *The Apocalypse; an Inquiry into the Mystical and Prophetic Meaning of the Revelation Granted to St. John the Divine*, The Rally, London
WIESER, Thomas 1985, "Community - its Unity, Diversity and Universality", *Semeia* 33.83-95
WILES, Maurice and SANTER, Mark (editors) 1975, *Documents in Early Christian Thought*, Cambridge University Press
WILKINSON, Richard H. 1988, "The στῦλος of Revelation 3.12 and Ancient Coronation Rites", *JBL* 107.498-501
WILLIAMS, James G. 1988, "The Innocent Victim: René Girard on Violence, Sacrifice and the Sacred", *Religious Studies Review* 14.4.320-326
WILLIAMS, James G. 1991, *The Bible, Violence and the Sacred; Liberation from the Myth of Sanctioned Violence*, Harper, San Francisco
WILLIAMS, James G. 1994, "Steadfast Love and not Sacrifice", in Wallace 1994a.71-99
WILLIAMS, James G. 1994b, "Sacrifice and the Beginning of Kingship", *Semeia* 67.73-92
WILLIAMS, James G. 1997, "Interview with René Girard," *Religion* 27 (1997)
WILLIAMS, James G. 2000, "King as Servant, Sacrifice as Service" in Swartley 2000.178-199
WILLIAMS, John 1992, "Purpose and Imagery in the Apocalypse Commentary of Beatus of Liébana", in Emmerson 1992a.217-233
WILLIAMS, Michael 1989; *The Power and the Kingdom; a Personal Look at Power, Politics and the Book of Revelation*, Monarch, Eastbourne
WILLIAMS, Rowan 1989, *Violence, Society and the Sacred*, The Oxford Project for Peace Studies, Oxford Project for Peace Studies Paper 18, Oxford
WILSON, Brian R. 1973, *Magic and the Millenium; a Sociological Study of Religious Movements of Protest among Tribal and Third World Peoples*, Heinemann, London
WILSON, Geoffrey B. 1985, *Revelation*, Evangelical Press, Welwyn
WILSON, J. Christian 1993, "The Problem of the Domitianic Date of Revelation", *NTS* 39.587-605
WILSON, Mark 2007, *Charts on the Book of Revelation: Literary, Historical,*

and Theological Perspectives, Kregel Charts of the Bible and Theology, Kregel Publications, Grand Rapids

WILSON, P. Whitwell 1921, *The Vision We Forget; a Layman's Reading of the Book of the Revelation of St. John the Divine*, Morgan and Scott, London

WILSON CARPENTER, Mary and LANDOW, George P. 1984, "Ambiguous Revelations; the Apocalypse and Victorian Literature", in Patrides 1984a.299-322

WINK, Walter 1973, *Naming the Powers; the Language of Power in the New Testament*, Fortress Press, Minneapolis

WINK, Walter 1984, *Unmasking the Powers; the Invisible Forces that Determine Human Existence*, Fortress Press, Minneapolis

WINK, Walter 1992, *Engaging the Powers; Discernment and Resistance in an Age of Domination*, Fortress Press, Minneapolis

WITHERINGTON, Ben III 2003, *Revelation*, NCBC, Cambridge University Press, Cambridge

WITTREICH, Joseph 1984a, "'Image of that horror'; the Apocalypse in King Lear", in Patrides 1984a.175-206

WITTREICH, Joseph 1984b, "The Apocalypse; a Bibliography", in Patrides 1984a.369-440

WOLTERSTORFF, Nicholas 1995, *Divine Discourse; Philosophical Reflections on the Claim that God Speaks*, Cambridge University Press

WOOD, Harold F. 1954, *The Real Remedy for All the World's Ills, International, Political, Personal and Physical or, What Will Happen when Christ Returns? A Study Based on the Scriptures*, Volume 1, *The Millennium and its Impact on the World of Men and Nature*, published by the author, Guildford

WRANGHAM, Richard and PETERSON, Dale 1997, *Demonic Males; Apes and the Origins of Human Violence*, Bloomsbury, London

WRIGHT, Nigel G. 2000, *Disavowing Constantine; Mission, Church and the Social Order in the Theologies of John Howard Yoder and Jürgen Moltmann*, Paternoster, Carlisle

WRIGHT, N.T. 1992, *Who Was Jesus?*, SPCK, London

WRIGHT, N.T. 1996, *Jesus and the Victory of God*, SPCK, London

YAMAGUCHI, Masao 1988, "Towards a Poetics of the Scapegoat", in Dumouchel 1988a, 179-191

YARBRO COLLINS, Adela 1976, *The Combat Myth in the Book of Revelation*, HTR Dissertations in Religion 9, Scholars Press, Missoula

YARBRO COLLINS, Adela 1977a, "The History-of-Religions Approach to Apocalypticism and the 'Angel of the Waters' (Rev 16:4-7)", *CBQ* 39.367-381

YARBRO COLLINS, Adela 1977b, "The Political Perspective of the Revelation to John", *JBL* 96.241-256

YARBRO COLLINS, Adela 1979, *The Apocalypse*, New Testament Message 22, Veritas Publications, Dublin

YARBRO COLLINS, Adela 1981a, "Myth and History in the Book of Revelation; the Problem of Its Date", in Baruch Halpern and Jon D. Levenson (editors), *Traditions in Transformation: Turning Points in Biblical Faith; Festschrift Honouring Frank Moore Cross*, Eisenbrauns, Winona

Lake, 1981.377-403
YARBRO COLLINS, Adela 1981b, "Dating the Apocalypse of John", *BR* 26.33-45
YARBRO COLLINS, Adela 1984, *Crisis and Catharsis; the Power of the Apocalypse*, Westminster Press, Philadelphia
YARBRO COLLINS, Adela 1986a, "Vilification and Self-Definition in the Book of Revelation", *HTR* 79.308-320
YARBRO COLLINS, Adela 1986b, "Early Christian Apocalypticism", *Semeia* 36.1-11
YARBRO COLLINS, Adela 1986c, "Reading the Book of Revelation in the Twentieth Century", *Int* 40.229-242
YARBRO COLLINS, Adela 1988a, "Oppression from Without; the Symbolization of Rome as Evil in Early Christianity", *Concilium* 200.66-74
YARBRO COLLINS, Adela 1988b, "Numerical Symbolism in Jewish and Early Christian Apocalyptic Literature", *ANRW* 2.21.2.1221-1287
YARBRO COLLINS, Adela 1988c, "Early Christian Apocalyptic Literature", *ANRW* 2.25.6.4665-4711
YARBRO COLLINS, Adela 1989a, "Persecution and Vengeance in the Book of Revelation", in Hellholm 1989.729-749
YARBRO COLLINS, Adela 1989b, "The Apocalypse (Revelation)", in Brown, Raymond E. and others (editors), *The New Jerome Bible Commentary*, Geoffrey Chapman, London, 1989.996-1016
YARBRO COLLINS, Adela 1992a, "Revelation, Book of", in David Noel Freedman (editor), *Anchor Bible Dictionary*, Doubleday, New York, 1992.5.
YARBRO COLLINS, Adela 1992b, "The 'Son of Man' Tradition and the Book of Revelation", in Charlesworth 1992.536-568
YARBRO COLLINS, Adela 1993, "Feminine Symbolism in the Book of Revelation", *Biblical Interpretation* 1.20-33
YOUNG, Frances M. 1975, *Sacrifice and the Death of Christ*, SCM Press, London
YOUNG, Frances M. 1979, *The Use of Sacrificial Ideas in Greek Christian Writers from the New Testament to John Chrysostom*, Patristic Monograph Series 5, The Philadelphia Patristic Foundation, Cambridge Mass.
YOUNG, Frances M. 1982, *Can These Dry Bones Live?*, SCM Press, London
ZAHN, Theodore 1924 and 1926, *Die Offenbarung des Johannes*, Kommentar zum Neuen Testament 18, 2 volumes, A. Deichertsche Verlagsbuchhandlung, Dr. Werner Scholl, Leipzig
ZERWICK, Max 1988, *A Grammatical Analysis of the Greek New Testament*, Third, Revised Edition, Editrice Pontificio Istituto Biblico, Rome
ZIESLER, John 1990, *Pauline Christianity*, (Revised Edition), Oxford Bible Series, Oxford University Press

Scripture Index and Index to Other Ancient Texts

Genesis
    123, 212
1 2
1:2 2
4:10 216n
9 202
9:12-17 185
49:9 188n

Exodus
8, 35, 41, 44, 145,
   149, 191
7-11 44
12:13 160n
12:14 149n
16:4-5 145n
19:6 149n, 191
19:16 185
32 123n

Leviticus
11:39 190n
16:15 149n
26:21 197

Numbers
5:12-31 187n
11:7-9 145n
16:41-50 144n
17:25 181n

Deuteronomy
30:19 93
32:8 184n

Judges
5:4-5 185n

Joshua
    123

1 Samuel
15:22 134n

Ezra
16 19

Psalms
    xxv, 180n
2 167, 145, 194n
7:12 202n
11:2 201n
18:7-15 185n
29:3-9 185n
33:3 184n
37:14 201n
40:3 184n
40:6 134n
45 201, 203
46 167n
46:9 201n
47:8 172
48 167n
51:16-17 134n
72 220
74 220
76 167n
78:2 151n
78:23-25 145
78:57 201n
96:1 184n
97 172
98:1 173, 184
99 172
99:1 173
103:6 181n
110:1 194n
118:26 180n
144:9 184n
149:1 184n

Isaiah
1:10-17 134n

6 180n
8:16 164n
11:1 188n
11:1-9 141n
17:12-14 167n
29:11 187n
34:4 218n
34:8 218n
42:9-10 184
42:10 184n
53 110n, 190, 191
53:7 190
53:10 154
62.2 145

Jeremiah
7:21-22 134n
14:12 196
21:9 196

Lamentations
3:12-13 202n

Ezekiel
1 180n, 185
2:9-10 186n
2:10 187
5:15-17 198n
9:4 160n
14:21 197
33:27-29 198n
34 19
39 201n

Daniel
    23, 163n,
   184n, 187n
7 19, 180n, 184n
7:13 180n
9:25-27 180n
10:13 184n
12:9 164n

Hosea
6:6 134n
7:16 201n

Joel
2:11 218n
2:20-21 218n

Amos
5:21-25 134n
8:9 218n

Jonah
123

Micah
6:6-8 134n

Nahum
1:6 218n

Habakkuk
3:3-15 185n
3:5-9 201n

Zechariah
147, 201, 215
1:8 196
1:10 196
6:1 196
6:5 196
6:6 196
9:13-14 202n
12:11 44

Malachi
3:1 180n
3:2 218n

Matthew
3:1 180n
5:23-24 154n
6:12 153n
9:13 134n
11:3 180n
12:6 134n, 154n
12:7 134n

12:20 143
13:35 150
17:24-27 154n
18:21-22 154n
21:33-46 121n
23:8-10 17n
23:18-19 154n
23:34-39 121n
24 19
24:14 200
27:45 218
27:50-53 160n
27:51 218
27:55 109n

Mark
125
1:4 153n
1:12-13 154n
1:15 153n
1:44 154n
2:5 153n
2:10 153n
3:11 181n
6:12 153n
8.38 145
10:45 154n
11:9 180n
11:15-17 154n
11:17 134n
11:19 181n
11:25 153n, 181n
12:28-34 134n
13 10, 35, 37, 44, 48, 132n, 197
13:1-2 154n
13:10 204n
14:24 154n
15.40 109n

Luke
1:5-23 154n
2:22-24 154n
2:24 154n
2:25-38 154n
2:49 154n
6:37 153n
10:18 154n

11:22 143
11:49-52 216
11:50 150
12:49-53 132n, 204n
18:8 217n
21 203
23:12 160n
23:47 155
23:49 109n
24:47 153n
24:53 154n

John
45
1:1-18 45
1:29 45, 155, 190n
1:36 190n
2:12-21 134n
5:19-29 132n
8.32 132n
8:37 143n
8:38-39 147n
8.44 156n
11:49-53 87
12:31-36 155, 156n
14:6 156n
16:33 143, 155
18:36-38 156n
18.37 132n
19:25-27 109n
21:15 190n

Acts
2:22-36 194n
2:46 154n
5:28-32 194n
7:51-56 194n
7:55-56 190n
19:4 180n
20:28 155

Romans
1-3 205
1:4 207
1:16-32 205-214
1:18-32 132n
1:18-3:20 205

Scripture Index and Index to Other Ancient Texts 273

2 214
3:4 143
3:19-20 205
3:21 205, 214
3:25 157, 158n
4:7 157n
4:25 158n
5:9 158n
6:5-11 157n
6:10-11 156n
7:4-6 157n
8:18 206
8:34 194n
8:37 143n
8.38-39 147n
12:21 143
14:8-9 157n

1 Corinthians
1:23 207
2:8 147n
2:10 206
3:13 206
7:31 157n
14:30 206
15:3 158n
15:22 156n
15:24-26 147n
15:47 207
15:54-55 143

2 Corinthians
1:6 138n
2:15 207
4:3 207
4:4 213
5:11-21 156n
5:15 156n
5:21 158n
11:14 201n

Galatians
1:8 207
1:13-14 125n
1:16 206
3:13 158n
3:23 206
4.1-11 125n

4:3 147n
4:9 147n

Ephesians
1:7 157n
1:13 158n
1:20 194n
1:20-21 147n
1:20-23 194n
2:1-2 147n
2:1-10 158n
3:10 147n, 158n
3:13 138n
6:12 147n

Philippians
2:6-11 194n
3:15 206

Colossians
1:14 157n
1:16 147n, 194n
1:24 138n
2:8 147n
2:10-15 158n
2:15 147n, 194n
2:20 147n
3:13 157n

1 Thessalonians
1:10 207
4:16 207

2 Thessalonians
1:7 207
2:3-9 17n
2:3 206
2:6 206
2:8 206

2 Timothy
4:1 132n
4:6 138n

Hebrews
133, 159, 225
1:3 194n

4:12 204n
7:27 159n
9:14 159n
10:12 194n
10:26-31 159n
12:2 194n

1 Peter
158
1:18-19 158
1:20 149n
2.9 158n
2:24 158n
3:21 158n
3:22 194n

1 John
45
2:2 156n
2:14 143n
4:4 143n
4:10 156n
5:4-5 143

2 John
45

3 John
45

Revelation
128n, 129, 130, 134
1-3 48, 168n
1:1 29, 136, 163n, 224
1:1-2 135
1:2 136
1:3 14n, 164n
1:4 175, 180, 201
1:5 136, 142, 145, 148
1:6 44n, 191n, 204n
1:7 147
1:8 175, 180
1:9 136n, 137n, 138n

1:10 178, 183n
1:12-16 178, 183n
1:12-18 xxv, 132n,
   148
1:14 201
1:16 141n, 170n,
   204n
1:17-19 179
2:1-3:22 27n, 31,
   36, 37n, 141, 145-
   6, 178, 183n, 202
2:2 137n
2:3 137n
2:7 141n, 143n,
   145, 177n, 183n
2.9 36
2:10 145, 201
2:10-11 136n
2:11 141n, 145,
   177n
2:12 141n, 170n,
   204n
2:13 136n, 138n,
   142
2:16 141n, 170n
2:17 141n, 145,
   177n, 183n, 201
2:19 137n
2.22 181n
2.25 181n
2:26 141n, 145
2:27 177n
2:28 183n
3:4 145, 149, 201
3:5 141n, 145,
   177n, 183n,
   187n, 201
3:7 136n
3.9 36, 181n
3:10 137n
3:11 201
3:12 141n, 145,
   177n
3:14 136
3:18 149, 183n,
   201
3:21 141n, 145,
   146, 175n, 176n,
   177n
4-6 205
4-11 24n, 35, 44,
   48
4-22 141-142
4:1 27n, 33, 177,
   178, 179, 183n,
   224
4:1-11 xxv, 30, 55,
   163n, 172, 178,
   179-185, 194,
   195, 202
4:1-5:14 3, 56,
   179, 180, 194,
   215
4:1-8 182
4:2 183n
4:2-5:14 173, 178,
   179
4:2-11 168, 182,
   194
4:3 185
4:4 145, 183, 184,
   201
4:5 185
4:8 175, 180
4:9 180, 182
4:9-10 181, 182,
   183, 192
4:9-11 182
4:10 180, 201
5-8 8
5:1 10, 16, 24n, 38,
   39, 140, 178n,
   179, 186, 187
5:1-7 5n, 28
5:1-10 202
5:1-13 55
5:1-14 30, 51,
   146n, 169, 171,
   178-9, 182, 183n,
   184, 186-196,
   221
5:4 188
5:5 141, 142, 143n.
   163n, 182, 202
5:6-14 xxv
5:6 24n, 149, 175
190, 191, 194n
5:8 182
5:8-10 183, 184,
   192
5:9 141, 142, 145n,
   148, 184, 191
5:9-10 148n, 149,
   192
5:9-12 142n
5:10 136n, 145,
   175n, 176n, 182n
   191
5:11-12 192
5:12 145n, 184,
   191
5:13 49, 183, 192,
   218
5:14 182, 184, 195
6-11 25
6-20 53
6:1 23, 39, 182,
   196
6:1-2 28, 51
6:1-8 27n, 28, 37,
   41, 51
6:1-17 1, 19, 28,
   29, 37, 39, 44,
   48, 51, 178, 196-
   221
6:2 18, 30, 32, 37,
   39, 141, 142n,
   200, 201, 202,
   203, 215
6:3 182
6:3-8 18
6:4 149n, 181n,
   191, 192
6:5 182
6:6 37
6:7 182
6:8 39, 169n, 197,
   198
6:9 136n, 191
6:9-11 8, 9, 18, 28,
   52, 138n, 191,
   192, 216
6:10 193n, 220
6:11 145, 201, 204

6:12-17 8, 18, 28, 37, 39, 47, 52
6:14 5n
7 21, 198
7:1-8 36
7:2-3 160n
7:3-8 175
7:9 201
7:9-11 183n
7:9-17 xxv, 171, 179n
7:11-12 184
7:13 163n, 182, 201
7:13-14 145
7:14 149, 201
7:15 177n
7:15-17 177n
7:17 175, 177n
8:1 161n, 181n, 182n
8:1-5 218n
8:1-9:21 25
8:2-22:6 38
8:2-9:21 1
8.2 5n
8:5 1, 179n, 185
8:6-9:21 38
8.6 5n
8:7 12
8:7-12 169n
8:8 36
8:10 5n
9:1-21 9n, 36
9:1 5n, 204
9:4 181n
9:7 201
9:14 37
9:20-21 221n
9:20 181n
10:2 140, 186n
10:7 182n
11 19, 25, 140
11-12 18, 19, 24, 25
11:1-13 186n
11:3-13 136n, 140
11:5 175

11:7 136n, 141, 144, 182n
11:8 36
11:15 171, 172, 173, 175, 182n, 194
11:15-18 xxv, 46, 146n, 172
11:15-19 1, 38, 39, 40, 47, 171, 173, 194
11:16 182, 184, 185
11:17 171, 173, 175, 180
11:19 179n, 185
12-22 48
12-19 25
12 2, 4n, 13, 194n
12:1-17 2
12.1-18 42
12:1 35, 36, 38, 201
12:4 182n
12:5 194n
12.6 145
12:9 146n
12:10 146n, 172
12:10-12 152n
12:11 136n, 141, 142, 146, 152n, 192
12:14 204
12:17 136n
13:1-18 44, 175
13:1-8 175
13:1 175
13:3 149n, 175, 191
13:4 175
13:5 204
13:6 17n, 146n
13:7 141, 144
13:8 149, 150, 187n, 191
13:10 137n, 181n
13:11 175
13:11-18 175

13:12 152n, 175n, 181n
13:14 146n, 152n, 175, 204
13:14-15 175
13:16-17 175
13:18 175
14:1-5 190n
14:12 136n, 137n
14:13 181n
14:14 201
15:1 1
15:2 141
15:3-5 46
15:3-4 xxv
15:3 44n, 191n
15:7 182
15:7-16:21 1
16:1-21 38, 39
16:1-19 41
16:1-18:24 146n
16:2-10 169n
16:4-6 43
16.4 42
16:5 175, 180
16:10 221n
16:12-14 18
16:12 37
16:13 146
16:16 44
16:17-21 47
16:18 185n
16:18-21 185
17-18 34
17:1-18:24 36
17 18
17:1 163n
17:3 175
17:6 136n
17:7-18 163n
17:8 175, 182n, 187n
17:9-14 175n
17:10 182n
17:11 175
17:14 142
18:8 182n, 217n
18:9 175n, 182n

18:24 191, 192, 217n
19 170n
19:1-8 xxv
19:1-22:21 169n
19:4 182, 183, 184
19:6 173
19:8 149, 204
19:10 136n, 140n
19:11-22:5 146n
19:11-21 169, 170, 175
19:11-20:15 149n, 169
19:11-16 xxv, 8, 9, 200, 201n
19:11 136, 142n, 201, 203
19:12-13 175
19:12 145n, 177n
19:13 45
19:14 145, 201
19:15 141n, 170n, 177n
19:16 177n
19:18 149
19:21 141n, 170n
20-22 5
20:1-7 5, 9
20:3 146n
20:4 136n
20:4-6 175n, 177n
20:6 145
20:7 182n
20:7-10 175
20:8 146n
20:9 175
20:11 201
20:11-14 176n
20:12 177n, 187n
20:14-15 145
20:14 177n
20:15 145, 177n, 187n
21-22 9
21:1 176n
21:1-6 177n
21:1-22:5 xxv, 145

21:2 177n
21:3 176n, 182n
21:4 176n
21:6 32
21:7 142, 176n
21:8 176n
21:9 163n
21:10 177n
21:10-22:5 169
21:22 175n
21:23 176n
21:24-26 176n
21:25 176n
21:27 145, 187n
22:2 145, 177n
22:3 175, 177n
22:5 175n, 176n, 177n
22:6 179n
22:7 14n
22:10 14n, 26n, 164n
22:14 149
22:15 176n
22:16 136n
22:18-19 14n, 164n

Books of Maccabees
143

1 Maccabees
188n

4 Maccabees
138, 143
1:11 144
6:10 144
6:28-29 144
9:6 144
9:30 144
11:20 144
14:5-6 144
17:11-12 144
17:21-22 144
17:22 157

4 Ezra
19, 163n
4:35-37 217n
11:1-23 188n
11:46 188n
13:1-57 141n
16:13 202n

Wisdom
143
2-3 217n
16:10 144n
18:20-25 144

Sirach
40:9 197

1 Enoch
163n, 189, 196n, 216n, 217n

2 Enoch
163n

3 Enoch
163n

Jubilees
163n

2 Baruch
163n, 197n

3 Baruch
163n

Apocalypse of Abraham
163n

Testament of Abraham
216n

Testaments of the Twelve Patriarchs
189-190

Testament
of Joseph
  189n

Testament
of Benjamin
  189n, 197

Testament
of Levi
  163n

Testament
of Naphtali
  163n

Testament
of Judah
  188n

Ascension
of Isaiah
  163n, 192n, 194n

Epistle of
the Apostles
  5n

Gospel
of Thomas
  5n

Gospel
of Truth
  5n

Sibylline
Oracles
  5n

Corpus
Hermeticum
  1:42

Martyrdom
of Polycarp
  138n

Odes of
Solomon
  186n

Shepherd
of Hermas
  174n

War Scroll
  165n

Sanhedrin
  201

Pseudo-Philo
  185

Author Index (prior to AD1850)

Abelard 152
Alcazar 25, 35
Ambrose 14
Andrew of Caesarea 13-14
Anselm 152
Apringus 14
Aristotle 65, 71
Augustine xxvi, 5, 11-15, 11n, 22, 86n, 142

Bale, J. 22
Beatus 11, 14
Bede 14
Bellarmine 24n
Blake, W. 168n, 202n, 218n, 225n
Bonaventure 16n
Bruno 14

Caesarius 14
Calvin, J. 20, 176n
Cassiodore 14
Cervantes, M. de 64
Clement 9
Cranmer, T. xxv
Cyprian 9

Dionysius of Alexandria 6

Eusebius xxv, 5-7, 13, 152n

Foxe, J. 23

Geneva Bible 23
Grotius 25

Hammond, H. 25
Hentenius 25
Hermogenes 8
Hippolytus 8-10, 186
Hobbes, T. 96n

Irenaeus 5-8, 5n, 10, 137n, 168

Jerome 10-11, 11n, 14
Joachim of Fiore xxvi, 5, 11, 15-17, 18
Josephus 35, 86n, 167n
Justin Martyr 4-6, 8

Luther, M. 17-19, 20, 21

Marlorat, A. 23
Mede, J. 23, 25, 40n
Melito 10
Menno Simons 20-21
Methodius 10
Müntzer, T. 19-20

Napier, J. 23
Newton, I. 23
Oecumenius 13
Olivi 16
Origen 6, 9-10, 10n, 13, 18, 138, 150n, 186n

Plato 61n, 64, 76, 78n, 81n, 106
Primasius 14
Pseudo-Philo 185n

Ribeira 24-25

Shepherd of Hermas 171n
Stendhal 64

Tacitus 184n
Tertullian 7-8, 8n, 10, 138, 142
Tyconius 5, 11-15, 11n
Tyndale, W. 21

Westminster Confession 17n
Whiston, W. 23
Winstanley, G. 86n

Victorinus 10-11, 14, 38, 186, 200

Zwingli, H. 19-20

Author Index (since AD 1850)

Abir, P.A. 2n
Abrams, M.H. 21n, 171n
Achtemeier, P. J. 179n
Aldington, R. 53
Alison, J. 59n, 85n, 95n, 114, 212n
Allen, L.C. 181n
Allison, D.C. 132n, 171n, 195n, 225
Allo, E-B 3, 4n, 21, 37, 38, 187n, 196n, 200n, 216n
Anderson, B.W. 2n
Anderson, G.A. 134n
Andrews, I. 57n, 177n
Argyriou, A. 14n
Ashby, G. 113n
Ashcraft, M. 165, 187n, 199n, 216n
Atlan, H. 102n
Auerbach, E. 66
Aulén, G. 131n, 135n, 146
Aune, D.E. 41, 46n, 49, 56, 163n, 164n, 166, 171n, 186n, 188n, 193n

Bachmann, M. 196n, 200n
Bachmann, T.E. 17n, 18n
Bailey, J.W. 5n
Bailie, G. 88n, 98n
Bainton, R. 18
Baker, J.A. 53
Baldensperger, G. 196
Balthasar, H.U. von 96, 110-114, 116n
Bancroft, S. 32n, 199n, 216
Bandera, C. 97n, 98n
Barclay, W. 37, 187n, 198n
Barker, M. 42n, 49
Barnett, P. 174
Barnwell, E.A. 31
Barr, D.L. 46n, 50, 56, 163n, 170n, 172n, 192, 193n
Barr, J. 3
Barrett, C.K. 45, 189
Barrow, S. 152n
Barry, F.R. 131n
Barth, K. 157, 177n, 211

Bartley, J. 152n
Bassoff, B. 98n
Bater, B.R. 119-120
Bauckham, R. 20n, 21n, 22, 27n, 44, 53n, 132n, 139, 140, 150, 164n, 165n, 166n, 169n, 170n, 171n, 185, 186n, 189, 190n, 192, 219, 221n
Bauer, W. 62n, 173, 182n, 189n, 207
Bauernfeind, O. 141n, 142n
Beagley, A.J. 36n, 43
Beale, G.K. 43n, 50, 180n, 187n, 195n
Beasley-Murray, G.R. 26n, 33n, 39, 53n, 55, 179, 187n, 193n, 195n, 199n, 216n, 217n
Beattie, J.H.M. 99
Beckwith, I.T. 4n, 26n, 37, 48n, 140n, 181n, 187n, 196n, 198n, 216n
Beker, J.C. 157n
Bell, A.A. 168
Bellah, R. 220n
Benson, E.W. 28, 166n
Berger, P.L. 220n
Berkhof, H. 147n
Bettenson, H. 138n
Betz, H.D. 42-43
Bietenhard, H. 4n
Black, M. 162n
Blevins, J.L. 26n, 46, 164n
Böcher, O. 4n, 54n, 163n
Bock, E. 31, 179n
Bockmuehl, M.N.A. 206, 211
Boesak, A.A. 50n, 199n, 216n, 218n
Boff, L. 139n, 155n, 160n
Boismard, M.-E. 48
Boll, F. 41, 196
Bonner, G. 11n
Bonsirven, J. 28n, 39, 200n
Borg, M.J. 121n
Boring, M.E. 53n, 164n, 169n, 174n, 176n, 198n, 217n
Bornkamm, G. 38, 186n, 202n, 207-210

Bousset, W. 3, 4n, 41, 196, 198, 203, 216, 217n, 219n
Bowman, J.W. 46, 164n, 166n
Boxall, I. 128n, 199n
Boyarin, D. 125
Boyd, R. 166n
Bradley, I. 113n
Brady, D. 21n
Bredin, M.R.J. 191n
Brewer, R.R. 46n, 164n, 180n
Brightman, F.E. xxv
Brogan, J.R. 22n, 27
Brooks, T. 29n
Bruce, F.F. 10, 11n, 33n, 39, 198n, 218
Brütsch, C. 54n, 55
Buchanan, G.W. 43, 48, 49, 52, 170, 187n, 189, 218n
Büchsel, F. 157
Buis, H. 200n
Bull, M. 176n
Bultmann, R. xxvn, 52, 110, 121
Burch, V. 56
Burdon, C. 21n
Bureau, R. 99
Burgess, A. 163n
Burkitt, F. 164n
Burnet, A.W. 163n, 187n, 188n
Burr, D. 15n, 16n, 17n
Butler, J. 64n

Cabaniss, A. 46n
Caines, G.A. 27n
Caird, G.B. 29, 51, 53n, 134n, 139n, 147n, 149n, 157, 170n, 187n, 188, 189, 190n, 191, 194n, 196n, 199n, 200n, 203-204, 209, 217n, 218n
Calloud, J. 191n
Camille, M. 15n
Capel, E.F. 31n
Capp, B. 21n
Carnegie, D.R. 46n
Carr, W. 147n
Carrington, P. 30, 46n, 53n, 199n, 216, 217n
Carter, J. 134n
Casey, J. 43n, 44n, 191

Cazes, B. 97n
Charles, R.H. 4n, 36, 37, 39, 44, 47n, 48, 148n, 161n, 162n, 163n, 169n, 170n, 171, 178n, 181, 182, 186n, 190n, 197-199, 203, 216n, 217n
Charlesworth, J.H. 183n
Childs, B.S. 49
Chilton, B. 99-101, 102n, 104n, 121n
Cho, P.Y. 32, 180n, 218
Christe, Y. 15n
Clouse, R.G. 26n
Coffin, H.S. 187n
Cohn, N. xxvn, 2n, 15n, 128n, 220n
Cohn, R. 176n
Collins J.J. 82n, 164n
Collins, R. 110n
Comblin, J. 46n
Congar, Y.M.-J. 53n
Considine, J.S. 196n, 202
Corsini, E. 9n, 12, 30-31, 182-183, 184n, 199n, 216n, 218
Couchard, P.L. 52n
Court, J.M. 3, 4n, 39, 53n, 161n, 163n, 164n, 166n, 168n, 170n, 187n, 194n, 199
Cowley, R.W. 15n
Craddock, F.B. 43n, 194n
Craigie, P.C. 167n, 194n, 201n
Cranfield, C.E.B. 157n, 210-211
Cross, F.M. 164n, 167n
Crossan, J.D. 121n
Culler, J. 67n, 69n
Cullmann, O. 165, 193n, 200n, 202

Daalen, D.H. van 190n
Daley, B.E. 4n, 13n
Daniel, R.R. 15n
D'Aragon, J.-L. 198n
Darr, J.A. 95n, 121n
Daube, D. 191n
Davies, W.D. 156n, 157n
Davis, C. 102n, 105, 115n, 116n, 120n, 121n
Davis, R. 180n, 184n, 187n
Day, J. 2, 42n, 44, 167n, 173
Deguy, M. 59n
Dehandschutter, B. 136n
Deichgräber, R. 46n

Delarge, F. 104n
Delcor, M. 2n, 164n
Delling, G. 46n
Derrida, J. 57n, 61n, 96n, 103n, 106, 110,176n, 218n
Descombes, V. 69n
Detienne, M. 100n
Deutsch, C. 192
Dewey, 122n
Dillistone, F.W. 131n
D'Iribane, P. 90n
Dix, G.H. 189n
Dodd, C.H. xxvn, 29, 52, 157, 189n, 194n, 208-209
Domenach, J.-M. 97n, 115n, 116n, 119n
Douglas, M. 77n, 81n, 98, 163n, 220n
Draper, J.A. 43n
Dumézil, G. 82n
Dumouchel, P. 59n, 63n, 90n, 96n, 99n, 129n
Dunn, J.D.G. 210, 212
Dupuy, J.-P. 96n, 102, 119n
DuRoussea, C. 13n
Dussaud, R. 134n

Eagleton, T. 67n, 69n, 75n, 166, 167
Eaton, J.H. 167n
Eco, U. 53n
Efird, J.H. 50, 199
Eliade, M. 77n, 99, 101n, 106n
Élie, B.-W. 97n
Elliott, C. 101n, 109, 116n, 118n, 120n
Elliott, E.B. 4n, 13, 23-24
Elliott, N. 120n, 157
Ellul, J. 31, 178n, 196n, 200n
Emmerson, R.K. 15n
Enroth, A.-M. 41n

Fanon, F xvii
Farrer, A. 40, 43n, 46, 166n, 192, 194n, 200n,202n
Feenberg, A. 96n
Fekkes, J. 43n
Féret, H.M. 28
Feuillet, A. 1, 4n, 35, 44n, 140n, 168, 183n,196n, 197n, 199, 216n
Fiddes, P.S. 131n

Finamore, S. 117n
Firebrace, A. 32
Firth, K.R. 17n, 21n, 22, 23
Fitzmyer, J.A. 43n, 209, 212
Flanigan, C.C. 15n
Fodor, J. 117n
Ford, J.M. 44n, 48, 49, 52, 129n, 170, 174, 186n, 187n, 189, 200n, 216n
Forestell, J.T. 155-156
Forster, J.W. 24n
Forsyth, P.T. 131n
Frazer, J.G. 69, 96, 99
Fredriksen, P. 11n, 13
Frémont, C. 59n
French, S.H. 22n
Frend, W.H.C. 137n, 138n
Freud, S. 64, 70n, 71n, 74, 82n, 104n, 118n,166
Friesen, S.J. 37n
Frye, N. 117n
Funk, R.W. 202n
Furcha, E.J. 20n

Gadamer, H.-G. 107n
Gager, J. 56, 163n
Gans, E. 97n, 103-104, 114n, 124n
Garrow, A.J.P. 50
Gascoyne, R. 24n, 189n
Geertz, C. 220n
Geneva Bible, 23
Gennep, A. van 77n, 176n
Georgi, D. 1n, 163n, 164n, 174, 220n
Giblin, C.H. 33, 38, 48, 140, 166n, 170n, 216
Giet 25n, 35-36
Girard, R. viii-vv, xxvi-xxvii, 57, 59-94, 95-130, 132-134, 138-139, 142, 147, 150-151, 153, 158, 159, 160n, 166, 169, 174, 175, 176, 195, 202, 211-214, 217, 219, 223-226
    Anthropology 69-83
    Myth 79-83
    Prohibition 75-76
    Ritual 76-79
    Gospel 85-93
    Narratology 166-167
    Martyrdom 139-140
    Mimesis 61-63

Reading strategy 64-69
Sacrifice 87-89, 133-135
Satan 147n
Teleology 83-85
Glasson, T.F. 3, 37, 176n, 179n, 216n
Goertz, H.-J. 19n
Goldingay, J. 113n, 133n, 134n
Goldsworthy, G. 135n
Goodhart 123
Gordon, R.L. 199n
Gordon, R.P. 44n
Gorringe, T. 97n, 99n, 101n, 110, 132n, 134n, 152, 154, 156n, 159n
Goulder, M.D. 46
Granstedt, I. 97n
Gray, G.B. 134n
Grayston, K. 131n, 178n, 180n, 187n, 191n
Green, K.M. 88n, 119n
Greve, A. 140n
Grey, M. 131n
Grier, W.J. 26n
Griffiths, F.T. 98n
Grimsrud, T. 97n
Gudorf, C.E. 113n
Gundry, R.H. 175
Gunkel, H.J.F. 2, 41, 42, 196, 199, 219n
Gunther, J.J. 168n
Gunton, C.E. 131n

Hadorn, D.W. xxv
Hall, R.G. 180n
Hamerton-Kelly, R.G. 60n, 99n, 120n, 124-125, 158n, 174
Hanson, A.T. 29, 51, 205n, 208-209, 255n
Hanson, P.D. 42n, 164n, 167n
Hardin, M. 123n, 159n
Harrington, W.J. 28, 44, 48, 182n, 183n, 189n, 198n, 218n, 219n
Harvey, A.E. 121n
Hasitschka, M. 191n
Hauerwas, S. 119n
Haussleiter, J. 10n, 200n
Hayes, T.W. 86n
Hegel, G.W.F. 64n, 96

Heil, J.P. 193n, 216n
Hellholm, D. 164n
Helms, C.R. 4n, 6-11, 8n
Hemer, C.J. 37n
Hendriksen, W. 11n, 26n, 200n
Hengel, M. 3
Hengstenberg, E.W. 180n, 200n, 217n
Hensen, H.J.L. 98n
Hermann, J. 157
Herzman, R.B. 21n
Heusch, L. de 99n, 100-102
Hill, C. 22n
Hill, D. 154n, 157, 164n
Hillyer, N. 190n
Hobbs, H.H. 198n
Hodges, H.A. 131n, 152n
Holtz, T. 191n
Hooke, S.H. 41-42, 45, 167n
Hooker, M.D. 154n, 167n, 189, 190n, 212
Hopkins, M. 25n, 35, 164n, 182n
Horbury, W. 138n
Horsley, R.A. 121n
Hort, F.J.A. 168n
Hough, R.W. 98n
Howard-Brook, W. 51n
Hre Kio, S. 43n, 44n, 191n
Hulmes, E. 113n
Hurst, L.D. 45
Hurtado, L.W. 183n
Hurtgen, J.E. 163, 174

Inman, A. 190
Irigaray, L. 97n, 104n, 108, 109n
Isaacs, M.E. 159n
Isaak, H. 20n

Janowski, B. 110
Janzen, E.P. 46n, 193n
Jay, N. 109, 111n
Johns, L.L. 123, 159n
Johnson, A. 27n
Johnson, A.R. 42n
Johnson B. 67n, 106n
Johnston, R.M. 13n
Jones, B.W. 164n
Jonge, M. de 190n
Joplin, P.K. 98n

Author Index (since AD 1850)

Juilland, A. 59n, 95, 96n

Kallas, J. 164n
Kaptein, R. 97n, 117
Karrer, M. 164n
Käsemann, E. 164n, 210-211
Kearney, R. 97n, 105
Kee, A. 6n
Keim, P. 98n
Kelly, J.N.D. 4n
Kepler, T.S. 46n, 164n, 198n, 216n
Kerkeslager, A. 199
Kermode, F. 176n
Kerr, F. 115n, 119n
Keynes, G. 168n, 218n, 225n
Kiddle, M. 183n
Kirby, J.T. 41n
Kirk-Duggan, C.A. 98n
Kirwan, M. 59n
Klassen, W. 53n
Klein, P.K. 15n
Kleinknecht, H. 219n
Knappen, M.M. 22
Knox, R.A. 174n
Koch, K. 164n
Koester, C.R. 4n
Kofman, S. 107-108
Koppisch, M.S. 98n
Korshin, P.J. 21n
Kovacs, J.L. 4n
Kraft, H. 48n, 191n
Kraybill, J.N. 193n
Kreitzer, L.J. 5n, 46n
Krodel, G.A. 39, 182n, 187n, 188n, 198n, 216n
Krondorfer, B. 105n, 126n
Kumar, K. 176n
Kümmel 17n

Lacoue-Labarthe, P. 61n, 106-107
Ladd, G.E. 33n, 40, 140n, 164n, 183n, 194n, 200n, 218n
Lambrecht, J. 166
Lampe, G.W.H. 136n, 139
Lancellotti, A. 162n
Lane Fox, R. 137n, 138n
Lantz, P. 97n
Lascaris, A. 96n, 97n, 115n, 123

Lasine, S. 123
Lawrence, D.H. 52-53
Laws, S. 52n, 53n, 170n, 174, 189n
Le Grys, A. 53n
Lee, H. 15n
Lefort, G 97n
Lehmann, P. 140n
Leivestad, R. 143n
Lerner, R.E. 15
Lévi-Strauss, C. 56, 64, 69n, 81n, 82n, 96
Levine, B. 67n
Lewis, S. 15n
Lilje, H. 33, 34, 46n, 187n, 198n
Lincoln, A.T. 157n
Lindars, B. 189
Lindsey, H. 27n, 32, 140n, 180n, 199n
Littleton, C. 82n
Livingston, P. 95n, 97n, 117n
Lo Bue, F. 11n
Loenertz, R.J. 166n, 179n, 187n, 200n
Lohmeyer, E. 166n
Lohse, E. 33, 166n, 180n, 187n, 199n, 218n
Lorie, P. 32
Lund, N.W. 166n
Lust, J. 43n, 44n, 166n
Lyon, D. 60n

Mabee, C. 123
MacIntyre, A. 119n
Mack, B.L. 99, 120-121
Mackay, T.W. 4n, 11n
Macquarrie, J. 131n, 152n
Malina, B.J. 98n
Manson, T.W. 157
Martyn, J.L. 194n
Marx, K. 23n, 74, 82n, 96
Mason, J.R. 77n
Mathews, A.C. 105
Matter, E.A. 11n, 15n, 185n
Matheson, P. 19n
Matties, G.H. 123
Maurice, F.D. 37n
Mazzaferri, F.D. 43, 44n, 164n, 166n, 186n
McGinn, B. 4n, 15n
McHugh, J. 13n

McKay, J. 28
McKenna, A.J. 59n, 106n, 116n
McMahon, E. 123
Mealy, J.W. 51, 170, 187n, 216n
Meeks, W. 99n
Megivern, J.J. 17n, 31n
Metzger, B.M. 50, 142n, 198
Metzing, E.H. 144n
Meyer, B.F. 121n
Milbank, J. 57n, 101n, 104n, 107n, 112n, 115-117
Miller, M.E. 110n
Milne, B. 27n
Minear, P.S. 152n, 169n, 170n, 179, 215
Moberly, R.B. 168
Moberly, R.C. 131n
Moffatt, J. 173n, 209
Moi, T. 108
Moore, S.D. 46-47, 193n
Morgan, R. 99n
Morin, L. 97n
Morón-Arroyo, C. 98n
Morrice, W.G. 53n
Morris, L. 33n, 157, 181n
Morrison, K.F. 15n
Moses, J. 101n, 113n
Moule, C.F.D. 181n
Mounce, R.H. 33n, 187n
Mowinckel, S. 42n, 43n, 167n, 173, 180n
Mowry, L. 46n, 180n, 186
Moyise, S. 43n, 189
Müller, H.-P. 41
Munk, L. 98n
Muñoz-León, D. 166n
Murray, I.H. 26-7n
Murray, R. 2n, 220
Murrin, M. 21n, 23n
Mussies, G. 162, 173, 182n
Myers, C. 98n, 100n, 109n, 134n, 152n

Nelson, R.R. 23n
Nemoianu, V. 95, 119n
Newbolt, M.R. 35
Newman, B. 5n, 168n
Newport, K.G.C. 142n, 162n
Nicholls, D. 132n

Niditch, S. 2n, 99n, 123, 170n
Niles, D.T. 46, 51, 187n, 199n
Nolan, A. 121n
Norris, C. 176n
North, R. 59n, 103n, 112n, 116n, 121n

Oberweis, M. 44n
Oden, R.A. 2n
O'Donovan, O. xxv, 50n, 111n
Oesterley, W.O.E. 134n
Olsen, C. 77n
Oman, J. 49, 179n
O'Neill, J.C. 121n, 189
O'Rourke, J.J. 41n, 46n
Orléan, A. 97n
Orsini, C. 59n, 76n
Orzech, C.D. 104n
Oughourlian, J.-M. 97n

Palaver, W. 96n
Parker, T.H.L. 20n
Patrides, C.A. 21n
Paulien, J. 26n, 42n, 46n
Pavel, T.G. 69n
Pedersen, J. 134n
Petersen, D.L. 196n
Pelikan, J. 17n, 19n
Piper, O.A. 46n
Pippin, T. 57n, 129n
Placher, W.C. 130n
Pobee, J.S. 132n
Popkin, R. 21n
Popper, K. 97n
Porter, S.E. 162n, 163n, 181n
Poulton, E.B. 62n
Preston, R.H. 29n, 182n
Prévost, J.-P. 183n, 187n, 200n
Price, S.R.F. 138n, 193n
Prigent, P. 4n, 8, 9, 13n, 14, 46n, 117n, 176n, 178n, 179n, 187n, 191n, 192n
Pucci, P. 98n

Quispel, G. 36, 198n, 220n

Raber, R.W. 195n
Rad, G. von 164n, 170n, 218n
Radcliffe, T. 114-115
Radkowski, G.H. de 97n

Ramsey, W.M. 37n, 186n, 187n
Rashdall, H. 131n
Rawls, J. 96n
Reddish, M.G. 137n, 190n, 191n
Reeves, M. 14n, 15n, 16n, 17n
Resseguie, J.L. 50
Richard, P. 51n
Riches, J. 98n
Ricoeur, P. 66, 83, 107n
Riddle, D.W. 137n
Rinaldi, G. 178n
Ringgren, H. 134n
Rissi, M. 170n, 197n, 199, 201n
Rist, M. 166n
Robbins, R.F. 50
Roberts, R.H. 115n
Robinson, J.A.T. 168n, 210
Rogerson, J.W. 134n
Roller, O. 186n, 187n
Rollins, W.G. 164n
Rosaldo, R. 99
Ross, J.R. 27n
Rowland, C.C. xxv, 15n, 19n, 40, 50n, 51, 53, 164n, 166n, 168, 169n, 178n, 179, 180n, 183, 184, 185n, 187n, 205n, 215
Rowley, H.H. 134n, 164n
Russell, D.S. 164n
Ruiz, J.-P. 46n

Sacks, J. 57n, 119n
Sanders, E.P. 121n, 134n, 157, 156n, 158n
Sanders, J.N. 138n, 168n
Sandler, F. 21n
Sarup, M. 67n
Saussure, F. de 60n
Scherrer, S.J. 46n, 193n
Schmidt, D.D. 162n
Schüssler Fiorenza, E. 4n, 33, 34, 39, 40, 45, 46, 47n, 48n, 51, 56, 121n, 137n, 139n, 148, 149n, 163n, 164, 165n, 166, 169n, 179n, 190n, 191n, 193n. 194n, 198n, 215, 216
Schwager, R. 110, 112-114, 123-124, 155n, 159, 160n, 215, 216, 219n
Schweiker, W. 66n, 107n, 111n, 116n
Schweitzer, A. 121n, 225

Scobie, C.H.H. 37n
Scott, C.A. 40, 179n, 190n
Scubla, L. 95n, 99n, 104n, 108, 113n, 119n, 121n, 153n
Scullion, J.J. 28n, 48, 187n
Seel, T.A. 46n
Segal, C. 98n
Seibel, C. 97n
Shaffer, E. 21n
Shea, C. 108, 166n
Shepherd, M.H. 45
Siebers, T. 106n
Siegman, E.F. 35
Simonetti, M. 4n, 5n, 9, 12, 13n
Smith, C. 166n
Smith, T.H. 97n, 117, 166n
Sollers, P. 111n
Southern, R.W. 14n
Stagg, F. 172
Stanley, J.E. 56
Staples, P. 41n, 43
Stauffer, E. 137n
Stefanovic, R. 188n
Stein, S.J. 23n
Steinhauser, K.B. 11
Stendahl, K. 157n
Stetkevych, S.P. 77n
Stone, M.E. 164n
Strack, H.L. 201n
Strand, K.A. 43n, 166n
Strathmann, H. 136n
Strauss, W.A. 98n
Strenski, I. 81n
Summers, R. 198n
Surridge, R. 165n
Swanson, T. 104n, 111n
Swartley, W.M. 59n, 117n
Sweet, J. 43, 51, 136n, 139, 147, 184, 186, 200n, 201n, 204, 205n, 217n, 218, 219
Swete, H.B. 36, 187n, 198n, 216n
Sykes, S.W. 104n, 113n, 154
Szittya, P. 15n

Tannenbaum, L. 21n
Tate, M.E. 184n
Tatford, F.A. 27
Taylor, S.J. 95n

Taylor, W.S. 38n
Theissen, G. 121n
Thistleton, A.C. 172
Thomas, K. 97n
Thompson, L. 46n, 56, 137n, 138n, 163n, 166n, 171n, 193n
Thompson, S. 162, 172, 173, 181n, 182n
Todorov, T. 167n
Torrance, T.F. 28, 39, 180n, 199n, 216
Tout, C.A. 22n
Trites, A.A. 136n, 137, 139
Trudinger, L.P. 43n
Turner, H.E.W. 132n
Turner, V. 77n, 98, 99n, 176n
Tuveson, E.L. 23n

Ulfgard, H. 43n, 44n, 179n, 191n
Ulrich, S. 53
Ungar, S. 98n
Unnik, W.C. van 41n, 193n

Vanhoye, A. 43n, 44n
Vanni, U. 1, 4n, 41n, 46n, 165, 166n
Vassiliadis, P. 136n
Vaux, R. de 134n
Vawter, B. 164n
Vermes, G. 121n, 170n
Vielhauer, P. 164n
Vigée, C. 123
Vögtle, A. 178n, 179n
Vollman, H. 32
Vos, L.A. 45, 150, 198n, 199, 201

Waddell, R. 189n
Waddy, S. 46n
Wakeman, M.K. 2n
Wainwright, A.W. 4n
Wall, R.W. 50, 142n, 149n, 199n
Wallace, H. 2n
Wallace, M. 59n, 60n, 88n, 106n, 110
Wallis, N.H. 21n
Walpole, G.H.S. 200n
Walvoord, J.F. 32, 180n, 195n, 199n, 218
Ward, G. 61, 125n
Warner, S.M. 27, 27n, 182n, 200n

Watson, F. 57n
Weaver, J.D. 152
Weber, H.-R. 53n, 189n
Weizsäcker, C von 47, 48
Wellesley, K. 167n
Wenger, J.C. 20n, 21n
Wengst, K. 144n, 215n
Wenham, D. 44, 198n, 203
Wenham, G. 2n
West, M 53n
Whale, P. 45, 190n
Whealon, J.F. 48n, 52
White, H. 85n, 95n, 96n
Whitwell, R. 27, 30, 199n
Wieser, T. 119
Wiles, M. 6n, 10n
Wilkinson, R.H. 46n
Williams, J.G. 14n, 59n, 96n, 125-6, 133n
Williams, M. 189n
Williams, R. 99n, 110, 118-119
Wilson, B.R. xxv
Wilson, G.B. 39, 199n
Wilson, J. 168n
Wilson, M. 166n
Wilson, P.W. 31
Wilson Carpenter, M 53n
Wink, W. 104n, 105, 110, 117-118, 121n, 147n, 153, 154, 167, 169n
Witherington, B. 50
Wittreich, J. 21n, 54n
Wolsterstorff, N. 172n
Wood, H.F. 27n
Wrangham, R. 71n
Wright, N.G. 152n
Wright, N.T. 121n

Yamaguchi, M. 99
Yarbro Collins, A. 2, 27n, 38, 39, 42, 43, 48n, 50n, 53n, 55, 56, 137n, 139, 163n, 164n, 166n, 168, 170n, 171n, 179n, 180n, 184n, 186n, 187n, 194n, 198n
Young, F.M. 131n, 133n, 134n, 151n

Zahn, T. 33
Zerwick, M. 173, 181
Ziesler, J. 156n, 181

Subject Index

Aesthetics 97n
Adam 15, 30, 32, 156, 157, 199, 213
Anthropology 69-83, 98-105
    Communitas 77n, 176n
    Liminality 77n, 176n
    Myth 79-83
    Prohibition 75-6
    Ritual 76-9
Antichrist 17n, 21, 22, 24n, 25, 41, 199
Anti-Semitism 121-5
Apollo 199
Aqedah 191
Armagedon 44
Arms Race 110
Atonement 131-5, 151-60

Biblical Studies 120-6
Buddhism 104n

Cain and Abel 86, 126, 150, 216
Chaos 1-4, 8, 26, 40, 42, 50, 56, 57n, 60n, 68-9, 72, 80, 81, 93, 109, 128, 129, 132n, 147, 148, 151, 160n, 166-9, 171, 174, 178, 179, 180n, 181n, 212, 219-21
Chiliasm 4-13, 26-7, 152
Combat Myth 2, 42, 117-8, 167, 170, 173, 181n
Conquering 141-6

Day of the Lord 3, 39, 55-6, 219, 221

Feminism 107-9

Gnostics, Gnosticism 5-7, 5n

Herod 160n, 167
Holy War 48, 49, 123, 165n, 170, 178, 189n, 192, 218

Horsemen of the Apocalypse 196-204

Inca Empire xvii, 104n
Ireland 97, 123n

John the Baptist 32, 48, 90, 225
John XXII 17

King, Martin Luther 97, 117

Lamb, the 188-96
Literary Criticism 21n, 64, 65n, 98, 105-7, 132n, 163,

Martyrs, see Witness
Marx 23n, 74, 82n, 96
Millenarianism, see Chiliasm
Mimesis 61-3
Mithras 199
Mohammed 18
Montanism 6, 8

New Jerusalem xxv, 9, 20, 145, 169, 174-7, 187n, 219n, 221
Nietzsche 83n, 88-89, 106n, 115

Orpheus 104n

Parables 44, 117

Parthians 28, 36, 37, 39, 50, 198

Passover 31, 149n, 154n, 155, 160n, 191

Paul, the Apostle 124-5, 138, 205-15

Persecution 24, 137-8

Peru xvii, 226

Post-structuralism 61, 66-8, 106-7

Revelation, Book of
    Authorship 6, 20, 168
    Date 168
    Exegesis 178-222
    Genre 163-5
    Interpretation 169-78
        Anabaptists 20-1
        Apocalyptic 50
        Canon-Critical 49-50
        Church/World Historical 27-9
        Critical Readings 26-51
        Early Church 4-15
        English Protestants 21-4
        Futurist/Eschatological 32-5
        Historical 35-41
        Historical-Critical 41-9
        Jesuits 16th-17th Century 24-6
        Joachim of Fiore 15-7
        Political 50-1
        Preterist/Contemporary-Recapitulation 11, 38-40
        Reformation Period 17-21
        Source-Critical 47-9
        Spiritual 30-2
    Language 161-3
    Literary Structure 163-6
    Outline 166-9
    Theology 51-4

Revelation 85-93
Roman Emperors:
    Domitian 36, 48, 50, 137n, 168, 199
    Galba 168
    Nero 48, 167, 168, 184n
    Trajan 24, 168
Romulus and Remus 86

Sacrifice 87-88, 99-102, 135
Scapegoats 71-5
Schofield reference Bible 27n, 32
Science, Philosophy of 97n
Scroll, the 186-92
Social Sciences 64, 96n
Structuralism 60n, 69-70
Synoptic Gospels 35, 37, 41, 44-5, 110, 134n, 145, 147n, 150, 153-4, 197-9, 203

Teleology 83-5
Terrorism 97
Theology 109-20

Vesuvius 36

Witness 135-40

www.ingramcontent.com/pod-product-compliance
Lightning Source LLC
Chambersburg PA
CBHW050622300426
44112CB00012B/1619